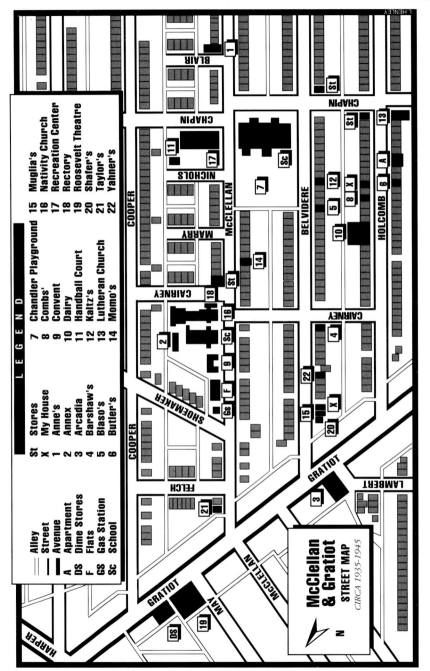

McClellan & Gratiot
STREET MAP
CIRCA 1935-1945

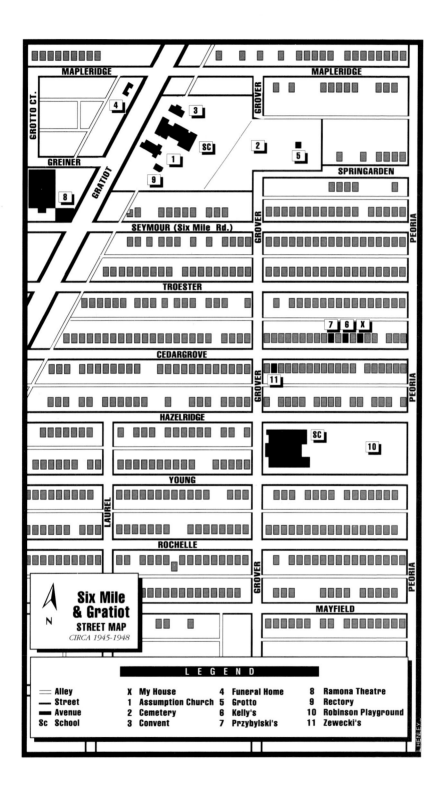

Six Mile
& Gratiot
STREET MAP
CIRCA 1945-1948

N

L E G E N D			
=== Alley	X My House	4 Funeral Home	8 Ramona Theatre
— Street	1 Assumption Church	5 Grotto	9 Rectory
▬ Avenue	2 Cemetery	6 Kelly's	10 Robinson Playground
Sc School	3 Convent	7 Przybylski's	11 Zewecki's

Streets labeled on map: MAPLERIDGE, GROTTO CT., GREINER, GRATIOT, SEYMOUR (Six Mile Rd.), TROESTER, CEDARGROVE, HAZELRIDGE, YOUNG, LAUREL, ROCHELLE, GROVER, SPRINGARDEN, PEORIA, MAYFIELD

HI...GOOD-BYE, DETROIT!

by
Robert Beckwell

This book contains a dash of fiction. Some characters are composites or have been misnamed to protect their privacy.

My sincerest thanks to:

Mary Beth Smith, Mary McNair and Donna McNorton for editing, encouragement and advice.
Lisa J. Henley for creating presentable maps from my crude drawings.
Family, acquaintances and former Nativity students for clarifying hazy memories.
Paula Morrissey, Alice Nichols and all my writing-class classmates for listening so attentively.

ISBN 0-9634988-0-0

Cover by R. Beckwell

Published by Rebel Times, Detroit, MI.

TO READERS

If with Hammett-type myst'ries
you seem to be smitten,
Call on Dashille.
But if clever short poems
you'd rather have written,
Ogden Nash'll.

—Eddie J.

Dedicated to Dona

(Although she's not a blessed virgin, she's still maDona.)

Dedicated to Dona

(Although she's not a blessed virgin, she's still maDona.)

I

Once upon a time, more specifically February 1935, in the midst of the Great (What was so great about it?) Depression, a plumpish, 32-year-old brunette disembarked from a train at Detroit's Michigan Central Station. Only 4-foot-11, she suffered the jostling crowd to help detrain her seven children: Elizabeth, 10 years old; Edward, 9; Mary, 7; Patricia, 6; Robert, 4; Charles, 2; and Dolores, 1. Her auburn-haired husband, four years her senior and six inches taller, pushed through the throng, hugged and kissed her, took her traveling bags and led them through the station's portals and into the night. Crisp, snow-filled winds strived to turn those venturing outdoors into icy figurines. I was the four-year-old and easily endured the cold. Before we left Midland, Pennsylvania, for the eight-hour train ride to Detroit, an aunt had provided me with an oversized red velvet snowsuit and a dark brown pilot hat that buckled under my chin. My brothers and sisters also were warmly dressed. Baby Dolores was so bundled up that only her eyeballs showed. We all crammed into a large taxi and drove through Detroit's downtown district. I marveled at the soaring buildings, the lights, the bustle. "Hi, Detroit!" I whispered, fell asleep, and didn't wake up until the taxi stopped in front of our new house.

Two months earlier my dad had quit his job at Pittsburgh Crucible Steel in Midland. His hours were cut to two work

1

days a week which didn't earn him enough to support his growing family. His brother, who lived in Detroit, assured him a job was available if he could get there. He did, using a popular mode of travel; hopping freight trains. I never discovered how Dad knew what train went where. I'm sure railroad companies didn't provide freight train schedules on request or pass out Triptiks.

Dad arrived in Detroit cold, hungry and wet. His brother welcomed him, provided a place to stay, and Dad got a job at Packard Motors the same week. Once Dad felt the job was steady, he visited Father Geller, the autocratic pastor of Nativity of Our Lord church on Detroit's east side, asked for help in finding a house to rent, and Father Geller steered him to a two-story frame house not far from the church. The house owner's son, who lived in the basement fruit cellar, stipulated that he didn't wish to rent to anyone with more than four children. My father, known to embroider truth at times, said that by coincidence four was the exact number of children he had. He sent for his family.

The Detroit house, on Belvidere street, had seven wooden steps ascending from the sidewalk to a wide front porch. There were two entrances. The left entrance door opened into our new home where my father had our furniture in place. The only one who got her own bed was baby Dolores. A double bed for my parents and a crib for Dolores were in one bedroom. My three older sisters slept in a twin bed in a second bedroom. Edward, Charles and I slept on the other twin bed in the front living room that Dad had converted into a third bedroom. We slept sideways to maximize space.

The boys' bedroom was the coldest room in the house. Every night Dad fueled and banked the furnace at bedtime, but by four a.m. I'd awake trembling to find that wetting the bed hadn't helped. It only provided a temporary warmth that eventually turned into a stimulating freeze. I'd get up, high-step across the bone-chilling floor to the chifforobe, put on clean underwear and return to bed in search of a dry section. If Chuck had also wet the bed, and he seldom

2

missed, it took some discreet feeling around to find a dry spot. An overpowering, nose-high mist hung in that room at all times. Ed, who was the oldest, had seniority rights when it came to selecting his sleeping spot. He, of course, chose the place next to the head of the bed known as the "high ground."

The only alluring part of that room during winter months was the beautifully intricate pictures of ferns, leaves and castles Jack Frost painted on its windows. Unfortunately, I never saw Mr. Frost at work for he was as elusive as our other night visitor, the Sandman, who dumped sand in eyes every night of the year.

For the first weeks in our new home, we explored our surroundings and gathered information. We discovered the second front porch door opened to steps that climbed to another residence where an aged woman lived a solitary existence. She spoke little English and my mother was the only one who seriously communicated with her. Their conversations consisted of animated hand waving, pointing, smiling, nodding, and two- and three-word sentences spoken in English and Italian. My mother liked her and dubbed her "Mrs. Up-a-stair," which was how the nice lady explained where she lived.

The landlord owned a fenced empty lot on one side of our house, which gave us a private playground. The Wolfes, an elderly couple, lived in the house next to the lot. She was short and petite; he was tall and reedy. They graciously welcomed my parents to the neighborhood and always had an amicable word for us, but despite these pleasant characteristics I avoided close contact with either for a time. The Three Pigs and Red Ridinghood tales had made me extremely wary of wolves, friendly or otherwise.

Mr. and Mrs. Muglia owned the house on the other side of us. Living with them were two sons, Joe and Mike, both in their early twenties; a four-year-old daughter, Rose; a twenty-five-year-old daughter, Yolanda; Yolanda's husband, Joe Gullo; and the Gullo's four-year-old daughter,

Virginia. Rose was Virginia's aunt...even though both were four years old. This puzzled me since my aunts and uncles were much older people, like my parents. That two little girls my age lived next door didn't really interest me, except for their odd aunt/niece relationship. There were more than enough girls in our house. I was still a few years away from discovering that little girls grew into big girls who can be very intriguing when they comb out their long curls and stop being a pain in the ass.

Next to the Muglia household were the Shafers. Mr. and Mrs. Shafer had three sons — Jack, 21; Tom, 19; and Joe, 13. With only two people living in the Wolfe house and five in the Shafers' I often speculated about what they did with all their extra space.

A side alley abutted the opposite side of the Shafer house and across the alley was the rear of a store, the front of which opened onto Gratiot (pronounced Grash-it) avenue; the biggest, widest street imaginable with a multitude of lanes and traffic! Alas, any independent exploration of Gratiot was forbidden for the next year and a half. My horizons expanded only if accompanied by my mother or oldest sister, Betty, who often shopped at Gratiot stores and sometimes took me along.

Grocery stores were wondrous places for a young boy to discover. In this neighborhood they were all owned by people named Guido, Angelo or Tony and if you couldn't get good fruit and vegetables from those guys you weren't trying. It was worth the trip just to watch clerks retrieve a box of Rolled Oats off the top shelf, twelve feet from the floor. They deftly used a magnificent invention that was nothing more than a long pole with a clamp on the top; the clamp controlled by a grip at the pole's bottom. The able clerks never spilled an oat.

Most grocery stores had a butcher shop at the back of the store. Since we were far from well-to-do, I never had much contact with meat. The first time I saw a butcher shop with all cuts of meat displayed, I thought they'd had a hideous

4

accident. The floor was always covered with sawdust and newspapers. Occasionally the butcher, in his haste to weigh and wrap a customer's pork chops, dropped one on the floor, but without hesitation he'd pick it up, wipe it off, smile and say, "Fellah right on dah paper."

In the summer, all grocery stores displayed their fruit on wooden racks set up on the front sidewalk. Each day older neighborhood boys looked over the displays and asked grocers for any fruit with rotten or dark spots. The grocers usually found a few for them and the boys used their ever-present jackknives to cut out the spots before eating. This way grocers kept them from stealing their best fruit. Grocers would have loved to have had the same deal with policemen walking the beat who often relieved them of prime produce.

There were other marvels and curiosities on Gratiot. In a shoe repair shop window a mechanical shoemaker soundly hammered a shoe heel. Only his arm and hammer moved.

There was a three-chair barber shop with a red, white and blue striped pole beside the front door. The pole resembled a giant candy cane and rotated slowly, giving the impression that the stripes were screwing themselves into the pole's lighted, domed top. Customers having their "ears lowered" were usually reading the *Police Gazette*.

Next to the barber shop stood a small tobacco shop with a sentry — an imposing, life-sized, wooden Indian who appeared angry and willing to divest you of scalp or extremities.

A nearby gas station had a flying red horse sign mounted on a towering stanchion. At night the horse was outlined in red neon lights and by some electrical miracle the wings flapped. I wanted to see a real flying red horse, but Betty smugly informed me that there wasn't such an animal — one of the first of many illusions to be shattered. Older sisters were good at that.

I also savored Gratiot's attractions during extended, leisurely, summer walks with my mother while she pushed her wicker, rubber-wheeled baby buggy. A few months earlier, in January 1936, a new baby sister was delivered to our house in a large black bag carried by a doctor. They named her Ann, which as far as my parents were concerned was another word for final. Mom would load Dolores and Ann in the buggy and with Chuck and me hanging on to it, and Pat, Mary and Betty beside her, she'd stroll up to Gratiot and head south. These outings took place once or twice a week affording opportunities to observe a teeming assortment of humans on foot and in vehicles; cheery, grim, rushing, dawdling. The oooga and blare of car and truck horns, the clack and clang of streetcars, the teasing aroma of fresh bakery goods and overripe fruit along with the smell of hot paving tar, horse manure and exhaust fumes, stimulated me and these walks became the highlight of my young life. Ed always stayed home, which made little sense because I knew during our journey Mom would stop at a sweetshop to buy Popsicles. I considered Ed peculiar. However, in future years I wondered if it didn't have something to do with that girl down the street. This was after I found out eating frozen suckers wasn't necessarily tops on a list of things for a growing young lad to do.

Chuck and I always clamored for ice cream cones when we reached the sweetshop. Mom always ignored us and bought the usual Popsicles that had two wooden stick handles and could be easily broken in two and shared. We'd start home licking our icy treats and if, after consuming, the word "free" appeared on any sticks, one of my older sisters would run back to the store to get another. "You'll never find the word 'free' on the inside of an ice cream cone," Mom told us, "so stop asking for them."

* * *

September arrived. First grade beckoned. Our idyllic summer walks ended. Hand in hand, my mother and I walked to McClellan street and Nativity school. I already had attended Nativity church numerous times and wasn't fond of it, but my mother assured me I'd love school. "Just do what Sister tells you," she advised.

Mom turned me over to an imposing person who looked like imposing church statues, with robe and veil, and promptly deserted me. She'd entrusted Chuck, Dolores and Ann to a nervous Mrs. Up-a-stair while she walked me to school.

I quickly became accustomed to first grade and learned to be quiet at all times and concentrate on everything taught. We had a couple free-spirited students in class, but even they became docile when the nun invited them to the front of class next to her desk and instructed them in "Nunal Authority," punctuating her remarks with several well-aimed slaps to their torsos. Nuns always had a way of letting you know that when entering their classroom you were no longer in a democratic environment. I often contemplated what nuns did in summer when there was no school to teach and decided they went to places like California's Camp Pendleton to teach U.S. Marines to fight dirty.

In a class of fifty-five students it was easy to keep from being noticed and I actually started to enjoy the learning process, but still welcomed Christmas vacation.

As Christmas drew near, my parents dropped ominous hints that Santa Claus would again be less-than-charitable. Although Santa hadn't been excessively generous the year before, I concluded it had something to do with our address change. Surely he'd have this oversight corrected. Betty, a harbinger of gloom, told Chuck and me that Santa, somewhat like our all-knowing God, watched kids closely and she felt sure our disobedience during the year would cause him either to skip our house altogether or stuff our stockings with chunks of coal. This baffled me. With an abundance of coal in our basement bin we didn't need more, Besides, Santa didn't seem the vindictive sort. The Christmas poem said he was jolly; not exactly the type to stiff kids with coal chunks. So I continued to happily anticipate the big day but, just in case, my behavior improved.

At sundown on Christmas Eve we sat in the dining room (converted into a living room) gleefully contemplating Santa's visit and admiring the naked fir tree in the corner. Betty, Ed and our parents sat in the kitchen looking worried, whispering. Any minute I expected Santa's reindeer to hit the snow-laden roof. He'd step from his sleigh, plunge down our chimney, open the furnace door, leap out fast to avoid the flames, climb our basement stairs to the kitchen, give us our toys, ho-ho a few times and rush off. Instead, the doorbell rang. Mary opened our front door and yelled, "Momma! The police are here!"

Two gigantic policemen stood at the door holding two large cardboard boxes. "We're from the Goodfellows organization and have more in the car, Ma'am," one told my mother.

Each box contained a toy — wind-up vehicle or wooden blocks for boys and a doll for girls — books for older children, and caps, mittens, underwear and a bag of hard candy for everyone. There were long stockings for girls, knee socks for boys, and shoe coupons redeemable at a downtown shoe store. Mom explained that the delivering policemen helped out busy Santa because there were so many children in the world to visit. I understood. I'd been to school so I knew there were an abundance of kids. (Besides, I still bought the entire Santa premise. Like the vaudeville comedians used to say, "You buy the premise, you buy the bit.") Santa might return later to help trim our tree, Mom added. Sadly, we didn't see him. I discovered a noisy wind-up truck and clacking wooden blocks caused parents to firmly suggest that all youngsters should be in bed.

Early Christmas morning Chuck and I crept into the dining room. Santa had beautified our tree with glass balls, strings of lights and silver tinsel and by the time everyone else arose, Chuck and I were devouring our bags of hard candy. Pat delighted in showing me her candy whenever she found a soft center so I jealously bit into all my remaining candy trying to find a soft one. I was left with a bag of unappetizing crunched-up candy and sore gums. As I contemplated my survival chances if I awarded Pat one jarring punch, we again heard the doorbell. Another of Santa's helpers stood at the door, a driver from the St. Vincent DePaul Society, his truck parked at the curb. With help from Dad and Ed, the driver unloaded a ham, turkey, canned goods, gallons of milk, shirts and knee-length pants, called knickers, for boys and dresses for girls. No toys. I silently wondered when Santa went into the food and clothing business.

Years later I learned that Betty had filled out forms provided at Nativity school for a Goodfellows delivery and Barney Yahner, Dad's friend who lived a few houses down the street, had informed the St. Vincent DePaul charity of our need. It was a smile-filled Christmas. It didn't occur to me at the time, but we were Cratchit poor.

* * *

Chuck got sick three months after that memorable Christmas. He lay in our bed, gasping, shaking, sweating. The same doctor who'd delivered Ann arrived that evening with his black bag, but this time it held no babies. My parents hustled their other children from the sick room and closed the door. We waited in the living room. Everyone spoke in whispers. Something was dreadfully wrong. A half-hour later the doctor opened the bedroom door, mumbled "I'm sorry," and quickly departed. Mom, who had followed him to the door, returned to our living room, eyes tormented, and sank slowly to her knees in front of the sofa. She buried her head in its cushions and, shoulders heaving, began to sob.

Dad appeared in the bedroom doorway, seemingly stunned. Then his face grew rigid. "Get up, Claire, and start

9

frying onions," he said quietly.

She looked at him, lips quivering, and said, "But you heard the doctor."

"I don't give a goddamn what any doctor says!" he exploded. "No kid of mine's going to die!"

Betty joined them in the kitchen slicing onions, Ed ran next door to Muglias to borrow another frying pan and any onions they could spare, and Mary gathered every pillowcase in our house. Mrs. Muglia returned with Ed to help. Dad ladled hot onions into two pillowcase poultices and, holding them with a towel, carried them into the bedroom, gently placing one on Chuck's bare chest, the other under his back. When they cooled, more awaited. A curious Mrs. Up-a-stair, attracted by the onion aroma, knocked on our back door and, after Mrs. Muglia explained the situation in Italian, Mrs. Up-a-stair joined the onion slicer's ranks. I sat wide-eyed in our living room with Mary, Pat and Dolores, watching, puzzled. Once Mrs. Muglia left the kitchen, her eyes red and teary, to see how Chuck was faring. She told us Chuck had double pneumonia, the doctor said he wouldn't live through the night and that we should all pray. I didn't understand. Chuck was a nice little kid, too young, just starting out. God wouldn't let it happen.

I fell asleep and awakened seven hours later on a caseless pillow on the floor. Chuck was still breathing. His fever broke that morning and my mother cried again.

A month passed and Virginia Gullo, the six-year-old grandchild of the Muglias, also contracted pneumonia. After their doctor said he could do no more for her, Mrs. Muglia called Dad and they started the onion cure. Virginia also lived and the story of these two miracles spread. Soon neighbors with sick children called "Doctor" Beckwell first; requesting advice or a house call. He readily obliged.

Dad specialized in children's ailments and initially tested all curative measures on his own kids. For earaches, Dad inhaled a deep mouthful of cigarette smoke and blew it into the sensitive ear. Even if it didn't mute pain, after a couple

10

treatments we said it felt better. Nobody wants someone blowing into their ear — at least at that age.

Father strongly recommended an enema to cure stomach problems. He poured soapy water in a small hole at the top of a hollow, hand-sized, red rubber ball, used Vaseline to grease a thin, hollow, black, three-inch tube, then jammed one tube end into the ball hole and the other into us. We dubbed this torture instrument "The Ballies." (It was a name I offered to sell years later to the C. B. Fleet Company. I resented their snide rejection letter.)

For fever, Dad soaked aspirins in a spoonful of water and thrust the mixture down our throat. Two hours later we were fever-free and still sucking particles of bitter aspirin from between our teeth.

Wonderful Dream Salve was Dad's sure cure for infected cuts and he mixed other strange concoctions, but if all remedies failed Dad resorted to castor oil, knowing the acrid taste would inspire children to forget discomfort and strive for full recovery.

Luckily, none of Dad's patients died and no one reported him for practicing medicine without a license.

* * *

In school, Jane, Dick and their pets, Spot and Puff, visited farms and ran-ran-ran all over the countryside. As a six-year-old with a little-used, absorbent brain, I relished returning to that primer to read their latest escapade.

At home Mary or Betty read books and Sunday newspaper comics to Dolores, Chuck and me. Sometimes I took literature literally. After hearing the *Arabian Nights* flying carpet story, I sat on a small mat in our front hall for an hour — willing it to take off.

When my sisters tired of the comic-reading ritual, a local radio program took up the slack. "The Joe Gentile and Ralph Binge Show" found a gentleman named Toby David to read to us. Chuck, Dolores and I laid Sunday comic pages

11

on the floor in front of our radio and followed each panel as Toby described it and read its dialogue.

By 1937 summer vacation I was attempting to read comics alone, only having to ask older people for help with a third of the words, and my literary universe expanded.

When not reading I loved to sit on our back porch and watch Ed and his pals play games. One afternoon they brought home a large female dog with long, reddish hair and flapping ears that they had named "Ruby." Seeing me on the porch steps Ruby playfully bounded over and licked my cheek, inducing surges of affection. After chasing and romping, the older boys used a small spongy ball to test Ruby's retrieving ability. She easily passed the test so Ed lobbed the ball directly at her and Ruby deftly caught it in her mouth. The boys took turns tossing the ball higher and higher, finally throwing it straight up in the air and Ruby circled under it like an outfielder and caught it every time. It was uncanny. Ed ran to the porch and called our mother. When she stepped outside he said, "Watch this, Ma!" and threw the ball straight up, higher than our two-story house, and Ruby snagged it before it hit the ground. He demonstrated a second time to suitably impress Mom and asked excitedly, "Can we keep her? She followed me home!"

Ruby loped up the porch steps and tongued Mom's hand, getting some personal "Please keep me" licks in, and Mom patted Ruby tenderly. "You know how your father feels about dogs, Ed," she said.

Ed gave her more pleas and I squeezed in a couple until she promised to talk to Dad as soon as he came home from work. "It does seem like a nice dog," she admitted.

When Dad came home I heard Mom through the back screen door telling him how Ed found a friendly, pretty dog and the kids should have a pet. He grunted, came out on the back porch, called to Ed and told him brusquely, "Get rid of that dog."

Ed explained Ruby was a stray, had followed him home

and liked our yard. This really didn't daunt old Dad. He said, "Just take the damned thing back where you found it!" Ed, his friends and Ruby left our yard through the alley gate, and I tried not to cry. I really loved that dog.

Ed returned alone, dogless and unhappy, and sat with me on the steps, cradling his chin. After a long silence, I asked, "Howcum Pa won't let us have a dog, Ed?"

"Why? Because of you."

"Me?!"

"Yeah. You probably don't remember, but we used to have a dog named Harv back in Midland. I found him limping after he got hit by a car, took him home and bandaged his leg. He was my dog but you played with him a lot."

"Why'd ya call 'im Harv?"

"'Cause he was a hit-and-run victim."

"What kinda dog? What color?"

"Just a regular dog; about this high. Black with a white chest. Then when you were three years old and didn't walk or talk, Pa and Ma got worried. Someone told them to take you to an East Liverpool doctor who knew about kid problems. East Liverpool was in Ohio, ten miles away, and Pa didn't have a car so he borrowed one from Mr. Avis who lived on the next block. Pa called him "Avis-loan-a-car" because so many people borrowed that car. After awhile Mr. Avis started charging a fee when he loaned it out. I wonder whatever happened to him."

"I remember goin' ta the doctor, Ed."

"Yeah, maybe you do. It was only three years ago. Anyway, Ma and Pa drove you to the doctor's office and told him you didn't walk or talk so he checked you over and asked if you made any sounds. Ma told him you barked and growled chasing Harv around the house on your hands and knees and made panting noises when perspiring through your mouth. The doctor said not to worry. As long as you made sounds you'd talk when you got ready.

"The doctor also said he had a friend with Barnum and

Bailey, and if they taught you to jump through a fire hoop, roll over and play dead, chase cats, lift your little rear leg, and do unspeakable things with the collie next door, he could get you a full-time circus job; then maybe Pa could pay his bill. 'Otherwise,' he said, 'get rid of your dog.'

"Pa took Harv for a one-way walk and hasn't allowed us to have a dog since."

"What's a one-way walk?"

"You take a dog out in the woods and throw rocks at it 'til it runs away. I personally think he made a wrong choice. Maybe he should've taken you on that one-way walk. Maybe Harv wasn't the problem."

II

Through second grade and another summer vacation my stature and imagination grew, but not necessarily my intellect. By the time I entered third grade I led a double life. While quietly and obediently attending school, forcing myself to digest real world facts and figures, I anticipated my return home to a fantasy world. I was deep into reading newspaper comic strips and spent a lot of Sunday time just staring at "Puck," the Hearst comic section symbol at the top of the first page. I reflected on the significance of the words on Puck's banner, "What fools these mortals be," and whether curly-haired Puck was a naked boy or girl.

I greatly admired Popeye's strength, wishing to be as strong, but couldn't fathom his addiction to spinach. I eagerly followed the adventures of Prince Valiant and Buck Rogers, but, because they lived in the past and future, knew I could never emulate them. King of the Royal Mounted became my hero. He was contemporary, bold, and captured every criminal he chased. I loved his uniform; red jacket with black epaulets, dark blue pants with wide yellow stripes down the sides, knee-high black boots, a pistol in a covered holster hanging from a thick black gun belt, and a thin black shoulder strap. The most unique item of his uniform, however, something no cowboy ever considered, not even the Lone Ranger, was a cord attached to a small ring on his pistol butt. The cord turned into a noose at the middle of his chest and the noose fitted loosely around his neck. If he dropped his pistol, or it was knocked or shot out of his hand, it would always be retrievable. King was a policeman working for Canada, a country north of us where it snowed constantly, and he sometimes rode a black stallion that was as fast as Silver. When tracking criminals, he ofttimes wore snowshoes or hung onto the rear of a sled pulled by husky dogs. These dogs resembled wolves, but lacked ancestral loyalty for they helped King stave off starving, marauding wolf packs.

Heavy snowfalls of 1939 turned our large backyard into Canadian country and I fashioned a Mountie uniform using my red velvet snowsuit. The jacket, though tight fitting, was wearable. The pants were red without yellow stripes and way too short, but I covered the bottom part of the leggings with my brown, knee-high, zipper-up-the-front canvas boots. Other parts of my uniform consisted of a cowboy belt and holster with a tin gun; a thin belt found in my sisters' bedroom, used as a shoulder strap; and a long piece of butcher's string noosed at the neck and tied to my pistol grip. King frequently wore a fuzzy fur cap. My old pilot's cap with ear flaps turned up resembled the cap when I used my fuzzy imagination. Not owning gloves or mittens, I slipped two pairs of my sister's pink anklets onto my hands to complete my Royal Mounted uniform.

Ed thought my uniform bizarre and joked, "He looks like Santa Claus with a gun." I noted that this was not one of Ed's funnier lines. Fortunately his comedic talent later improved.

There were many lengthy shoot-outs in my backyard between me and Canada's most wanted criminals as I happily practiced for the day I'd enlist in King's intrepid Mountie organization whose motto was "They always get their man." This was the first time I considered a future occupation and I was sure I'd never want to be anything else.

The third grade nun had other career plans for me brought on by an occurrence that challenged my never-draw-attention-to-yourself policy. I drew a picture. At the beginning of art class the nun passed out art paper, told us to draw anything we wanted, color it, turn in the papers at the end of class, and we'd be graded on our work. This would keep us busy and she could catch up on other duties. I drew a picture of a tan-colored horse's head and neck sticking out of a brown barn window munching on a yellow haystack. Early the next day the nun pointed to my picture taped to the wall, told the class how lovely it was and proclaimed: "Robert has artistic ability."

Every kid in class turned around to stare at this talent sitting in their midst — last seat, last row — and I felt a flush spread from my forehead to neck. There were chuckles and good-natured remarks about my talent and red face, which led to a deeper shade of red when I realized that well-meaning nun had just put me in a very bad light with my peers. If there is one thing I didn't need it was to be referred to as an "artistic talent." Even at a young tender age, there is something about being called "artistic" that makes macho boys look askance at you and derisively remark about your sexual preference; whether you preferred being with boys (good) or girls (bad). Finally the nun stopped praising the picture, started teaching and the class returned to normal. That should have been the end of it. However, when final bell sounded at 3:30, the nun called me to her desk and said she'd like to talk to my mother. While walking home I considered not delivering the message since she hadn't pinned a note to my shirt. Then I imagined myself trying to explain to the nun why I hadn't.

I entered the house, yelled "Ma!" and received a familiar "Yoo, hoo" response from the kitchen. I relayed the message and she assumed the worst. She kept asking what I did wrong and why I didn't know what I did wrong. I didn't know.

At school the next morning I gratefully noted the absence of my horse picture from the wall. At ten o'clock my mother knocked on the classroom door, the nun called me and the three of us stepped into the hall. The nun showed Mom my horse picture, pointed to the horse's rounded jaw line and anatomically correct chin, nostrils, eyes, ears and mane and suggested private art lessons. I didn't understand. Horses pulled wagons in streets and alleys. King, Tom Mix, the Lone Ranger and Tonto rode them in comic strips. Movie cowboy heroes all had favorite horses. Even gas stations had flying red ones. Everyone should know what a horse's head looked like!

My mother patiently explained that she had difficulty paying twenty dollars a year tuition (tuition was twenty dollars a year per family whether you had one or ten children in school) so she certainly couldn't afford private art lessons. Whew! I got out of that one!

But the nun said she understood the financial problem so she would give me extra art assignments to refine my latent talent. My stomach churned. No one asked if I wanted art lessons or extra work. I wanted to be a Mountie, not an artist.

The interview ended, I became the "artiste laureate" of the third grade, and the nun started paying attention to me. So did two blond curly-haired boys whom I hadn't noticed before. I quickly rejected their offer to carry my books.

* * *

Two movie theaters, the Roosevelt and Arcadia, were within easy walking distance of our house. Both sat on the other side of Gratiot avenue so to attend either required an older person's company. The Roosevelt was two blocks up from Belvidere near Harper, a major cross street. This ornate building had a large seating capacity that included a balcony, showed second-run movies after they closed at downtown movie houses, and charged a dime admission for children, twenty-five cents for adults. We rarely attended this expensive theater. (Three years later I developed serious doubts about the Roosevelt management when it hired Ed and a few of his friends as ushers over the summer months. Listening to their conversations I discovered there were such things as usher groupies; young worldly ladies who attended Saturday matinees, admired guys in uniform, or "out of" as the case may be, and didn't mind foregoing a few love scenes in movies in order to create their own with the hired help. According to overheard conversations, these trysts took place either in last balcony rows or in what was known as the "letter room," a little second floor room where management stored cleaning supplies and letters used on the theater's marquee. Now I don't know what actually went on in that room, but I once noticed a young lady standing in line at the church confessional with impressions of block letters pressed into the back of her coat that read: Coming Attractions.)

The Arcadia, directly across from Belvidere, was much smaller, no balcony, scheduled movies weeks after the Roosevelt finished with them, charged children a nickel and adults a dime, and gave adults free dinnerware, one piece at a time, every Tuesday, as an attendance incentive. These plates, saucers, bowls, cups and tumblers usually were see-through pink- or amber-colored with flowery designs and became known as Depression glass.

Chuck and I, with an older sister or neighbor, attended the Arcadia's Saturday matinees, which featured westerns, comedies, or other movies approved by the Legion of Decency. The Legion, a Catholic organization, screened all movies, rating them "A" suitable for children, "B" suitable for adults, and "C" for condemned, suitable for no one. A list of current movies and their Legion ratings was printed in the Michigan Catholic, a newspaper available in Catholic church vestibules. This Legion of Decency seriously hampered our sex education so we resorted to such things as the underwear section of the Sears Roebuck catalog.

The movie creating the biggest stir among the kid-set and much of the adult-set was *Snow White and the Seven Dwarfs*. It was held over at a downtown theater. All Detroit children whined to go downtown and many parents, to quiet them and save money, promised to allow them to see it the instant it hit neighborhood theaters. In our case, this meant the Roosevelt.

When Snow White arrived at the Roosevelt, Mary, Pat, Chuck and I went together. I found myself bristling with anticipation because, even at that early age, I thought a young girl living with seven guys might have a hidden connotation that could happily lead to a couple little sins. I thought somebody might have slipped one past the Legion of Decency; but, alas, I found the Legion did its usual good job of protecting our morals.

Snow White was a great adventure movie except for two nagging inconsistencies. It seemed unrealistic that the mirror changed its mind about who was the fairest, since the Queen always looked seductive, more beautiful and much shapelier than Show White — until she messed herself up with the "ugly" potion. And then Snow White, after many dire warnings from the dwarfs to beware of suspicious strangers, became friendly with a suspicious, strange hag. After committing this blunder, she stupidly bit into a suspicious-looking apple. The apple appeared suspicious because it was oversized, bruiseless and wormless, unlike ordinary apples.

Taking advantage of this Snow White craze, a Detroit bakery held a contest. The grocers who sold this bakery's bread distributed thin booklets, whose pages contained black-on-white drawings of Snow White characters. Each loaf of the bakery's bread included a full-color picture of a Snow White character. Contestants were required to paste this picture over the booklet's corresponding one and, when the booklet was full, they'd qualify for a prize. Three times a week I volunteered to help my mother shop to be sure she bought bread. Time passed and my booklet was filled, except for Grumpy. I had many duplicates of characters, but no Grumpy. The grocer tried to help. Although you could see through part of the bread's wrapping paper, the pictures always faced inward. The grocer pushed, squeezed and poked the loaves until we could see part of the pictures inside...but no Grumpy.

When the contest ended I felt disgusted and skeptical. Why didn't Grumpy show up? After all those loaves of bread...after pushing and squeezing and poking the loaves on the shelf...so what if that wasn't completely honest. I had all the other pictures and deserved Grumpy, too. No one in our neighborhood won the contest. We never heard about anyone in Detroit who won the contest. Maybe there never was a Grumpy, anywhere, in any loaf on any shelf in any store in the whole city. I'd wasted so much time. All those shopping trips...searching for Grumpy...pasting and sticking those stupid little dwarf characters into the booklet. I'd raised my hopes so high —for nothing. It was totally disappointing. I knew I'd learned a bitter but valuable lesson, yet I couldn't figure out what it was. In retrospect I realize now that it helped prepare me for all that mail from Ed McMahon.

III

A rich kid, Jimmy Bacon, my age and an only child, lived on the other side of the Wolfes and occasionally went to the Arcadia with us. We knew he was rich because his parents bought him every new toy he wanted, Christmas or not. After a heavy rain when children gathered at the curb to float homemade wooden boats with paper sails, Jimmy would bring out his tin, wind-up speed boat that cut through water against the current. He even owned a rocking horse, a pedal-driven automobile and a Mickey Mouse watch. After he saw a gangster/G-man movie, he described it to his parents and they bought him a G-man badge and a wind-up tommy gun that rat-a-tat-tatted and shot muzzle sparks. A week after he raved about a western movie, he showed up to play "cowboy" wearing a cowboy hat, a red bandanna around his neck, a fringed vest, two-gun holster set with silver-painted wooden bullets interspersed around the belt, wrist covers, and artificial leather chaps wrapped around his legs. A sheriff's star, pinned to the vest, made him a good guy. Between his legs was a wooden pole with two wheels on one end that rolled along the sidewalk and, on the other end, a painted horse head that he held up with real reins. My horse, a worn-out broom named "Old Paint," suddenly looked like a worn-out broom named Old Paint. My holster was shabby and the gun belt didn't hold bullets. Even Dad's white handkerchief around my neck felt fake.

I resented Jimmy and I resented my parents. They should have just had me and skipped my brothers and sisters. Then they could afford to buy all the toys I wanted. I started looking at baby Ann, thinking what a terrific deal it would be to trade her for a complete cowboy ensemble.

Upon reflection though, I had to admit Jimmy always was generous with his toys. A quiet lonely boy, he always seemed to be searching for company or playmates. So maybe I was lucky to have brothers and sisters. But why so many of them?

* * *

A Sunday comics hero had an astonishing adjustable flashlight that could cast a regular, red or green beam. It would be a superb signaling device at night. Red if by land — green if by sea; attack if green — don't attack if red. An advertisement at the bottom of the comic page explained how anyone could own a duplicate of this amazing flashlight by mailing two box tops from Ralston cereal boxes. I asked my mother to buy the cereal, promising to eat it myself if no one else would, for it wasn't the most tasty of breakfast foods. Because Mom fretted about my eating habits and saw this as an opportunity to add healthy food to my diet she even helped mail the box tops.

When the flashlight arrived five weeks later I loved it although it wasn't quite as big as it was pictured in the comic strip hero's hand or in the advertisement. (But as my wife so caustically noted many years later, "Some things aren't as large in actuality as previously advertized." Until she made that remark, I had always thought she called me "Shorty" because of my height. And since the Legion of Decency might check this book when it's made into a movie, I won't even discuss why I call her "Lucy.")

The flashlight was about the size of a penlight battery, which it used, and over the bulb was an adjustable wheel

24

with three small holes, each covered by either red, green or clear cellophane. My parents' bedroom closet door shut tightly, providing total darkness, so I tested it there. The flashlight didn't cast a long beam — three feet maximum for the clear light, a foot for the red and green — but it still could be used for signaling at night so it satisfied me. Flashing the clear light around my surroundings I discovered a square opening at the top of one end of the closet, big enough for a small human to explore on his hands and knees. I pulled my mother's vanity bench into the closet, stood on it and, using my forearms, cautiously lifted myself into the opening. It was like exploring a deep secret cave. I studied its contents with the flashlight and the first three objects I saw were hat boxes. I carefully opened each, illuminated their insides and found hats. This adventure could prove disappointing, I thought. However, while squeezing by the boxes, my hand closed around a soft, furry body!

My first instinct was to throw myself backwards through the cave mouth and, if I survived the fall, scream for my mother. But after my initial terror I noted the furry body didn't move, bite or growl. This calmed me. Turning my flashlight fully on the creature, I saw two deep-set staring brown eyes. It was smaller than a wolf and obviously lifeless. Bravely, I reached out and touched it. Its body felt flat, like someone had emptied its insides.

Nothing else interested me except some old clothing at the rear of the cave that I could investigate later, so I dropped the animal out of the opening, hung by my elbows, eased myself down until my toes touched the vanity bench, grabbed my prize and raced to the kitchen shouting, "Look what I found way back in your closet, Ma! Someone musta left it who used ta live here!"

My mother frowned. "What were you doing in my closet?"

I explained about testing my new flashlight, while wondering why she seemed unexcited about my discovery.

"That's an old fox neckpiece your aunt Paula gave me years ago...the ugly thing! I don't know why I kept it, as ratty as it is."

I carefully worded the next question. "Can I have it then?"

"All right, but keep it away from Dolores and Ann. I don't want you frightening them."

I couldn't believe my ears. How could someone give up such a treasure? "Thanks, Ma!" I yelled while heading for the back porch to closely examine my loot.

The fox had reddish-brown fur; a face tapering to a black nose; a long, white-tipped, bushy tail; four loosely-hanging, black legs with clawed feet; ears that laid flat against its head; and two authentic-looking eyes, until you poked them with your finger and found they were glass. The only other thing fake was the lower steel jaw. When I pressed the jaw's inner end, the outer end opened like a gaping mouth. Let go and the mouth snapped shut! If I wrapped the fox around my waist and snapped the mouth on the tail it couldn't fall off. Ingenious! I played with this pelt for two days, carefully keeping it from Dolores and Ann.

Then an incredible idea materialized. If I mutilated the fox by cutting off the head, tail and legs, bisected what remained and tied the two pieces to the front of my legs, I'd look a lot like movie cowboys who wore fur chaps. I measured the fur against my leg and discovered that if it were cut in two, my chaps would be too short. I needed another fur piece. My mother didn't want this one. Perhaps the neighbors also had unwanted ones. I pictured Jimmy Bacon's envious gaze when I rode Old Paint wearing my fur chaps that would put his fake leather ones to shame. Thus began my fur quest.

I memorized my question — "Do ya have an old fur piece ya don't want?" — and started at the Shafers. Mrs. Shafer answered the door, said she didn't think so, smiled, then yelled into the house, "Anyone have any old fur pieces they don't want? It's for the neighbor kid. You know, the odd one?" I heard male laughter inside and Mrs. Shafer started laughing too, so I thanked her and hastily left.

Mrs. Muglia was furless as was Mrs. Wolfe. Mrs. Wolfe had to hear the whole reason for the fur request, which evoked the same reaction I'd received from Mrs. Shafer, only this was more fun since Mrs. Wolfe had false teeth and had all she could do to get both hands in front of her mouth in time to hold them in place while she guffawed around her front porch. After regaining her composure she asked, "Has your mother ever considered selling tickets to watch you play?" I wasn't sure if I was being laughed at or with, but I thought it sounded like a good idea.

I even tried Jimmy Bacon's house, although I didn't tell his mother the truth. I told her I needed another fox to fight the fox I had. Who could fault that for a reason?

Bobby Yahner, who was in the same grade as me at Nativity, answered the door at the Yahner residence and called his mother. Mrs. Yahner told me I'd be hard put to find an old fur, fox or otherwise, in our neighborhood. She meant that this was the type of neighborhood where you'd hear people use the phrase, "Our house looks the way it does because we're too poor to paint and too proud to white-wash." Now this wasn't a new or original phrase even then, but poor people borrow everything else, so why not phrases.

The next house, Mrs. Hill's, I skipped entirely, and worked my way to the corner Barshaw house. In between were all "No" answers, often accompanied by smiles and chuckles. Mrs. Barshaw didn't have an old fur but suggested I try Mangold Cleaners across the street. Maybe a customer left a fur to be cleaned and forgot to pick it up. I thanked her, debated for ten seconds whether I should cross the street since I wasn't allowed to, and crossed.

The Mangold house, in mid-block, could easily be seen from our front porch and I prayed Mom wouldn't wander outside, see me, and start yelling. She'd be sure to tell Dad, and that could be horrendous. Nothing distinguished Mangold Cleaners from other frame houses on the street except for the sign attached to their front porch railing: Mangold Laundry and Dry Cleaning. The Mangold sign consisted of a square, wood-framed window screen. The letters were wooden block, painted white, and thin wires nailed to the back of the letters were woven through the screen, then twisted to hold them in place. They had laundry and dry cleaning machines in their basement and I overheard my parents say they had opened a dry cleaning store on a big street in another neighborhood. The Mangolds were expanding.

Mrs. Mangold answered my knock, listened patiently to my plea for any old fur she had lying around and asked where my clothes were that needed cleaning. When I told her I had none she smiled, shook her head, and gently closed the door. The closing of the door was accompanied by laughter I now had become accustomed to, yet resented, and I hoped some new cleaning process would come along to put Mangolds out of business. I envisioned some guy named Martin developing it and quickly made up a great brand name — *Martinizing.*

My disappointing fur quest ended. I contemplated appearing on the street with one fur chap, figured it would look silly and rejected the idea. Instead I mentally changed the fox into the pet dog I always wanted — one that didn't bark or bite and slept a lot. It would be tragic to deform such a beautiful animal anyway, I reasoned. Besides, I hadn't used it yet to scare hell out of my little sisters.

* * *

Dad saved enough money for a car and purchased a 1929 Model A Ford from Mr. Shafer, drove it into our backyard and spent hours tuning the motor to perfection. My two brothers and I watched and halfheartedly listened as he explained what he was doing to the engine and why, like a surgeon performing a delicate operation. Dad was a machinist and tool maker and thought everyone should be enthralled by machinery. To me the only enthralling thing about our new car was the thought of long drives to escape summer doldrums.

During summer, people passed leisure time on their front porch gently swinging to and fro while sitting on a contraption appropriately called a "porch swing," a legless wooden bench with a back, armrests on each end and suspended about eighteen inches above the porch floor by chains leading from armrests to the porch ceiling. Numerous single, young men and women spent warm, starlit, entrancing evenings swaying on a swing together and woke up the next morning betrothed.

These were pre-motel days, before Bing Crosby and Fred Astaire invented the Holiday Inn, so amorous encounters required a lot more improvisation than current swains have to muster. The porch swing was a very poor substitute for a motel room, but much better than the alternative, the backyard hammock.

For kids, a porch swing presented a challenge — get it swinging fast and hard enough so it banged into the porch railing or the house front. Either way, the noise guaranteed a visit from a screaming parent.

We didn't have a swing, nor did the Muglias, but they did have a porch glider, five feet long, suspended on a framework by straps, hinges and springs, and completely covered by padding and vinyl-like material. It was more comfortable than a suspended swing but only glided back and forth a short distance.

Rose Muglia, Virginia Gullo and my sisters, Pat and Mary were sitting on the glider one morning when I joined them. Sitting on the porch steps, I dispassionately eavesdropped on their conversation while trying to think of something more exciting to do. (When an energetic boy relies on the conversation of four young girls for excitement, then excitement must have been very hard to come by that day. I don't recall what they talked about when I joined them, but I doubt if every sentence started with, "He goes,"

"She goes," "They go" or "I go." This was long before "go" replaced "said" in the English language.) When they started talking about kissing, my attention intensified. From the discussion it was evident none of us had much firsthand experience with the subject. We all had suffered our adult relatives quick-kissing us and observed parents kissing hello and good-bye and even in-between at times. The romantic-comedy movies, approved by the Legion, usually ended with single people kissing, but we knew they got married a fast minute after the credits stopped rolling. This almost explained why my heart pounded with fright when Mary suggested Virginia and I kiss and describe how it felt. Virginia, Rosie and I were all eight years old, Pat was ten and Mary a year older, so we were all much too young to get married. However, for the sake of experimentation, I reluctantly agreed. Virginia wasn't enthusiastic about it either, but after a little cajoling and catcalling (Don't be a fraidy-cat!) she said she'd participate.

Instinctively, we knew we couldn't engage in public kissing, but Mary had a solution. Virginia and I could crawl under the glider whose skirt would safely conceal us from prying neighbors who might inform parents. We scrambled under the glider, carefully avoiding any undue touching in the process, and ended up facing each other on our sides.

Although wishing to be elsewhere, I felt I'd rather be there than anywhere. That Virginia was a comely, young lady hadn't escaped my notice and though I disliked girls, Virginia definitely appealed to me. We held a brief, whispered conversation: "What do we do now?" "I don't know." "I've never done this before." "Neither have I." "Let's not do it." "They're gonna ask us about it." "Okay, let's try it." We tightened our lips and kissed.

Later, neither Virginia nor I could clarify our feelings except to say it was okay. It was. My face stayed flushed for some time and I knew I wanted to do it again, but another opportunity never presented itself. I considered spending a lot more time under the glider hoping Virginia would one day return, but knew if Mr. and Mrs. Muglia discovered me there I'd have an awful lot of explaining to do. They'd probably tell my parents, mention that I didn't know why I was under there, and suggest I be committed — a thought that had also crossed my father's mind a time or two. The memory of that kiss and the feelings it evoked remained with me for weeks. Eventually I resumed a more normal "girl avoiding" attitude as the memory faded, but it never, ever, faded completely.

* * *

Often after eating the evening meal, called supper, my younger brother and sisters left the table, stood next to our mother and proudly exclaimed, "Feel my tummy, Mummy!"

Rubbing their stomachs she'd say, "That's a good (boy or girl)," for their stomachs were full and extended from eating all food placed in front of them. This was referred to as "cleaning your plate," an action valued by Depression era parents who paid food bills.

I never had a tummy rub. Supper had become a contest between me and my parents. There were only so many types of food I ate. Round steak and pork chops were okay, but every bit of fat had to be removed. Potatoes were great with butter, not gravy. Broccoli, cauliflower and lima beans weren't edible; peas and string beans were. Corn on the cob was delicious; canned corn wasn't. Bread was edible, but not its crust. There had to be at least a quarter-inch space between all foods on my plate. If one food mixed with another I wouldn't eat it. These and other finicky "rules" naturally upset my parents. Mom explained about the poor starving children in China and Dad threatened to jump down my throat and gallop my guts out. All their yelling and pleading was useless. At least once a week Dad lifted me bodily out of the kitchen chair, slapped me on various parts of my body and dumped me onto the living room couch to cry and meditate on the unfairness of life in general and parents in particular. Other times Dad told me to sit at the table until I had eaten every morsel on my plate. Three hours later I'd be staring at cold potatoes, dried lima beans and bread crust turned hard as a nut.

Gradually I triumphed. Only certain pre-approved foods were put on my plate with an inch of space between each. I discovered if you were bullheaded and could put up with a little physical pain for a principle, no matter how stupid, you could turn people around — especially your mother.

Although victorious in this culinary dispute, I developed a deep resentment for poor starving children in China. I couldn't fathom why my dislike for broccoli and cauliflower should have anything to do with a bunch of kids in a faraway country. Even to this day, when I see a fat person, I find myself muttering, "Good for you for trying to help those damned Chinese kids. I hope they put too much starch in your shirts."

* * *

Cardboard boxes, crayons, orange crates and cord are useful in fashioning toy armor, once you borrow your father's hammer and saw and your mother's kitchen knife. Dismantle an orange crate, saw a point and tie a hilt on each slat and you have enough swords to outfit every knight on your block. Draw shields on sides of boxes, color them, cut them out with the butcher knife and attach them to forearms and hands with pieces of cord and you have all the armor needed for good sword fights, until someone gets rapped on the head and goes home crying, as Jimmy often did. Prince Valiant would have been proud.

I found another use for a cardboard box. My mother had a sailboat-shaped, blue-glass ink blotter. The sailboat sat on a curved base. The actual green blotter on the bottom of the base wore away so the sailboat became a dust-gathering table decoration. Mom surprised me by saying I could have it.

Taking it out to the back porch, I idly pressed down on one end of the curved base, released it, and tried to count the times it rocked back and forth before stopping. The sailboat appeared to be in a raging storm for about six seconds and then slowly calmed down. If only it continued to rock without being touched....

I had an inspiration. Using a 3x1x1 cardboard box retrieved from our garage, along with Scotch tape, rubber bands, string, and two saplings with leaves removed, I rigged a fine contraption. When finished, a sapling extended out of one side of the box, its thin end taped to the tip of the sail. The boat could be moved by pulling a string hanging out of a small hole in the box's opposite side. I felt completely divorced from the boat. Just pull the string and the boat rocked. I wasn't sure about the concept of perpetual motion, but I could feel immortality looming before me, and I didn't even have to fly a kite in a thunderstorm.

"What do you have there, Robert?" My dad stood inside the screen door where, oblivious to me, he had observed the rocking boat for some time.

He came out on the porch, stooped down, and I opened the box, showing him the sapling, anchoring string and rubber bands that created the movement of the sapling attached to the boat. He yelled, "Claire! Come on out here. I want you to see something!"

Mom came out and patiently tried to look interested as he pointed out the intricacies of the box. He kept shaking his head while making admiring remarks. "This is amazing! Look how he strung this stick between the sides of the box. And the rubber bands put just the right tension on the stick. Look over here. Watch what the sticks and rubber bands do when he pulls the other string!"

He finally stood up, turned to Mom and said, "I'm telling you, Claire. This kid is going to be a great inventor someday. He has imagination."

As they disappeared into the house I felt a mixture of pride and humility, for much of the inner workings of the box had been pure dumb luck. Yet the thought of being a great inventor sounded easier than being a Mountie and I seriously considered a shift in my future ambitions.

Sadly, Dad's admiration for my inventive genius was short-lived. He didn't think it so imaginative a week later when I decided all legs should have feet and nailed two pairs of his shoes to the legs of a basement chair.

What shall I do next?, I wondered. My parents voiced a similar question: "What will he do next?"

Brother Ed gave Chuck and me a great idea by telling us a geographic fact. If we burrowed straight down into the earth we'd end up on the other side of the world in China. Chuck and I raced into our backyard, I pointed out the spot where we'd begin digging and sent him into the kitchen to swipe two of the largest spoons he could find. He returned with two soup spoons and we began our venture.

It was easy at first, the ground was soft and we progressed nicely. Then Chuck mentioned we'd have to go through hell to reach China and we paused to discuss this new, hideous thought. Neither of us wanted to go to hell, but, we reasoned, only dead people became permanent residents and we were alive and just passing through. Besides, it would be a provocative experience to talk about upon our return. We continued digging.

The hole was two feet deep when we struck clay. Previously our sole problem was the soft dirt rolling back into the hole, but this clay was hard, heavy and difficult to cut with spoons. Our hands were burning and developing blisters.

Mom came outside and asked what we were doing. When I told her, she smiled and asked, "Are those my spoons?"

I explained that we just borrowed them and we'd clean them when we got back from China. She said, "You'd better," then waved to Mrs. Wolfe who was in her yard pinning wet laundry to her clothesline. "My boys are digging a hole to China," she announced loudly. Mrs.

Wolfe also smiled.

I couldn't help noticing that grownups always seemed to be excessively smiling when I worked on one of my important projects. Usually they didn't come right out and laugh. They just glanced at me and my current project, then exchanged furtive smiles.

We continued digging at a slower pace, until Chuck said, "My hands hurt. I quit," and walked away rubbing his palms.

I felt abandoned but couldn't stop — not now. Relentlessly I chopped at the clay. If I could get through the clay, maybe more soft sand would follow. My palm blisters broke, exposing raw flesh, and any pressure on the spoon caused searing pain. When the spoon clanked against a large embedded rock, I knew my journey had ended. The rock was impenetrable and a legitimate excuse to give up. I quickly filled the hole and returned the spoons.

I neglected to tell Mom the uppermost reason we had dug the hole, since it was a failed endeavor. The hole sat conveniently under our kitchen window. After suppers, all she would have had to do was open the window and drop leftover food directly down the hole to help feed all those starving Chinese children.

Ed was usually a wealth of information so, while sitting on the front steps one evening, I asked him if everyone saw things in the same color. He answered, "Of course."

I pointed out that if I didn't know my colors and saw the sky as green, he saw it as blue and he told me it was blue then for the rest of my life I'd think green was blue. And if I saw the grass as red, someone told me it was green, then red would be green to me. He patiently explained it to me this way: "That's the dumbest idea I ever heard." He shouted through the front screen door, "Hey, Ma! Where'd you get this kid? He's nuts!"

I immediately noted that Ed hadn't resorted to a furtive smile. He wasn't quite grown-up yet, so he came right out and said what some smiling grownups were thinking. He then leaped off the steps and loped down the sidewalk in search of his friends, leaving me wondering, "Are his brown corduroy knickers really orange?"

IV

Our maternal aunt from Cleveland visited us. I developed an instant love for Aunt Paula when she walked Pat, Chuck and me to Morley's ice cream and candy store for chocolate sodas. The proprietors of this magnificent Gratiot avenue store manufactured ice cream, candy and other sweets right on their premises. It was tantalizing to watch Morley's candymakers create chocolate in the store's front window.

After consuming a soda I wondered if it was possible to slurp so many you couldn't slurp another. How could anything tasting so delectable not be available at all times? Why couldn't it be made at home? Couldn't it be sold for a nickel and put Popsicles out of business? When I asked Aunt Paula if she'd buy us another soda before returning to Cleveland she said, "No, but if I come back next year I certainly will."

So now I looked forward to two visitors per year — the unreal Santa Claus and Aunt Paula. (Chuck and I accidentally discovered Santa wasn't real the previous Christmas season when we came upon toys and wrapped presents stashed way back in our parents' bedroom closet. We quietly discussed our findings and other evidence pointing to a Santaless world and determined never to tell anyone, especially our parents. Besides reprimanding us for snooping in their room, they might not give us the toys on the big day. But we also kept the secret for a couple more years so we could remain on the dole. What convinced us to admit we no longer believed was when we became too big to sit on Santa's lap at Sears. Santa didn't seem too thrilled about it either.)

Before Aunt Paula departed she bought some going-away presents. I received a small iron bank shaped like a finely-detailed house, gold-painted with green roof. The roof peak had a slot for coins and she slipped a nickel in the slot and made me promise to save up for a soda. I promised, and after she left, had a difficult time shaking out the nickel. The bank came in handy, but not for saving coins.

One day my exasperated mother told me, "Robert! Go outside and get the smell blown off you!" This was her quaint way of telling me to leave before I drove her to infanticide. Taking her advice, I decided to build a town in the backyard using my house bank, toy car and truck. One house doesn't make a town, but I could construct more out of cardboard or mud. First I'd check the neighbor's garbage for materials.

That's where I found a treasure. Mrs. Wolfe's garbage included an empty Log Cabin syrup can. This ingenious tin can had a log cabin shape; its sides painted to resemble logs. Also painted on its sides were a door, windows, bearded languid mountaineers holding rifles and, on one end, a red chimney leading up to the peaked roof where the can's cap was situated. Unscrew the chimney cap, invert the can and out poured syrup instead of smoke.

I searched through every garbage receptacle on both sides of our alley — even examining Mrs. Hill's garbage while keeping a wary eye on her back door — and found two more syrup cans. I gave each garbage container a good kick before rummaging to assure it didn't harbor foraging rats, a precautionary measure always employed by those of us who spent a considerable amount of time in Detroit's alleys and counted garbage-can-rummaging among our favorite outdoor sports. Rats were plentiful and Ed once told me the rat had been designated "State Rodent." I didn't know whether the State of Michigan had chosen a state rodent, but it sounded plausible.

After sweeping stones and debris from a small area of ground near our back porch, I smoothed the dirt, set up my four buildings, used a stick to draw a sidewalk and street and added the car and truck. But something was missing — grass. Wandering around looking for anything green, I saw moss growing on one side of our backyard tree and, using a kitchen knife, easily peeled off sheets of it. The neighbor's trees also had a ready supply. It was a bonanza of toy-town grass that could be effortlessly removed and shaped into lawns.

When finished I stood back and proudly admired my miniature streetscape. Later my dad also admired it and I heard him tell Mom, "Claire, the kid's built a town out there. He might get into designing buildings someday. Maybe even become an architect."

Architect! I didn't know what it meant but it sounded important and I considered giving up my Mountie dream.

Two days later my moss died; my syrup cans started looking like what they were, duplicates of each other; my finely-detailed bank house appeared out of place with rustic log cabins; and the car and truck weren't in proper proportion. I learned that first impressions sometimes mislead before reality settles in. Regretfully, I destroyed my creation.

* * *

Many pedestrians passed our house at all hours. Mom, when she had time, loved to sit on our front porch and watch them go by. She waved or said hello and they often stopped to chat for a minute or two. Sometimes she learned their names and other times she herself named them. One bald, portly man, about 55-years of age, completely ignored her greetings. He moved at a deliberate pace, carrying a lunch bucket, never glancing to either side, concentrating on his objective —either getting to work in the morning or getting home to his evening meal. He weighed at least 300 pounds, yet still had slack in his trousers' waist, so he wore suspenders and a wide leather belt. Mom called it "double security against embarrassment." Right after he passed our house one late afternoon he reached back and scratched his left buttock. From that moment on he had a name. Mom dubbed him "Mr. Pick-a-seat." Seeing him coming from Gratiot, her announcement, "Here comes Mr. Pick-a-seat," guaranteed an outbreak of giggles from her children. She tried to shush us, but our snickers still escaped. Mr. Pick-a-seat noticed our amusement and began speeding up his pace when passing our house. I felt a little sorry for him, but he could have been friendlier.

Mom had names for others who passed by regularly. There was an old, bearded gentleman with a German accent who walked very slowly and, regardless of weather, wore a gray homburg hat. He always had a cheerful "Gud day, Ma'am," as he made a slight bow and raised his hat about ten inches off his head. He became known as Mr. Tip-a-hat.

There was a man with a limp named Mr. Step-and-a-half and a rather shabby character who wore a loud plaid jacket and walked each day to a Gratiot avenue store to purchase a racing form. He'd be reading it upon his return and always had a toothpick in the corner of his mouth. He wanted everyone to think he had eaten recently. He was dubbed Mr. Bet-a-horse.

Mr. Stuff-in-the-eye got his name on the day we found a bat — the kind that ordinarily hang around caves — at the base of the tree in front of our house. It lay face up on the berm area between sidewalk and curb. A small crowd of children and adults gathered to stare and comment and at first no one knew it's genus. It had brownish-black, slimy fur, and its wings wrapped completely around its body. A knowledgeable naturalist in the crowd pronounced it a bat and theorized it flew blindly into the tree, cracked its head on the trunk and died. One man picked up two thin sticks and pried a wing apart from its body. It definitely was a bat. I'd heard bats were just rats with wings, but this one looked a lot uglier than a rat. When the man removed the sticks, the wing slowly refolded across its body, like an insect closes its legs when dead. We all sighed with relief, nodding and muttering, "It's dead."

Except it wasn't. Slowly it started moving its wings and feet, and abruptly we all had feet with wings. Everyone scattered with shouts of, "Get outta here!" "It's alive!" "It'll get in your hair!"

The bat turned over on its stomach, tested its wings twice, then with loud flapping noises soared straight up and disappeared into the tree leaves above. There were nervous comments and laughter, mainly because we'd been so close to a live bat without losing blood. The adults quickly left the scene, but we continued staring warily up at the tree. No one could quite believe the resurrection, but we all witnessed it and began lying to each other about how we were never scared, not for an instant. However, after all our bravado was put to rest, it was pretty much agreed that if we had to have a bat in the neighborhood, it would be better if it had *Louisville Slugger* engraved on it.

Mom, who remained on our porch through the whole episode, sat on her chair enjoying our excited chatter. A well-dressed young man heading for Gratiot avenue walked under the tree and noticed us staring at the tree top. He paused and asked, "What's up there? What are you kids looking at?"

Almost in unison we told him "A bat!" and one boy explained, "It just flew up there!" Another said, "It's near the top!"

He peered upward, and at that moment a robin flew into the tree and ejected a large portion of waste matter that struck him directly alongside his nose. He reached for his face and muttered a loud "goddamn!" when he realized

what had happened. He also made some less-than-compli-
mentary comments about the ancestry of the robin while he
fumbled for his handkerchief. Mom went into our house
and returned with a wet towel.

We did our worst to contain our amusement. The young
man cleaned his face and appeared both embarrassed and
angry. He thanked my mother for the towel, apologized for
his language and speedily departed.

Our laughter subsided, but we agreed it was the funniest
thing we'd ever seen. Mom reminded us we shouldn't make
fun of another's misfortune. "Put yourselves in his place.
How would you like it? Do unto others." Yet, from that day
forward, she always referred to him as "Mr. Stuff-in-the-
eye."

Luckily, we had no professional baseball players in the
neighborhood. Mom would have been in a dilemma. It's
well known what part of the anatomy they're famous for
scratching, but it wasn't in her nature to be crude. Even
when angry, the strongest phrase she ever used was "Heck
on it!"

Mom had a penchant for creating words. She often
served us scootled eggs for breakfast. As a teenager, Betty
considered herself sophisticated and somewhat of a speech
purist and one day gently chided, "Mother, why do you call
them scootled? Everyone else calls them scrambled."

"Because," Mom explained, "I put them in the skillet and
scootle them around." You can't argue with that logic.

"Flink" was another favorite word. I'm not sure what it
meant, but it seemed to fit in enough places to make it
worthwhile. If we asked Mom about a person she didn't
care for, she dismissed him by saying, "He's flink." If I
brought her one of my harebrained schemes or projects and
solicited her opinion, she gave it in two words. "It's flink."

She didn't need stronger words than "flink" because she
married a man who made cursing and swearing into an art
form. Dad could speak extemporaneously on a multitude of
subjects to any person or, preferably, group of persons, and

in the process spew enough vitriolic words and comments to hold the attention of a Marine Corps drill sergeant. He told stories using words and phrases so expletively that we listened to the same stories over and over and still hung on every syllable. He did not have to use the eff-word or variations of it because he did such an artistic job with the more common words of the day: Flop-eared sonovabitch, goon-headed bastard, and so on. I never heard him speak to men who worked for him in later years, but I imagine when he had a bad day, and they were not doing their job to suit him, he embellished their vocabulary.

Dad's good friend, Barney Yahner, who lived down the street, often came to our house to visit. Barney's father, a gentleman in his 80s, seldom left the Yahner house, but always asked Barney to take him along when he visited my dad. He added little to their conversation, mostly sat and listened. One day Barney asked his father why he liked going on these visits. "Because," he answered, "it's just such a pleasure to hear Mr. Beckwell swear."

This acclamation wasn't a Medal of Honor or academy award, yet when one excels at something, it's nice to receive even a modicum of recognition. When Barney told Dad what his father had said, Dad's reaction was very much what we expected. He laughed and said, "Well I'll be a goddamned sonovabitch!"

The subjects on which Dad would speak at the drop of a hat, question or comment were many and varied. They included baseball, his days in a Pennsylvania grade school, time spent working in coal mines and steel mills, the life and times of his brothers, and tales of his father who came to this country in the late nineteenth century from Ireland and could easily be included in anybody's list of "Unforgettable Characters."

In addition to Dad's talent for salty, and sometimes ear-burning language, he had a phenomenal memory. He had instant recall of the names of all the children with whom he had attended the first five grades of school (the extent of his formal education), and names of almost anyone else who crossed his path in his early years. But what set his performances apart from those of other good tellers-of-tales was his presentation. Once he had the attention of his audience, his thespian artistry emerged and we were treated to a couple hours of unbridled dramatics, gestures, quotations, possibly a small dance, an impersonation of his fifth-grade teacher trying to get out of a tipped-over outhouse behind the school or a demonstration of how to whip a mule in a dark coal mine. Dad picked slate in Pennsylvania mines when he was seven and drove mules at age 12. All mules in his stories had human names and characteristics. Jim Mule was intelligent and industrious; Bob Mule, obedient and gentle; Pete Mule, lazy and ornery. A careless miner once turned his back on Pete Mule and found his shoulder clamped in Pete's mouth. Miner lore held that a mule can't reopen its jaws until they are closed completely, causing the miner to scream in terror, as well as pain, for a shoulderless existence loomed. Dad's older brother, Edward, a brawny man, picked up a pick handle and knocked Pete Mule unconscious with one powerful blow to the skull, loosening its jaws. When the mule staggered to its feet, Edward volunteered to change Pete's temperament permanently. The mine foreman gave permission and Edward with his whip and Pete Mule with his bad attitude were quartered in an empty stall. Two hours later they emerged and mean Pete had become meek Peter.

I once asked Dad why horses weren't used in mines since they seemed to be more docile and trainable. He answered, "Mules stepping between railroad ties are sure-footed bastards; horses trip and break their goddamn legs. Also mules don't react when their ears rub the top of a mine tunnel, but it drives horses crazy."

Dad liked poetry. Even if he couldn't justify the incongruity of it, he might slip into a recitation of *Casey at the Bat, Face Upon the Floor, Dangerous Dan McGrew, In School-Days* or any other of that ilk he'd committed to memory.

44

Dad's favorite subject was baseball. Even in his 40s he loved joining neighborhood kids in the street or alley for a baseball game. Bat in hand, he'd declare loud and clear for all to hear, "The old man can still hit a few fungos." Kids loved it for they knew when the game was over they'd end the evening sitting all over our porch, steps and railings as he regaled them with stories about the greats of baseball. They'd hear the exploits of Ty Cobb, Babe Ruth, John McGraw, Christy Mathewson, Joe Cronin, the Dean brothers and so many more. Dad quoted batting averages, fielding averages, and even drinking averages of the more free-spirited legends of the game. He even claimed that his mother was the midwife when Steve O'Neil, a Detroit Tiger manager, was born in Manooka, a little town outside Scranton, Pennsylvania. I never knew if this was true, but we kids enjoyed the story. Dad never let mere facts get in the way of a good tale. He was at his best when surrounded by a throng of children, and with eight of his own he always had an excellent start toward a large gathering.

Dad often offered us advice and instructions: Stop the monkeyshines; quit the shenanigans; hold the noise down to a roar. He seemed uninterested in how other parents raised their children. His rules were: No playing on the street; no climbing on roofs; no unnecessary noise, especially when he tried to sleep; obey your mother; go to church on Sundays and holy days; respect elders; do your home and school work; no profanity; no dogs; no bikes; be fully clad before leaving your bedroom...no bathrobes or pajamas allowed; and no smoking. Breaking rules got you yelled at or smacked. If bumper stickers were in vogue his would have asked, "Have you slugged your kid today?"

So we usually didn't break these rules — until he left for work. Mom, who was less restrictive and often squeezed and kissed us, only asked that we be careful and play nice, so we naturally supposed she cared more for us.

Dad never verbally expressed his love for his children. Yet he arose every workday at five a.m. and never took off sick. On icy winter mornings he stoked the furnace before leaving for work so we woke up warm. When we did something praiseworthy, like bring home a respectable report card, he smiled, said "Good going" and patted our shoulder. He made sure we were clothed, fed and sheltered, and obviously worried about our safety. I developed a distinct impression that he would have died to protect us. As the biblical passage says, "Greater love hath no man—"

Like many another good Irish lad, Dad was known to take a drink, although he would say he limited his drinking to St. Patrick's Day, Sundays, Holy Days of Obligation, and those days ending with "Y." He thought a balanced diet was a bottle of beer in each hand. I used to get calls from concerned bartender friends in later years who asked me to come and retrieve Dad from their taverns. When I arrived he'd be stoned, but he maintained his sense of humor. Once I walked up to him at the bar and asked, "Drunk again, Father?" He turned to me and answered, "So am I, Rob."

Another time I found him lying on his back on the floor in front of a bar with drink in hand. I always tried to be gentle with him so I asked, "Pa, would you like to sit here on a stool?"

He said, "No thank you. I'll just stand here."

After Mom died, Dad's drinking became a big problem, but I won't go into it since the problem has been written about so many times by so many people about so many people. Let it suffice to say that he did kick the booze completely and spent quite a few happy sober years before he left us.

And if by some chance he caught the UP, instead of the DOWN, escalator, I'm sure that St. Peter and all his cronies are well versed in the intricacies of baseball. I wonder if Dad has been able to contact those old-timers like Ruth, Gehrig, Cronin, et al., and point out to them what they did wrong in their careers. I would like to have been there when he told Cobb how to steal bases.

But I hope that wherever he is, and the jury is still out, he has a cold bottle of beer (it can't hurt him now) and a bunch of kids to sit around on steps and listen to those wonderful, vivid stories. I also hope he'll still be telling them when I get there.

V

The pony photographer ambled down Belvidere on a sunny afternoon. He carried a large tripod camera and was followed by his teenage son leading a spotted, saddled pony. Cowboy paraphernalia was stacked on the saddle. The pony guaranteed a Pied-Piperish trail of neighborhood children. If the children lived on the street, he sent them ahead to ask their parents if they could have a picture taken astride the pony. Of course I begged my mother and of course she said, "No, we can't afford it."

To her credit, she did appear on the porch to talk to the photographer, but the verdict remained, "We can't afford it."

I dreaded the entourage arriving in front of Jimmy Bacon's house for I was positive his mother would be proud to have her son experience the thrill of sitting on that pony — no matter what the expense.

I was right. The photographer helped Jimmy mount up, tied a blue bandanna around his neck, added a black studded vest, a two-gun holster set and topped it off with a white Stetson hat. He folded leather chaps attached to the stirrup straps over Jimmy's legs, positioned the pony on the lawn in front of Jimmy's house, set up his camera on the sidewalk, slipped under the camera's black hood and prepared to snap a picture of smiling Jimmy.

That should be me up there, I thought, and fantasized the pony suddenly bucking and tossing Jimmy over its head while making a break for freedom. Instead the camera clicked and Jimmy was allowed to remain on the pony all the way to Yahner's house. I wrestled with an urge to yell something about there being one horse and two horse's asses in the picture, but decided it would sound like sour grapes. The photographer lifted Jimmy from the saddle uniting him with the rest of us earthbound kids following the pony, but when Jimmy started talking about how great his ride was I turned and slowly walked home. I crossed our backyard, entered our garage, leaned against the wall, sank to the floor and wept.

All I wanted in the whole world was money to have a pony picture taken when the photographer showed up next time, but there were few ways for children to acquire money. The most popular was an allowance, an outright grant with no strings. Once a week parents handed you a nickel or dime. I had heard about it but never experienced it, unless the dime my mother gave me for almost weekly Saturday matinees at the Arcadia counted as an allowance.

You could sell old newspapers, rags, furniture, metal or other assorted junk to any of many sheenies who daily drove horse-drawn wagons through the alleys of Detroit, blowing tin horns to announce their presence. I don't know why we called them "sheeny" — a better name would be junkman or hornblower — but that's the only name we used. In future years I learned "sheeny," when used in an opprobrious sense, meant Jew, but I never understood why because the sheenies who plied their trade in our alleys were of many ethnic and racial backgrounds and spoke various dialects. In those young years we didn't know one dialect from another and trying to understand those trades-people was part of the bartering fun. They bargained astutely, doled out a minimum number of pennies, and I used to think behind their stern countenance lurked a sly smile.

You could cash in empty soft drink bottles at a neighborhood store and get two cents each, but there was enormous competition for these bottles, even from adults.

On rare occasions older relatives or your parents' friends would visit and hand you a nickel or a couple pennies and tell you, "Go play outside for awhile." Although this seemed like accepting a bribe, it also seemed honorable. You were paid for delivering a service — serenity. I toyed with the idea of going from door to door selling serenity to the neighbors. When I mentioned this great, surely profitable, plan to Dad he said it bordered on extortion. He'd rather I didn't get involved, but admitted that having me put away for a few years as a guest of the State certainly had a nice ring to it.

Many times I had an opportunity to steal money. However, this was specifically forbidden in the Ten Commandments with no exceptions, conditions or qualifications — no ifs, ands or buts. Just don't do it! No excuses! Thou shalt not steal! Don't even think about it! Even if you think about, don't do it! If God doesn't get you, your parents will! I decided not to steal.

Instead Chuck, Jimmy and I opened a Kool-Aid stand. Mrs. Shafer loaned us an orange crate to use as a stand; Mom supplied Kool-Aid, sugar, two pitchers, water and ice; I mixed the Kool-Aid and made the *Kool-Aid 5 cents* sign; and Chuck and Jimmy positioned the crate on our front lawn. We sat two pitchers, one containing orange Kool-Aid, the other strawberry, on top of the crate along with four clean glass tumblers and a long handled spoon, the spoon doubling as a stirrer and a ladle to rescue an occasional flying insect with a swimming urge. By two o'clock on a hot steamy afternoon we were in business.

The only thing lacking was customers. Passersby either ignored our sales pitch, which consisted of a pleading look and a "Cool drink, Mister?" whine, or said, "No, thanks." The sympathy spiel didn't work well at all. It's hard to look like one of those starving Chinese kids.

One woman complained, "Five cents is too much." I changed the sign to two cents and within a half-hour sold four glasses. Then Mrs. Wolfe and Mrs. Shafer each bought a glass and, with a few more sold to strangers, sales were definitely picking up. It looked like we were going to run out of Kool-Aid and we didn't have any more in the house. We didn't want to spend the money we just earned to buy more. Our solution: Add more ice.

Chuck was in charge of supplying clean glasses and ice. After one of his trips into our house to rinse glasses he reported Mom was getting upset. She had to use an ice pick to chip slivers off the block of ice in our wooden ice box and it was depleting the block. Wouldn't you know that in our haste to enter the business world, we had started our little refreshment company on a day when the iceman wasn't peddling in our neighborhood. Had he been, we could have replenished our supply quite handily by swiping chunks of ice off of his truck, a practice at which we all were adept.

In later years, with the advent of electric refrigerators and demise of ice trucks and ice cards in front windows, I determined that icemen played games with us. On real hot days there were always nice chunks of ice of swipeable size lying on truck floors, and although drivers hollered and climbed down from their truck cabs looking angry, we always seemed to have time to jump off the back and get away. I think our "Ice Men" were "Nice Men."

Chuck, Jimmy and I took turns waiting on our customers — one standing behind our stand while the other two rested on our porch steps or fetched more ice. Traffic picked up. Mr. Pick-a-seat passed and gave no heed to our plea. Mr. Stuff-in-the-eye tried a glass, probably to prove he wasn't afraid to stop under the tree in front of our house. A limping Mr. Step-and-a-half bought a glass and only drank half of it.

The Kool-Aid was losing its flavor and color. One man spit it out and said, "That's awful!" As he walked away he muttered, "I know what it is, but whose?"

We tried it ourselves and agreed it tasted terrible. Besides, we were tired and bored with the storekeeper routine. We counted our profits, split thirty-two cents three ways (Jimmy got ten cents), emptied the tinted water on the ground, returned pitchers and orange crate, and concluded that our little entrepreneurial endeavor left much to be desired. I also concluded I'd never have a photograph taken on a pony.

However, fifty years later, when touring Ireland, I visited the beautiful cliffs of Moher, one of Ireland's more breath-taking sights. In front of a tourist's gift shop stood a nice old gentleman holding the reins of a donkey. On the donkey's back sat a little dog with a pipe in its mouth. The man said for a pound note he'd take my picture in front of the donkey. I said, "Get the dog off there and let me on and I'll give you a five pound note for a picture."

Minutes later, as I paid him five pounds for the Polaroid picture and walked away smiling, I could see he wondered why I murmured, "Eat your heart out, Jimmy."

* * *

I didn't return to Nativity's main school building for fourth grade. Fourth and fifth grades were located in an annex behind the main building. Whoever designed the school didn't foresee the neighborhood's population explosion, but once it happened school officials quickly built the annex and purchased and modified three two-story flats on McClellan, converting them into classrooms. The annex was a wooden, one-story, four-schoolroom, barrack-type structure with slanted roof. Fourth and fifth graders felt a little like outcasts, but we were still closer to the main building than sixth-, seventh-, eighth and ninth-grade boys who were taught in the flats located between the convent and a corner gas station at Shoemaker street. When the wind was just right on hot, muggy days and windows had to be open to sustain life, these boys were blessed with lovely

53

aromas of oil, gasoline, grease and exhaust wafting around classrooms. This did very little to improve their already waning attitude toward formal education.

After fifth grade all girl students returned to the main building. By separating boys and girls after fifth grade the school officials probably felt they did their part to mute the population explosion. It didn't work completely because separated-by-sex grade school students did manage to find ways to overcome such barriers, yet it made little difference since, for the most part, our sex lives were still only in our minds.

All of us in grade school, except first graders who hadn't made their first confession and communion, did get together daily at 8 o'clock Mass. Each morning at 7:45 we lined up in front of classrooms and nuns, with a minimum of difficulty, marched us silently, except for sounds of shuffled feet and muffled whispers, over to, and into, church. The timing and control were astounding. We all agreed most nuns should be named "Sister Mary Sergeant," although we never dared call them that. By 8 a.m. students were in church and ready, or unready as the case may be, to participate in the sacred rite.

On rare occasions when students were late all they had to do was sneak into church, sneak down the side aisle (walking on the sides of shoes quieted footsteps) and sneak into the end of a pew without their nun spotting them — but she usually did and they usually stayed after school a half-hour. The only time students ever appreciated Father Geller officiating at 8 o'clock Mass was when they were late, for that meant he wouldn't be standing around in front of church when they made their sneak attempt. He was bad news and could make students wish they'd been born Protestant.

One morning I was late. I had stayed up later than usual doing homework I should have done earlier, and just didn't want to wake up. There was excessive morning commotion and my mother didn't miss me right away and when she did

54

it was too late. I was late. Everyone else had left for school. I didn't eat; just dressed, grabbed my books and took off running. As I approached the intersection of Cairney street I noticed the safety boys had already returned to school. Boy, was I late! Accelerating I made a quick left turn at the corner, raced into the street, slammed into the side of a fast-moving sedan and ended up lying next to the curb wondering what happened.

A milkman delivering milk to the Barshaws got to me first and asked if I was all right. I whimpered that my legs hurt, and then Mrs. Barshaw loomed over me along with the driver of the sedan and a couple of pedestrians. The driver said he didn't see me because I ran out from in front of the parked milk truck, the milkman said he had a right to park on any street and the driver was speeding, and Mrs. Barshaw said, "Be quiet! We have to find out if this kid is hurt."

They pulled up the legs of my knickers and there were large bruises on both sides of both knees. Even in my distraught frame of mind it embarrassed me that they could see the rubber bands around the cuffs of my knickers. It was a well known fact that elastic in knicker cuffs had a very short life span and, only a few weeks after purchase, had to be supplemented with sturdy rubber bands, which were never color coordinated with our knickers. These bands also had the responsibility for keeping our knee socks from slipping down over our shoes. I hoped they'd not further embarrass me by taking off my shoes and finding my Shredded Wheat carton insoles. I lamented to myself that I hadn't changed to a fresh pair of insoles, but our Wheaties box hadn't been quite emptied.

My mother came running, panicky, and when she calmed down asked if I could walk. I bravely said, "I'll try, but I don't think so."

The driver of the sedan, a burly-type person in his 30s, said, "I'll carry him." Someone retrieved my books that were knocked across Cairney and gave them to Mom and we all returned home where I was gently laid in bed.

There ensued some discussion between Mom and the driver about how I sustained four bruises and they determined his car hit one side of my knee smacking it into the other and the outside of that knee hit the curb. Mom told him I'd probably have to stay in bed for a week, and he said he'd drop by soon to make sure I was okay. This elated me. A week in bed, no school, waited on, and the driver returning and possibly slipping me some conscience money.

Three days later Mom caught me practicing a limp in my bedroom and I had to return to school. The consolatory nun helped me catch up on my homework and never inquired why I was late on my accident day. When I heard students whispering about me I tried to look pained, like I'd been through a horrible experience. It felt good to be the object of their conversations. At recess, students who never talked to me before asked sympathetically how it felt to be hit by a car. In a friendly tone I told them, "Not too bad. Ya oughta try it." They looked at me strangely, like they were sorry they'd asked, and returned to ignoring me. By lunch time they had all stopped glancing my way and my celebrity status ended.

The accident was another learning experience. I learned not to expect conscience money. I never saw that driver again. The accident had only one positive aspect. All the time spent practicing my limp comes in handy now when I get out of my car after parking in a "handicapped" zone.

* * *

Dad quit Packard and got a job at Gelatin Products, located in mid-Detroit. (This little corner plant eventually grew to be known as the R. P. Scherer Corporation.) Gelatin Products manufactured vitamin-filled capsules, so for the next few years we were probably the city's healthiest kids. Dad brought home many bottles of capsules, and every morning Mom encouraged us to sample multiple vitamins from A to Zinc. "Don't forget your vitamins" gained importance over "Be careful" in our mother's final admonition before we left our house.

To assure his daily on-time arrival at his new job, my dad sold his Model A and purchased a 1932 four-door DeSoto. This old DeSoto was in good mechanical shape, but needed a paint job. The used car salesman offered to have it painted, but the price he quoted wasn't included in the "out the door" cost. This didn't bother Dad since he always said an automobile is only "painted scrap iron." With this thought in mind he stopped at a Western Auto store on Gratiot and bought two quarts of automotive black enamel and a paint brush. Arriving home, he pulled the car into our backyard, opened the paint cans, and within an hour we had a shiny black car.

It was a pleasant, sunny day, so Dad left the drying process to the good Lord. He, of course, did His usual fine job, but somehow forgot to reduce breezes blowing dust from the alley and much of it landed on Dad's newly painted DeSoto. When Dad eyed the results of his labor he overindulged in much profanity. The Lord looked down, smiled, and said, "What the hell. It's only painted scrap iron." Earl Scheib gained a convert that day.

* * *

Excitement reigned in Europe. Someone named Hitler, a man equivalent to President Roosevelt, had his army invading and taking over other countries, including Poland. I learned this by reading newspapers, listening to radio and watching Arcadia newsreels. Hitler was the leader of Germany, Father Geller was of Germanic stock and the meanest, toughest person I knew, so I concluded if all German soldiers were similar it wasn't surprising they were winning.

I had gleaned this opinion about Father Geller a few months previously when doubts were raised about the legality of bingo in Michigan. Bingo, held weekly in the church basement, was a real moneymaker for Nativity and the thought that these funds might be imperiled angered our pastor. When Michigan's Governor Fitzgerald died in March of 1939, Lieutenant Governor Dickinson, a devoutly religious old man adamantly against everything resembling fun, took over the job and promptly banned bingo throughout Michigan. This caused a stir among Nativity's parishioners who wondered how a fighter like Father Geller would react. He wasn't used to any lay person, even a governor, telling him what to do.

The following Sunday at ten o'clock high Mass before a standing-room-only crowd he mounted the pulpit and, after a brief sermon, gave a long, fist-pounding, spirited (but less-than-spiritual) diatribe about our new Governor's mandate and included his priestly thoughts on the state mixing in affairs of church. When ranted out he ended his invective speech with, "Bingo will continue in this church!" It did.

* * *

A witch lived on our street. Not many neighborhoods could make that claim...or cared to. Our witch was Mrs. Hill, a tall, angular, sharp-faced woman, about thirty-five years old with dark hair pulled back in a bun. She was loud and over-bearing to every child within earshot, the antithesis of her quiet, withdrawn husband. Her blue-gray painted house sat farther back from the sidewalk than other houses and, consequently, had a large front lawn. The lawn was surrounded by a three-foot high hedge. Little children always passed Mrs. Hill's house with caution — my sisters even crossed the street — for invariably, if in her front yard, Mrs. Hill screamed questions and advice such as, "What are you looking at? Keep going!" or "What are you up to? Go home!" She obviously disliked children and we were convinced if she caught us in her yard we'd end up in her caldron as a main stew ingredient. Of course she was a prime target for Halloween pranksters.

The celebration of Halloween changed considerably over the years. My father, who was raised in a small, eastern Pennsylvania mining town called Murray Town, told us the favorite kids' prank at the beginning of the 20th century was to tip over the neighbor's outhouse, preferably while the man of the house was having a post supper respite with a Sears catalog. Deodorants hadn't been invented and Father said that one guy in town smelled so bad he could count on being tipped over at least twice.

The closest Belvidere Street came to Halloween pranks was on Doorbell Night, the night before Halloween. It was just what it sounds like. Kids rang a neighbor's bell and then ran and hid while feeling absolutely malicious. Most neighbors knew about Doorbell Night so they ignored the ringing and continued listening to *Amos 'n' Andy*. That is, all except the "Wicked Witch of Belvidere," Mrs. Hill.

On one of these occasions, Ed had just rung her bell for the third time when he found she had stationed Mr. Hill at the side of their house and Mr. Hill had thoughts of ringing Ed's bell. Thus began one of the grandest foot races in the annals of Belvidere history. Ed cleared the front hedge, but found that "old man Hill" wasn't that old. He also cleared the hedge and was running as he hit the sidewalk, and Ed wondered why a man who could run so fast couldn't get away from Mrs. Hill. Ed managed to stay a couple strides ahead of him until they rounded the corner at Barshaw's house where Mr. Hill tripped and did an impressive backflip, before flopping on the sidewalk. Ed wasn't going to underestimate Mr. Hill again so he never slowed down. He ran around the block, circled to Gratiot, cut through backyards, and took refuge at home. Fifteen minutes later one of Detroit's finest stood at our front door. Mrs. Hill had called the police and Ed received a lengthy, verbal reprimand.

Today if you called 911 and reported that a kid rang your doorbell and ran away a Detroit operator would consider you deranged. Doorbell Night is now called Devil's Night and some with a faulty "Motown mentality" think burning people out of their homes is the proper way to celebrate. The arson taking place now makes previous Halloween pranks seem exceedingly tame.

VI

Russia invaded Finland and our nation's armchair generals predicted the much-larger Russian army would easily win, but Finnish ski-troops swept down from snow-covered mountains and stopped the surprised, befuddled Russians cold. Russian soldiers didn't hear the Finns coming on their silent skis or see them until the last moment because the Finns wore white uniforms that blended into snowy backgrounds. The Russians were getting massacred. It was a David/Goliath war and few people pulled for Goliath. The white-clad Finnish troops reminded me of my radio hero "The Shadow" who attained invisibility by "clouding men's minds."

* * *

For Christmas I received Tinkertoys and Chuck received a Lincoln Log set. But Betty received the most remarkable present of all — a two-sided jigsaw puzzle. Our whole family worked to put it together. I could tell the lighter-colored pieces filled with newsprint, when assembled, would form a newspaper page, an obvious observation I was sorry I blurted out for all to hear, for everyone glanced at each other with that "Why don't we take him out back and stone him" look.

Completed, the puzzle became an ordinary front page with a masthead, weather report, political happenings, foreign news and a farm report except for the banner headline proclaiming WAREHOUSE ROBBED. A related story detailed how an employee arrived at the warehouse office and discovered someone had broken into a company safe. The yegg escaped with thousands of dollars.

We pulled the puzzle pieces apart, turned them over, reassembled them and there before us was a picture of a masked safecracker crouched in front of an open, flashlight-illuminated safe, his burglar tools at his side as he reached for stacks of money.

It was the only two-sided jigsaw puzzle I ever saw and it's odd that more weren't made and sold. For instance on one side could be a picture of happy travelers waving from a deck of an ocean liner. On the opposite side the same people standing on a slanted deck singing, "Nearer My God to Thee." Or a priest officiating at the marriage of a happy couple on one side. On the opposite side a Justice of the Peace officiating at the marriage of the same priest.

* * *

January of 1940 brought a deep, good-packing snowfall and Ed and his friends built an oblong snowhouse. It began as a snowfort for protection during snowball fights, but after building a wall close and parallel to our garage, they decided to fill in the two sides. They covered it over with branches from discarded Christmas trees, dumped more snow on top, opened a small side entrance and Presto! A snow-house! They all disappeared into the house, covered its entrance with cardboard for privacy, and talked and did whatever young male teenagers are prone to do and talk about. I didn't know because I wasn't a teenager, nor allowed to enter this sacrosanct edifice. Even in my tender years, I realized that if I happened to be a female-type teenager, I would have little trouble entering this inviolable site. Yet, I didn't see any female-types lining up outside, so I started to suspect a snowhouse was not a good place to carry on a romantic tryst.

Two days later the Detroit Times' Sunday comic section contained a detailed diagram of how to construct an igloo. It was easy! Pack cardboard boxes with snow, add water, wait until the combination froze into icy blocks, remove from boxes and start building. I envisioned a five-foot-high dome with a crawl-through entrance, putting Ed's snowhouse to shame.

Feeling this huge construction endeavor couldn't be handled alone, I secured the aid of Bobby Yahner, Jimmy Bacon and Chuck. We could have called another boy for help — he was our age and lived far down Belvidere — but decided not to. We usually avoided him most months of the year because of his nasal problem that made him very hard to look at. His nose flowed from October through April — the flow resembled tiny lamb's legs — and he constantly wiped it on his jacket sleeves. His sleeves accumulated so many layers of dried fluid that he could have cut them into little squares and sold them as pocket mirrors. His nose action also caused two deep red rivulets to form from his nostrils to his upper lip, which wasn't too pleasing to look at either. In May his nose stopped draining, the redness faded and by August only a faint pinkness remained. His mother washed his jacket, October came and the whole ravaging process began anew.

The boxes for our igloo blocks had to be a uniform size. Concluding that Shredded Wheat cereal boxes would be ideal, we raided garbage receptacles and gathered six of them. I thought we'd find a lot more but, obviously, there were other neighborhood kids who preferred the flexibility and tensile strength of Shredded Wheat boxes for making insoles. I wonder if that's the way Dr. Scholl got started.

We stuffed the boxes with snow, poured in cold water and encountered our first problem. The temperature didn't go below freezing until nighttime so we had to leave the boxes overnight. The next morning Chuck and I ran outside to our backyard and found a second problem. The blocks of snow were frozen to the boxes and we had to tear the cardboard to free them. This brought up a third problem. Where to get more boxes? We doubted neighbors would cooperate and eat more Shredded Wheat. Even obtaining two or three boxes a day I calculated it would be mid-August before we completed our igloo. Apparently the Detroit Times comic section editors neglected to mention that Arctic residency was imperative for igloo construction. I told my mother about my igloo problems and she had no suggestions on how to build one but did offer some wise advice: "Don't believe everything you read in the funny papers."

Ed and his friends eventually tired of their snowhouse and we smaller children quickly commandeered and loved it —shortly before it collapsed.

* * *

In school, on St. Valentine's Day, I received a grand total of one comic-variety valentine from a boy named Bill Stellon. It reminded me of something. I wasn't very popular with classmates. Not that I did unpopular things — I just didn't associate or talk with them very often. Around home I was exactly the opposite, but with the same result. I talked too much and did do unpopular things.

Stellon, a round-faced, dark-haired, olive-skinned, out-going kid had contracted rheumatic fever early in life causing heart damage so he was prohibited from playing strenuous games. At recess we sat on the annex steps and watched our classmates romp. Stellon, older than most of us because he missed a whole year of school recovering from his illness, was in an enviable position because his heart problem made him smackproof. He clowned around in class with immunity. He became my best, and only, school friend.

When I mentioned my valentine disappointment at recess, he wisely pointed out a salient fact. Although I hadn't received any valentines besides his, neither had I given any to anyone, including himself. He further pointed out another not-so-salient fact, for the sake of conversation. If Adolph Hitler got four valentines that year, we could naturally assume that Father Geller got none; a remark good for a chuckle. Young disrespectful wags were fond of making little jokes about Father Geller. One, which we thought very funny, was that on Valentine's Day he not only didn't get valentines, but he was so miserable he had to return all the ones he got when he was a nice little kid. Another opinion was that he could never have been a nice little kid.

Returning to my heartfelt case, I countered Bill's "It's better to give than receive" argument by citing the fact that if I had given a valentine to all fifty-five students in our classroom, I still would have ended up with one and then I'd feel worse. Also, even if I could afford to buy everyone valentine cards I wouldn't because I wasn't fond of girls who made up over half the class, and it would feel odd giving heart-filled cards to boys — even the funny, insulting kind. Valentines should be done away with, I insisted. He just smiled and said, "Well, I don't know."

He smiled because he received twenty-three of them. I changed the subject, not actually able to put into words my hurtful feelings.

After school, while waiting for the safety boy to allow us to cross McClellan, a classmate named Pauline walked up to me, softly said "Here" and thrust an envelope into my hand. She continued walking while I, with thumping heart, pulled from the envelope an honest-to-gosh "Will you be my Valentine" card. I couldn't stop grinning, for although I wasn't too fond of girls, and the feeling seemed to be mutual, I always harbored a secret idea that out of the great throng of feminine pulchritude in school, at least one of them might fancy me.

I later began to suspect Stellon had put Pauline up to it, especially when he asked me the next day, "Did you get your card from Pauline?" But it was okay. I relished it and secretly promised myself I'd double my intake the next year, either by being friendlier to schoolmates or buying myself a few.

I was delighted not to get a valentine card from one boy in class. His name was Donald Blaso, a pleasant enough boy and musically talented, yet he talked and acted like a combination of two of the most disliked child stars in moviedom...Freddy Bartholomew and Bobby Breen. Actually they weren't disliked by everyone — I'm sure all mothers wished their sons could be as angelic and perfect — but they sickened most boys. We considered them sissies; boys who were cleaner than the rest of us and didn't argue when mothers told them to wear short pants. Even in youthful years, most boys have an innate feeling that male-type kids should take bigger steps when walking. I felt this way about Donald. Always friendly and smiling, he received many valentines from girls, with whom he preferred to associate.

The fourth-grade nun also thought him adorable and when she heard he took accordion lessons, asked if he'd play for our class someday. Naturally this little child prodigy agreed.

The day, too soon, arrived. Donald's mother drove him and his accordion to school and the nun informed us we would give up our half-hour recess to partake of the musical feast. This didn't endear him to me because even though I didn't participate in recess games, the conversations with Stellon were enjoyable. Also, I had no interest in hearing a budding Lawrence Welk perform because, although Mr. Welk was just coming on the entertainment scene, I had already decided that we didn't need two of him.

At recess time the nun inquired, "Donald, are you ready?"

He smiled sweetly and answered, "Yes, Sister."

Donald looked rather pudgy and, although of Italian

heritage, had sandy-colored hair. He sashayed to the cloak-room where he'd temporarily stored his accordion and as he adjusted its shoulder straps the nun pulled her chair from behind her desk and positioned it facing the class. Donald sat down, the nun faded to the room's rear and the recital began.

He started with *Chiribiribin* and I noticed something. He was good! He moved on to *The Blue Danube Waltz* and I turned to Stellon sitting in the row of seats next to me and made a distasteful face. He nodded. We didn't want to admit that this kid, whom we didn't particularly admire, had a real talent. When he went into *Lady of Spain* and started to sing along in a praiseworthy, falsetto, "Bobby Breen" voice, I placed my palms over my ears, caught Bill's eye and grimaced. I then stuck my fingers in my ears and closed my eyes, almost blocking out the musical world. While in this posture, I busied myself by wondering if all accordion players played Lady of Spain. I also found myself wondering if all accordion players were circum-cised at birth, or if it happened accidentally during a spirited rendition of that fine song.

The real world returned with a rush when I felt what had to be a lightning bolt slam the top of my skull and my face almost hit the desk top. "What do you think you're doing? Sit up straight and listen!" the nun hissed.

She raised her hand while debating whether to smack me again, then lowered it when Donald's music and singing faltered as he glanced our way. She waved for him to continue and returned to the back of the room.

Most kids in the vicinity heard or saw this flurry of violence and were staring at me — some solemn, some amused. I glared at Donald who continued entertaining and thought he had a happier expression on his face. Blushing, still feeling the sting on my cranium, I took an oath to pound darn old Donald into the ground at some future date, although it was really my fault. I had broken an unwritten survival rule in the Catholic school system. Namely, never do anything untoward in the presence of a nun unless you know her whereabouts, and her back is turned.

This recital episode was worrisome. It could adversely affect my report card "conduct" mark. When nuns announced report cards were due to be passed out soon, even the best students became nervous and tense for they knew their conduct grade depended on the whim of these Dominican sisters. If you were liked and/or rarely gave them problems, you could expect an "A" or "B," very passable grades. If you disrupted class, were insolent or disrespectful, you could count on a "C" or "D." Then you faced your parent's anger. This wasn't your main worry, though. Your chief concern was the reaction of Father Geller.

Father Geller distributed report cards. He rarely missed. If Pope Pius XII summoned him to Rome on report card day he'd say, "Okay, your Holiness. I'll be right there — right after I pass out some cards." He had a perpetual scowl and resembled every pro-football coach's dream of an offensive guard. He was a massive figure, his large head sitting midway between immense shoulders on an almost nonexistent neck. We knew he had a neck because he managed to don his, probably special-made, Roman collar each day. He wore his black, ankle-length cassock during most morning hours, the buttons straining to hold in his thick chest and stomach. His black hair was thin and cut short; his voice gravelly and bellowing. He was every child's daytime nightmare — terror incarnate.

There were two unsubstantiated, but believable, rumors about him. One, that a local brewery delivered a good supply of beer periodically to the side door of the rectory for his consumption; not surprising in view of his German descent. The other, that he was a former heavyweight prize fighter. This rumor explained why he never struck anyone with fists. It would have been illegally using lethal weapons.

He once ordered three young hooligan-types who had taken up residence on the front church steps to leave. They mistakenly decided to challenge his authority, considering that they lived in a free country. He slapped and threw all three down the cement steps. They quickly scattered, suddenly willing to forego a few freedoms to keep their bones intact.

Father Geller sang the requiem high Mass at 8 o'clock most mornings. This was the grade-school student Mass and it would behoove you to be very attentive. If he spotted kids talking, giggling or nudging each other he interrupted mass, came down from the altar and took them to task. It didn't matter if they were in mid-pew. He'd point at the wayward children, say "Yes, you two" and they had to step over the other kids' feet to get to the aisle where he stood. He'd slap their faces, explain in a few thunderous words why the sanctity of the mass should be respected and return to the altar. He then continued Mass where he left off while students and nuns tried to breathe quietly lest they, too, face his ire.

It was roundly agreed that the worst place in the entire world to be at 8 a.m. on a school day was on Nativity's altar while serving as altar boy. Even the smallest infraction in an altar boy's duties brought Mass to a halt, a pall fell over the congregation, and St. Gregory looked down and wondered who the hell put that long pause in his chant. Father Geller would turn to the offending party and go into one of his award-winning tirades. If you were that poor altar boy, the least you could expect was complete humiliation in front of your peers, with a distinct possibility of expulsion from the sanctuary. It was not unheard of for an entire four-boy crew to be banished. Baseball-minded kids referred to this as "being sent to the showers."

Father Geller finished more than a few Masses by himself. Unfortunately, he also finished all wine in the cruets, leaving nothing for the altar boys to enjoy later in the sacristy.

No one felt safe until they returned to their schoolroom. Once, when lined up to leave church through the side door for the short march to the annex, a commotion ensued and the line momentarily halted. Father Geller, aware that boys acted up while leaving church, had quickly doffed his priestly robes after mass, rushed to the other side of church and caught two boys roughhousing. He gave them a new meaning for "rough-house." The first words new kids in school heard from fellow students was, "Watch out for Father Geller." If they didn't, they paid dearly.

Three report card marks were most important to Father Geller — Religion, Effort and Conduct. Religion meant religiously memorizing prayers and the catechism. A low mark in Effort (later changed to "Study") meant you weren't applying yourself, and if you would, in the nun's opinion, your grades would be higher. Laziness wasn't tolerated. Conduct was later changed to "Courtesy" but it still meant the same, whether you conducted yourself with courtesy and respect. No rudeness, loud comments or insolence to nuns. No elbowing, tripping, fighting, whispering or pushing fellow students.

For nuns, giving low marks on report cards was akin to hiring a "hit man." The executioner, Father Geller, entered the classroom; we leaped to our feet and said, "Good morning, Father;" he sat at the nun's desk; she handed him the cards and moved to the side. From there she'd be available to fill in any details of questionable grades. These visits were never scheduled. The nun always had the cards ready for distribution on the proper day, but they remained stacked on her desk until Father Geller arrived at his convenience. He realized that if we were made aware of the exact day of his arrival it would cause an epidemic of horrific diseases that would miraculously clear up after one day of absenteeism.

Father Geller would read aloud a name from a card and as the student approached the desk he'd read the student's grades. "Andrew has an 'A' in Spelling, a 'B' in Arithmetic, an 'A' in History," and so on, until he reached the last three marks —Religion, Effort and Conduct. A "C" in any category assured a strong lecture and the student had better appear properly contrite. A "D" guaranteed some kind of physical mayhem, depending on details the nun provided, and a promise of more if the grades didn't improve by next quarter. To be slapped by one of his slab hands left a lasting impression on both body and psyche.

Each class had a group of less-than-studious boys who had little regard for rules and regulations of the parochial education system. It's hardly necessary to mention that this rebellious group was not made up of mental giants or Rhodes scholar candidates. Most of us realized this when one of the group stood up during literature class and asked a nun if Moby Dick was a book about venereal disease. I never became overly friendly with them, but I was glad to have them around because they took up a lot of a nun's time, leaving her less time to concentrate on me.

They also were the source of comic relief on card distribution day. The cards were passed out in alphabetical order, and since my surname started with "B," I'd have my "trial by fire" over with and be safely back in my seat before the entertainment started. As each malcontent's name was called, a rustling of anticipation stirred the room as he rose and walked reluctantly towards the desk. Father Geller would be apprising us of the ne'er-do-well's inadequate grades and approaching the dreaded Religion, Effort and Conduct. The room would be very quiet and, as he read the final three grades, Father Geller would slowly rise from his chair. We had to admire his ability to coordinate his reading of the Conduct mark with the booming, open-handed right cross to the student's head. We'd then be treated to a flurry of arms, legs and ass slamming to the floor in a corner of the room. The recipient would return cautiously to the desk to receive his card and Father Geller would give it to him along with some inspirational words such as, "I expect to see a better-looking card next time." We knew he wouldn't.

We'd all sit back in our seats and mentally go through the alphabet to see how long it would be until the next burst of entertainment.

Evaporated milk cans challenged the ingenuity of every kid on Belvidere. The milk was mixed into coffee by adults who punched two small holes in the top of the can for pouring. The milk congealed at the pour holes, but it was a simple matter to re-open them using any pointed object.

A ready supply of empty evaporated milk cans could always be found in garbage receptacles. Because they were almost intact (other discarded cans had tops removed by manual can openers leaving jagged edges capable of shredding flesh) they were perfect for clip-clopping; laying a can on its side on the ground and crushing it with a shoe heel so the can's top and bottom curled around and attached itself to your heel. Do the same with another can on your other heel, jump on Old Paint, hustle down the sidewalk and the cans sounded exactly like a two-legged, galloping horse: clip-clop, clip-clop. Cans wouldn't attach to cushiony rubber sneakers or tennis shoes, so we had to wear leather shoes, but the noisy effect was worth all the discomfort. Adults who worked nights and slept days didn't appreciate our creativity, and parents who had to replace loosened shoe heels didn't appreciate it either, but we thought we were brilliant, and so did all shoemakers. I think shoemakers invented evaporated milk cans right after they invented roller skates, which were secured to your shoes by tight-fitting clamps. These clamps could tear off a sole and heel with dispatch.

Parents did manage to circumvent shoemakers in a couple of ways though. When holes first appeared in our shoes, they resorted to the popular cereal box insole method mentioned earlier. Only a temporary measure, a box could be cut to fit any size shoe. Cardboard didn't wear well, but there was always an abundance of it.

When holes became larger, parents had one more way to forestall a need for a shoemaker's services. They went to five-and-ten-cent stores and, for about 40 cents, bought a pair of rubber soles and a tube of glue to stick them to the old soles. These soles were guaranteed to outlast shoes, but we couldn't confirm that claim because they never stayed stuck long enough to wear out. After a couple days the new soles started coming off at the toes and, when you walked down an aisle in a quiet church, made clippity-clap sounds. If you also happened to be wearing new corduroy knickers, you'd sound like a Mexican maraca band.

Empty evaporated milk cans also were perfect for playing an alley game called "duck-on-the-rock." Each boy in a group had a milk can, someone was chosen to be IT, a brick was placed in the middle of an alley, and IT had to place his can on the brick and then tag someone before his can was knocked off the brick. The other boys could only knock ITs can off with their cans. As soon as ITs can was placed on the "rock," cans flew from every direction. If the others missed, IT had an excellent chance of tagging someone since they had to retrieve their own cans for another throw. Once a boy was tagged, it was his turn to be IT. Being IT entailed a certain amount of risk because some trigger-happy boys threw before IT finished gingerly setting up his can. This breach of rules resulted in the thrower becoming IT, or fisticuffs — if a hand, shin or more important body part was injured. IT was very vulnerable when he squatted down to place can on brick and, in a squat position, wide open for an "accidental" well-aimed can that could raise his voice an octave or two. He'd then grab all offended body parts that fit in both hands, hop around on one leg, and loudly decry the thrower's parentage. He'd also talk to the good Lord, mentioning His name loudly for all to hear.

It was a good game that could be played for hours and turn cans into unlabelled, twisted metal. All mothers hated the game, believing it dangerous.

Breakfast conversation at our house often centered on the ubiquitous can. Every morning I'd irritably stare at it. We always used the Pet Milk brand whose label had a picture of a Pet Milk can turned on its side with a cow's head sticking out one end. This picture had a picture of a Pet Milk can with a cow's head, that had a picture of a Pet Milk can with a cow's head, and so on, each Pet Milk can getting smaller until only a dot remained, which made me wonder if a powerful magnifying glass would turn up more Pet Milk cans. I asked Betty and she said, "I doubt if you could see more with a magnifying glass, but they're there, reaching into infinity."

I asked, "How many more?"

She replied, "Maybe millions. It's something like the number of angels on the head of a pin. No one knows."

I thanked her for clearing it up for me, while thinking maybe she shouldn't have skipped the seventh grade.

My other all-knowing sister Mary perpetuated a fallacy that if equal parts of evaporated milk and water were mixed, regular milk would result. "Evaporated milk is regular milk with most water removed," she claimed.

It wasn't true. I tried it on my Wheaties and it tasted exactly like what it was — a mixture of canned milk and tap water. After two spoonsful, to give it an honest test, I garbage-canned the rest. I always suspected whoever told Mary this lie had something to do with the development of powdered milk, which is about as tasty and appealing.

I believed Mary's milk story because she should have been a food expert. She was healthy and well fed, so much so that she looked like she beat the Great (it wasn't so great) Depression. Some people might be so callous as to describe her as chubby.

All my brothers and sisters had similarities. Although some started life as blond, we all ended up with various shades of brown hair, which seemed odd since our Mother had black hair and Father, auburn. And we all grew to the same size...short. Similarities between us ended there.

Scholastically Betty was quiet, determined and an all-A student. The only time she received Bs was in eighth grade after she skipped the seventh, but by ninth grade she had returned to an all-A status. She was a perennial honor-roll type and a hard act to follow.

Edward chose not to enter the honor-roll race. Perhaps I should note that, in spite of his cavalier attitude toward the educational system, he did make Nativity's honor roll one year on all four card markings, which made him extremely happy and he thought the nun should have been a little more appreciative. Unfortunately, he had to learn not to expect compliments because, in his quest for knowledge, he always followed closely behind Betty and had the same nuns, who found him comparatively lacking. He gleaned solace only in the happy realization that his grades, fluctuating between As and Bs with an infrequent C in conduct, were always good enough to avoid that smash to the head by Father Geller. Ed was a comedic cut-up who enjoyed school because he found so much humor in it. He served the church as an altar boy and I'm sure the paramount reason was the looks of Sister Mary Linus who taught altar boys Latin. She was beautiful with a lovely personality, and Ed always appreciated those attributes. To this day, he can recite all the Latin responses of the Mass, but there doesn't seem to be much call for it, and it's awfully difficult to work into conversations.

Mary was a talkative, jolly person with many friends. Sometimes she attained honor-roll status, but didn't worry when she didn't.

Patricia, another good student, had an excellent singing voice and once sang a solo in a grade-school Christmas play. This was the "Shirley Temple" era when every mother curled her daughter's hair and encouraged her to tap dance and practice singing *The Good Ship Lollipop*. The mothers then waited for a Hollywood scout to miraculously drop by their houses and sign up their little darlings for lucrative acting careers. In the meantime they bought cereal containing Shirley Temple dishware, and I suspect they thought if their daughters ate out of blue-glass Shirley Temple cereal bowls they'd suddenly break into song and dance. I knew this never worked because I was a bona fide "Ralston Straight Shooter" who sent Ralston box tops to Checker Board Square in St. Louis for everything Tom Mix ever offered and I still had never been on a horse and, with only one fur chap, I certainly didn't look like a cowboy.

Pat could already sing, so when Nativity's gym teacher offered tap dancing lessons for 25 cents per week our mother jumped at the chance. Little taps were placed on little shoes and this tap-dancing craze lasted at our house for months. Pat practiced on the hardwood floor of our rugless dining room, no doubt endearing us forever to the landlord's son in the fruit cellar. I don't know why Mom didn't call him Mr. Down-a-stair.

Our family's record of scholastic achievement came crashing to earth with Charles and Dolores. They both were completely indifferent to and disinterested in school, although Chuck did excel in one envious talent — ear wiggling.

Baby Ann wasn't old enough to go to school so her main purpose in life was to have her hair curled so people would say, "Isn't she cute? She looks just like Shirley Temple!" I considered Shirley an insipid twerp.

* * *

One war in Europe ended. Russian soldiers started clouding the Finns' minds by also wearing white and painting tanks and trucks white, removing a distinct Finnish advantage. This, on top of Russia's overwhelming edge in troops and equipment, wore down Finland's army and they surrendered in mid-March of 1940. Goliath won one.

In June, Hitler sent his armies into Belgium and France. England, who'd declared war on Germany when Germany attacked Poland, had troops stationed in France and lost thousands while evacuating Dunkirk, a small port in northern France. Germany acted very uncivilly to our civilized world.

Also in June, both Betty and Ed bid adieu to Nativity; Betty the conventional way by graduation from high school, Ed because Nativity boys weren't educated past the ninth-grade. Nativity had a three-year commercial high school for girls, so Betty actually graduated from eleventh-grade. This, plus her skipping seventh-grade, made her one of Nativity's youngest graduates. It also created a situation where she was, at 15, too young to get a job. Sister Mary Theophila, Nativity's principal, told her to enroll at Comptometer and Secretarial Institute, a business school downtown, to hone her skills at shorthand and typing while awaiting her 16th birthday. Sister Theophila was the one about whom students used to say, "School isn't really so bad; it's just the principal of the thing."

Betty always did as she was told so immediately applied at CSI and arranged to pay her tuition by correcting papers and performing other clerical duties. She disappeared into a downtown-bound Gratiot streetcar in the morning and reappeared ten hours later, spending her days honing and correcting. When she turned 16 our family's insurance agent got her a downtown office job with his company and Betty became a "Piece of the Rock."

Ed wanted to attend Eastern High School where most of his buddies were going, but Dad, who worked with and admired a graduate of Cass Tech High, thought Ed should go to Cass and take drafting. Dad won the argument, as dads usually do. Ed did well enough with his drawings, yet it didn't take long to see that he wasn't a budding Henry Ford. His mechanical aptitude was next to nil. He passed machine shop and foundry class because his teachers didn't want him back the following year. They were afraid he might hurt somebody since he had his lathe doing things lathes aren't meant to do. Ed did, however, flunk Metal Pattern-making for it was all handwork, and he could only hurt himself, which didn't seem to unduly concern his teacher.

I envied Ed because, by going to a Protestant school (Catholic school children always thought public schools were Protestant), he'd be obligated to attend mass only on Sundays and Holy Days. Going to a Catholic school meant being present at mass Monday through Friday, plus you'd better appear for Sunday Mass or suffer the pain of mortal sin. During the school year we went to Mass six days a week and sometimes seven if a holy day of obligation fell on a Saturday.

A Saturday holy day, and ones that came up during summer vacation, like Assumption Day in August, were especially resented. Contrarily, a holy day falling on a weekday during the school year caused elation because we were excused from classes. I loved Ascension Day for this reason because it always fell on Thursday, 40 days after Easter, in the warm spring season. Protestant kids simmered when they had to do a whole day in the school mines while we, after doing our church duty, had the remainder of the day to loaf.

Easter was tolerable. It was a two-for-one; you had to go to church on Sunday anyway. And although Christmas Day occurred during Christmas vacation, I never minded going to church on that day since it seemed special with the church so beautifully decorated.

The least appealing holy day was the feast of the Circumcision celebrated on New Year's day while we were still on Christmas vacation. I disliked even the sound of the word "circumcision," but always enjoyed the story about Moses asking God on the Mount, "You vant us to cut a half-inch off our VHAT?!! Catholic school children loved jokes concerning religion, the more sacrilegious the better. Such as the joke about the three wise men, one of whom fell off his camel in front of the stable. As his head painfully hit the ground he shouted, "jesuschrist!!" Mary looked at Joseph and said, "You know, Joseph, that vould be a nicer name than Irving."

VII

A tree and a rosebush stood in our backyard, both about twenty feet from our porch steps. Eight feet of ground separated the bush from the tree trunk. The bush grew wild for it knew no sane person would try to destroy it. Its thorns reminded me of a wolf's fangs, but razor sharp, and there were thousands of them. If you passed within an arm's length, it reached out and snagged your clothes, your skin, or both, and injured you grievously. In Spring its buds bloomed, and we had hundreds of gorgeous, pink roses. Alas, three days later the petals fell leaving a gargantuan, overgrown, hideous, menacing monster — six feet tall, six feet wide and getting larger every year. I detested that bush and knew the feeling was mutual. I also knew if it ever got a good grasp on my body it would pull me into its depths and tear me to shredded wheat.

The bush had one minor redeeming feature, excluding its yearly two days of beauty. On Good Friday, when Christ's crown of thorns was mentioned, I sympathized for I knew what pain and damage thorns could inflict. I hated that bush.

On the other hand, the tree I liked. In addition to it's cooling shade, at its roots lived a colony of black ants. Though half as large as carpenter ants, they were the meanest, fightingest ants I ever saw in the city.

Trees lining Belvidere Street in front of our house harbored an abundance of carpenter ants. (They were easily distinguished from other ants because they usually wore miniature union buttons and carried little saws.) I'd gather about 50 carpenters in an empty glass milk bottle, carry the bottle into our backyard, give the backyard colony a few swipes with a spoon and hundreds of angry soldier ants rushed out. (I always wondered what the soldier ants said when they were angry. Were they calling me a son of a something, and did they have an eff-word? If they were like soldiers I later met, they did). I'd dump the carpenters into their midst and furious, deadly encounters ensued. Each carpenter killed two or three before being swarmed over, but the ant colony always won. I found some aggressive orange ants, smaller than the black ants, in another section of the yard, who were fighters also, yet no match for the black colony. Digging deeply into the orange ant nests I'd found hundreds of reserves to throw into battle, but the blacks slaughtered them.

One Sunday my parents loaded their four youngest children into the back seat of our DeSoto to visit friends who owned a small farm near Mount Clemens, a town north of Detroit. At nine years old I was the eldest and most educated of the four, so as we set out on our journey I enlightened Chuck, Dolores and Ann on what farm animals they could expect to see: ponies, cattle, horses, sheep, pigs, goats, rabbits and the possibility of sighting toads, skunks, snakes, lizards, possums, deer, foxes, buffalo, beavers, bears and wolves. They were greatly impressed with my knowledge of rural life and became visibly excited at the prospect of being so close to such a variety of domesticated and wild beasts. Mom, sitting in the front passenger seat, turned and smiled at our expectant, vivacious chatter and suggested, "Don't count your chickens—"

As we passed through Mount Clemens the car's air took a decided turn for the worse. Mount Clemens was famous for sulfur mineral baths and attracted people worldwide to its fine hotels that featured this healthful and healing water. However, since these were pre-air conditioning days, all hotel windows were open on hot, muggy, summer afternoons and the sulfur odor, akin to rotten eggs, could not be confined. It requires little imagination to understand what it was like to be with a bunch of children in a '32 DeSoto driving through this town in July. Unpleasant aromas always bring out silliness, or sometimes cruelty, in kids. For instance, one girl in my class at school had a personal hygiene problem, making it difficult to sit downwind of her. Some unkind boys in class whispered that she wore a perfume called "Hot Summer Night in Mount Clemens."

When we reached the farm I was distressed to find that it had a large coop holding innumerable chickens. Four cats were the only animal life available to view. No ponies. Chuck, Dolores, Ann and I, along with the farm wife, Mrs. Popkie, watched the chickens for a time and to salvage some of my siblings' respect for my rural acuity I asked Mrs. Popkie, "When are ya gonna cut off their heads?"

"Oh, we rarely eat them," she said. "These are laying chickens. We sell their eggs."

Discouraged, my interest in chickens quickly waned. I wandered alone to a dirt road abutting the farm property, sat on the remnants of a rotted fence post, and weighed the danger of a lone foray through the farm's radish and lettuce patches. Poisonous reptiles probably thrived there, and in the short pants I wore I'd be particularly vulnerable to bites. My adventurous thoughts were abruptly interrupted by a sharp, stinging sensation. Leaping up I found a red ant clinging to my thigh, its pincers clamping my skin. I pulled it loose, and it bravely tried to bite my finger. Many of its fellow citizens scampered helter-skelter over the fence post looking to attack the disturber of their tranquility. Surely these ants could provide a challenge to the fighting black ants in my backyard. They were the same size and just as ferocious. All I needed was a container to transport them home.

I ran to the farmhouse porch where my parents and the Popkies were relaxing and excitedly explained to Mrs. Popkie what I had found (the ant nest), what I needed (an empty quart milk bottle), and why I needed it (to start a war in my backyard). She smiled and said, "Sure. C'mon. I've got a bottle."

My dad warned me, "Make sure you put a cap on it. I don't want damned ants loose in the car."

Following Mrs. Popkie into her kitchen I explained that a cap wasn't necessary. An ant couldn't traverse the tapered neck of a glass milk bottle; its feet slipped on glass. Besides, I intended to add dirt to the bottle to keep the ants too busy burrowing to think of climbing out. She listened politely, handed me a bottle and cardboard cap, suggesting I use both.

I enlisted Chuck's aid, and we ran to the fence post to gather ants. We worked diligently popping them into the bottle, one at a time. When picked up between thumb and forefinger the ants fearlessly twisted and maneuvered for opportunities to bite. When Chuck got bored, antsy, and left me alone, I persisted, figuring the more red ants the better the war.

I stopped counting after 200, but continued adding recruits to my red army. I filled the bottle a third full with sandy dirt and those ants crawled all over themselves digging out and tunneling in. I figured there were 400 ants housed in the glass barracks.

It was dusk when we started home. I capped the bottle before entering Dad's car to keep him in good spirits and placed it on the back seat. It amused me to think of Dad's reaction if I uncapped and upended the bottle and hundreds of angry ants swarmed through the car. The thought helped pass the travel time, but I never seriously considered it for his reaction would eventually be aimed at me. Besides, I needed my red ants for battle.

It was too dark to start a war when we reached home, so I uncapped the bottle to give my red army oxygen and put

82

it on our back porch. The ant war of the century would begin the next day and for the first time in my life I wanted to retire early. The attack would be launched at dawn.

The morning broke cloudless and cool. I scrambled out of bed, dressed swiftly and tried to make it through our kitchen to the back porch, but Mom collared me and insisted I eat a breakfast of champions. Mothers never understand that there are things more important than eating.

When I got to the milk bottle, I saw my red ants had worked all night building a labyrinthian, underground settlement and were ready to enjoy it. They were going to be highly annoyed at its destruction. I returned to the kitchen for a soup spoon and received an admonition from Mom not to return the spoon bent, "like you did on your China trip." I promised, thinking, aren't they ever going to forget my ill-fated China venture?

I picked up the ant-filled milk bottle, walked quietly to the tree and gazed down on the peaceful black ant village. The natives were leisurely starting out on their morning food hunt unaware that the red-ant general secretly observed them from high above, savoring the thrill of the coming battle.

My plan of attack was simple. Scrape the nest with the spoon and when soldier ants angrily poured out ready to annihilate someone, dump about one-third of my red troops on top of them. It worked beautifully. I scraped and hundreds of black ants rushed from their holes, scurrying, in a frenzy, bumping into each other, trying to find someone to kill for wrecking their village. I dumped some bottle dirt on the ground right next to the nest and red ants clambered out, also incensed because someone just earthquaked the home they'd spent all night building.

Those red ants were brutal. Though outnumbered, they tore into their enemies, lopping off black legs and heads. My red army's winning! I gleefully told myself and committed the last of my troops to battle, which gave them an antpower advantage. Some courageously tried to enter the black ants' holes, intending to find and kill the queen, but were thwarted because of a steady stream of black ants popping out. The tide of battle slowly changed, and I woefully realized there were almost unlimited black reserves underground. Many more reds were needed to win. I did proudly note that, though vastly outnumbered, my reds were far ahead in kill ratio...about three to one.

I watched for hours. The weather warmed, and Mrs. Wolfe came outside to work on her flower garden. She noticed me and after a time became curious enough to yell over the fence, "Robert! Why are you staring at the ground?"

"I'm watching ants fight," I yelled back. "Do ya wanna see?"

She smiled and shook her head.

Every ant was in the fray. Wounded red ants staggered around with black heads attached to their legs searching for another enemy to attack and having no problem finding one. Reds were biting blacks who were biting reds who were biting blacks. Chuck joined me, watched impassively for awhile, then wandered off. Pat appeared, stared, shook her head, commented "How repulsive!" and hastily departed.

My mother called me and insisted I eat lunch. While in the kitchen I invited her to watch the ant battle, but she refused — she was too busy. I gulped a sandwich and returned to my observation post.

I found if I picked up one ant, ten to twenty more would be attached to it and each other. If I pulled one loose it instantly grabbed hold of an enemy when returned to combat. They didn't believe in rest and relaxation. (However, I did see a male red ant talking to a female black ant. She wasn't the queen, but, for a moment I thought I saw him offer her a very tiny chocolate bar and nylon stockings. I didn't quite understand the significance, but stored it in my memory bank for later, in case I ever went into the Army). I watched the struggle until nightfall, breaking only for supper.

The following morning black ants were carrying dead bodies into their holes and I noticed some red ants were still alive, but barely moving. (The one exception seemed to be the male red ant with the chocolate bar and nylons. He was eight feet away, under the rose bush, doing lascivious things to his new-found friend. I made another mental note.)

By the third day there was little evidence of the momentous battle. The village had been rebuilt, all dead and wounded bodies were removed and black ants were again engaged in peaceful foraging and other assigned chores. Maybe a black ant got out a tiny bugle and played "taps" the evening before. I truly hoped so. I didn't know. I did know I'd witnessed a supreme contest, a phenomenon rarely seen, and no one seemed to care. It saddened me. "Rest in peace, red-ant warriors," I proudly whispered. "You were magnificent."

* * *

The doorway leading from our kitchen to the back porch had a dual purpose. It provided a quick passage to and from the backyard, of course, but its door jamb provided a growth record of all children in our house. Periodically Mom complained that we were growing out of our clothes and Dad would say, "Let's see. Someone get the yardstick."

We'd all take off our shoes (if we were wearing any), line up, and when our turn came, place our back against the jamb while he leveled the yardstick on our head. He'd draw a pencil line on the jamb, write our name and the date next to it, measure from the floor and make an observation, "She's growing like a bad case of bacteria," or "He'll be a six-footer for sure."

Sometimes the difference in the new pencil mark and old was an inch or more for me, and I'd feel I'd made progress. Then Mom would disappoint me at supper by saying, "You're too short. You have to eat to grow," and I'd look at the selection of food before me and think life as a circus midget couldn't be all bad; although I couldn't forget what Ed once told me: "Crowded elevators smell differently to midgets."

Every two or three weeks I'd walk up to the jamb alone and try to measure myself with my hand, checking for any height improvement. Growing up was a man-sized goal in my life.

I passed the door in early August and noticed all height marks were washed away. This had to be an enormous mistake —probably on the part of one of my older sisters. I yelled out "Ma!" and heard a "Yoo, hoo!" from the basement. I found her scrubbing clothes on a washboard and she wasn't fazed as I babbled about the loss of our growth records. When I finished she said, "Yes, I know. I did it."

"Why?!" I asked, incredulously.

"Because I'm trying to clean up around here. We're going to move to another house. You can tell the younger kids. The older ones already know."

"Moving! Where are we going?" A scene of returning to Midland with benevolent, doting grandparents and hilly streets crossed my mind. I wanted a chance to sled down a hill and I'd never seen a hill in Detroit.

"It's a house on Holcomb," she replied.

The sledding image faded. We shared the alley behind our house with people on one side of Holcomb street, which ran parallel to Belvidere. "You mean we're moving across the alley?"

She patiently explained, "Yes, but about two blocks down near Chandler school. We need more room. You kids are getting big and the Holcomb house has four bedrooms. We'll be leaving at the end of the month...in three weeks." Feeling she had answered all possible questions, she turned back to the wash tub.

"We're going to Chandler school?"

"No, you're still going to Nativity. You'll just have to walk farther."

I ran upstairs to pass on the news to Chuck and Dolores. Neither were moved by our moving. To excite them, I suggested we'd probably be allowed to go to Chandler. They still didn't care. Attending Nativity or Zachariah Chandler school made little difference to them, since a college scholarship didn't loom in their future.

The next three weeks passed slowly, but at times sped up. Time passed slowly when I looked forward to moving, sped up when I pondered about things I was leaving and would miss. Our large basement held many memories. It had a smooth cement floor made for roller skating. The furnace sat directly in the middle allowing you to skate around it with no impediments, like a miniature roller rink.

As long as adults were unaware of it, the basement's gas-operated hot water heater could be lit and used to play a quiet game of "camp fire." Adults frowned on children playing with fire or matches so quietness was essential. Jimmy, Chuck and I once charred potatoes in this heater, but they stayed raw inside making them inedible. We fared much better with marshmallows, although the gas flavor didn't enhance their taste.

This water heater had to be lit manually when hot water was needed and turned off when the need was satisfied. On Saturday, when eight children were run through the bath cycle, the last one out of the tub was admonished to turn off the heater. This usually was Ed and he, of course, had more important things to do on Saturday night than worry about water tanks. After all, there were girls with dallying in mind and dumb teenage things to accomplish. After an hour or two the hot water tank built up a torrid pressure. (This was before the advent of thermostats and automatic shut-offs.) When someone turned on a spigot upstairs and steam blasted forth, pandemonium prevailed, and there was a mad dash by everybody to open all hot water spigots in the house. After the steam dispersed, brown rusty water flowed and we once again had the cleanest tank and pipes in town.

The basement was a refuge in the summer of 1936 when

87

a heat wave struck Detroit. Temperatures soared into the 90s and 100s and Mom decreed her family should live in the cool underground. She believed all that she read in the Detroit Times, except for its comic section, and if it said people were dying from heatstroke and she should protect her children by keeping them cool, then she'd certainly try. Those days of basement living were a new adventure, like camping in, with Mom and Betty inventing games and homemade toys to keep the younger children amused. Another positive aspect was permission to stay up later than usual because it took so long for the temperature to go down in our bedrooms, even with windows opened wide.

Mom invited Mrs. Up-a-stair to join us in the basement during this heat wave but she declined, no doubt deducing that heat and quiet were more attractive than coolness and noise, so Mom walked upstairs three or four times a day to check her condition. Upon returning from one of those errands of mercy Mom worriedly reported that Mrs. Up-a-stair moaned, "Eet so hot I tink I gonna takea dah beeg schleep." After that frightening statement Betty volunteered to also visit upstairs periodically to assure the old woman drank enough water to survive.

The landlord's son, who worked days as a truck driver, probably felt his space defiled when he entered the side door on those hot evenings, came down into the basement, and had to walk through a gauntlet of rackety humanity to reach his living quarters. I never went into the fruit cellar — he wisely kept it locked — but I heard he had a bed, dresser, lamp and hot plate for coffee. He ate and bathed elsewhere. He also had the patience of a saint or was partially deaf. Bless him. He rarely complained about our noise.

I'd also miss our late afternoon Popsicle or ice cream cone walks on Gratiot. I doubted Mom would continue walking us to Gratiot when Betty told me there was a small corner grocery store that sold these refreshments a half-block from our future Holcomb address. Our walks had changed mostly to ice cream cone walks, probably because

Ed worked and brought home a weekly wage so Mom had extra money. Ed worked for Mr. Ronkhol who lived directly across Belvidere from us and drove a truck for Wegener's Rock and Rye, delivering a variety of soft drinks. During school vacations he hired Ed as a jumper on his truck, five days a week, to carry full cases of pop into stores and taverns and pick up empties. He paid Ed fifty cents for a ten-to-twelve-hour day, plus bought him a daily lunch. Ed gave Mom $2 out of his weekly wage, kept the remaining fifty cents and, no doubt, spent it foolishly.

I proudly thought of the celebrities on our block. There were real live radio celebrities in the Shafer family. Mrs. Shafer was a fair to middlin' piano player and Jack, her oldest son, played a wild banjo and did well on guitar. He was good enough on banjo to be invited to New York to appear on Fred Allen's show and, the night he played, Belvidere street shut down for an hour while everyone enjoyed his performance.

The younger Shafer sons, Tom and Joe, also were talented. They sang and Jack played each Sunday afternoon on "Uncle Nick's Talent Show," a local radio program. The Shafers occasionally took Ed with them to the station, where he immediately fell in love with all of the little girl singers and dancers (Yes, they danced on radio), and he'd be very smug and even more repulsive than usual for days after.

The Shafers were good friends with the two best known and most popular people in Detroit area morning radio — Joe Gentile and Ralph Binge. Joe and Ralph were on CKLW, a Canadian station in Windsor, and although we all enjoyed the music they played, they were best known for their commercials. They wrote all the wacky messages themselves and may have originated the concept of treating sponsors with disdain. Their audience loved it. Toby David was another cast member who made intermittent appearances on their show. A multi-talented performer, he added considerably to skits. One skit involved Joe and Ralph throwing Toby down an elevator shaft. They did this with much grunting and hollering, along with the banging, breaking and slamming together of cans, bottles and anything else available in the studio, and it ended with the eventual smashing of Toby on the far away bottom of the shaft. This skit was so well received that it had to be repeated frequently. When listeners wrote in requesting a record, they usually added a postscript: "Don't forget to throw Toby down the elevator shaft." In later years Toby David became a well known local television personality named Captain Jolly.

Joe Muglia, who lived next door, was the leader of one of the finer musical aggregations in our area, despite its name, The Buccaneers, and its billing, A Treasure Chest of Rhythm. The group patterned itself after Guy Lombardo's band with a singing trio and a male soloist. However, Chris Hild, their very large soloist, was not a Carmen Lombardo. He sounded more like he might have been vaccinated with a Bing Crosby phonograph needle.

Another fine entertainer, Bob Durant, lived a couple blocks down the street across from Chandler school. Bob jammed a little with Jack Shafer and later formed his own band.

On warm summer nights The Buccaneers rehearsed in Muglia's garage and it turned into a social event. Even children were allowed to stay up late to enjoy the entertainment — and free entertainment was always the best kind on those halcyon summer evenings.

The day before we left for Holcomb, Mrs. Wolfe motioned me over to her backyard fence. "Robert! Come here. I want to show you something," she whispered. "Look!" She pointed to a tree in her backyard. "Can you see it? What kind of bird is that?"

It was a bird I'd never seen before — golden yellow with black wings. "Maybe it's a canary that escaped," I suggested.

"No," she said. "I think it's an oriole."

We watched it until it flew away in the direction of Baltimore and I thought, I bet they don't have orioles on Holcomb. I'll probably never see another.

"You're leaving tomorrow, are you?" she asked. When I told her we were, she said, "Well, you aren't moving too far, so drop in and see me. I'd like to know how you kids are getting along."

We talked for awhile, mostly about her granddaughter Carol who was in my room at school, and then we parted. I felt a regretful pang, for she and Mr. Wolfe were considerate, helpful and courteous neighbors. They treated each other the same, with never an unkind word passing between them. When together — walking to Gratiot, sitting on their porch — they held hands. Theirs was a tender, gentle love.

I never again saw another oriole and I never again saw Mrs. Wolfe, at least in person. Years later a 10-inch picture of Mr. and Mrs. Wolfe appeared in a local newspaper. They were standing very near each other, gazing out a large window, almost in silhouette, with their backs to the camera. The window was at the end of a hall in a rest home. The story accompanying the picture explained that Mr. and Mrs. Wolfe were celebrating their 75th wedding anniversary and mentioned they were both in their 90s. Except for growing older they didn't seem to have changed much, at least from behind. He was still tall and thin, she was petite. And, plainly, their love had endured. They were holding hands.

On moving day, I didn't have to say farewell to Bobby Yahner, Rose Muglia or Virginia Gullo. I just told them I'd see them in school in a few weeks. I said good-bye to Jimmy, then went into our backyard and said, "Good-bye, backyard." I loved that yard. A huge section had never suffered a lawn mower blade. During summer months it was covered with tall weeds, wild flowers and raspberry bushes teeming with enchanting insects. Tobacco-spitting

91

grasshoppers leaped and played; plump spiders stretched intricate silken parlors to capture unwary winged prey; and caterpillars of varied shapes, sizes and colors clung to leaves and stems dreaming of a happier, soaring life. Delicate butterflies were plentiful, mostly small and white; but often larger yellow, orange or blue ones joined them in their frantic, fun-filled flitting.

I wished good luck to the black ant colony. They'd have a more peaceful existence without me around and their queen could start putting in a regular day, without overtime, replenishing her troops. I even said good-bye to the rose-bush — from a safe distance. It was time to leave.

VIII

The Holcomb house, wooden and two-storied like every house and flat on the street, wore weather-faded white paint. In front, on its left, grew a large horse chestnut tree in a thinly-grassed front yard, the tree's branches partially extending over the front porch roof. To the porch's right, two sets of bay windows, one atop the other, reached to the eaveline. A lone attic dormer extended from the roof.

The front door opened into a foyer. A stairway to the left led to the second floor; an archway on the right led to the bay-windowed living room. A kitchen and dining room were at the rear. Mom and Dad converted the dining room into a bedroom for themselves by hanging thick drapes over the entryway between it and the living room and for extra privacy Dad placed our living room sofa across the draped entrance so the only unencumbered entree to their bedroom, except climbing over the sofa, was a door in the kitchen that they usually kept closed.

Kitchen access was gained by either using a short hallway off the foyer, the converted dining room, or a rear door that opened onto a small porch.

There were four bedrooms and a bath upstairs. Of two front bedrooms, Mom assigned Betty and Mary a large bay-windowed one; Ed a small closetless one with area enough for a twin bed, chifforobe and walking space between. Pat, Dolores and Ann received a spacious rear bedroom; Chuck and I a rear one similar to Ed's and furnished the same way with twin bed and a chifforobe.

My lone disappointment was the stairway leading to the second floor. I always dreamed of sliding down a banister, but this staircase had a bottom newel post uniquely topped with a lampshaded light fixture. Sliding backwards and miscalculating the travel distance would slam sliders into this delicate lamp. I believed someone deliberately placed it there to discourage kids from doing what I wanted to do.

I sat on the back porch and studied our new, grassy backyard enclosed on both sides and along its alley line with wire fencing nailed to unpainted, intervalled, wood posts topped and connected with 2-by-4s. Most neighborhood backyards had this type fence. A two-car garage stood on the right side of our yard, thirty feet from where I sat. A narrow concrete walk started from our back porch, sliced straight through the yard, then veered slightly to run alongside the garage to our alley gate. Left of the gate, a distance of five feet, sat a concrete garbage receptacle.

Leaving our yard, I strolled through the alley and noticed most houses were blessed with these three-foot high, square-shaped receptacles. Permanent and immobile, each had three-inch thick walls and two large, square openings, one on top and one facing the alley, covered by hinged lids of thin steel. A resident simply lifted the top lid and dumped his garbage. Every week a city truck came through the alley, its workers lifted the other steel cover and shoveled out the week's trash accumulation. In time these covers rusted, bent, loosened, and rats feasted.

Across the alley, three backyards from our yard, I spotted a familiar figure. Donald Blaso stood smiling behind his gate and shrilled, "Hello there." I nodded, looked away, kept walking. I hoped he wasn't the only boy my age in this neighborhood.

He wasn't. Within a week we'd settled into Holcomb life

and became familiar with neighbors, especially ones with children. Directly across the street were the Butlers. Mr. and Mrs. Butler were from England, retained their English accents and had six children, five still living at home. The youngest of the five, Robert, eight years old, had red hair. Everyone called him "Red" except his parents, who feared he'd forget his given name. Their other living-at-home children were Joseph and his twin sister Gladys, ten years old, Mary Jane, thirteen, and Frank, seventeen.

The Butler house included a side driveway and, consequently, a garage with entry doors that opened onto Holcomb. Most garages on the block opened facing alleys. Residents wishing to park cars in these garages had to drive through narrow alleys, stop near their garage, leave the car, open the garage doors, then jockey the car into position while avoiding telephone poles, cement garbage receptacles, fence posts, garage doors and jambs. Everyone with a car and good sense parked on the street.

Two houses from us lived the Combs family. Mr. Combs was a city policeman who owned the house between us and rented it out to adults. Mr. Combs and his wife had an eleven-year-old son Clifford.

Across Holcomb, three doors from Butlers, stood a six-unit, red-brick apartment building with two apartments each in the basement, on the ground floor and second floor. An eleven-year-old boy, Ray Allis, lived in one basement apartment. Chuck and I became good friends with Red and Joe Butler, Cliff Combs and Ray Allis.

The six of us often walked over to the Morning Star Dairy to watch employees bottle milk. This dairy, located in a wide paved clearing, six doors from our house, four from Combses, had a small operation with creamery buildings set back near the alley. The bottlers were a nice group. On hot summer days they worked with the big front door open, which allowed us to admire their labor. One phase of the bottling process involved cream cascading over horizontal pipes. The pipes were obviously very cold because cream solidified and built up on them and eventually workers broke off big chunks of that delicious confection for us to enjoy. It was our cheap answer to Good Humor bars.

The dairy owners lived in a house on the opposite side of the paved clearing and if neighbors ran short of milk the owners conveniently sold them a bottle from their back porch. They had six delivery trucks. We watched truck drivers return from routes on late afternoons and I considered someday being a milkman. It had to be less strenuous than an iceman's job that entailed lugging 50-pound blocks of ice up and down stairways.

For the few remaining days of summer vacation, we played alley baseball behind Butlers' house, spending lots of time retrieving balls fouled into neighbors' backyards. We also spent lots of time listening to ballgames on radio as the Detroit Tigers sought to win a pennant.

Then the school bell rang.

* * *

I suffered a great deal of anxiety when returning to Nativity for fifth grade. One of the two fifth-grade classes had a lay teacher, so there was a fifty-fifty chance I'd be taught by a civilian. I never dared ask why they were called "lay" teachers, but assumed they were stricter than nuns; possibly because nuns, with veils and ankle-length robes, resembled church statues of the Blessed Virgin and Saint Theresa, whose faces had beatific, gentle smiles.

I was relieved when I got the class with the nun. Unfortunately, she felt her mission in life entailed scaring hell, literally, out of all her charges. Some students referred to her as Sister Mary DeSade. She loved teaching religion so she could describe the everlasting torment of the damned who'd be sitting in flames for eternity and, since all of us had been burned accidentally at least once, a finger or arm, we realized to be burned over our entire body forever was horrifying. To explain eternity she told us to think of a faucet dripping water on a huge boulder and, after millions of years, the water constantly dropping on that rock would wear a hole through it. The time it took wouldn't cover the first day of eternity. Eternity was definitely hard time.

Purgatory was just as hot as hell; except after suffering for a few million years for venial sins, we'd be allowed to join God in heaven. There was one other stipulation regarding a purgatorial stay. If the world ceased to exist while we were being cleansed, all venial sins were erased and we went directly to heaven. I imagined a lot of purgatory inmates hoped for a quick end to our world.

Still, the picture of hell in our religion book didn't look quite as terrible as she described it. The people weren't smiling, but they weren't covered by flames either; just climbing and flopping about on, presumably, hot steamy rocks. I found myself committing a venial sin or two by straining my eyes to see certain features of the suffering, naked women.

The nun told us another destination for dead people was limbo, a place restricted to unbaptized infants or righteous folk who died before the coming of Christ. It was comparable to heaven with one difference...the babies never saw God. I felt sorry I didn't die at birth because seeing God wasn't exactly my top priority. God, in paintings, always looked like a robed, unsociable gentleman with Father Geller's sense of humor. Since I couldn't remember being born, or even two or three years after birth, I didn't think not seeing God would be fretful. I hoped these babies were allowed to grow up to be nine- or ten-years old so they could appreciate their idyllic surroundings. I also hoped they didn't fault their cretin parents for not splashing a little water on them and saying the magic words.

And I thought it a little unfair for the other poor souls the nun mentioned who were unfortunate enough to be born in the four thousand or so years B.C. to be relegated to limbo. They shouldn't have been shut out so long because God seemed to have learned scheduling techniques from present day airline schools. He could have sent somebody a lot sooner. I also hoped those nice folks, when they heard of their limbo destination, didn't think they were going to get lessons in how to bend over backwards and dance under horizontal poles.

A student asked the nun, "What does the soul look like?"

With chalk she drew a large, white circle on the blackboard and said, "This is your soul at birth with original sin. See how it's completely black?" Using the chalk's side she filled in the circle. "After baptism your soul looks like this, completely white and pure. This is the way it remains until you commit sins, venial or mortal."

Picking up a chalk eraser, she dabbed at the circle leaving small, black marks. "These are venial sins like swearing, talking back to your parents or teachers, being selfish, telling lies, (speculating as to the chastity of a young lady who stayed a long time in a confessional), and not doing homework. If you die with these on your soul they have to be burned off in purgatory."

They didn't look too ominous, I thought.

She then erased all chalk inside the circle and announced, "This is how your soul looks when you commit a mortal sin —completely black. If you miss Sunday Mass, eat meat on Friday, go to communion without fasting from midnight, commit adultery (by getting lucky enough to make the acquaintance of the young lady who seemed to require extra time in the confessional), or murder someone, and die without going to confession, you'll go straight to hell for eternity."

The class murmured. She had said the word most of us didn't fully understand — adultery. We knew adults did it, but what was it? Stellon raised his hand and I thought he intended to ask, but instead he said, "Sister, what if you commit two or three mortal sins. Does your soul get any blacker?"

"No. That's as black as it gets." She punctuated this

answer by rapping the middle of the blackboard soul with her eraser leaving marks of chalk residue. She quickly erased them and added, "It doesn't matter if you committed one or one-hundred mortal sins. You still go to hell."

This didn't seem fair. The flames should be hotter for someone who killed people and missed Mass every Sunday than for some poor Catholic who choked to death trying to swallow a meat morsel on Friday.

Leroy Kolassa, one of the boys who flirted with disaster every time Father Geller passed out report cards, asked, "What about Protestants, Sister? Are they going to hell?" I think he liked to say "hell" out loud in front of a nun.

The nun seemed pleased that Leroy even participated in a religious discussion. "No," she answered. "If they live lives according to their religion, they can go to heaven, too, but they won't be able to get as near to God. Catholics hold a unique position on earth. Since they're the custodians of the one, true faith, they have an opportunity to get closer to God when they reach heaven."

More unfairness. Born Catholic meant I had to follow a lot more rules, just to get a better heavenly seat. Joe and Red Butler were lucky. They were born Protestant and didn't have to worry about Fridays, fasting, filching, fibbing, or fighting. They went to church, silently expressed sorrow, and their souls were wiped clean. Also, it appeared, there were a lot fewer things in their religion which were considered sinful. Being Catholic did have unpleasant aspects.

At lunchtime, I asked Stellon to explain adultery. "It's when someone is married, and they kiss and touch and do other fun things to the opposite sex, and the opposite sex isn't the one they're married to."

I thought of my first kiss with Virginia Gullo. "What if ya ain't married and ya kiss somebody?"

"Oh, that's okay," he said. "Kissing is just a venial sin — depending, of course, where you kiss them and how much verve you put into it."

"What if ya accidently rub up against a girl?"

"You have to be careful where you rub them and how many times. Three rubs equals a fondle, and that's mortal."

We discussed the locations on a girl's body to avoid, and I concluded I was a sure bet for a heavenly reward. I'd never miss Mass on Sunday or holy days, eat meat on Friday, murder anybody, snatch a kiss (or vise versa), touch the communion host with anything but my tongue, go to communion right after eating or drinking, worship idols, touch myself to excess, or fondle females on off-limit places since I wasn't fond of them anyway. Mortal sins were easy to avoid. (However, even in those youthful days, the sixth and ninth Commandments had a nice ring).

* * *

Dad purchased a brand-new, 1940, 2-door, maroon, deluxe-model Chevrolet and it was a great way to acquaint himself with the neighbors. People naturally gravitated towards a new car to marvel at the latest engineering and designing feats and features. Ed also gravitated to this car since Joe Shafer from Belvidere street once drove him to a cemetery and let him take the wheel. After that test drive Ed fancied himself an ace driver and wanted to be referred to as "Mr. Motorist" or, even better, "Sir Malcolm Campbell," who raced the fastest car moving across the Utah Salt Flats. Ed had recently turned 15 years old and felt ready for the highway.

Every automobile manufacturer made sure its vehicles had distinctive, easily-recognized characteristics like grilles, hood ornaments, hub caps, tail lights and chrome trim. These characteristics were modified yearly, but never radically, and never in unison. This made it simple for kids to play a game called "Name-That-Car." As we walked to the candy store or theater, we called out names of cars parked or driving past —Ford, Packard, Chevy, Desoto, Hudson, Nash, Studebaker, Pontiac, Dodge, Plymouth, Chrysler, etc., and, at the same time, tried to keep track of how many we were first to identify correctly.

We never saw an Essex, Cord or Duesenberg, but were sure, with our superior knowledge garnered by studying automotive advertisements, we'd have no problem recognizing them. We became so expert at this game that we stipulated an additional rule — yell out the car's year. This caused spirited arguments, especially when the vehicle had passed and was out of sight, though it did increase car familiarity. Anytime I read in the newspaper about criminals escaping in, for instance, a light-blue, 1938, 2-door, Hudson sedan, I imagined a boy my age smugly saying, "Yes, officer. I saw it all. They got away in a light-blue, 1938, 2-door, Hudson sedan." The policeman would grin and say, "Thanks, son. You've probably solved this case for us. We'll see you get rewarded."

Automobiles were alike as far as accessories were concerned, but some local Lotharios, desiring to impress girls or guys hanging out in front of the local sweetshop, could find a beautiful array of items to hang on, or attach, to almost every part of their cars. They only had to visit a Western Auto Supply store. There they'd start with a mandatory raccoon tail that attached to their hood ornament or radio antenna. This would be followed by an expensive set of Van Auken grille guards that attached to bumpers. Then a set of white metal rings that fit on wheels to make black tires look like whitewalls; a set of wire curb feelers to protect these fake whitewalls; a spinning, steering wheel knob to facilitate steering; a small rubber-bladed fan to defrost the rear window; an exhaust deflector with a small, round red reflector that attached to the tail pipe; a compass on the dashboard; a fancy, marble, gear-shift knob; a pair of fender skirts for rear wheels; a pair of red reflectors for the rear license plate and green for the front; a set of musical horns that only seemed to be able to play *Mary Had a Little Lamb;* and a set of plaid, fabric seat covers. Nobody ever wore out the original scratchy, mohair upholstery.

* * *

Our Holcomb house was in mid-block between Cairney and Chapin streets. An attraction on this block was a small, grocery store on the corner of Holcomb and Chapin. The proprietor and his wife catered to youthful customers by selling everything growing children craved such as ice cream cones, Popsicles and soft drinks. However, the greatest enticement for the majority of neighborhood children was a glass display case positioned just inside the store's entrance, filled with an eye-catching, mouth-watering variety of succulent, penny candy. This candy (probably designed with the American Dental Association's blessing) tested the mettle of tooth enamel. The enamel always lost.

There were spearmint-flavored gumdrops shaped like green leaves and embedded with sugar crystals; licorice sticks, both black and red; Squirrels, oblong-shaped candy with walnuts; Walnettos, square caramels that should have been shaped like walnuts, but weren't; and Mary Janes, also oblong with a folded-in streak of peanut butter. With Mary Janes, you usually felt cheated because they rarely contained enough peanut butter. I preferred peanut butter kisses — small, round pieces of taffy-type candy filled with peanut butter that had paper wrapping twisted at two ends. It made a nice package, but in summer heat you usually got to eat some paper stuck to the candy.

If you desired quantity, you could buy what we called "buttons," hard quarter-inch balls cut in two with their flat sides stuck to paper resembling adding-machine tape. These buttons were precision-spaced on the paper and came in various colors like pink, white and yellow, yet all had the exact same flavor — sweet. They were supposed to be sold by the foot, but if a proprietor was of a magnanimous spirit, you could receive 15 inches of button-covered paper. The one objectionable feature of these buttons was the work involved in removing paper residue attached to their flat side.

You could buy miniature, Coca-Cola shaped, wax bottles with sealed-in, dark-colored liquid. Bite off the top and, if the whole bottle didn't crumble and spill onto your clothing, you drank the liquid. It was supposed to be pop, but tasted suspiciously like Kool-Aid. We then chewed the wax, although I never knew why. It was almost as bad tasting as the tar we chewed when we could steal a piece from a roofing job in the neighborhood. Somebody said it made teeth whiter. Obviously, gullibility was one of our strong suits.

Jaw Breakers were a good buy. You could suck on them for days before they became small enough to crush with your jaws. They were large, round, hard, and if placed between cheek and teeth, gave you the appearance of a kid with a nasty toothache, or of Hank Greenberg with his usual large tobacco chaw. Root Beer Barrels, barrel-shaped with a root beer flavor, were another good sucking candy.

If you wanted to splurge you could buy a Guess What? for two cents. This was a small box with two little caramels, plus a surprise prize. The prize might be a tiny plastic gun, soldier, doll or, in one impressive case, a rubber-band popper. The popper was a contraption you wound tightly, placed carefully in an empty, sliding matchbox, handed to a friend and enjoyed his frightened reaction when he opened it and the popper flew by his face. One kid opened one and was known as "Blinky" for a long time afterward.

One of our favorite candies, "Tar Babies," so called because they were black and shaped like a baby, gave rise to some racial epithets from kids who had trouble embracing the then, fairly new, equality programs. (We believed "affirmative action" meant moves older boys used to get close to their girlfriends.)

The store also stocked a variety of gum. Since I was becoming interested in the Detroit Tigers, I'd buy gum that included baseball cards. Invariably I'd get cards with pictures of Joe Dimaggio, Ted Williams, or other lesser known

103

ballplayers and either give them or throw them away. All I wanted was a Charlie Gehringer or Hank Greenberg. I've rarely been accused of far-sightedness.

There was also bubble-gum with war cards. Japan had invaded China and one ghastly card depicted thousands of Chinese farmers charging Japanese machine guns with pitchforks and other farm implements. The Chinese were vividly being butchered. The back of the card explained the Chinese were defending their homeland against the dastardly Japanese and, at times, actually reached the Japanese machine-gunners and gave them a good pitchforking. As a susceptible ten-year old, I began to dislike the Japanese Empire's expansionists who, clearly, were the bad guys.

There was a reason this candy and gum had become affordable. My mother had more pennies available than previously and it became easier to beg her to part with them. On Sundays I noticed she had doubled the amount sealed in our collection envelopes from one penny to two. It took some time to get used to an envelope that rattled.

These envelopes were packaged in small cartons and distributed to Nativity school children yearly. There was a dated envelope for each Sunday, plus one for each holy day of obligation. Also imprinted were the church name with spaces to identify a student's name, grade, and amount enclosed. Our nun told us that, even if we couldn't afford to put money in these envelopes, we should drop them in the collection basket empty so they'd know we attended mass. I never quite believed this, and I wondered what Father Geller would do if he found an empty in the basket. The thought of excommunication unnerved me.

The adult parishioners picked up their envelopes from card tables in the church vestibule. They were larger than student envelopes, perhaps anticipating a more liberal contribution, conceivably even paper money. It rarely happened. The contribution pattern at our house, and probably the same for most parishioners, was: One or two pennies from grade schoolers, a nickel from high schoolers and a dime apiece from parents. Dad did put a quarter in his envelope one Sunday and, while walking home from church, found a dollar bill. This unexpected blessing prompted him to loudly declare to all that, "Bread cast on waters doth come back a thousand-fold," yet this fractured, biblical quote didn't inspire him to make a weekly habit of quarter donations.

The two cents in my envelope inspired me though. Every Sunday, during the walk to church, I was inspired to figure out a method to relieve the sealed envelope of its contents and still avoid discovery by people in authority. After overhearing parts of a whispered conversation one school morning between a fellow student and our nun concerning the absence of his envelope from the previous Sunday's collection, I decided to abide by the *Thou Shalt Not Steal* Commandment for a few more years. A minor temptation, I reasoned, and not worth the risk.

* * *

Dad was doing well at Gelatin Products and receiving promotions and raises. The company expanded so fast it needed more room and built a new Grinnell street plant only 15 blocks from our Holcomb address. Now we could afford to have our first telephone. Installed in our living room, it resulted in calls placed by my parents to everyone they knew who had a phone. Long-distance calls to relatives in Pennsylvania and Ohio necessitated using a louder voice since the distance between them was so much more than from neighbors and friends a block or two away, and Father talked so loudly we wondered why he bothered having the phone installed.

A new car, more money in church envelopes and a telephone signaled we were doing better financially, but the real tip-off was the spreads on our sandwiches. Over the years they evolved from butter sprinkled with sugar to apple butter and now peanut butter. Surely nothing could be so delicious on a slice of bread. And surely the Great (it was actually rather wretched) Depression was over.

IX

Winter was full of snowball fights and belly flopping with sleds. Belly flopping required mental and physical coordination. To land improperly on a sled at full gallop could render one incapable of producing offspring. Joe Butler and Ray Allis received Flexible Flyers for Christmas, and we took turns running on the sidewalk holding a sled, then throwing it, and ourselves on top of it, onto the snow-covered walk. It was never a long ride, but what else could be done in flat country? No one had a big dog trained to pull a sled so the only other alternative was to attach a rope and pull ourselves. This was splendid if you were the pullee, not so splendid if you were the puller; especially pulling someone heavy like Cliff Combs. If you suddenly came to a section of sidewalk that was shoveled and strewn with coal ashes the sled would slam to a sudden, jarring stop, threatening to separate your pulling arm from your shoulder. Then you silently cursed those safety-minded citizens who cleared their walks to spare themselves falls and lawsuits and wished they cared as much about a sled puller's physical welfare.

* * *

In school our class absorbed History, Geography, Spelling, Reading, Arithmetic, Handwriting, Drawing, English,

Health and Religion. One day in Religion class the nun told us to memorize the Apostle's Creed and, once learned, to come to the back of the room and whisper it to her. We'd get extra credit in Religion, and after reciting we could read anything we wanted for the remainder of class. This appealed to me because I wanted an opportunity to leisurely stare at the picture of those poor, suffering female souls in hell.

The whole class sat for a quiet twenty minutes, some with lips moving silently, trying to be the first with confidence enough to attempt this recital. I thought I had it memorized but didn't want to be the first to arise for I still avoided attention. Finally, a boy named Frank Baccala got up, walked to the rear, and we heard his voice murmuring. The nun said, "Very good, Frank," and he smugly returned to his desk. Audrey Hoch recited next, and I came in third. A satisfactory position, I reasoned. (In race track parlance, I finished in the money.)

The Apostle's Creed mystified me. When Jesus died, "He descended into hell, the third day He rose again from the dead. He ascended into heaven, etc." The next day I talked Bill Stellon into asking the nun what Jesus did in hell for those three days. She explained it wasn't really hell but purgatory and He went there to free all the people without mortal sin, a kind of general amnesty.

This nun had answers for every question, and I really started to appreciate her; especially when she gave my "class artiste" title to Walter Stein who, I had to admit, drew better than I did. She now gave him extra artistic assignments. I passed on the symbolic mantle happily, yet with a touch of melancholy.

The last picture I drew for additional credit in Drawing class was of Notre Dame Cathedral in France. Copying from a photo in a text book, I discovered it had about 150 statues of saints in its niched facade making it the most difficult drawing I ever attempted. It took a week to finish, I printed my name and *Grade 5* at the bottom, and turned it in. The nun liked it and prominently displayed it on a wall of the main school building's first floor hallway. One kid in our class, never a threat to cop any scholastic honors and certainly not considered an artistic zealot, took one look at my picture and said, "So big deal! Where's da hunchback?" He was obviously more concerned with movies than the arts.

* * *

England was the only country still actively opposing Germany and she was getting strafed and bombed almost nightly by German Luftwaffe. Most Americans pitied the English people. Not my dad. His opinion: "The English bastards deserve every rotten thing they get," and he didn't give a damn about bluebirds over their white cliffs of Dover.

Dad, whose parents immigrated from Ireland, had no love for bloody Englishmen although this hostility apparently didn't extend to partially English women like my mother who was half-Irish and half-English. Dad's father, whose original name was Robert J. Bakewell, disliked England so much that when he came, some said illegally, to this country he gave himself a new name — Beckwell. He thought Bakewell sounded too English.

He came from Antrim county in Northern Ireland near the end of the nineteenth century, settled in Pennsylvania, met and married Bridget O'Gallagher who came from county Mayo, and they raised eight children, an average-sized Irish family then. Grandfather came here as a young man, but spent enough time in Ireland during what was called "The Troubles" to develop and maintain a practiced distrust and hatred for anything English. He was fluent in Irish so he cursed England in two languages, which he'd do with little provocation.

On his only visit to Detroit, when we lived on Belvidere, Grandfather took Chuck and me for a ride in his big 4-door

Chrysler. Standard gas stations sold red, white and blue crown gasoline, and each gas pump was topped with a large crown of corresponding color. When he mentioned a need for gas, I pointed to a Standard station up ahead. His shoulders stiffened and, with the brogue he never lost, he said, "I'm not sure, but with the crown on the pumps, the goddamn English must have something to do with it, and I'll not be after buying their goddamn gas."

My dad's dislike for the English, engendered by Grand-father, wasn't shared by his children, for we thought the whole Butler family were okay people. Mrs. Butler never raised her voice in anger and her accent was refreshing. When playing in the Butler backyard, I found myself hoping she'd come outside and talk to us, just for the pleasure of hearing it.

Mr. Butler was a quiet, educated gentleman I rarely saw for he worked long hours, came home, ate supper and spent evenings in his easy chair reading newspapers, books or magazines. Every Sunday he loaded his family into his sedan and drove them to church, and we didn't see them for two or three hours for he insisted his children not only go to services but also Sunday school. He had a subscription to both the National Geographic and Esquire, two magazines that were mandatory scanning for boys approaching puberty. Naturally he was never home when Joe and Red allowed us to examine these enlightening publications. We enjoyed the National Geographic for its educational features. Somehow we knew seeing African native women in their natural habitat, in varied stages of undress, would be beneficial in our geography classes. We learned art appreciation while staring at paintings of pretty Petty girls in Esquire and liked the cartoons, although we weren't sure what was meant when the caption said, "Why didn't you tell me your husband was coming home?"

Dad's aversion to the English didn't extend to Red and Joe who spent considerable time on our side of the street. He said of Red, "That boy is all-boy." Red was a nervy kid with a quick temper and could easily be goaded into fisticuffs. Dad admired fighters, especially fighters with red hair and a temperament like his own. Red's freckles were also a plus. Dad watched Joe for a time and pronounced that he had natural athletic ability and would probably play in the Majors someday. Joe had a wicked, accurate pitching arm, as anyone struck by one of his rifle-shot snowballs could attest.

During one of his frequent fireside chats, Franklin D. Roosevelt, our president, announced a new government program called "Lend-Lease" to aid England. The United States would rent arms and equipment to England to help overcome the Nazi menace. After England won the war they'd repay us. This riled a few of our more spiteful citizens on Holcomb since England didn't seem to be winning and hadn't repaid much of their World War I debt. To others it appeared Roosevelt was choosing sides and easing us into another European war. They weren't quite convinced when Franklin D. had solemnly declared, "I hate war."

Our president disturbed some people for another reason. He didn't seem capable of controlling, or didn't care to control, his wife Eleanor. She did a considerable amount of traveling throughout the world, and there were those who thought the president could have done more toward keeping her closer to home. These people were those who had never seen a picture of her. She was a brilliant, plain-looking, politically-active woman and publicly spoke her mind on controversial issues.

Some mildly-amusing neighborhood wits were asking, "Did you hear Roosevelt's latest speech?" Then, imitating Franklin's slow, dignified tones, they'd say, "I hate war. Eleanor hates war. I hate Eleanor." How much you laughed at this quip depended on how much you disliked one, or both, of the Roosevelts.

* * *

111

Nativity students performed school plays in the church basement. It was generally conceded among thinking students that missing one of Nativity's plays wasn't the worst thing that could happen in your lifetime. They were directed by a nun who was not, I repeat NOT, known as Sister Mary Cecil B. DeMille and, if you attended, you could be reasonably sure to see at least one kid waving a crutch and shouting, "God bless us, everyone." This could even happen in the Easter play. At the annual Passion play there was usually a difference of opinion as to whether an actor or the director should be nailed to the cross.

The few good seats at these plays were in the first two rows. The stage stood two-feet above floor level and though the rows of metal and wooden folding chairs were staggered so the audience could see between heads in front of them, few students could see through the head two rows forward. Those who actually had a good view of Nativity plays were the aforementioned first and second row students, overgrown students, students who didn't find a seat and had to stand along the walls, and actors. Everyone else could just as well have listened to the plays on radio. To them the most interesting part of any play was the oil cloth curtain rolled down between acts on which was imprinted, in blazing colors, the names, addresses and sales pitches of neighborhood stores and businesses. Also interesting was the possibility that a mouse might run across your shoes while on its way to wherever mice are on their way to. When it occurred, shrieks rang out in the darkened audience and the play would be suspended while nuns tried to soothe grated nerves and get the remaining students to remove their feet from chair seats. No one subscribed to the "Show must go on" theory.

The mice probably enjoyed the bedlam created, but on one occasion a hapless mouse chose the wrong row of chairs to invade. A sixth-grade heroine heard the screeches and saw the mouse coming her way. She deftly stepped on its little body, grasped the end of its tail, and stood up smiling while holding the wriggling animal for all to see. Folding chairs scraped and collapsed as fellow classmates forsook her immediate vicinity. We had all heard the expression "Poor as a church mouse," but this little intruder received no sympathy.

Someone turned on the lights, and a nun warily approached and told the student to bring the mouse and follow her. They headed to the girl's lavatory with the nun staying five feet in the forefront and turning often to make sure the student didn't close the gap. Once the lavatory door shut behind them the rest of us nervously snickered and talked about what guts the girl had. Most boys bravely said they would do the same thing if a chance came. I wasn't convinced. Most of us wore knickers, but what if we wore long pants, tried to step on a mouse, missed, and it ran up our pant leg. Not a pretty thought. Then again, the luckless boy might start a new, very animated, dance craze.

The nun and still-smiling girl returned to their seats after presumably flushing the poor critter down the toilet. I wondered if, as it went kicking and thrashing, it waved a little crutch and yelled, "God bless us, everyone!"

This episode shattered a widely held illusion that all girls are afraid of mice. Further, it was generally conceded that the entertainment value of a mouse-in-the-audience far surpassed the production on stage.

Our pastor bought a mostly vacant city block on McClellan, directly across from Chandler school, to build a recreation hall (appropriately named Nativity Recreation Center). Completed in February 1941, it contained a basement kitchen and dining area and, on the main floor, basketball courts for the girls high school teams and a stage to replace the dud in the church basement. A handball court was erected outside, and the land was cyclone-fenced. Why Father Geller did this we could only speculate since he seemed to be so anti-recreation. Some caustic critics suggested the basketball courts and dining area could easily be converted into bingo game areas. Students still appreciated it.

It wasn't long before our whole parish realized why Father Geller built the Recreation Center. We already knew he had majored in money at the seminary, and now we saw that he had created the best little money-maker for miles around. In addition to bingo and basketball games, he quickly added meetings, weekly dances, proms, Catholic Youth Organization boxing matches, Father and Son dinners, Mother and Daughter dinners, fairs, galas and celebrations for every holiday and holy day, with the possible exception of Yom Kippur.

Nativity's weekly dances were terrific and drew fine crowds from parishes all over Detroit's east side. We had the best big bands in the vicinity, the hall was nicely decorated and the lights dimmed, but not dimmed enough so any amorous swains could get away with copping an extra squeeze, or anything else.

The stage at one end of the hall was a vast improvement over the church basement facility. It was elevated enough for easy audience viewing and had real curtains that moved horizontally instead of up and down like the oil cloth one. Sister Mary Lucille replaced the old play director and we all fervently hoped that we had heard the last of "God bless us, everyone!"

She started making changes in the senior plays, the most significant of which was booking plays with male roles. Since this was an all-girl high school, we wondered where she'd get actors for these parts.

Ed found out in a hurry. Although attending Cass Tech High School, he still served mass at Nativity. After he served a six o'clock mass one morning, Sister Lucille nabbed him in the sacristy and advised him that his dramatic career would start the following Tuesday at senior play rehearsal. Further, he had to recruit three males for other roles. Ed tried to convince Sister Lucy (as he called her behind her back) that one more production of *Little Women* wouldn't hurt, but when his argument fell on deaf ears he asked three buddies, Ray Wronski, Al Bussacca and

114

Joe Cortez to join the cast. They demurred, vehemently, until Ed pointed out what a great way this would be to get involved with many young ladies. Then they took a different view of thespian endeavors. A new, exciting era of dramatic arts was introduced at Nativity.

* * *

Chuck was in third grade, Dolores in second, when their nuns asked Mom to stop by school for a conference. Having a nun ask your mother to stop by for a conference is not unlike having a girlfriend's father ask you to stop by the house to discuss your intentions. You know somebody is in trouble. The nuns told Mom that Chuck and Dolores were both close to failing many subjects and there was a possibility one or both would have to repeat their grades. This appealed to Chuck, because he and Dolores were inseparable. If he failed, Dolores would catch up to him, and they'd both be in the same class.

When Mom told Dad he roared threats and warnings. I only worried that their nuns might give them a D or F in Effort, bringing on Father Geller's ill-humored wrath. When I mentioned this possibility they bravely gave me "who cares" shrugs. I admired their attitude.

The school day at Chandler started at 8:15 and lasted until 3 p.m. We at Nativity started at 7:45 and left at 3:30. Actual educating hours were the same; the difference was we spent our first hour in church. We always suspected the two schools deliberately staggered hours to minimize contact between students for there was a certain amount of animosity. They called us cat-lickers; we called them pup-lickers, and infrequent scrimmages occurred. The shortest route home for me was through an alley running from McClellan to Belvidere along the Chandler schoolyard and a cut through Blaso's backyard. To avoid public school children still lingering on their playground, I'd stick to a slightly longer, but safer, Cairney-to-Holcomb route. Short-

115

cuts led to uppercuts and I bled easily.

I had just crossed McClellan heading home on Cairney one fine May day when a BB ricocheted off a garage door I was passing and hit my thigh. I heard a maniacal laugh. Looking across Cairney I saw a boy my age standing on a second story back porch holding what appeared to be a rifle. He was yelling something unintelligible. Why am I standing here? I asked myself and sprinted forward as another BB struck the garage behind me. Turning left down a nearby alley I ducked behind a rusty, 55-gallon drum, but the kid had already forgotten me and was firing at other unsuspecting students. I didn't recognize him so I knew he didn't go to Nativity. He had to be a Chandler pup-licker. I raced through the alley until I was well out of his range.

Arriving home, I breathlessly told my mother the details of this little adventure expecting her to organize the neighborhood against this blatant misuse of firearms, but she just said, "You see? BB guns can hurt. You're lucky you didn't lose an eye." She didn't seem distressed about kids shooting kids.

As I headed to school the next morning and approached the sniper's area, I caught up with other students, figuring there was safety in numbers. No one was standing on the upper porch when it came into view, yet I imagined the kid suddenly jumping out his back door and letting loose a fusillade. I asked Bernard Harrington, a fellow student who used the same homeward route, if the kid shot at him. He said, "No, but I saw him shoot at you. You should've hung around. Right after you took off the kid's mother came out, grabbed the rifle, and slapped hell out of him. It was funny!"

I was sorry I missed it. With one burst of maternal fury our neighborhood Protestant-on-Catholic crime wave terminated.

* * *

Finally, summer vacation arrived. Nativity students didn't burst out the front door on the last day of school. We walked in a silent single file until one block from school at the corner of either Cairney one way or Shoemaker the other before breaking ranks. Only then could we jump, skip, scream, fall down, kick each other, wrestle, run, fight and shout dumb things kids shout on the last day of school like, "No more pencils! No more books! No more teacher's dirty looks!" Chuck and Dolores both lucked out in one way on this last day. Father Geller didn't pass out the final 1940 report cards to the lower three grades. They didn't luck out in another. They both failed to get promoted, prompting Dad to disgustedly comment, "They'll have to burn down the damned school to get them out."

Nothing is as exhilarating as awakening to the realization that you don't have to wake up, and every day for three months would be the same. Vacation is like a succession of Saturdays when you can sleep in, wear comfortable clothing and do whatever you like within reason, except, of course, for the annoying interruptions for church services on Sundays and holy days.

As soon as we ate breakfast, if Chuck and I hadn't been called by friends, we went to their house and called them. Phones weren't involved. Calling friends consisted of standing on the sidewalk in front of their house and calling their names in a sing-song voice. We never considered knocking on doors or ringing doorbells. If they didn't come to the door after three or four calls, we moved closer to their front steps or went around to their back porch where the kitchen was located. If friends didn't show after a few more calls, a parent usually did and explained the kid was still sleeping, eating, not home, or being punished and wouldn't be outside playing for awhile.

Most names were simple to call. Joe-whee-eee, Cliff-fee-eee, Ray-mee-eee. We never called Red Butler. Red-dee-eee just sounded too fruit-eee-eee.

We still played baseball in the alley, but now we also played at Chandler playground. It had a backstop behind home plate and bases at each corner, but not a blade of grass.

The entire field was covered with small, hard, sharp gravel. If stretching a single into a double required a slide into second base, we usually stopped at first. Our games weren't important enough to take bark off our bodies.

Joe played in a Fireman Midget Baseball league and his manager gave him worn-out balls at times. Joe also had bats and a couple of well-used, right-handed, baseball gloves he let Chuck and me use. Since I was left-handed my little finger fit into the glove's thumb, making it highly susceptible to pulverization on hard-hit, slightly-misjudged line drives, but when I complained about pain Ray suggested I either buy a lefty glove or shut up. "Beggars can't be choosers," he added. Ray was a realist.

With Red still attending Chandler and Joe, Cliff and Ray alumni, they knew lots of the kids who showed up every day so we could always field a team. We played baseball for hours, losing track of innings and score.

Eventually we knocked the cover off the ball, due more to it striking gravel than bats, and someone would cover it with friction tape. There always seemed to be a boy with tape in his pocket or one who could run home for a roll. We also used this black tape to wrap bat handles. Bats were prone to cracking or breaking at the handle when the fat end forcefully struck a hardball. When learning batsmanship, boys were told to always grip bats with the Louisville Slugger trademark facing upward so the ball struck the bat on its grainy, or strongest, side. Despite this precaution, boys got careless, the handle cracked, and tape had to be applied. More sensible bat owners were pessimists who taped bat handles before they cracked. In addition, a taped handle acted as a bat glove, preventing a bat from slipping out of sweaty hands when we took a mighty swing.

When we tired of playing ball, Chandler had swings, teeter-totters, slides and chinning bars. I'd look across McClellan at Nativity's recreation center and the empty glass- and rock-strewn field next to it and wonder when Nativity would get all these good things to play with.

Protestants always took better care of their children's recreational needs.

When we weren't playing in the alley or at Chandler we played marbles and mumblety-peg in our front yard, two games needing ground devoid of grass. On the left side of the walk leading to our front porch, where the horse chestnut tree grew, even weeds couldn't cheat death. On the other side there were grass clumps but still plenty of wide, bare spots. "Manicured" and "postage stamp," cliches describing lawns, definitely didn't apply to ours. Theories abounded why grass didn't grow on the tree side: too much shade; ground too sandy; the tree sucked up all nutrients and moisture from adjacent soil; the neighborhood dogs' ongoing love affair with the tree. These reasons didn't explain the absence of grass on the other side.

My dad probably came closest to the real reason. "Grass and kids can't grow on the same side of the street." This was another of Dad's little sayings. He liked to lay one on us now and then, either to help us through this troublesome world or because he thought of himself as the poor man's Will Rogers. My favorite was the one he'd say as he came home from a long day at work and found us doing very little, which was what we did best. As he hung up his hat and coat, he'd exclaim, "It's the old dog for the rough road and the pups for the pavement."

Playing the game of marbles required a sharp stick or knife to draw a circle in a flat section of ground and a supply of small, colorful, glass marbles. Players mastered snapping a larger shooting marble, called a taw, from between their thumb and forefinger with enough velocity and accuracy to strike an opponent's marble and roll it outside the circle. It then became the shooter's property. Every neighborhood had a game going during summer daylight hours, each game not unlike a small gambling casino with the more adept and skillful shooters winning all the marbles. Boys practiced for hours before challenging better players and risking their loveliest agates or minnies. There always seemed to be one boy who became so good at the game he'd be banished from playing or required to shoot with his other hand. Often he took his skills into other neighborhoods where, being a stranger, hustling could earn him a solid punch in the mouth. No one thought to break his thumb.

We played mumblety-peg with pocketknives and every boy with a pants pocket carried one. We took turns and the winner was the first boy to run out of ways to flick or flip their knife into the ground. We flipped the knife from our hand, wrist, elbow, shoulder, chin, nose, ear and forehead.

We carried pocketknives or jackknives for two reasons: to play mumblety-peg and to whittle. Few boys carried a knife for protection because most realized by the time they got a knife out of their pocket and opened, their assailant would have punched them twelve times.

Joe Butler didn't carry his pocketknife in his pocket. He was one of those lucky boys who wore high-tops — smooth leather, knee-high boots that laced up in front. The comic strip hero Jungle Jim wore them, and so did every movie hero we saw stomping around jungle or desert terrain.

We all envied Joe, not only because boots looked so good with knickers, but because of the slim leather jack-knife compartment on the side of one boot. The knife that came with the boots, a cheap, one-bladed number guaranteed to break with the first whittle, had to be replaced anyway because two blades were required to play mumblety-peg. The knife compartment had a snap-over top making it impossible for the knife to fall out and get lost.

Joe, sensing our envy, explained he had to have high-tops for protection against animal bites while on his annual Boy Scout outing to Belle Isle. This scenic island rested in the Detroit River, accessible by bridge, and although it had many picnic and recreation spots, most of it was covered by woodland and underbrush, the natural habitat of lurking, long-fanged snakes and sharp-toothed rodents waiting to pounce on some high-topless Boy Scout's unprotected calf.

High-tops were expensive, so I knew it was futile to ask

my mother to buy me a pair. Besides, if she did, she might insist I join the Boy Scouts, an unpleasant idea. Boy Scouts wore short khaki pants during summer months, and I realized my knobby knees weren't my most attractive feature.

The highest-top footwear I ever wore was sneakers that reached a little above the ankle. Every active boy wore sneakers through most of the summer. They were made of canvas, trimmed with rubber, and had thick, treaded, rubber soles whose treads were designed to grip whatever they contacted, be it sidewalk, grass, tree bark, roofing or playground. Sneakers always had thin, round pieces of rubber that covered each protruding ankle bone. In our boyhood discussions we decided the rubber either protected ankles against minor injury from thrown objects such as stones and baseballs or reinforced the canvas where it tended to stretch. Maybe it was a combination of both. Or maybe, as cynical Ray mentioned, it was merely a place to identify the manufacturer since most had a U.S. Keds logo.

When wearing sneakers I felt capable of outrunning the wind — or anyone chasing me — and climbing the highest tree or rooftop. Sneakers only had one bad aspect. After wearing them all day in a hot playground, it was best to put them on the back porch for an overnight airing. They could lay a very bad assault on sensitive noses.

X

In late June, Germany invaded Russia taking pressure off England and highly irritating my dad. He thought the Irish prime minister should have invited Germany to use Irish ports to invade England and, at the same time, kick the English out of Northern Ireland. "That goddamn Hitler's crazy!" he ranted. No one ever accused Dad of being a great military tactician, but Irishmen have been known to be intractable in their contempt for "Brits." Even Dad admitted the Irish had faults for he often said, "Some Irishmen are as thick in the head as a mule is in the ass."

We schoolchildren also thought Hitler crazy, but for a different reason. We judged a country's strength by how large it appeared on maps, and Russia and England governed much more territory than Germany. Even with Italy helping we figured Germany couldn't win since about half the world in our Geography books was pink, the color of the British Empire, including a vast expanse of North America directly above the United States.

While Europeans blazed away at each other with Howitzers, bombs and rifles, we Holcomb boys spent many hours blazing away at each other with toy pistols. If we didn't own one, we drew a gun outline on plywood and cut it out with a band saw. We chose sides and played cops and robbers, cowboys and Indians, but mostly we just played "guns." The noise our guns made, furnished by our mouths, wasn't "BANG!" It was a loud, guttural "KKOOUUE!" In some circles POW! was acceptable, but not preferred. Our gunfights always caused lively discussions about whether we were shot or not. "I got you!" "No you didn't!" "I got you in the head!" "Heads don't count!" "Who said?!" "Joe said before we started!" Rules made before gunfights started had to be adhered to all that day. All rules were subject to change the following day.

Or "I got you." "No, you just got me in the arm!" Movie heroes always got shot in the arm and it healed two minutes later. They called it a flesh wound.

The only way to unequivocally "kill" your opponent was to sneak up behind him and from three feet away, KKOOUUE him.

A second floor vacancy developed in Ray's apartment building and a new kid, Danny, moved in with his parents. Danny was an only child, eight years old, and his parents bought him anything he wanted. Ray disliked this small family and called them "Mr. and Mrs. Rich Bitch and their little bastard." He had a reason for this assessment. Danny owned many toys, but unlike my friend Jimmy on Belvidere, he objected to sharing them. Included in his toy array were a spark-shooting machine gun and two cap pistols. When he pulled the pistols' triggers the caps made a most realistic bang, and smoke poured from their barrels. That about fifty shots could be fired from these six-shooters without reloading didn't strike us as unrealistic since movie cowboy's six-shooters had the same ability. We allowed Danny to play guns with us just so we could use his arsenal. Soon after, Danny and his parents moved away taking all this fire power with them, but this exposure to realism evoked a strong desire for my own cap gun and caps. I was tired of saying KKOOUUE. My mother, who didn't equate want with need, refused my cap gun request saying, "They're too noisy and they smoke so they're probably dangerous." Extremely disappointed, I considered asking for a bow and arrows, so I could dispense with sound effects altogether, but quickly put the thought aside. In cowboy and Indian games, I invariably ended up an Indian and knew from watching Saturday afternoon movies that Indians who shot cowboys with arrows ended up dead. Being an Indian was hazardous anytime. Even good, old Tonto got pretty well misused at the hands of town folks when he stupidly let his "kemo sabay" send him to scout a town while the Ranger stayed safely out on the prairie making silver bullets.

(They still play "guns" in my old neighborhood, but with the advent of real guns there's a whole new meaning to "I got you in the head." When somebody gets it in the head now, he doesn't say, "Heads don't count." He usually doesn't say much at all unless he might have just enough time to make a quick remark about the shooter's mother.)

* * *

Summer vacation ended, and I faced sixth grade in the flats — the two-story houses converted to classrooms. Only boys went to school in these flats. It saddened me because girls were becoming tolerable, and even likeable. Yet, school life without girls had one advantage. It wasn't embarrassing to say something dumb or make a mistake in front of class. With only boys around it just didn't seem to matter.

For the first five years at Nativity the nuns prepared us for this complete disengagement by separating boys and girls whenever possible. Apparently nuns spent a great deal of time worrying about us and the adultery Commandment. "That's where they got their name," a boy told me. "Ain't had 'nun,' don't want 'nun,' ain't gonna get 'nun,' and neither are you kids if we can help it." We were segregated when marching to and from church, during recess games, mass, plays, confession, and any other school-sponsored activity outside our classroom. So it wasn't a formidable adjustment.

* * *

125

Ed got his driver's license in October on his 16th birthday. He had many days of practice beforehand using Dad's car and, according to Dad, wore out the clutch. I think Dad was just looking for a good excuse to buy another new car for he came home with a green, 1941 Chevy, and declared, "I'm going to buy a new car every damn year from now on. No more used cars for me." It was the last new car he'd own for a long time.

When I awoke on Sunday in early December I quickly donned three pairs of shorts. It was my 11th birthday and Dad would, at times, give his children playful birthday smacks that hurt like hell. Mostly the last two — the one for good measure and one to grow on. I never understood how an extra swat was going to make me grow and, after looking at our whole family, I could see it obviously didn't work.

We didn't receive any gaily wrapped presents on our birthdays, but we did get recognition, including the Happy Birthday song and deference during altercations. For example, Chuck might say, "Ma! Robbie won't give me my Lincoln Logs!" and Mom would say, "Let him play with them for now. It's his birthday." You were monarch-for-a-day.

Two unpleasant things happened that particular 11th birthday in 1941. I still had to go to church, birthday or not, and my country went to war.

Late afternoon a newspaper boy walked down Holcomb excitedly shouting, "Extra! Extra! U.S. fleet bombed at Pearl Harbor! Extra!"

Neighbors gathered around living room radios or outside in small clusters on sidewalks trying to understand what it meant. "Where's Pearl Harbor?" they asked each other. Some thought it was a naval base in California. Others, who had listened closely to the radio or invested three cents to read the newspaper extra, said it was on Oahu, one of the Hawaiian Islands in the Pacific. "What's our fleet doing in a foreign country?" was the logical next question. "I don't know" was the answer.

And they said, "I thought we were going to war with Germany. Why's Japan getting into it?" No one knew.

Then someone asked, "Where's Japan?"

Wherever Japan was, it declared war on the United States and Great Britain after its attack on the U.S. fleet, an attack which struck people as underhanded — like clubbing someone with a baseball bat and then asking, "Do you wanna fight?"

People were confused, frightened and excited. Above all, they were patriotic. World War One veterans and men with many children — like Dad — wondered aloud if they'd be called to the colors, and some actually wished they would.

Of course there were those who hoped they wouldn't become a part of the Selective Service program. Some remembered old back and knee injuries. Some started to develop a little cough. Others began to talk about all sorts of mayhem that had been inflicted upon them in their quest for football immortality on college gridirons. I also heard about guys who started to step a little higher and shake hands a tad more loosely than before.

Yet, most young, eligible, single men lined up at Army and Navy induction centers, ready to do battle with the sneaky Japanese who had sent peace ambassadors to Washington while secretly planning war.

Four days after Japan's Pearl Harbor attack, Germany and Italy declared war on the United States. World War Two began in earnest. Security was tightened by the FBI, Army and local police at defense plants and at the tunnels and bridge leading into Detroit from Canada to stop German secret agents or saboteurs from infiltrating and blowing up vital installations. Soldiers also guarded the entrance to Waterworks Park near Belle Isle to keep German agents from poisoning Detroit's water supply. There was little fear that Japanese secret agents, with their unique features, could infiltrate.

A radio hero, The Green Hornet, had a powerful black

car driven by his faithful Japanese companion and chauffeur named Kato. Soon after December 7th, however, through the magic of radio, Kato became his faithful Filipino companion faster than President Roosevelt could tell us the date would live in infamy. After that I often wondered why people didn't protest about the Lone Ranger's faithful companion, Tonto. It seemed a change might be warranted when I learned in history class about the unpleasantness with General Custer.

Monday, December 8th, was a holy day, the feast of the Immaculate Conception, so we went to church but not to school, and I expected to get the rest of the week off. Enemy bombs should start falling any minute, and a well-placed one dropped on Nativity could wipe out our student population. Instead we went to school, and no bombs fell. Our nun discussed the war and showed us Japan's location on the rolldown world map attached just above the blackboard. I knew it would be somewhere near China because of the Japan-China War bubble gum cards I'd seen. Comparing the size of Japan with the combined land area of China and United States made me wonder if they had maps in Japan. Couldn't they see they were outlanded? Japan's leaders were as dense as Germany's.

I tried to imagine the conversation between Emperor Hirohito and his wife at breakfast on December 8th. I figured his wife would start out with, "Now look, Emp! Just what in hell do you think you're doing picking on a country that big?"

He'd reply, "I declared war on America out of a sincere desire for Japan's self-preservation."

She probably retorted, "Preservation this! I told you to drink your tea, not sniff it. Have you looked at the size of that country? Hawaii isn't even a state yet and you still got those people angry!"

"But Empress, baby, I'm concerned about the well-being of our subjects and the solemn obligation foisted upon us by our imperial ancestors."

128

"Don't 'Empress baby' me, buddy, and screw our ancestors. They never saw a John Wayne movie. And besides him, America has Tyrone Power and Errol Flynn. Now there's a guy who can loosen my obi anytime. They'll also have Humphrey when he gets back from Casablanca, so we're in deep trouble, Emp."

"You could be right," Emp says, looking grave. Then he brightens. "But look at it this way. If we win, we take it all at once. If we lose, they rebuild our country, and then we buy theirs. It will take a little longer that way, but we could own it all by the year 2000."

The school week ended, the excitement wore off and life settled down to abnormal.

* * *

At the breakfast table adults drank coffee. Children drank cocoa and pretended they were adults drinking coffee. Adults enjoyed giving children sips of unsweetened coffee to watch their childish faces squinch up in bitter distaste. This made us kids appreciate cocoa that much more.

We even appreciated Ovaltine. It wasn't that we liked the taste. We just needed the round, thin, metal foil under the lid so we could send away for Little Orphan Annie decoder rings and so many other things we could never do without.

Mothers thought cocoa great for warming our stomachs before sending us off to school on cold winter mornings. I thought the greatest thing about cocoa was the fudge recipe on the back of the container. Often while babysitting siblings, an older sister, either Betty or Mary, asked, "Who wants fudge?" No one ever answered "Not me." That answer was reserved for questions like "Who wants liver?" or "Who wants spinach?"

The babysitter mixed a concoction of cocoa, butter, milk, corn syrup and sugar in a saucepan and cooked it over a low flame. After it thickened, she added vanilla and beat the mixture until the mixing spoon bent and her wrist and fingers ached. She spooned it into a buttered cake pan, and after cooling, cut it into two-inch squares and distributed it to well-behaved children. Sweets were as good as threats to control kids; especially threats to withhold sweets.

Then a decision had to be made: Who was going to lick the spoon and pan? Betty or Mary usually made their determination based on disciplinary considerations. One pan of fudge controlled a group of children for several hours.

I liked chocolate fudge and candy. Chuck loved them. This love led to the 1941 Christmas Chocolate Candy Caper.

On Christmas Eve, Betty came home from her job at Prudential Insurance Company with a two-pound box of chocolates; a Christmas bonus given to loyal employees in lieu of a raise. At 9 p.m., as an enticement to get us to bed, she opened the box and offered Chuck, Dolores, Annie and me one piece each —a no-lose situation since we knew we had to go to bed anyway.

When Chuck saw all that chocolate candy his eyes popped and glazed. I saw his hand tremble when he reached for the box. His reaction was understandable, for we had never seen so many delicious, appetizing candies in one small space — available and free. We crammed the chocolates into our mouths and looked voraciously at the box as Betty replaced the lid.

Mom followed the four of us upstairs and tucked us in bed. I don't know why being tucked in felt so good, but it did. A blanket tucked under your chin and around your body by a mother's hands made you feel protected, warm and secure. You hated to move and lose the feeling.

Chuck and I lay wide-eyed in bed listening to the downstairs murmuring and laughter as our parents, older brother and sisters trimmed the tree and played with our toys.

Chuck whispered, "Robbie. Are you awake?"

"Yeah."

"I want some more candy."

I did too. The one I had eaten was tasty looking, but under its chocolate cover lurked marshmallow and green jelly. Yuk. I figured Betty owed me a creme. "Let's wait 'til everybody's asleep; then get some," I suggested.

Chuck agreed. We forced our eyes to stay open, concentrating on the drone of voices downstairs. Once, when there was a burst of laughter, we silently got out of bed and tiptoed part way down the stairs, almost to the landing, to gaze across the darkened foyer at the living room activity. Dad was trying to assemble a wind-up train, muttering under his breath every time a railroad car fell off the track. This project was a ten-expletive job for him. Betty, Mary and Pat jabbered happily while adding tinsel to the lighted tree. Mom sat in an armchair smiling at one of Ed's remarks and Ed sat on the couch trying to think of another witticism.

"There it is!" Chuck blurted. He spotted the open box of candy on an end table at Mom's elbow. Unfortunately, Chuck's blurt was loud enough to cause her to notice us.

"You kids get to bed!" she cried, jumping up from her chair.

We scrambled up the stairs as she questioned aloud, "Why are they still up? It's almost ten-thirty!"

Chuck and I dived into bed, pulled the covers up to our chins and waited breathlessly, listening for the ominous sounds of Dad's slippers ascending the stairs. After a few minutes of silence we started to giggle.

For two hours we talked about everything we could think of to keep each other awake. We wondered if Joe and Red were already asleep, who would get the wind-up train, when should we tell Annie there wasn't a Santa Claus or Easter Bunny, who would get a spinning top this year. Every Christmas Dad gave one of his younger children a colorful, pumping, humming tin top so he could play with it.

131

We discussed mean nuns and nice nuns, kids we liked and disliked at school, and what we were going to be when we grew up. He wanted to be a fireman. I still wanted to be a Canadian Mountie. We also speculated about the chastity of some neighborhood ladies, although such thoughts didn't seem to be in keeping with the spirit of the holy Christmas season. Mostly we wondered how long those people downstairs could stay awake, because we were certainly having difficulty.

Twice I dozed off and Chuck awakened me. Once he dozed and I awakened him. When we heard footsteps ascending, our eyes snapped open. Finally! Patiently, quietly, we waited for all activity to cease; the laughter, levity, mumbles, murmurs, faucets, flushing.

After fifteen minutes of absolute silence, we slipped out of bed and soundlessly, with the exception of a couple stair creaks, reached the living room. The Christmas tree, dimly illuminated by moonlight pouring through the curtains of our front windows, emitted a fresh balsam fragrance. As I admired its darkened beauty, Chuck grabbed my arm and said, "Let's get the candy."

The candy wasn't on the end table. It was nowhere in sight! Did Betty take it to her bedroom? She wouldn't be that rotten!

She wasn't. Chuck found it where she'd hidden it, under wrapped presents behind the tree. He possessed some uncanny chocolate sense, either smell or intuition. He gently lifted the lid exposing a candy gourmand's delight — a feast! We began to feast.

We sat crosslegged near the tree, the box between us, happily staring at each other's bulging cheeks as we swiftly stuffed piece after piece into our mouths — cremes, fudges, nuts, cherries — all delicious. After we each ate seven pieces, the realization struck that Betty could easily detect the absence of so many chocolates. Not to be daunted, the Chocolate Candy Caper Kids seized candies from the second layer underneath and deftly shifted them to the top layer. Brilliant! Stuffing two more delicacies into our mouths, and glancing longingly at the toys, we retreated to our bed and safety.

Our successful caper was over but Chuck wasn't satisfied. He whispered rapturously, "Geez, they were good. I wish we had some more. I could eat the whole box. Geez, they were good." Then he said, "Let's go get some more."

"Ya wanna get us killed?" I cautioned. "If Betty figures out who stole her candy she'll tell Pa and he'll knock our heads off."

"I don't care. I still want more." He was having a chocolate fit! He closed his eyes and visions of chocolates danced in his head. He would have had visions of sugar plums, but we didn't know what they looked like.

"Maybe we can steal some tomorrow," I told him. "Maybe Betty will give us another one. Take it easy. Go ta sleep." He didn't hear me. He was already sleeping — smiling.

If Betty noticed the missing candy, she didn't mention it. We each received two more pieces on Christmas Day. She loved Christmas and considered it not only a day of festive merriment, but also a day for indulgence and magnanimity.

She still feels the same. In 1986, the Detroit Free Press printed her letter when the editor asked readers to answer the question, "What does Christmas mean to you?"

She wrote: "What can you say about Christmas that hasn't been said a thousand times before? My memories go back many years. A big family growing up in the 1930s, I suppose we were poor by today's standards, but we were rich in so many ways. We were blessed with loving parents who instilled in us a strong sense of family and caring and faith. I don't know how they did it, but there was always something under the tree for each of us. What a thrill to get up on Christmas morning and see and smell the real Christmas tree. Today we've substituted an artificial tree, but I still love to sit and look at the pretty lights and dream of happy years.

"What does Christmas mean to me? It means shopping for just the right gifts for all those special people in my life. It means twinkling lights and gaudy decorations in the stores and sparkling houses up and down the street. It's the warm feeling you get standing by the creche looking down at Baby Jesus and remembering why we celebrate this day.

"But above all, Christmas means love."

XI

Whenever our coal supply diminished, Mom or Dad phoned for a delivery. Our basement coal bin was situated right under the living room. The fuel truck parked at the curb, one of the older kids rushed down and opened our front basement window, and the coalman filled our bin. He used a steel-wheeled wheelbarrow to convey coal from truck bed to window —crossing and recrossing our lawn.

Burning coal for heat had disadvantages. Besides the labor of shoveling it from bin to furnace, there was also the labor of washing away soap-resistant blackened stains that accumulated directly above wall registers in each room. And when fresh snow fell on wintry days, children who had a penchant for eating snow had to get it done quickly. Every chimney in Detroit's homes and factories blasted and spewed smoke, and within hours snow became dotted with soot. After a deep snow, tardy snow-eaters had to scrape an inch or so off the top to get to nice, clean stuff underneath.

Detroit's factories were definitely spewing smoke. The automobile plants ceased manufacturing civilian vehicles and totally geared up for war production. Workers were needed and they came, mostly from southern states. They were joined by women who ably took the place of young men drafted into military service. "Rosie the Riveter," wearing blue coveralls and a matching snood, was born.

The plants, Chrysler Manufacturing, Motor Products, Budd Wheel, Briggs Beautiware and others, were working around the clock turning out military equipment. Detroiters believed, with the masses of people swelling their ranks, that the city would eventually surpass Philadelphia in population, thus making Detroit the country's third most populous city, behind New York and Chicago. The city vigorously boomed. Prefabricated corrugated metal shelters, called Quonset huts, were erected on any available land to help house Detroit's new citizens, and portable schoolrooms were added to schoolyards to teach their children. Everyone wanting a job easily found one and Holcomb's lunch bucket pedestrian traffic zoomed.

To our dismay, the newspapers reported a Japanese invasion of the Philippines and capture of our troops stationed there. When Colonel Doolittle staged a daring, successful Tokyo air raid from an aircraft carrier, it raised our morale and, we hoped, lowered theirs. In May, American and Japanese fleets both lost an aircraft carrier in a Coral Sea battle fought strictly with carrier-based planes. Planes were destroyed on both sides, but the battle discouraged a Japanese invasion of Australia.

Some Holcomb neighbors questioned why our army occupied the Philippines in the first place, but after Pearl Harbor, they weren't surprised. Our armed forces appeared to be all over the Pacific. In the meantime, Holcomb life continued.

* * *

We boys developed a talent for climbing any pillar, post or pole, plus any tree we could get our legs partially around. Once we reached the lowest limb, the remaining limbs were easily reached.

We climbed as high as nerve allowed. The higher we went, the more we felt like Tarzan. The more we felt like

136

Tarzan the more apt we were to let loose with a mighty Tarzan yell. However, with our, as yet, unchanged voices, our Tarzan yells weren't very mighty. Johnny Weissmuller's job was secure.

Wooden telephone poles provided more thrills, particularly shinnying to the first rung. The first rung wasn't high, but reaching it could be hazardous. Shinnying involved wrapping arms and legs around the pole and pulling your body upward. Telephone poles were notorious for having very sharp slivers and if you weren't careful, you could find a sliver in your arm, legs or other tender frontal parts. The only thing worse was sliding down a telephone pole in a hurry. When this was necessary a boy could end up with more wood in his dick than Pinocchio ever had.

Rung by rung we scaled poles until we reached the first wire. We carefully avoided wires since it was common knowledge they all contained more electricity than the electric chair and touching one brought instant death. We concluded that every dead bird or squirrel found without a BB embedded in its body must have touched a live wire.

Whoever erected alley telephone poles surely had boys in mind for many were placed adjacent to garage corners. Our garage had such a pole. We climbed the pole until we could step onto the slanted roof corner, walked to the peak, sat down and viewed our neighborhood from on high.

Joe, Red, Chuck and I initiated a yearly custom that impressed my mother. She thought it cute and told many neighbors because it wasn't often she could tell them anything about her boys that had an ethereal motif. Every Good Friday, the four of us spent afternoon hours between 12 and 3 sitting on our garage roof while whittling, discussing religion, or simply trying to be quiet and reverent.

During one of these devotional times, I asked Joe why his family drove to church every Sunday when they could walk to the Protestant church down the street, an austere, wooden, Lutheran church located at Holcomb and Chapin. He explained about the diversity of Protestant churches, how they didn't all agree on biblical interpretation. How some, like his Evangelical and Reformed church, appealed to people because it was more ritualistic than the corner church. He told me what fun he and Red had in Sunday school and how inspirational the minister's sermons were. Just as I became convinced to change religions at the first available chance, he smiled and finished lamely with, "Besides, my oldest sister, Virginia, married the minister."

We noticed during our Good Friday sits that, invariably, dark clouds rolled in as noon approached, blocking the sun and making us nervously whittle a little faster as we marveled at this minor miracle. No rain fell and three hours later the clouds dissipated. Surely God was reminding us of His Son's agonizing crucifixion. We didn't realize there might be cloudless skies over Chicago and Toronto. In our world there were dark clouds for three hours and it deeply moved us.

We all agreed the best garage to play on was the one behind Ray's apartment, a 6-car, flat-roofed, tar-covered type, accessible by telephone pole. From this flat roof, with a running start, we could leap over to the neighbors' pyramid-shaped garage roofs at either end, emulating Batman, one of our comic book heroes. The gaps between garages were three and five feet, respectively, and became tests of courage and stupidity for there were concrete walks to fall on if we miscalculated.

Cliff Combs thought of another use for a garage. His parents' aged, wood-rotted, two-car garage had never suffered the indignity of a coat of paint or housed an automobile. It was used for storage. It had a decided list in the manner of Pisa's tower and was piled rafter-high with every discarded relic and souvenir known to man: musty couches, mattresses and armchairs; rusty iron pipes and bed frames; broken-legged chairs and tables; damaged toys, radios, lamps, dishes, tools, sinks and stoves; various lengths of warped wood; old moth-eaten clothing; and at least two hot-water tanks with busted seams. There had to be a thousand dollars worth of treasured antiques or five dollars worth of junk in there, depending on who did the appraisal. I asked Cliff why he didn't sell its contents to the first passing sheeny and he answered, "The junk's the only thing holding up the garage." So he couldn't use that garage when he had his brilliant inspiration.

Since the house between the Combs family and us belonged to the Combses and their tenants weren't interested in using the small empty garage that came with the lease, Cliff turned it into a chicken coop. He built two rows of wooden shelves along its inside walls with more shelves down the middle and lined them with straw. Outside he erected a large chicken-wired enclosure against one side of the garage and cut out a small aperture in the garage wall near the bottom so chickens would have free access to either the garage or enclosure. He then stocked his coop with thirty-five hens and two happy roosters. The roosters led an active, fighting and funning life. They avoided, stalked or attacked each other and, in between, jumped on the hens' backs. This kept the hens alert and perpetually clucking disapproval of this fowl play.

Each morning Farmer Cliff gathered eggs from his garage, and neighbors began lining up at his back door to buy fresh eggs at cut-rate prices. Now we not only had a dairy six doors down the street, but an egg farm next door. My mother appreciated it because she shopped for food almost daily at her favorite Gratiot market (the market owner accepted her penny wagers on numbers) and carried her heavy purchases home in paper bags. The convenience of sending her children on short trips for milk and eggs lightened her load. The only inconvenience was washing birth residue from Cliff's eggs. Cliff had not yet mastered marketing techniques.

Mornings, near dawn, when the two roosters had a crowing competition, lively neighborhood grumbling ensued regarding this undesirable noise, but no one considered complaining to the police. Jack Combs, Cliff's father, was the police.

With the exception of Batman, Superman was my favorite comic book hero, so when Mom presented me with a new, navy-blue-with-white-belt swimsuit, I instantly recognized I could now make a Superman costume. Gathering crayons, safety pins, scissors and an empty cereal box, I retreated to my bedroom, cut two triangles from the box and, using crayons, drew a red Superman "S" with a yellow background on the blank side of each. From the bathroom I got my Superman cape, a light-blue towel. I pinned one triangle to the cape, donned long underwear, pinned the other triangle to my chest, slipped into the swimsuit, pulled on dark-blue knee socks, and pinned two corners of the cape together at my throat. I stuck two pairs of rolled-up socks inside the bicep area of my sleeves and, faster than an express train, raced into my sisters' bedroom to admire the results in their dresser mirror. Except for color discrepancies, the costume was perfect. I only had to convince my mother to dye the towel, swimsuit and knee socks red, and my long underwear blue.

I returned to my bedroom feeling strong, mighty and invincible and resolved to perform heroic feats. I removed my cape and put on a Clark Kent disguise over my costume, consisting of a long-sleeved shirt, knickers and sneakers. No one paid attention to me as I descended the stairs, walked casually through the hall and kitchen, and slipped out the back door. I was completely ignored quite often, and it happened mostly when in one of my disguises. I ran for the alley, scaled the telephone pole, stepped onto our garage roof and walked to the edge facing the yard. I knew I couldn't jump OVER a tall building, but at least I could jump OFF one.

The distance to the ground was a mere nine or ten feet, but when looking down it seemed higher. I knew it would be best not to land on the narrow sidewalk running alongside our garage; that leaping outward to land on grass would be safer. After three tense minutes of debating whether I was Superman or a cowardly 11-year-old kid, I chose Superman and jumped.

My feet hit the grass and a split second later so did my buckled knees. With hip bones lodged in armpits I knew my growth was forever stunted.

But soon pain receded and I stood tall, thinking, geez, that wasn't so bad! I AM a man of steel! If only Lois Lane had been here to see my performance.

Looking for more adventure, I returned to my bedroom, removed my disguise and pinned on my cape. I gathered pillows from all the second floor bedrooms, arranged them on my bed and spent hours smashing the murderous Pillow Gang. I caught them harassing Lois and buffeted them terribly. I pummeled them, hurled one into the others, tossed them over my shoulder, jumped on them, slammed their heads together, bashed them across the room, and inflicted many another just retribution before turning them over to the proper authorities for confinement. Don't mess with Lois when Superman's around!

But the Pillow Gang broke out of jail and before I recaptured them my sister Pat missed her pillow, and whined to Mom when I wouldn't return it. Mom came upstairs to settle the dispute and when she saw the condition of the pillows — two were shedding feathers and all pillowcases were grimy from sliding across floors — she demanded I return them to their proper beds. I decided this would be an inappropriate time to ask her to dye my costume. After duly reprimanding me, Mom asked, "What kind of get-up is that?"

When I told her who I was a smile flickered and she suggested I use my super strength to throw all pillowcases down the clothes chute, along with my cape when I finished wearing it. With only two pillows left with which to do battle, Chuck's and mine, I temporarily suspended Superman's adventures. Most members of the notorious Pillow Gang spent the remainder of their days sleeping with my sisters — an appropriate punishment for their crimes.

The aforementioned clothes chute, a simple convenience, was a metal chute extending from our upstairs hallway to the basement. It was between walls and had two access doors, one in the hallway and the other in our kitchen. Most homes still have clothes chutes and they present no problem, but in our house at least forty percent of the entire family wardrobe was caught in the chute because eight impatient children simultaneously tried to send all dirty clothing to the basement at the same time. On washday, Mom had to use broom handles and clothes hangers to unload the chute. Each time she dutifully reported this to our father and he dutifully warned us that if it happened again, stern measures would be taken. This warning, for the most part, went unheeded, so one day Dad got a hammer and a hand full of large nails and permanently solved the clothes chute problem. He nailed the access doors shut. From then on, clothes had to be carried to the basement.

Dad's solutions to problems were unimaginative, but effective. When as Superman I crawled out my bedroom window onto the back porch roof and Mom discovered me getting ready to jump, she told Dad and he nailed all our second floor windows closed. Living with Father was a real trip. With his little hammer and nails he'd have been a big hit on Mount Calvary.

* * *

The war started to affect our neighborhood during that summer of '42. Shortages of life's staples developed and the federal government's Office of Price Administration (OPA) instituted a rationing program for all citizens. Car owners were issued an "A" card, plus a white on black "A" sticker for their windshields, entitling them to purchase three gallons of gas per week. Upper echelon personnel in industries who supplied material to the military received a

"C" card which entitled them to unlimited gas. Dad, who had risen to a supervisory position at Gelatin Products got a "C" card because the company supplied our armed forces with medicine-filled capsules. This pleased Ed who drove Dad's car regularly during evening hours.

With the advent of gas rationing, most people grudgingly used their cars less and public transportation more. Still, some devised inventive ways to obtain gas with duplicate cards and a few others even resorted to the very unlawful siphoning method.

Food rationing also was launched. An OPA bureaucrat created an ingenious plan to ration meat, butter, oleomargarine, cheese, sardines, catsup, coffee and the coffee additives, sugar and canned milk. Caffeine addicts suspiciously thought it a government plot to wean them from their favorite beverage.

Consumers were issued war ration books with red, blue, green and brown stamps, each worth a certain amount of points. The rationed food was assigned a point value and the point value of food and stamps changed at times just to make sure everyone involved paid attention. Red tokens and blue tokens, worth one point each, were introduced to be used as change. Shoppers and grocers not only had to keep track of fluctuating food costs, but also fluctuating point values. The whole process involved housewives, grocers, food wholesalers and banks. Grocery retailers and wholesalers began to encourage their children to become accountants and lawyers. They needed accountants to track points, prices and cash; lawyers to interpret directives from the OPA.

After the war the OPA bureaucrat who invented the ration book point system was amply rewarded. He became head of the Bureau of Internal Revenue.

Rationing significantly changed one of America's eating preferences. Butter was much more expensive than oleomargarine and its point value was four times as much, so patriotic and practical housewives began to replace butter with oleo. When Mom introduced it to our dinner table, she heard disapproving howls from her children. The taste wasn't so different from butter, but it resembled a pound of lard. Evidently the oleo companies heard our howls for they began to enclose an envelope of orange-colored powder to be added and mixed into their product. It miraculously changed the oleo from lard-white to butter-yellow. Then my mother howled as her mixing arm and hand throbbed. The companies heard again, and they packaged the oleo in sealed see-through bags with an orange dot inside. Simply puncture the dot and knead the color into the oleo. The one time my mother gave me the bag to knead I thought I'd need to grow new little thumbs.

Finally the companies began coloring oleo before selling it. Then the dairies howled, because fewer people bought their high-priced spread.

In order to aid the war effort, the government also suggested that all home front citizens plant Victory gardens and organize scrap drives. Almost everyone in our neighborhood had at least a small section of backyard devoted to tomatoes, peas, rhubarb, beets, carrots, radishes, lettuce and cabbage. Some over-zealous neighbors, obviously frustrated farmers, turned half their backyard into corn fields and tomato patches, then worried who would harvest their crops first: birds, insects, themselves or neighborhood children.

My mother's modest Victory garden of tomatoes, peas and lettuce was relegated to a space near our garbage container. Mrs. Combs had given the vegetable seeds to Mom, cautioning, "Listen, Claire. These are really fast-growing seeds. Just put them into the ground, splash some water on them, then jump back out of the way." My mother followed directions precisely, including the jump, and realized Mrs. Combs had a peculiar sense of humor.

I appreciated our garden because it diminished the grass area to be cut with our rusty lawn mower. Mom occasionally assigned the job to Chuck and me to relieve us of excess energy. For the same reason, she gave us the job of beating on rugs hung over our backyard clotheslines. Swinging a long, wire, wooden-handled rug beater and slamming it into those rugs guaranteed to improve one's baseball swing and raise clouds of dust. Continuing for any length of time also raised blisters on hands.

Chuck and I never succeeded in knocking all the dirt out of those rugs before sinking exhausted onto our back porch steps. It was impossible. After we quit Mom would come outside, pick up the beater, hit the rugs a couple times raising small clouds, and say, "There's still dirt in these." There was. It billowed out when we hit the rugs, then floated back in as if the rugs were magnetized.

The whole neighborhood joined in scrap drives. Chandler and Nativity schools provided space to drop off metal, paper and rubber tires and both schools became engorged with flattened tin cans and toothpaste tubes, treadless rubber tires, radiators and other metal car parts, stacks of old newspapers, broken lawn mowers, spades and shovels, and even silk and nylon stockings. My sisters thought their old run-ribbed stockings would be turned into parachutes and I pictured a poor pilot bailing out of a plane, pulling his ripcord and watching horrified as 2,000 sewed-together, holey stockings billowed out over his head.

The stockings actually were used to make powder bags for naval guns. Old tires were turned into gas masks, old shovels into hand grenades, and other metal into shell casings. I pointed out to Mom that giving up our rusty lawn mower might speed up the war's conclusion, but she demurred. She found another way to contribute to the war effort.

Since our government recommended that all bacon grease be returned to grocers in a covered can to be used to make ammunition, Mom started buying more bacon. And because ours was a large family with more-than-enough food stamps, she gave her surplus to our neighbors and suggested they also buy bacon. The proprietors of groceries and markets not only had to deal with food stamps, they now had the added responsibility of handling fragrant bacon grease. Some regretted not opening in orthodox Jewish neighborhoods, but in our neighbor-hood they kept smiling, and none closed.

Nativity parishioners collected scrap in a courtyard between the church and school. When Chuck and I borrowed Red's wagon to deliver flattened cans and an old tire, we joined a long line of patriots who patiently waited while their contributions were deposited in huge separate piles of metal, paper and rubber. Two weeks later all scrap drives temporarily halted because Uncle Sam was up to his bushy, white eyebrows in scrap.

Fearing that German and Japanese air forces would eventually bomb Detroit and other large cities, the government established a Civil Defense agency that included neighborhood air raid wardens and plane spotters. Every now and then we had a nighttime air raid drill called a "blackout." Sirens blared, spotters manned posts on high buildings scanning the sky through binoculars for enemy aircraft, and wardens wearing CD arm bands and white World War One helmets ran up and down side streets screaming, "Turn out those lights!" These Civil Defense volunteers took their jobs very seriously.

German planes, we were told, would drop incendiary bombs that would crash through our roofs and end up on attic floors before bursting into flames. All houses should have a bucket or two of sand in the attic to smother bombs. Everyone dutifully complied, including my dad. Protecting the house from bombs was the least he could do for our good landlord. Surely in some Detroit attic there still sits a lonely bucket of sand waiting patiently to snuff out a blazing incendiary bomb.

Eventually we were bombarded, but with silhouettes of enemy and Allied planes. Magazines and comic books printed a bottom and side view of German and Japanese bombers and pursuit planes and American and English aircraft as well. Every kid playing outside automatically looked skyward whenever we heard a plane motor, hoping to be the first to yell, "It's a Stuka!" or "There goes a Messerschmitt!" before heading to our basement bomb shelter and supposed safety. In Detroit's burgeoning inner-city, some kids hoped the first enemy plane to fly over would be a Fokker so they could shout, "There goes a little mutha-Fokker." Alas, we never saw an unfriendly plane in the friendly skies.

The Butlers' oldest son, Frank, joined the Army entitling them to hang a small satin service flag in their front window. This flag was white, rectangular, with a wide red border and gold fringe. The amount of blue stars in the middle signified the number of household members serving in the military. These flags proudly hung in windows all over the country with a fervent prayer that they would not be replaced by flags with gold stars representing family members who would not return.

I fervently hoped Ed got a 1-A selective service classification when he became old enough to enlist. A colorful flag would certainly dress up our front window and detract from the ice card's unsightliness.

XII

One member of the Butler household didn't captivate me —Mitzi, a dog with a killer instinct. She was an over-fed, short-haired, black-with-tan-and-white-trim, 15-pound, rat terrier, but rats considered her a terror, mainly because she was lightning fast and pounced on them before their little feet could turn to flee. No rats could expect to have a long, happy, fruitful life if they ventured outside with Mitzi around. She'd bite the nape of their neck, give them five or six vicious shakes, drop their lifeless bodies, then run up to Joe or Red wagging her tail as if to say, "Not bad, eh? How about a pat on my head!"

Her heroics with rats notwithstanding, she wasn't a perfect pet. She also bit people. It only took one leg bite each to convince Cliff, Ray, Chuck and me not to give Joe and Red playful shoulder punches or make other gestures that Mitzi might construe as threatening.

She had one other failing. She fell in love with every male dog lucky enough to amble down our street. Behind Red and Joe's back, Ray referred to Mitzi as the neighborhood whore. "I never saw any money exchanged," he said, "but I did see her accept a couple bones."

Therefore, the Butlers' dilemma was: Do we let Mitzi roam outside to rid the neighborhood of unwanted rats or do we keep her inside so we won't have to rid ourselves of unwanted puppies? They decided to let her go outside, supervised by Joe or Red, when she wasn't in heat. Unfortunately, there were times she didn't appear to be in heat, but was, and supervising got lax, resulting in unexpected litters. She was "with puppy" often. When her puppies were six or seven weeks old she, being a protective mother, still wouldn't let strangers, including me, touch them.

I also had unpleasant encounters with two dogs on Belvidere. Every time I walked down the alley, they dashed from their back porches and slammed into their alley gates — frothing, growling. One, a large, black-on-brown, short-haired, long-eared hunting dog, lived directly across the alley from the dairy. I had no doubt it would relish even a small part of my body and be positively enraptured with a larger portion. Two doors from that dog lived a wire-haired mutt with the same ambition. It was small, white and old with stained, snarling teeth. Yellow muck flowed from its red-rimmed eyes. I wanted neither for a friend and when passing their yards I often said a quick prayer that the gates would hold.

An acrimonious canine even stalked me at a social gathering. Chuck, Dolores and I were among thirty invitees at a backyard birthday party for one of the Barshaw children, delighting in games, cake, ice cream, pie and corn-on-the-cob. Just when I started to relax and enjoy the festivities, the next door neighbor opened his back door and released his dog. With no warning or provocation, it hurtled a growling into the fence upsetting both me and the plate of food in my hands. This was the biggest dog I'd ever seen. It had long, coal black hair and, I was fairly certain, timber wolf in its recent family tree. I was also fairly certain that if anyone called it by name it would be "Blackie."

Mrs. Barshaw hurried over to assure me it was simply a big, playful puppy as it barked and loped back and forth along the fence, colliding with and denting it at times. It stopped barking and ran to her when she called "Come here, Blackie" and stood on its rear legs resting its front paws on the fence top, panting and slobbering. "It's really a friendly dog," she said. "Go ahead. Pet him."

I hesitantly reached up and touched the top of its head, warily eyeing its open mouth and brown-stained teeth. Its hair felt soft and silky. Encouraged, I patted its neck while thinking, this is a nice friendly dog, my kind of dog, nice and friendly.

Other children lined up to pet this friendly dog so I stepped aside and picked up the plate and food I had dumped, hoping it could be replaced with more. Worrying about germs had changed my eating habits. I didn't eat grass or dirt anymore.

A month passed before I again saw the black, friendly dog. After a breakfast of Ralston wheat cereal (I was trying to accumulate enough box tops for a siren ring), I barreled out our front door and came to a hasty stop. There were five dogs of various sizes on Butlers' lawn and the biggest was the friendly black one. Joe and Red sat on their front steps and Mrs. Butler stood on the porch waving a broom and shouting, "You dogs get out of here! Shoo! Shoo! Go home!" To her sons she said, "Bobby! Joe! Don't let them onto the porch!" She gave a final broom wave and disappeared into the house. Red saw me standing on our porch and yelled, "Come on over."

"Not with all those dogs!" I yelled back. Two of the dogs looked like they'd eat right out of your hand...the others like they'd eat right out of your arm or leg.

"They won't hurt you. They're after Mitzi." I hoped they wanted to eat right out of Mitzi's leg.

Cautiously, giving the dogs a wide berth in passing, I joined the Butlers on their steps. Joe explained Mitzi was in heat, and all these male dogs wanted to cool her off. I asked how the dogs detected the heat; why some, like Blackie, traveled so far to gather in front of her house. Did she emit a strong scent that wafted through the air? Did a dog pass the house, catch the scent, then pass the word to others? Did Mitzi publicize it herself using a certain coded bark?

Joe didn't know. "It could be a scent," he said, "but Mitzi's been whining to go out all morning, so maybe the dogs just heard her."

Mitzi's plaintive cries continued to emanate from behind the screen door until we heard Mrs. Butler's voice, "Get away from there!" and she closed the front door completely.

Chuck, Cliff and Ray showed up and sat on the steps with us. Once he saw Butlers' front door was shut, Ray made a few crude remarks about the dog pack's intentions, which brought forth many sheepish giggles. Ray believed his mission in life was the sex education of every boy on our street.

Except from someone like Ray, whose picture should have been in the dictionary illustrating "horny," it wasn't easy to learn about sexual rituals of animal life, but, on rare occasions, I could rely on my brother Ed for information. A few years before, while walking with him on Gratiot, I saw for the first time two dogs locked in amorous embrace. "What are they doing, Ed?" I asked with all the innocence of those early years.

Ed furrowed his brow and rubbed his chin, as though in deep thought, then said, "Well, Robbie, the dog in front is sick and the one behind is pushing her to the veterinarian's office." I was lucky to have a sophisticated older brother.

I described to Ray my previous encounter with Blackie and remarked, "He seems to be a lot quieter today." Blackie was flopped on the lawn facing Butler's house with lolling tongue, panting and drooling.

Ray said, "Let's let Mitzi out and see how quiet he'll be."

As the weather warmed and noon approached, the dogs became discouraged and started drifting away. Maybe other wayward little girl doggies in the neighborhood had needs as great or greater than Mitzi's. Finally the only one remaining was old Blackie. He looked absolutely relieved that the "gang bang" element of the tryst had been removed and he had a better crack at Mitzi. I felt sorry for him.

Unaware of Mitzi's small size he definitely wasted his time. It was physically impossible for him to do what he wanted to do to Mitzi. Since he hadn't laid eyes on her, maybe he thought her loud whining implied "big, female dog."

Cliff went home to feed his chickens, and the rest of us assembled in divergent positions of repose on the lawn crowding around Blackie. After a time Joe went into his garage, returned with a rubber ball, shoved it under Blackie's nose and tossed it down the sidewalk. Blackie, welcoming activity, leaped up and retrieved it. We all took turns throwing the ball and giving Blackie a good head rub every time he dutifully returned with it. Even after everyone else had tired of the game and re-sprawled on the lawn I continued, amazed that a dog so large could be so docile. Also, he seemed to like me more than the others and gave my hand extra tongue licks.

At last I too tired of the game, dropped the soggy ball, and sprawled on the grass. But then a problem arose. Blackie wasn't tired and still wanted to play. He put a paw on my chest, and I gently removed it. He put both front paws on my chest, and I pushed them off. He started panting loudly and his eyes appeared vacuous. A stab of apprehension shot through me as I got to my feet and said, "Down, boy. Take it easy. Nice boy," and patted his head and finally put a little pressure on it because he began pawing up my chest. I said to no one in particular, "There's something wrong with this dog."

The others now were standing, watching, as I backpedaled around them, making inane comments like, "Be good, Blackie. Nice doggie. What's the matter, boy?" I grabbed Ray, pulling him between me and Blackie, hoping Ray could get his attention and calm him down. He didn't. I was beginning to panic.

Blackie bounded around Ray and encircled my waist with his big forelegs. I spun in his grasp intending to run, but couldn't loosen his powerful paws that were crossed in front of me in a sturdy grip. I slowly started walking toward home pulling him along. As we gained the street I took a quick glance over my shoulder, the shoulder where Blackie's salivating head wasn't, and my good friends were rolling on the grass laughing hysterically. I could expect no help from them. I wanted to cry but feared the dog might get irritated and bite my neck.

It flashed through my mind that Blackie might be trying to do to me what he wanted to do to Mitzi, but I wasn't a dog nor female and surely Blackie knew the difference. Then I thought of the oft used phrase "dumb dog" and said to myself, whatever you do, don't fall on your hands and knees. The term "dog fashion" also came to mind.

Starting up our front porch steps, I called out, "Ma! Ma! Help me! Help!"

Mom came to the screen door and asked, "What are you doing to that dog?"

"It won't let me go!" I whimpered.

She shook her head, opened the door, pried Blackie's front paws open, pulled me into our house and slammed the screen door. I felt like a great weight had been removed from mind and body.

Blackie stared longingly at me through the screen and I almost felt sorry for him, but he sure knew how to bust up a budding friendship. My other friends continued knee-slapping, ground-pounding and holding their stomachs in amusement as Blackie left our porch and leisurely strolled toward them. He crossed the street, rambled over to Joe and tried to give him a big hug. The laughter changed to shrieks, Ray dashed for home, and Joe, Red and Chuck stumbled over each other getting in the Butler front door with Blackie at their heels. Maybe this really is funny, I thought.

Stepping out onto our porch, I called Blackie to distract him, and he raced toward me. When he got close I quickly stepped back into the house and slammed the screen door. Then Joe, Red and Chuck went through the same routine across the street. Blackie abandoned me, rushed to them, and they slammed the door at the last second. We continued this routine with Blackie running back and forth across the street from porch to porch until he tired of the game and trotted away, a very slow trot, and I figured that even if someone turned Mitzi loose she wouldn't get much attention from old Blackie. When he disappeared from sight, Ray and I returned to the Butler steps, and I explained how it felt to have a large, amorous dog infatuated with you. After we were giggled out, I realized I now had another dog worry. When mutts galloped towards me they might not just want to bite. They might have something more sensual in mind.

* * *

Mr. and Mrs. Combs organized a neighborhood block party. They distributed notices to people on both sides of Holcomb, from Cairney to Chapin, announcing the party would be held in the street on the coming Saturday, starting at noon. Police barricades would be erected at the intersections, so car owners were encouraged to park their cars in garages or on side streets. The notice ended with: "Bring Food and Drink, Come Meet Your Neighbors and Share a Jubilant Celebration."

My dad refused to attend. "I'm not hobnobbing with no damned Englishman," he told Mom, referring to Mr. Butler.

"Now, Sree," she patiently cajoled. "The kids say he's a very nice man."

"Sree" was a pet name she always called Dad. For years I thought it short for "Yessiree," even though she didn't always sound like she was agreeing with him. When I asked her, she explained it was a simplified "Sweetie."

"I don't care what the kids say. I'm not going."

"Well, then, I'll go alone," she said quietly.

"You'd go to that shindig without me?"

She nodded.

For the rest of the week they continued to kiss when he

left for work and returned, but an uncommon pall settled between them.

Mom and Dad were usually very tolerant of each other's foibles. They were partners and knew that, to maintain their non-turbulent relationship, cooperation was necessary. If one felt especially strong about a subject the other deferred. They either supported each other or remained silent. They provided family sustenance in different ways, he by working and bringing home wages, she by running the household while he worked. When both were at home and their roles overlapped they presented a united front. We all knew that Mom thought Dad's child-raising rules were too stringent, so Betty once asked her why she didn't try to convince Dad to modify them. She answered, "I love him. And besides, you kids are going to grow up and leave us someday. He and I will be together the rest of our lives."

Saturday morning Dad drove off in his car and returned with a case of cold beer. "You can't go to a party with just food," he declared.

"Does this mean you're going?" Mom asked.

"No, but I'll help carry your food."

Mom gave him a little knowing smile. What she knew was that if Father donated a case of beer and did not aid in the imbibing of it, he'd fear the leprechaun's wrath. The life of a practicing Irishman is not always easy.

All children were outside well before noon hour, helping and watching, as folding tables were set up in front of the Combs' house. The few cars still parked on the street, including Mr. Combs' sedan, didn't interfere with any festivities and actually were useful for men to gather around, sit on, lean on, or use bumpers as footrests while discussing war, sports, politics or their jobs.

At noon adults brought out pans and bowls of food along with silverware and Depression dishes. I watched from down the street as my parents added their contributions. Dad set the case of beer near the curb by Mr. Combs' car, uncapped a bottle and spoke with Mr. and Mrs. Combs and others. Mr. and Mrs. Butler weren't in sight.

We kids greatly appreciated this get-together. With no moving traffic and only a small number of parked cars to contend with, we had full use of wagons, roller skates and scooters and arranged races and a softball game while adults completely ignored us. Since police barricades were erected after milkmen made their early morning deliveries with their horses and wagons, we had to be careful where we ran our races. And before we stepped onto second base it seemed a good idea to find out what it was made of.

I glanced around at the adults and spotted Mrs. Butler talking with Mrs. Combs and Mom at the food tables while Mr. Butler stood among a group of men standing near Combs' car. Dad stood next to him.

Word of our party spread. Kids from other streets arrived. The party continued until late afternoon, and everyone had a splendid time.

I overheard my parents discussing the party later that evening. Mom told Dad how much she enjoyed herself, how she loved Mrs. Butler and her charming accent and then asked, "How did you get along with Mr. Butler?"

Dad grunted and said, "He's okay...but he's still English."

Two days later, following supper, Dad took the newspaper to read on our front porch. Chuck and I finished eating soon after and, intending to play with Red and Joe, rushed out our front door and stopped—dumbfounded! Mr. Butler and Dad sat on Butler's top porch step deep in conversation. Instead of going to the Butler house, we ran around to our backyard; enthralled by this astonishing, unexpected event.

Visiting Mr. Butler for a front porch chat became a regular part of Dad's routine. Chuck and I never knew what they talked about, but were sure Mr. Butler received a liberal education in baseball, steel mills, coal mines and the manufacture of gelatin capsules. We never ventured near enough to listen, fearing we'd break the spell. Dad's anti-English rhetoric diminished significantly from that time on.

One early evening in our backyard, Joe, Red and I had a discourse about Adolph Hitler. We had seen *The Great Dictator* movie starring Charlie Chaplin, and the consensus was that Hitler was a total buffoon. Joe mentioned his dad had a book written by Hitler. I expressed doubts so we all went over to his house, entered the living room where Mr. Butler sat reading a newspaper, and Joe asked if I could see the book. He said "Certainly," walked across the room to their bookcase and pulled out a volume entitled *Mein Kampt.* It was an English version, the cover red and white with a black swastika prominently displayed. He handed it to me, and it was mind-boggling to hold in my hands the words of a person who had started a world war. Mr. Butler said, "Hitler had some good ideas and many not so good. It's a tragedy England's leaders didn't closely read this book before dealing with him. They didn't understand his thinking. If they did they could have been ready and stopped him. You could predict everything he's done so far, including the attack on Russia, just by reading this book."

It was the most I'd ever heard Mr. Butler speak on any subject. I thumbed through the pages and pages of print and Mr. Butler smiled and asked, "Would you like to read it?"

I think he anticipated my stupid answer, which was, "No, but it sounds great." I thanked him for showing it to me and we hurriedly departed.

I thought later that a better answer might have been, "No thanks. I think I'll wait for the movie." The sole books I read with actual interest were comic books and Big-Little books. If they didn't have pictures they didn't appeal. Even school books in Religion, Reading, Social Studies and English had pictures to pique interest.

I knew I'd never read Mein Kampt. The thought of reading a book of that size for leisure was beyond my vision and I wondered about the mentality of a person who'd attempt to write one. (...or of a person who'd write an autobiography.)

XIII

Dominican nuns wore layers of clothing year around. I and my fellow students believed they wore a type of undershirt because we could see tight, white sleeves from elbow to wrist. They wore black stockings rising to an unknown height and, except for an occasional glimpse, we saw little of them either. Their black shoes with one-inch heels reached above their ankles and were unlikely to attract anyone with a shoe fetish. Their ankle-length, white robes had long, loose sleeves neatly folded up to their elbows. A black leather belt encircled their waist. Attached to the belt was a small purse of unknown contents and hanging from the belt was a key chain, a regular rosary and a 15-decade rosary. I figured the 15-decade rosary was for heavy-duty, industrial-strength praying and hoped they never needed that one if praying for me. Students appreciated this large rosary. The oversized beads and cross hanging to the nuns' knees collided with each other alerting us to their approach. It was like the cat belling itself.

There was another white, wide, free-falling cloth loosely hanging from their shoulders almost to the hem of their robe. Our unverified supposition was that it acted as an apron, bosom-size concealment, or both.

Their heads were swathed in white, tight material called wimples that covered hair, foreheads and ears. This led to much speculation about their hearing ability. We also speculated whether they were baldy-sours or just wore a very short hairdo. Among the guys you could get 6 to 5 either way, but none of us ever found out for sure.

Over the top of their robe was a short, white, cloth mantelet that fitted around the neck and covered shoulders, upper chest and presumably the upper back area. We weren't positive because an ensemble, consisting of a soft black veil over a stiff white fabric, was hat-pinned to the wimple material on top of their head and hung down their backs.

The only other item of apparel we ever saw them wear, but solely for inclement weather, was a black ankle-length cape-like affair that buttoned down the front and had two large arm slits.

We had no knowledge of anything worn underneath the obvious, which is no doubt the way they wanted it. Did nuns wear brassieres, bloomers, garter belts and slips? We never knew, although boys thought it would be fun to watch nuns get dressed. Watching them keep wimples, mantelets, veils, belts and beads in order would be worth the price of admission. As far as the height of the black stockings, it made very little difference since we pretty much agreed that donning all those clothes was a lot like covering an abandoned gold mine.

Entering the seventh grade forever dispelled my illusion that nuns were heavenly-type individuals. Sister Mary Rosella had an apt name. Her face, the only skin visible besides her hands, was the color of a radish. I could easily imagine her joyfully turning in her black and white habit for a black and white storm trooper uniform as she forcefully declared on our first day of school that we'd obey her or suffer. She said as a baby her parents accidentally placed her too close to an active radiator, her heels were horribly burned and they still hurt. If her extremities were going to hurt so were ours. She explained if we didn't do homework, gave her any back talk, were late for school, or fooled around in class or church, then she had a wooden ruler and would use it on us liberally. I feared the seventh grade would be a long nine months.

We often went to confession. Nativity had at least three other priests assigned by the diocese to assist Father Geller in tending to our spiritual needs. The church's four confessionals consisted of three small connecting rooms, each room the size of a telephone booth. The priest sat in the middle one, and the other two were for penitents. The priest had access to each penitent by opening a small, sliding window covered by what looked like cheese cloth, and he could hear, but not see clearly, through the cloth. The penitents lined up on each side of the confessionals and waited their turn. As each cleansed sinner left, he or she was replaced by another uncleansed one who entered, closed the door, sank down on the kneeler inside and anxiously waited for the window to slide open.

The week before major holy days, such as Christmas and Easter, the diocese usually assigned an extra priest to help hear confessions of the expected penitent onslaught. This presented a horrible situation for us sinners because Father Geller gratuitously gave up his confessional to the visiting priest, then took a portable wooden kneeler to the church's side altar and set up an open-air confessional. The kneeler had a wood frame attached to its top with a linen cover, but Father Geller, sitting on a folding chair on the opposite side, had a good view of all lined-up transgressors. He bowed his head and pretended not to be peeking, but we knew he did and would make mental notes about us to be used in later encounters. Once on the kneeler we couldn't get away with whispering lower than in the regular confessional because he made us repeat our sins until he, and all waiting penitents, heard them clearly. The two times nuns forced me into this dreadful situation I realized I had but one recourse — lie. I simply forgot my juicier sins and told him the easys. I knew if I died I'd be in big trouble, but facing Saint Peter seemed much less petrifying than facing Father Geller.

161

During the school year we were marched over to church every two weeks on Friday to participate in this soul-cleansing sacrament. The exception was when we confessed on the day before the first Friday of every month. First Fridays were special. If we received communion for nine consecutive first Fridays we'd be assured a "happy death," a term that always seemed somewhat contradictory. A happy death meant dying in a state of grace and going to heaven. If, when dying, you happened to have a mortal sin on your soul a priest would always be near to hear your last confession and send you happily heavenward. I never understood how this priest would materialize if I happened to drown in the waters of Pago Pago with an "eat meat on Friday" sin on my soul, but it seemed like a good deal, and I honestly tried to reach the nine-plateau. At some time in the count though, I'd forget and take a sip of water or eat something (we had to fast from midnight to receive communion) on a first Friday morning and I'd have to skip communion and start recounting. The best I ever did was seven in a row. Yet, with all the changes in church laws in recent years, seven in a row should rate an unordained deacon in attendance as I depart this vale of dross and tears.

Student confession was also required every other Saturday during the summer, putting a small crimp in vacation enjoyment. The church rarely let you stray too far from her influence.

All over the world 500 million Catholics started confessions with the words, "Bless me, Father, for I have sinned." Except at Nativity. Father Geller determined this was redundant, first, because the priest automatically blessed you when he opened the little window; second, you wouldn't be in the confessional if you hadn't sinned. We began our confessions with: "My last confession was two weeks ago and I have committed the following sins—" Then we launched into all moral mistakes we had engaged in since our last confession, making sure to mention the total number of times we committed them. The numbers were de-

162

cided upon while examining our conscience prior to entering the confessional. Some of these sins were definitely not mistakes, the most enjoyable ones were usually on purpose, but we hoped we could get to confession before we died. It was like a religious Russian roulette.

I had developed into what many considered a swearmouth. I didn't curse so much at school, except to myself, because of lack of opportunity and because of my surroundings. Nuns and priests were everywhere, and I was sure one overheard "damn" would mean instant expulsion and loads of trouble at home. In addition, swearing in the vicinity of a church struck me as bordering on sacrilege. I didn't swear at home either. Even "geez" wasn't tolerated because Mom thought it was half of Jesus. But in alleys, backyards or playgrounds, kids, including myself, expressed themselves freely.

When examining my conscience I tried to remember how many times I played in alleys, backyards and playgrounds since my last confession. I calculated swearing a modest average of three times per playtime, then multiplied and came up with a nice, believable total; unless the total became too high. Then I cut it down to a figure under 20 since many of my words were damns and hells, and they were even used in Religion class, though in a different context.

I got a distinct impression that damns and hells weren't serious because the priest usually asked if you used the Lord's name when swearing and if you answered "sometimes," he gave you a little lecture. I gathered from this reaction that "goddamn" and "jesuschrist" were so profane they were in a class by themselves so I started giving them a "C" rating like the Legion of Decency system. Bastard, sonovabitch, asshole, and dickhead I rated "B" and were some of my favorites. The "A" words, damn and hell, were hardly worth using since they didn't really get the job done. Words like darn, gosh, goshdarn, heck and egad were unrated substitute profanity used by mothers, girls, and boys leaning toward ordination; they contained no vitality and didn't even have to be confessed.

I rarely told a priest I swore over 20 times because he might think he had a problem swearer on his hands and give me a rosary for penance. No one wanted to say a rosary on hard wooden church kneelers, and if a nun saw you saying one after confession, she might start thinking about you in a different light, like maybe you needed an extra dose of religion or, in Sister Rosella's case, an extra dose of her ruler.

I started to include "impure thoughts" in my confessions. They weren't that impure, usually just wishing when a running girl's dress flew a little above her knees that she could run faster, or the women pictured in blurred underarm deodorant ads in my sister's *Cosmopolitan* magazines were a little more explicitly photographed.

I always ended my sin list with an, "I disobeyed my mother, eight times," a truthful statement since just about everything I did outside home, and many things inside, my mother had warned me against. Furthermore, it might take the priest's mind off my impure thoughts — sins I didn't want to discuss at length or in detail. If he asked how I disobeyed I mentioned forgetting to take out garbage or not jumping out of bed when called in the morning. Then I imagined him saying to himself, "Well, this kid doesn't seem so bad. Nobody wants to take out garbage or get up in the morning."

After the priest's short lecture he'd say, "Now say five Our Fathers and five Hail Marys and make a good Act of Contrition," and he'd start praying in Latin. This presented a challenge — timing your Act of Contrition so you'd both end your prayers somewhat in unison. It was always embarrassing when he finished first, said, "Go in peace and sin no more," and slammed the window. You were left praying out loud to a closed, square, piece of wood, and the next person in line had heard the window slam and wondered what the hell was taking you so long.

164

XIV

Dad had replaced a furnace grate the previous winter and hauled the broken one out to our garage. Since he intended to allow a neighbor to store a Model A Ford in our garage, Chuck and I were told to clean the garage and sell the grate to the first passing junkman. We rushed to the garage to examine this treasure. It was rusty and heavy; so heavy we calculated we'd get at least a dollar for it, or even more.

In our dealings with junkmen we usually sold old newspapers. We waited until we accumulated a good-sized bale, tied it together with old rope or rag strips, and offered it for sale. The junkman went through the ritual of getting out his hooked hand-scale, lifted and weighed the bale, and after a significant pause while he pondered the poundage he'd announce his offer — three cents. We'd explain this bale was bigger and heavier than the last one we sold for three cents. He'd say, "Three cents." Junkmen had one-track, three-cent mentalities. Some enterprising kids resorted to hiding a brick inside the bale or soaked a good portion of the middle paper with water to add weight. The junkmen still said, "Three cents." They were tough, astute bargainers and seemed to automatically deduct for bricks and soaked paper.

This grate was made of iron and a lot heavier than a bale of paper. Chuck and I agreed it must be worth much more, and we were surely on the brink of solvency. Financial independence would be ours.

Ray appeared the next morning as Chuck and I sat impatiently on our back porch steps waiting for the familiar sound of a junkman horn. We went to the garage and showed Ray our prize, and even though Ray was almost 14 years old and muscular, he still had trouble hoisting it. He said, "You guys are lucky. You should get at least fifty cents." Financial independence wavered somewhat.

A junkman's horn could be heard at least a block away giving us plenty of time to rehearse our sales pitch. The horses pulling junk wagons had long since lost any desire for galloping, cantering, loping, pacing or trotting. These animals moved at a slow gait, completely oblivious to blasting horns, barking dogs, inclement weather, adoring kids, mean stone-throwing kids or dickering, wishful-thinking kids. Their two horsely pleasures were eating oats and eliminating digested oats. This always caused conster-nation among alley baseball teams whose members dis-liked becoming temporary groundskeepers and they some-times objected in earthy language, causing reactions that sounded suspiciously like horselaughs from both junkmen and horses.

I personally admired the horses and felt sorry for them, not only because (unlike postmen) they started their work-day with a light load and finished with a heavy one and their work environment was a breeding place for tormenting flies, but because most junkmen didn't seem to be charter members of any licensed humane societies. Many horses appeared to be leaning towards lean, and I hoped they had led fuller lives in their youth, perhaps out on the range punching cattle, or charging happily out of the starting gate at Churchill Downs. I always wanted to ring a loud bell and shout, "They're off!" just to see what would happen. I had a vision of this suddenly animated steed charging haphaz-ardly down the alley, the junkman pulling vainly on reins as soaked papers, bricks, grates and other wagon junk scat-tered in all directions.

The first horn blare heard that day was a junkman coming through the alley behind the Butler house, so Ray and I had to pick up the grate, lug it across the street and through Butlers' backyard. Red and Joe joined us as we waited for the horse, wagon, junkman and our bonanza payoff. I couldn't stop smirking and hoped the driver brought a lot of money with him.

The driver, an old, Italian gentleman with a gray, walrus mustache, slowly stepped down from his wagon and asked, "What you got?"

Proudly pointing to the grate I said, "I wanna sell this and it's real heavy!"

He hardly glanced at it before saying, "I givva you ten cents." I felt like someone had dropped a grate on my head. Financial independence flew out the window.

"Wait a minute," Ray said. "You haven't even weighed it."

"I no need weigh. Ten cents," he said. "Dis ting ten cents."

We argued for two minutes, but he wouldn't weigh it, and we couldn't change his mind. Rather than wait for another junkman, I reluctantly agreed to accept his ungenerous first and final offer. We could buy a lot of penny candy for ten cents. I took the dime.

He had an almost full wagon so he lifted the ten-cent grate onto the wagon's rear, leaving a good portion sticking out. He climbed up to the driver's seat, gave a click-click to his horse and slowly pulled away. Knowing this junkman earned at least a "B" word, I muttered, "Damn! The sonovabitch didn't even weigh it."

"Well, let's go get it back then," Ray suggested.

"What do ya mean?" I asked, but I knew what he meant. I wondered if the seventh Commandment covered stealing from sheenies.

"Come on! Let's go!" Ray said and we ran after the wagon.

It had only traveled about 70 feet. We swiftly covered the

distance and Ray reached up, grasped the grate and gave it a pull. It crashed down on the concrete alley and Ray hissed, "Grab it, grab it!"

The wagon halted as we each lifted the grate with one hand and headed back toward Butlers' gate. Our friends had disappeared, but at least they left the gate open. The junkman yelled, "Stop! You boysa, stop!"

We didn't stop. Although running with that grate seemed more awkward than running a three-legged race, we were fast enough to discourage a much older person from pursuit. We staggered through Butlers' yard, stumbled across the street, and didn't slow until we returned to our garage where everyone else was hiding. When we finally released the grate my arm felt like dropping off. My fingers ached, my heart pounded, and I feared the old guy would burst into our garage at any second, take back his dime, give us a kick, and worse yet, tell our parents and his Mafia relatives.

Ray had a different reaction. He couldn't stop laughing. "Did you see the look on that sheenie's face!" he gasped, then started another round of giggling.

The laughter was contagious and soon we all joined in, even Joe who up until then was shaking his head and saying things like, "You guys are nuts," and "We're going to get in big trouble."

We continued discussing and laughing about this dastardly crime until Red said, "Shut up! Listen!"

We fell silent and heard the unmistakable sound of a junkman's horn. As the seconds passed it got louder — closer. Joe volunteered to scout the wagon to see if it was our crime victim. He returned quickly, smiling. "It's a colored guy," he reported. He also assured us there wasn't an old Italian roaming the neighborhood threatening mayhem to two, young, smart aleck thieves.

We pushed open one of our garage doors, dragged the grate out to the alley and waited. When the wagon pulled abreast of us I yelled, "Hey, mister!" Wanna buy some iron?"

The driver stopped the horse with a "Whoa," jumped down, checked out the grate and said, "Dis all y'all got?" I told him, "Yeah" and he said, "I'll give ya ten cents." Ray said, "Christ, you didn't even weigh it!"

I said, "Geez, Ray, don't start," and to the driver, "I'll take it."

We didn't even consider stealing back the grate. That sheeny looked like he could run. When he jumped off the wagon I thought I heard the rattle of Olympic gold medals.

Ray didn't want any of the stolen money — he said the laugh was better than any pennies — so I split the twenty cents with Chuck. It was a profitable, fun day with one nagging worry. My next confession I'd have to make sure I went to Father Burroughs. He didn't ask for too many details — just told you not to do it again.

* * *

United States forces were breaking even in the war. The Japanese sank two of our aircraft carriers, the Wasp and Hornet, and we sank two of theirs. We shot down forty of their planes, they shot down thirty of ours. They sank our cruisers and destroyers. We sank theirs. Major land battles took place between our Marines and Japanese ground forces on a Pacific island called Guadalcanal. Newspapers reported the Japanese fought fiercely and when I mentioned this to Ed he said, "Apparently the word is out that I'm almost of enlistment age and the Japanese want to win before I get there." I don't know how Ed could say that with a straight face. I envisioned all five feet, five inches and 130 pounds of him in full battle gear storming Guadalcanal's beach. He wouldn't need a rifle. Japanese soldiers would laugh themselves to death.

It was different in movies. Americans were winning. Tyrone Power helped the Royal Air Force turn back the German air threat to Britain and John Wayne blasted Japanese planes out of the sky and Japanese snipers out of jungle palm trees. Errol Flynn also did his part — between trysts with young ladies of the teen-age persuasion.

We watched these inspiring movies at the Dawn, a theater we discovered on Gratiot near Iroquois street. We never took the Gratiot route, which entailed walking a long block-and-a-half to Gratiot and turning left for another five and a half blocks. Instead we walked the opposite way to Chapin, a half-block away, turned right and walked only five blocks. Chapin veered toward Gratiot and ended at Seneca street. A short jaunt to Gratiot and another half block and we arrived at the Dawn.

The Chapin route, though one block shorter, had a disadvantage. We had to run a gauntlet of Italian boys bent on either maiming us with thrown objects, punching us, or relieving us of movie money. Since there was safety only in numbers, we usually visited the Dawn en masse.

Our section of Detroit was predominately Italian with large portions of Polish, German and Irish and a smattering of English and French. My dad had one comment to make about Italians: "They put the "O" at the wrong end of their names." We even had people of another race on Holcomb. A Negro couple lived three houses off Cairney next to the Cortez family. Joe Cortez, a friend of Ed, said they were both pleasant, she a lady, he a gentleman, which made their move onto Holcomb probably the first unrecorded case of Detroit gentrification.

A shorter way to reach the Dawn theater and avoid Italian boys we called, "as the crow flies." We headed to the theater in an almost straight line by cutting through yards and crossing side streets and alleys. Most people didn't mind children using their backyards for shortcuts as long as we were quiet and closed gates behind us. We avoided yards harboring vicious dogs. When not sure if a yard had a dog, we shook the gate before entering which brought forth any hidden, angry animals. Then we tried another gate. This always worked, except in one notable case.

Chuck, Dolores and Ann were returning from the Dawn

one Saturday afternoon using the backyard, cut-through method. They shook an unfamiliar backyard gate, received no response and proceeded through. A large, sneaky dog suddenly jumped out from under the back porch causing instant terror. Chuck and Ann managed to slip safely through the alley gate, but Dolores wasn't so lucky. The dog sank its fangs into her left buttock and wouldn't let go until the dog's owner, hearing her screams, rushed out to rescue her. As Chuck later commented, "That dog was pissed!" Luckily the owner had first aid training and sent Dolores home reasonably patched up.

When Dad got home that Saturday (he often worked Saturdays) and examined Dolores's wound, he angrily admonished Mother: "Claire, I told you to watch these kids."

Indeed he did. Every morning. It was a ritual. Mom walked with him to the front door, they kissed and he'd say, "Now, Claire, watch the kids." While listening to these morning partings from our kitchen, Ed would silently and simultaneously mouth the words, "Now, Claire, watch the kids," causing muffled laughter among us younger children. We anticipated these words knowing the next sounds would be a door shutting, footsteps descending, Dad's car starting and driving away. Once the noise of the motor faded a sense of relief prevailed. We knew Mom instantly forgot Dad's final advice, and we'd be practically on our own until he returned in late afternoon.

It wasn't that she didn't want to watch all of us. She just knew the impossibility of it with all her other wifely and motherly duties. She could have required us to stay indoors at all times, except for school or church, but that was totally unacceptable to us and to her. She needed peace and quiet. She decided instead to trust in the Lord and our common sense, giving us credit for much more common sense than we possessed.

Dad, on the other hand, didn't think we had enough sense to pour liquid out of a boot, as he often commented. If left

171

up to him, his younger children would go nowhere unless accompanied by an adult; otherwise they should be confined to house, backyard, or within eyesight/earshot. He constantly worried about our being killed either while crossing streets or falling off high structures. He even considered nailing our shoes to the floor, putting us into them and tying knots in our laces. If he knew how far we roamed, of the games we played in the street, and the garages, poles and trees we scaled while he was at work, he probably would have killed us. For this reason, after a few unpleasant disciplinary episodes, Chuck, Dolorie, Ann and I developed an uncanny sense of timing. It was either the position of the sun or a survival instinct, but we were always safely home before Dad arrived.

Dad's reaction to Dolores's dog bite was characteristically loud and disapproving. Mom, who could remain calm through a hurricane, answered, "Well, I can't watch them every minute of the day and I'm certainly not responsible for every stray dog in our neighborhood." She wasn't about to tell him she let a six-, eight- and ten-year old walk six blocks to a movie theater by themselves.

Dad poured iodine on the dog bite and rebandaged it, Dolores didn't develop rabies or any other fatal disease, and the following Monday as Dad left for work he exhorted, "Now, Claire, watch the kids."

Mom worked very hard at being devout. She attended mass and received communion almost daily. She once said that God sent her these eight children so He should help raise them and keep them from harm's way and when He didn't, He heard about it in her next communique. I suppose this puzzled even God since He didn't have much to do with the actual conception of her problems. Nevertheless, I imagine He got a good chewing out about Dolorie's ass chewing.

XV

As the 1942 Christmas approached, we heard a rumor that Santa Claus at Sears, Roebuck was giving away a spectacular item. Ordinarily he gave each kid a coloring book or something equally as unimaginative.

The Sears store was only four blocks past the Dawn theater so Chuck, Red and I decided to investigate by making the trek on a Saturday morning using the cut-through-yards method. On the way, Chuck pointed out the yard where Dolores lost a lot of her dignity and a small bit of flesh and we rattled the alley gate hoping to see if, as Chuck claimed, the dog stood taller than a large horse. No dog appeared, but we pictured it under its back porch saying quietly, "C'mon, c'mon." We passed through another yard. Looking down, God breathed a little easier. He didn't need to hear from Mother again.

Sears had turned the rear section of its store into a toyland. When we arrived, there were at least 50 kids, some with parents, lined up to make a pitch to Santa so we chose to forego the line for awhile to look over the toy crop. Tops on my wish list was a Red Ryder air rifle but, since my mother thought eyesight more important than my complete happiness, I didn't spend too much time drooling over the BB gun display. I picked up and examined a Dick Tracy wind-up squad car. Dick was driving, and his face appeared twice, a full-face in the front window and a profile in the side. Chief Patton's face appeared in the rest of the windows. The uniformed Chief sat in the front passenger seat, and two replicas, or his triplet brothers, sat in the back seat. The toy manufacturers were slipshod, I mused. They could have painted different faces on the back seat policemen.

There also was a Fresh Air taxi cab. The windows pictured Amos in a cap and Andy in his ever-present derby. (These two lovably humorous characters had a long run on radio, tin taxis and television, but when Rosa Parks refused to sit in the rear of a bus, Amos 'n' Andy's days were numbered.)

The tin cars had one major defect. They were held together by bent-over tabs inserted into slots. The tabs tended to unbend with play, and if re-bent more than three times they broke off. Then you held the cars together with rubber bands.

Continuing to browse, I briefly considered asking for a bow and arrow set, complete with target, but my mother hated missile games, even though the arrows had rubber suction cups on their tips. She'd probably say, "They'll suck your eye out." She also disliked suction cup missiles because they put little round circles on wallpaper and a week after Christmas she'd be on a ladder dragging handsful of pink, gummy matter across walls to return them to their original beauty.

Both Erector sets and chemistry sets were too expensive, so I settled on a deluxe version of Tinkertoys, one with many more sticks, spools, blue-cardboard blades and structure plans. Maybe Mom would throw in the Dick Tracy car as a bonus if I ate all my mashed potatoes every day until Christmas.

Chuck and Red impatiently pulled me into the Santa line that wasn't getting any shorter. A boy in front of us exclaimed that Santa was giving away cameras, and I smiled and thought: What an idiot!

Chuck and Red received their Santa gift and then it was

my turn. Santa didn't seem too jolly as he asked, "What do you want for Christmas, young man?"

"Young man" was Santa's way of informing you he knew you didn't believe in him, you were too old to be bothering him, and he wished you'd go home and shave.

I answered, "Tinkertoys."

He reached down into a large box next to his chair, pulled out an oversized envelope, handed it to me and said, "Here. Merry Christmas."

Outside the building, Chuck had already opened his envelope. It contained sheets of light cardboard imprinted with what appeared to be camera parts. The kid in line was right. We rushed home, gathered in our basement and began assembling our camera kits.

First the parts had to be punched out on perforated lines. Each kit included a sheet of bond paper full of square drawings of a maneuvering airplane that had to be cut apart with scissors and slipped into slots on crank wheels. After folding parts, sliding tab A into slot A, tab B into slot B, etc., we each ended up with a thin box camera, its exterior resembling simulated brown leather, with a viewer on top and a crank on the side. With a turn of the crank, Action! Camera! As the pictures popped up into the viewer the plane started doing barrel rolls and loops, fast or slow, depending on how fast the crank was turned. It reminded me of thick Big-Little comic books that sometimes had a small, movie-like adventure on the top corner of the right-hand page. Just flick the pages and watch the performance. I thought it astounding and knew I had to have another one of these amazing cameras.

Chuck was less enthused about the Sears giveaway. He doubted a cardboard camera was worth another 20-block round trip, especially since it began to snow, but Red wanted a second one so he agreed to accompany me.

As we passed the Dawn theater, Red had second thoughts. He nervously wondered, "What if that Santa Claus remembers us?"

"How's he gonna remember us? He musta seen at least a million kids today. We'll be okay."

He wasn't convinced. After two more blocks he declared, "I'm not going to try it. He'll remember my hair."

He had a point. "Yeah, you're right," I told him. "We shoulda disguised ourselves and put on our damn Acecaps." I bravely added, "I'm still gonna try it."

When we reentered Sears, Red wandered off to look at toys while I fell in at the end of the Santa line. Though a little longer than the earlier line, it moved faster, or maybe it seemed to move faster as I became more fearful. I tried to figure a way to squint up my face so old Santa would think me a different kid.

Ten minutes later, as I neared the head of the line, Red started hovering around, ostensibly admiring the doll display, but actually testing out his peripheral vision with an occasional sidelong glance. Red didn't look the type who'd be interested in dolls, and I wished he and his red hair would go away. The kid in front of me departed with his camera, and I stood looking at Santa.

"Well, young man, what do you want for Christmas?"

"Tinkertoys," I blurted truthfully, and instinctively knew I'd made a mistake. I should have said an air rifle or baseball glove. That's what every boy in Detroit asked for.

Santa's brow contracted and recognition flashed in his twinkling eyes. "Hey, ain't you the Tinkertoy boy who was here two or three hours ago?"

"No," I said, shaking my head, heart pounding, trying to look shocked at his question, but feeling my face heat up. What a stupid answer, I thought. A simple, one-word "No." Couldn't I have been a little more inventive? I might have said, "Well, Santa baby, I have a kid brother named Cecil B who needs a camera to practice with." Or, "Look, Santa, one of these days Walt Disney might open a theme park in California or Florida, and I was just practicing standing in line."

"Yeah, you were here," Santa loudly proclaimed to

everyone within a two-mile radius. "You were with that red-headed kid over there! G'wan, get outta here."

Mortified, I swiftly turned and headed toward the door, looking neither left nor right, knees too weak to run, feeling like I wanted to cry. When I pulled open the door, a cold air blast chilled my burning face as I muttered, "Damn, damn, damn..."

Red and I said very little during our snowy walk home. I felt despair, not only because of my recent embarrassment, but also because, at twelve years old, I realized I'd never again experience an expectant wait in a Santa line, not even for a camera. I'd reached a painful plateau in my march towards adolescence by outgrowing a cherished, pleasurable, irreplaceable part of a child's Christmas. It was mournful and sobering. Jolly old Saint Nick had certainly given me my comedownance.

A week before Christmas all neighborhood stores ran out of Christmas tree lights because the war effort had diverted shipments of glass, metal and wire. When Dad heard our moans about the dull, lightless tree we'd have, he said, "Don't worry; I'll have some made at work."

On Christmas Eve he came home with two strings of tree lights, each string with fifteen, five-watt bulbs. The sockets were square, the wire heavy, and the bulbs handpainted either red, blue or green. The only imperfection was the four-foot spacing between lights. With 120 feet of unsightly, black, electrical cord wrapped around the tree, we had to use twelve boxes of icicle tinsel for concealment. This made the tree even more lovely, and our family agreed it was the prettiest tree ever trimmed.

I did get the deluxe version Tinkertoy set for Christmas, but all its plans for different structures included a small electric motor to make the wheels turn. A motor didn't come with the set, it had to be purchased separately, and without it the wheels had to be turned by hand. After showing Dad the many conformations and architectural possibilities with my set, I mentioned how much more exciting it could be with a motor to continuously move the parts, and how I felt a little stupid turning wheels by hand and making motor noises with my mouth. He concurred and two days later came home from work with an electric motor. It was larger, heavier, and more powerful than the one required, had two speeds and worked splendidly at low speed. When I turned it on full blast, it hurled Tinkertoy sticks all over the room, irritating my mother and making me jubilant. I appreciated non-conformity, even in a Tinkertoy set.

I'm positive Gelatin Products' owners would have been elated knowing they contributed an electric motor and tree lights to brighten our family's 1942 Christmas. I'm also positive Dad didn't mention it to them when he accepted his year-end bonus check.

XVI

With a dairy on our street there was never a shortage of cats and, consequently, there was an abundance of kittens. The dairy owner tolerated cats because they kept the dairy mousefree and almost ratfree. Rats aren't enthused about sharing living quarters with cats when there are so many safer havens under garages and concrete receptacles.

In return for discouraging rodents, the cats were rewarded with unlimited milk spillage in the dairy's bottling section. When they got underfoot, they also were rewarded with a good kick from the bottlers, but mostly a peaceful coexistence reigned.

Every few months I'd find a friendly kitten on the dairy grounds and bring it home for a pet. My parents didn't allow cats in our house so I used our garage to shelter my feline friends. Kittens were fun. After I fed them with food stolen from our ice box, I'd sit on the back porch and watch them scamper after a homemade ball made of balled-up newspaper wrapped in rubber bands. When they got tired of playing they usually nuzzled up to me, purring and asking for a gentle rub or more stolen food. During these peaceful times I sometimes stared at birds in trees, trying to will them to fly down and alight on my shoulders, kneecaps or fingers. If they only would, I'd imagine people coming from miles around to hear the saintly utterances of this wondrous boy who was beloved by all birds and beasts. I'd say things like, "Suffer the little animals to come unto me" or "Bring forth thy sick and maimed animals so I may heal them."

Of course there would be callous non-believers who would smirk and whisper, "Let's go see the idiotic kid who thinks he can get birds to alight on his shoulders and kneecaps while he's petting a cat on his lap."

There were three major flaws in my musings. Saint Robert of Detroit sounded stilted in comparison to Saint Francis of Assisi, the birds continued to avoid me, and even kitten friends, when they grew into cats, deserted me. They mysteriously disappeared. This was hard to fathom. They'd be fed, petted, played with, pampered, treated with dignity and allowed to roam at night, yet, when mature, they left me. I started feeling guilty. What did I do wrong? At times I didn't even name the kittens, because I knew one morning when I poured milk into the saucer on the back porch and intoned, "Here kitty, kitty, kitty," kitty wouldn't appear.

But I continued bringing kittens home, whenever possible, dreaming that one day I'd find one who'd be both faithful and grateful. Alas, my dream never came true. But then, I never became a saint either.

(Two years later my mother told me that as fast as my kittens reached cathood, that's how fast my dad took them on an early morning, one-way automobile trip to Gelatin Products. Unlike Lassie, none ever came home.)

* * *

Ed quit Cass Tech, giving up any aspirations of becoming a draftsman, and got a job as a salesman at Montgomery Ward and Company. When he saved enough money and became eligible for an employee's discount he brought home a phonograph, setting it up in our living room. He built a sizeable collection of 78 RPM records by various entertainment artists including Bing Crosby, Dinah Shore, Kate Smith, Tommy Dorsey, The Mills Brothers, Sammy Kaye and Artie Shaw. He told us to keep our sticky hands off his records and phonograph unless we wanted to suffer hideous punishment. Naturally Chuck and I ignored him. An off-limits sound machine capable of making selective music drew us like Lorelei drew sailors.

78s were fragile. Any rough treatment chipped, cracked or broke them altogether, so we were very careful when handling them during the many opportunities afforded us, because Ed spent a lot of time at work or dating. One of his dates was a young saleslady in the "Monkey Ward" music department, which partially explained his sudden interest in records.

One evening Ed came home from work with a package and announced he had a special treat for the whole family. The package held a two-record album entitled "Ballad for Americans" sung by a bass singer named Paul Robeson accompanied by a chorus. The song's lyrics detailed United States history, its birth and growth, its trials and tributes, its troubles and triumphs. The album fascinated me because it mentioned familiar characters and occurrences first discovered in U.S. history books at school. King George of England, Patrick Henry, Abe Lincoln, the carpetbaggers — all were mentioned — along with the 1776 Revolution, the Civil War and words from the Constitution and Gettysburg Address. It praised our nation's ethnic, religious and occupational diversity. One minor gaffe marred Paul's stirring rendition. He took an audible breath while stretching out the ballad's last word.

Chuck and I played this album often in Ed's absence and also played other records he brought home. We even became adept at recognizing when to change the needle in the playing arm. A needle was only good for a few plays and changing to a new one always brought a notable improvement in tonal quality.

Mom never told us to stop playing with Ed's phonograph, probably because as long as we used it we weren't outside getting into trouble. We still got into trouble.

After a long laborious day of schooling, Chuck and I both wished to hear some soothing music. We got into a loud discussion about which soothing record should be played first, so I gave him a slight, but firm, push to emphasize the fact that my selection should go on the turntable first. It might have been a little firmer than intended since it banged him into a wall. In retaliation he picked up "Ballad for Americans" and busted me over the head with it. This resulted in both album records neatly separating into four distinct, unplayable pieces. As ill luck would have it, the commotion also resulted in the appearance of our mother as Chuck and I vainly tried to figure a way to glue four, half-moon-shaped pieces back together. She slowly shook her head as I explained Chuck's violent reaction to my gentle push and declared, "I'll have to tell your father. Ed's going to be very angry." We then received a lecture that ended with, "I wish you kids would learn to play nice."

When she left the room I whispered, "Boy, Chuck, are you going to get it." I was half right.

The incident wasn't mentioned at supper that evening. Chuck and I finished eating before the others and went into the living room to read the newspaper. I didn't argue with Chuck when he wanted the comics section. He was in enough trouble. Besides, I wanted to read the latest war news.

I sat in my father's favorite reading chair, and Chuck sat across the room on the sofa absorbed in comic strips. I knew that soon Dad would finish eating, enter the living room intent on reading the paper, see me sitting there and say what sounded like, "Con vin da rune" and I'd give up the chair and paper. I think "Con vin da rune" was Gaelic for "Remove your torso from my space." I never asked for the English translation because its meaning was obvious when accompanied by a hand wave.

I continued reading the spread out paper as I heard Dad approaching and waited for the usual "Con vin da rune." Instead I felt a burning sting across my inner thigh. I dropped the newspaper and watched Dad swing his thin belt at Chuck while yelling, "Don't ever touch Ed's things again! Keep your damn hands off his property! If you ever go near that phonograph again I'll kill you!" Then he returned to me.

From experience Chuck and I assumed the prenatal position and made what we hoped sounded like legitimate mournful cries of remorse. In reality the belt didn't hurt that much, but the only way to make him stop swinging it was to make loud, howling sounds.

After visiting both of us with the belt a couple more times, he repeated his ominous warnings about touching Ed's property and then told us to get out of his sight. I'm not sure, but I think he meant "Con vin da rune."

Father had two modes of punishment depending on the situation at the moment and how much corrective measure he deemed necessary to cover infractions. The above mentioned belt beating was a "plan-ahead, deliberate, calculated, on-purpose" type of mayhem performed on our little bodies. The other was a "spur-of-the-moment" chastisement, usually administered for some minor mistake in demeanor. He could handle it without taking too much time from his busy day. It consisted of grabbing our left hand in his left hand and laying sound, well-aimed kicks to our buttocks while he simultaneously smashed his calloused right hand across the back of our heads. We, of course, started running in a counter-kickwise circle to lessen the severity of the kicks and slaps. After a few spins around, our now dizzy father would decide the infraction wasn't quite as serious as he had previously thought. Neither of these methods were very severe but, since Chuck and I were usually punished in tandem, the worst part was waiting your turn. It was better to be first.

Ed bought another Paul Robeson "Ballad for Americans" album and also a Bing Crosby version that was, in my humble opinion, superior. The words were more easily understood and Bing didn't take any audible breaths. Howbeit, Bing did admit that the song required a little more voice than he possessed.

After the war Paul Robeson fell into disfavor with a majority of Americans when he publicly expounded on the "superior" Russian system of government; sort of a "bite the hand that fed you" routine. This struck me as incongruous since the Ballad's words, that he sang so well, praised America's greatness. He spent many years living in England and Russia where he felt more comfortable. Curiously, he never gave up his American passport or citizenship.

Thirty-three years after Chuck brained me with that album the United States celebrated its bicentennial. To my knowledge, not once during the whole patriotic year did anyone in the entertainment media revive "Ballad for Americans." It would have been a natural. At least a radio station could have played the Bing Crosby version.

* * *

Sister Rosella was really getting on my nerves. We returned to the classroom after Mass each morning and she'd say, "Who didn't do his homework?" — a negative approach to the new day if I ever heard one. Those who didn't were required to line up at the side of the room; and I've seen better looking line-ups in James Cagney/George Raft movies. The rest of us passed our homework forward where she collected it from the first boy in each row of desks. Then she got a wooden paddle that hung on a hook near a side window and beat on the palms of all lined-up unfortunates.

At the beginning of the school year she used an 18-inch ruler, but after she complained aloud that the ruler didn't seem to bother some miscreants, and there were usually five to ten each day, a favor-currying opportunist offered to make her the paddle she craved. He said his dad had a well-stocked workbench at home and all he needed from her were the specifications. I sincerely hoped he'd become so busy making the paddle he'd forget his homework. The Italian members of our class, most of whom lined-up daily in the homeworkless line, started to mentally measure the kid's feet for a pair of cement shoes.

The paddle measured 3-inches wide, 16-inches long and a quarter-inch thick with a grip on one end. Although much heftier than the ruler, it didn't seem to alter anyone's behavior. Generally the same boys continued to line up each day to have their extended hands pounded by this saintly nun.

One oversized boy, whom we called "Big Tony," sat in the front seat of the row of desks next to the wall where the morning line-up occurred. He collected homework papers from students behind him, handed them to Sister Rosella, then stood up in front of the line. He rarely did homework. "It's bad enough coming to school," he once told me. Tony had already repeated two grades during his less-than-relentless pursuit of education and didn't seem too concerned about repeating another. In a couple years, when he turned sixteen, he figured he'd be driving his uncle's vegetable truck and he already had enough schooling to pass a driver's test. Even though I greatly admired Tony's cavalier approach to education, we never became fast friends. I always believed a person should not become too close with anybody who's name began with "Big." (However, this rule-of-thumb should be changed immediately if a fight starts in a bar.)

The students who lined up behind Tony appreciated him because he usually made Sister Rosella laugh. Their hope was that, in a better mood, she might swing the paddle with less enthusiasm. Tony started his daily routine by sticking out his hand, then snatching it away as she brought down the paddle. She'd grin and say, "Now cut that out, Tony" and he'd smile. They went through this same ritual a couple more times and she'd laugh and say, "Stop fooling, Tony! I have to get class started," and he'd whine, "But it's gonna hurt, Sister!"

After a little more of this repartee, and when it appeared she really was getting angry, he allowed her to smack his hands while he slouched and grinned at her and everyone in class. She'd finally give up trying to wipe the smile off his face and tell him, "Okay, sit down."

He'd plop down at his desk, start blowing on his hands and say, "Wow, Sister! Look what ya did to me! Ya really hurt me this time. Wow!"

She hoped he meant it and would turn with relish to her next victim. These disciplinary chores seemed to put her in a cheerful mood for the remaining school day. I figured if cheerleaders were hired for a hanging, she'd be well-qualified.

I wasn't fond of Sister Rosella and I'm sure the feeling was mutual. I believed we shared an intense dislike for each other. She preferred loud, boisterous boys to quiet, studious ones. She enjoyed good-natured bantering or jocularity in class. I never participated, not only because it wasn't in character, but because I didn't care to jabber with someone I didn't admire.

I only missed doing my homework twice with the resultant hand blasting. It may have been paranoia, but both times, when presenting my hand, I swear her eyes narrowed, the amusement left her face and she swung that board a little harder.

So as the weather warmed, flowers blossomed and trees leafed, I eagerly contemplated summer vacation when Sister Rosella and I could part company forever.

* * *

On the home front, shortages of luxury items continued. Silk and nylon stockings were difficult for girls to come by.

186

Thus was invented the "paint-on" stocking. Nativity girls didn't mind using this leg makeup, but Father Geller and nuns had no tolerance for the practice at school or at the Recreation Hall dances, contending painted legs were bare legs, therefore immodest. Done properly, it became almost impossible to tell by sight if a young lady wore hose or gave her all for the war effort, but Father Geller was determined to enforce the "must-wear-stockings" rule at dances. He stationed an usher at the front door with the job of unabashedly feeling suspect calves as they entered the building.

Ed worked part-time selling pop and other refreshments at these dances. He worked for Father Burcki who managed many Rec Center activities. When Ed witnessed this unique approach to maintaining modesty standards, he went to Father Burcki and volunteered to help handle the touching job at the door. But Father Burcki was striving to get Ed to consider the priesthood and felt a calf-stroking job wouldn't encourage him toward Holy Orders. The request was denied. Ed continued to sell refreshments.

Because of wartime shortages Betty often arrived home from work late. When she left the Gratiot streetcar at the end of her work day, she'd spot a line of people in front of Cunningham's drug store and automatically "queue up" as they say in the British Isles. She knew this dreary wait in line would result in either a pair of nylon stockings or pack of cigarettes, two items constantly craved.

For cigarettes she also had access to a tobacco shop in the downtown building where she worked that sold an under-the-counter brand named "Sano." Another brand was "Spud," one of the first menthol cigarettes on the market. Smokers avoided them at first because they feared "pneumonia of the throat." If people had a choice of brands they smoked Dominos, Bullseye, Sunshine and Raleigh with the coupon on the back. They "walked a mile for a Camel," smoked Chesterfield because "it satisfies," Pall Mall because some guy held a short cigarette next to a long one, Philip Morris because the world's only living trade mark called for them, and Lucky Strike because its "green went to war." The power of advertising is awesome.

Betty's remaining source for cigarettes was our pantry where Dad hoarded packs he purchased himself or received from salesmen visiting Gelatin Products. He always had a sizable accumulation and left opened packs on a high pantry shelf, safe from the prying eyes and fingers of smaller children. Betty, along with Ed, who also developed a nicotine habit, frequently pilfered from these opened packs. Dad never noticed the deficiency because he knew none of his children would ever smoke. Until the day he died he probably thought Chesterfield only sold fifteen cigarettes to a pack.

Leaving open packs of cigarettes on pantry shelves wasn't one of Dad's smartest moves, and not just because of pilferage. All of us liked to play tricks and practical jokes on him, but Ed reveled in it. Once, at a novelty and magic store, he bought little wooden pegs which, when inserted into a cigarette tip, exploded upon lighting. He stuck a peg into one of Father's Chesterfields on the shelf, only letting Betty and Mary in on the joke.

Then the waiting began. After supper our family gathered in the living room to listen to the radio, read the newspaper and do homework. Betty, Mary and Ed sat with high anticipation as Dad made a couple pantry trips for cigarettes. On his third trip their patience was rewarded. Dad reentered the room, sat in his easy chair, scratched a wooden kitchen match across the sole of his slipper, lit his cigarette and settled back to continue reading the Detroit Times. On his third puff it happened. With a small bang, not unlike a cap pistol, half of Dad's Chesterfield blew everywhere. An intense excitement ensued. Father shot from his chair, yelled "Holy, jumped-up, bally-eyed suzz!" threw down the cigarette and went into a diatribe about inferior workmanship and shoddy wartime merchandise. He also spoke to God and every saint he could think of about punishing those responsible. We younger kids snickered while Betty, Ed and Mary tried to keep a straight face.

Ed wasn't about to let a successful prank die. He pulled the same trick twice more in the following two weeks, deciding to quit only when he went to the pantry to filch some of Dad's cigarettes and found packs of Lucky Strikes. Dad clearly felt a change of brands was in order.

Dad never went back to Chesterfields. Betty, Ed and Mary never told him about the funny explosive devices, and Mom, when Ed told her about it, declared, "He could have blown his eye out."

* * *

There were only three more days of school remaining when I slipped my arithmetic book and loose leaf binder under my arm and headed out our back door into a bright, June morning, already warming. All I had to do was cut through my backyard, the alley and Blaso's yard, jaywalk across Belvidere, cut through the alley running along the rear of Chandler school-yard, turn left onto McClellan, cross it with the safety boy's permission, pass the rectory, church, main school building and convent, then turn into the lower flat near Shoemaker street. There I'd enter the classroom, and all would be fine with the universe. Simple.

I never made it. I decided to tarry a little and say good-bye to the black and white kitten in our garage. I had already fed it milk and bits of leftover bacon from my mother's war-effort bacon grease can, so it wasn't that enthused to see me. It even tried to escape out the open door. I grabbed it, closed the door and gave it a good petting, explaining how I'd be home at lunch hour and try to find it some meat before returning to school. I apologized for penning it up during the day, but it was for its own good. I asked it not to get a wanderlust attack and disappear like its predecessors and I told it I'd try to keep it happy if it stayed with me. I silently rejoiced at its contented purring. I also lost track of time.

It finally dawned on me that I was late for school,

extremely late. Sister Rosella considered anything over two minutes extremely late. She also beat on hands for extreme lateness. School suddenly lost all appeal. With my book, binder and kitten I climbed into the back seat of the neighbor's Model A Ford my dad had agreed to store.

At first my decision to pass up the rigors of academic pursuits and spend a day in the garage felt exciting and I was astonished at my nerve, but spending any length of time with an arithmetic book and kitten for companionship becomes tedious after a time. I tried drawing pictures of the kitten on my binder's blank pages but soon abandoned the idea for the kitten refused to pose and using a pencil, even for drawing, seemed to defeat the purpose of school-skipping. I laid down on the back seat and dozed.

The noise of children passing through the alley as they headed home for lunch awakened me. I heard Chuck, Dolorie and Ann talking as they went by the garage door. I shut the kitten in the car, waited for silence, slipped quietly out the door, then walked casually through the yard to the back porch and entered our kitchen. I hoped my mother wouldn't ask, "What did you learn in school this morning, Rob?"

Lunch on schooldays was the usual hurried, hectic affair. A few minutes before we arrived home Mom placed on the kitchen table a loaf of Silvercup bread, a stack of sliced baloney (we never heard of bologna), a pound of oleo, a large jar of mustard, some drinking glasses and a couple quarts of milk. Then she stood back and waited for the onslaught.

I swiped a slice of baloney from the table and jammed it in my pocket, then hesitated as Chuck, Dolorie and Ann started back to school. Saying I had to go to the bathroom I instead went upstairs to my bedroom and grabbed three comic books. Stuffing them down the front of my knickers and under my shirt, I walked stiffly down the stairs, through the kitchen, said "Goodbye, Ma," and left. When I got to our garage, I took a quick look back, didn't see my mother at the back screen door and ducked inside.

When he smelled the baloney, the kitten forgave me for shutting him in the car. For the rest of the afternoon I read and reread comic books, played with the kitten, dozed and planned my next day's events. I intended to skip school again and definitely needed more comic books.

After arriving home from garage that afternoon I went over to Ray's apartment and traded comic books. He had six I hadn't previously read and although I wanted to read them immediately, resisted the temptation. Instead I stashed them in the Model A's back seat.

I had trouble falling asleep that night wondering if anyone noticed my absence from school. If Sister Rosella did notice she probably didn't care since it was so close to the end of school anyway. Getting safely by the next two days meant the start of vacation, a happy thought. If Nativity expelled me I could go to Barbour Intermediate school the next year with Red, Joe, Ray and Cliff. Then maybe Dad would buy me a bike since Barbour was six or seven long blocks away, although more likely he'd tell me again how "I used to walk five miles to school through ten feet of snow...uphill...both ways." Skipping school began to look like my best idea ever. I didn't worry too much about laying awake thinking about it. I had all next day to sleep.

And the next day became a replica of the day before, except for new comic books to read. I heard my mother at different times exchanging back fence pleasantries with neighbors. At those times I laid flat on the car's back seat and prayed she wouldn't enter the garage. She didn't and the day passed.

The following morning I seriously considered returning for the last day of school. I'd tell Sister Rosella my mother was sick, so sick she couldn't even write an absence excuse, and I stayed home to spoonfeed her chicken soup. Then I thought I'd probably blush, she'd suspect I lied and doublecheck my story with my older sisters. Moreover, my mother insisted I wear the new, short pants she bought me for the summer months instead of my usual knickers. These pants were green, light-weight and didn't even reach down to my kneecaps. To make matters worse they had a matching short-sleeved shirt. I welcomed the garage's isolation.

I just settled down in the car's back seat for my first nap when the garage door opened and Mom entered. She called my name a couple of times, walked to the car, looked in, said "Come on," and walked out. I felt it would be to my advantage to follow her and fully cooperate. Though small, she was mighty under stressful conditions.

Her first words when I entered the kitchen were, "Where have you been for two days?"

I whispered, "In the garage."

"You spent two days in the garage?" she asked in amazement.

I nodded.

"Well, the principal called. They thought you were sick. When I told her I'd sent you to school she started talking about expulsion. Imagine that! A child of mine expelled! For spending two days in a garage yet! What's the matter with you, Robert? I told her I'd find you and get you right back in school, so turn around and get over there!"

I contemplated mentioning the time, almost ten o'clock, and it didn't make sense to go to school and return an hour or so later for lunch, and I should just stay home until lunch hour ended and go in the afternoon. Instead I silently turned and walked out the back door. She didn't appear too susceptible to reasonable arguments.

Reaching the alley I glanced back. Mom stood at the screen door watching to make sure I didn't duck into the garage. She was shaking her head, no doubt wondering if she should tell Dad, and if she did, would he nail the garage door shut.

I didn't take giant steps on the way to school. Somehow I didn't believe my last day would be its usual upper. I tried to act like James Cagney in *Angels With Dirty Faces,* boldly going to the electric chair, but didn't quite pull it off. I felt very apprehensive.

The principal's office door stood ajar, almost as if she awaited me. I hesitated and she said, "Come in, Robert." Sister Mary Theophila, a large, imposing woman with an authoritative voice, dressed exactly as all other Nativity nuns. I always believed a Principal should wear something distinctive, like a red veil, so she'd stand out from the rest, but the Dominican order didn't agree, being into black and white exclusively. She didn't rise from her desk when I timidly approached it — just leaned back in her swivel chair, spread both hands on her desk and stared at me for a few seconds. Finally she said, "Your mother told me you skipped school."

"Yes, Sister."

"Can you tell me why?"

"No, Sister." How could I tell her I couldn't tolerate her fellow Sister, Sister Rosella.

"Where were you for two days?"

"In our garage."

"You spent two days in a garage?!" I was beginning to think spending two days in a garage wasn't a normal childhood activity.

"Yes, Sister."

"Well, we aren't going to expel you this time, but it better never happen again. Skipping school is an extremely serious offense. Sister Rosella tells me you've passed all your subjects so that's in your favor. Now go to your classroom. Sister Rosella wants to see you and I suggest you apologize to her. You're dismissed."

I mumbled a "Thank you, Sister" as my heart sank. I hoped she'd tell me "Go home and sin no more." I sure didn't want to see Sister Rosella.

A thought formed. If I only had money I could walk past the lower flat classroom, continue to Gratiot avenue, catch a streetcar to the end of the line, then keep walking. Maybe a lovely movie star like Joan Crawford would find me, take me into her home and raise me as her own child. Then I could write a book later about how nice she treated me. But instead, being penniless, I turned, walked up the stairs of the flat and entered its front door.

All conversation ceased. Sister Rosella stared angrily at me, and everyone else just stared. A few boys, including "Big Tony," were grinning. Only the sound of my shoes broke the silence on the long trek to my desk. Sister Rosella let me sit down for a few seconds before speaking. She slowly arose from her desk and loudly proclaimed, "No one's going to skip school in my class!"

This remark prompted hearty laughter from those in class who'd been skipping school all year.

"Well, I didn't know you were doing it," she said to the laughers, and then to me, "Get up and bring the paddle."

As I walked over to the side window to retrieve the paddle, she told Tony, "Stand up. I need your desk."

As I handed her the paddle she said, "Now bend over that desk."

When she beat your hands you could cut down on the pain by slightly cupping them. I couldn't cup my buttocks. She smacked me five times before I leaped up crying, blubbering and pleading. She was ordering, "Get back down there!" and I was saying "Please, Sister!" when Tony spoke.

"Hey, Sister. Why don't you let the little guy alone?" There was a menacing tone to his voice.

They glared intently at each other for a long moment before she said to me, "All right, you can take the rest on your hands."

She pounded my hands to a scarlet pulp and told me to return to my desk and sit down. It wasn't easy.

I went home for lunch and Mom asked, "Everything okay?"

"Yeah," I replied, glad she didn't ask for details.

I returned to school and somehow got through the rest of the day, sitting stiffly and quietly, staring straight ahead. When I left Sister Rosella's classroom for the last time and headed home, Bill Stellon overtook me and asked, "Hey, Bob, what did you do on your skip days?"

"I stayed in my garage."

"You spent two days in a garage?" (I wished people would stop asking that.) "Why didn't you go downtown or to Belle Isle or something?"

"Because I didn't have any money." Actually I didn't think of downtown or Belle Isle. I kind of liked garage.

I never had an opportunity to thank Tony for literally saving my ass that day. He didn't return to Nativity the following September, preferring a freer, moneymaking environment on his uncle's vegetable truck. I never thanked him, but I always fervently prayed that he and his uncle sold many, many, many vegetables.

XVII

The advent of school vacation meant more time to build model airplanes. Mothers loved these planes. They were inexpensive, constructed indoors and kept young boys quiet and occupied for days. They were made almost entirely of balsa wood with a thin paper covering. The only exceptions were hardwood wheels, a small hardwood part of the propeller assembly, metal wheel axles, a thin metal hook-like part that attached to the propeller, and Celluloid cockpit windows. A long rubber band, stretching from propeller hook to a brace near the tail, powered a completed plane if, when we tightly wound the propeller, the brace didn't break.

In summer months, Joe, Ray, Red, Chuck and I used our basement to build these planes because of our long work-bench and because one basement section had room enough for a first test flight. Models most prone to a successful flight were biplanes and Piper Cubs. To be successful a plane had to take off from our basement floor, be airborne for at least ten feet, then glide in for a landing when the propeller stopped spinning. There were impediments to overcome before the ideal flight. If too much glue was used a plane became too heavy to take off. If not enough glue was used on certain sections, such as landing gear or rubber band brace, we spent a great deal of time back at the workbench repairing and regluing.

The model plane kits only included one small tube of glue, so we tried to use it sparingly, but sometimes we had to buy an extra tube. When we started to feel lightheaded and staggered a little, we failed to realize we were really having a great time. It wasn't until years later that manufacturers noticed they sold a lot more airplane glue than airplane models.

I devised a perfect fate for planes that didn't fly properly. Using a claw hammer from my Dad's tool box, I ascended to my bedroom and quietly removed all nails from the nailed-shut window opening onto our slanted, back porch roof. While Red, Joe and Ray waited in our backyard, Chuck and I carried all defective planes to the bedroom. I tightly wound the propeller of a plane and sat it on the roof for its last glorious flight. Chuck lit its tail assembly with a wooden kitchen match, I let go of the prop, and the plane sped down the roof, soared into the backyard like a plane taking off from an aircraft carrier, then plummeted and crashed in flames. We called it scuttling, and it made a dramatic sight. We repeated it with five more planes before Mom discovered our fun, appropriated all matches and threatened to inform Dad. She didn't, probably because she loved us and wanted us to reach maturity.

When models of war planes became available, they became our favorites. We felt it patriotically incumbent for us to build them even though they were weighed down with glued-on numbers, letters and insignia and rarely passed flight tests. We dreamed, if the war continued for a few more years, of flying the real planes. At the Army Air Corps pilot school we'd amaze training officers with our airplane knowledge. They wouldn't have to explain the meaning of elevator, aileron, cockpit, canopy, landing gear, struts, pants, prop, rudder, cowlings, fins, tabs, stabilizers, ribs, air intake, air scoop, gun mount, joy stick, fuselage and other aviation words. We learned them all building model airplanes.

There was another aviation-type summer diversion available to us that consisted of a fuselage, wings, and tail assembly made of flat balsa wood. After sticking wing and tail sections through slots in the fuselage we had a glider. There were no rubber bands or other means of locomotion. We threw it, it made a couple loops and came to a gentle landing. That was it. It was amazing how little it took to amuse us. We threw those damn gliders until our pitching arms gave out.

We avidly read everything we could concerning war planes. Our favorite for a time was the Curtiss P-40 Tomahawk, flown by the Flying Tigers, with an open, vicious-looking mouth painted on both sides of its front air scoop. We had no doubt it mesmerized Japanese pilots. We heard they also didn't like the Flying Tigers because no matter how hard they tried to say the name, it came out Frying Tigers.

We noticed the red ball inside a white star on American planes' insignia disappeared early in the war. Ray said it was removed because it looked too much like the larger red ball on Japanese planes. Apparently someone on our side, not as well-versed in plane silhouette identification as we neighborhood boys, mistakenly shot at one of our planes.

No one was too impressed with Lockheed's P-38 Lightning although it performed well against German planes. It had two of everything including two motors. We believed only bombers should have multiple motors. I thought maybe Lockheed had extra parts, so they made two planes and tied them together.

We weren't enamored with Navy fighter planes either. The Grumman Hellcat, Wildcat and Tigercat and the Douglas Corsair, a fighter plane with fold-up wings, were more than a match for Japanese planes, but, being aerodynamic experts, we assumed they were slower than Army Air Corps planes since they had blunt, not pointed, noses.

We considered the four-motored Flying Fortress B-17E our best long range bomber. It looked faster, more maneuverable and more heavily armed than our B-24 Liberator or the British Manchester. The B-17s were modified with much larger and flowing rudders early in the war when their original small tail assemblies were easily shot off by enemy planes. (Ben Franklin had a similar problem when flying a kite in a thunderstorm trying to discover electricity. Mrs. Franklin hollered out the window, "Hey, Ben! I think you need a little more tail!" Ben hollered back, "I told you that last night and you told me to go fly a kite!")

We all admired British Royal Air Force Spitfire planes and pilots for fighting the Germans to a stalemate because we originally suspected Germans were superior in aircraft design and pilot training. The German aces always shot down more planes than British and American aces.

The Japanese Zero received little respect. We felt it lacked speed, maneuverability, was cheaply made and a sitting duck for our much superior pilots. The feeling that Japanese products were inferior was engendered before the war when anything bought in dime stores marked "Made in Japan" broke or wore out within a day of purchase. We heard in order to lighten, and thereby improve, the Zero's performance, the Japanese war lords refused to provide cockpit armor protection for their pilots. This solidified our suspicion that they had no respect for life, a suspicion garnered from movies depicting their penchant for hara-kiri and murderous battle antics.

In movie dogfight sequences, Japanese pilots invariably sneaked up from behind to machine gun blissfully unaware American planes. The Japanese were known for sneaki-ness, and all came equipped with large sets of buckteeth, custom-made for leering. After American pilots bailed out, Japanese pilots turned their guns on their foes hanging helplessly in parachutes. They apparently had no ethical training, life wasn't too precious to them and sportsman-ship didn't seem to be their strong suit. Of course other American planes would get on their tails and blast the leers off their faces as blood streamed from cruel mouths. The Japanese pilots and their planes would go down in flames.

Ray, the great disillusioner, told us the blood was really chocolate syrup, but we didn't care. Revenge was sweet, and God was on our side.

Some of us believed the war in the Pacific would end when the United States began bombing Japan with incendiaries. The whole country would be set ablaze because their houses were all made of flammable rice paper and bamboo. Chuck predicted our scientists would invent a devastating rocket to end the war. Ray said he thought Chuck maybe played by himself a little more than necessary, and we shouldn't pay attention to him. After all, what the hell does a kid that age know?

* * *

On Sundays Mom required us to don our best shoes and clothing, go to church, and wear those duds the remainder of the day. I hated Sundays, not only because I was forbidden to do anything that could soil or tear my clothes, but also because all day I could detect a sweet, sickening, cloying aroma about my person. I called it the Sunday smell and suspected it came from my clothes or shoe polish. It was a constant reminder to avoid any enjoyable activity. I did a lot of sitting around waiting for the day to end.

This is what I was doing on the Butler's front steps one late Sunday afternoon — sitting with Red, Joe and Cliff — when Ray came running. He had startling and tragic news. A U.S. sailor and his pregnant wife were walking across Belle Isle bridge when they were attacked by a gang of Negroes. They cut out the sailor's eyes and threw him and his wife off the bridge. Racial fights raged all over Belle Isle, and the trouble was spreading throughout the city. We asked Ray for more particulars, but that was all he knew. This story seemed logical to us, especially the eye cutting, for the Negro's propensity for carrying switchblades and razors was well known. That the rumor wasn't true didn't occur to us, and it swept through our neighborhoods.

A similar rumor swept through the Negro community only the victims were a black woman and her child tossed off the bridge by Caucasians. In reality there had been many skirmishes on Belle Isle, and large groups of irate citizens roamed the city searching for people to blame and maim.

The news initiated a lively discussion about our familiarity, or lack of familiarity, with people of color. Red said Chandler school only had two Negroes, one in his sixth grade classroom and another in the fifth grade. They were brothers, he liked them, and called them both "chocolate drop." We thought this humorous, perhaps because many people referred to them more derisively, and Red's nickname seemed innocent and inoffensive.

I mentioned my theory about the origin of the least complimentary term for our dark-skinned brethren. After studying a map of Africa in a geography book, I concluded that when the first group of slaves arrived in this country a plantation owner asked them, "Where y'all from?" An African spokesperson answered, "Niger" and most Southerners have been mispronouncing the answer since.

Joe, the scholar, gruffly corrected me saying, "You're nuts! It derives from the word 'Negro.'"

The next morning we went over to Chandler schoolyard to play ball at a section we favored between the side of the school building and a fence. If we hit a well-taped baseball solidly enough from home plate, which was fashioned from a flattened piece of cardboard box placed close by the school, we could loft the ball over the fence onto Belvidere. We were getting into heroic home run hitting and knew one of us would certainly be the next Hank Greenberg.

At noon Joe had to leave to practice with his organized team, effectively breaking up our game. Other players went home to eat, so Red, Cliff and I wandered over to the chinning bars to see who could do the most chin-ups. I won the competition, which is easy to do if you don't plan to use your arms for a few days. Cliff expressed amazement at my performance and said, "Rob, I've just seen more chins than

I'd see in a Chinese telephone book." Most people don't realize that Cliff originated that line.

We noticed a crowd of mostly adult men mobbing-up across the street on Belvidere. A boy about 15-years-old suddenly broke from the crowd, ran across the street, and entered the schoolyard. As he approached us Cliff yelled out, "Hey! What's going on over there?"

The boy stopped long enough to explain that five carloads of dark-skinned people, intent on mayhem, were approaching from downtown via Warren, a heavily traveled major street two long blocks away. He was going home to get his older brothers, and they'd all be back to join in the coming skirmish.

We sauntered over to the schoolyard fence and stared at the group across the street. There were about thirty people gathered and more swelling their ranks. One of them abruptly shouted, "Let's go!" and, turning in unison, they began walking in the direction of Warren avenue.

When I suggested we follow them, Cliff wanted nothing to do with it. His father wouldn't approve. Being a policeman's son has its drawbacks, so he opted to draw back and go home.

Red and I fell in at the end of the procession, strangely excited to be part of this vengeful mob. As we streamed past houses more people, including women, fell in with us. Curiously, everyone kept to the sidewalk, being careful not to walk on anyone's lawn, so the horde stretched out quite a distance. I developed mixed emotions. I wasn't sure I should be proud of being part of a group bent on doing bodily harm to their fellow man. I decided instead to be proud of being part of a group who didn't walk on their neighbor's lawn.

The crowd reached Moffat, the street preceding Warren, and someone in the lead shouted, "There they are! They got 'em!" Everyone turned onto Moffat and rushed forward. When Red and I reached the intersection, the crowd was gathered around two cars parked in a small clearing near the mouth of an alley. One car was a four-door gray sedan, the other a police car.

We wended our way through the crowd and emerged about fifteen feet from the sedan's rear. A tall, thickset, uniformed policeman stood facing four young men lined up along the sedan's side. They were in their late teens or early twenties, a little swarthy, possibly Sicilian-Americans, and holding up their trousers with both hands. The policemen obviously had coerced them to remove their belts for four belts lay on top of three baseball bats and two heavy chains that were piled near the car's rear wheel. "These nice gentlemen are probably looking for the baseball diamond," I said to Red. "Maybe we should tell them where it is." Red gave me a quizzical look and suggested we stay out of any discussion.

Another policeman rummaged inside the sedan searching under lifted seat cushions. I figured it would be a plus for the four captives if he happened to find a baseball or two. A third policeman leaned on the patrol car parked in front of the sedan, warily watching the growing crowd.

The tall policeman approached the captive nearest to Red and me and asked quietly, "What were you going to do with those bats?"

"Play baseball," he answered.

"See!" I said to Red. He gave me that same look.

"How about the chains?" the policeman asked, a little more forcefully. Now here I could see that the guy should be more imaginative with his reply.

"Use 'em for bases," the young man said. I decided he wasn't very imaginative or a good liar.

The policeman didn't take kindly to this feeble attempt at humor. He must have trained at the same school of discipline as Father Geller for his open hand crashed against the humorist's face snapping his head to the side. The policeman then turned his attention to the next young man in line and asked the same "bat" question. The young man chose to answer with a statement, "Hey, we didn't do nuttin'." He just got the "nuttin'" out of his mouth when the officer slapped him.

The third young man, when asked about the bats, figured the best answer was no answer at all. It didn't work. He also got a hard slap. From the young man's silly grin I could see that Father Geller's face-slapping championship might be challenged. This policeman had at least a brown belt in the face-rearranging category.

No one named Donahue or Spock stepped from the crowd to point out that the policemen could be violating their captives' civil rights or suppressing their egos, nor did anyone object to the clearly visible police brutality, but some did loudly suggest that justice would be better served if the policemen were downtown doing what they were doing to Niger-Americans. In fact, the crowd seemed to be getting more agitated. Red and I found ourselves nudged closer and closer to the action and I detected an uncharacteristic panic in Red's voice when he proposed that we head home. The policeman also noticed the crowd's ill temper, so he slapped the last young man, just so he wouldn't feel left out, and told them all to "Get your belts, get in your car and get the hell outta here." He quickly confiscated the bats and chains and joined his fellow officers in the patrol car.

Many curses — and a few rocks — were thrown at the police car as it drove away. Red and I were happy to break free from these people, and we ran most of the way home. Red suggested we not mention the experience to our parents.

The National Guard moved into Detroit that day and within 48 hours, order was restored. Thirty-four people had been killed. Thousands more were wounded, injured and arrested. There was millions of dollars property damage.

There also were complaints from citizens wearing silly grins who said they had met a policeman who didn't seem to like chains and baseball bats.

I finally discovered the origin of the Sunday smell. It came from the white creme Mom combed into my hair to make it manageable. A switch to pure, odorless Vaseline ended my problem.

XVIII

When resting on Butler's front steps after a strenuous game of duck-on-the-rock, Ray asked, "Hey, did you guys hear they cut Bob Hope off the radio last night?"

We all shook our heads. I wasn't aware he was even on the night before. "Why?" Joe asked for the rest of us.

Ray replied, "Because he told a dirty joke. He said, 'Did you hear about the little girl who swallowed a safety pin and didn't feel a prick 'til she was eighteen?' and they cut him right off."

Ray smirked, Joe and Cliff snickered and Red, Chuck and I grinned while trying to grasp why we grinned. What was so funny? I easily pictured a safety pin rusting in a stomach for years, the catch weakening, then the whole thing snapping open. It was logical.

"Don't you get it?" Ray asked me. I admitted I didn't so Ray explained the joke. I still didn't think it funny. In fact, I thought it a little unfair. I just got used to calling it a dick, and now they changed the spelling and pronunciation. I assumed a lot of guys named Richard had something to do with the change.

Ray knew everything about sex and seldom passed up an opportunity to pass it on. He also had access to some interesting reading material that he willingly shared. Reading

Ray's booklets assured that we'd be in line the following Saturday at any confessional but Father Geller's, and could count on at least a decade or two of the rosary for penance. They were called "dirty comic books" and featured such stalwarts as Maggie and Jiggs, Popeye and Olive Oyl, Dick Tracy and Tess Trueheart, and even Little Orphan Annie and Sandy for those who appreciated bestiality. The comic books showed parts of our heroes that were never seen in the "Funnies" section — not even in Hearst newspapers — and they were depicted in every carnal position imaginable. I found them fascinating, but I protested to Ray that Jiggs, Popeye and Tracy weren't anatomically correct, sizewise.

Ray just smiled.

Mothers didn't like Ray. Mrs. Butler, Mrs. Combs and my mother all told their sons, "I wish you wouldn't spend so much time with Ray."

When we'd ask why, they'd say, "I just don't trust him," or "He's too old for you boys." Ray was older than the rest of us — he was going on 15 — but he was only a month older than Cliff, and Mrs. Butler and my mother didn't tell us to stay away from Cliff. Maybe it was his looks. His face was slightly puffy and his thin, tightly-waved light-brown hair was already starting to recede. He did look older.

They'd say, "He's too polite," but we were always told to be polite, so how could Ray be too polite? Then they'd say, "He's too wise," which meant he knew too much about birds, bees, girls and Tess Trueheart.

Our response was always, "Aw, Ma, he's okay."

The mothers were right. What really puzzled us was how they knew he corrupted us, because when holding seminars on life's baser details, he first made sure no parents were in sight and then lowered his voice a decibel or two. I concluded all mothers have an inexplicable instinct about their children's companions.

A young lady in her late teens lived on Belvidere, not far from Chandler playground. Her name was Laura, she was lovely to behold, and I dreamed of holding her, although I knew in my heart I never would. She was just too old and beautiful. She wore tight sweaters and short skirts in the Lana Turner tradition, but if Lana and Laura were placed side by side, Lana would look like a boy. When Laura strolled by Chandler playground, outfielders lost track of fly balls, pitchers stopped their wind-ups and batters casually stepped out of the batter's box to stretch, rub their hands in dirt and furtively ogle. A few of the older, nervier players whistled or made sexually obnoxious remarks.

After one of these sightings I remarked to Ray in a hushed, reverent tone, "That is one pretty girl and, if she goes by again, I'll be pole-vaulting home."

Ray grunted, "She's a whore."

This shocked me. Our understanding of the word was a woman who did what Popeye and Olive Oyl did in dirty comic books. These women were to be avoided at all times or you'd end up known as a whoremonger, or worse yet, dead and in hell. A weird thought crossed my mind. All good girls I knew wore scapulars and Blessed Virgin medals on chains or ribbons around their necks. I wondered if Laura wore a Mary Magdalen medal.

"How da ya know she's a whore, Ray?" I asked, thinking perhaps he was a whoremonger.

"Because I know a guy who took her out. He told me if she had as many dicks sticking out of her as she's had in her she'd look like a porcupine."

"I don't believe it."

"Well then, look at the way she dresses. Look at all the lipstick and rouge she wears. Look at her red hair. It's dyed."

Ray could be right, I thought. I'd heard housewives talking about older girls and women who dyed their hair. Their conclusions were the same: Any female who dyed her hair had loose morals. Housewives called the dyers "tramps" or "harlots."

No one who looked so perfect could be morally flawed, I reasoned, so I told him, "Ray, you're nuts. You don't know what you're talking about."

Ray smiled and said, "You'll see."

Three mornings later Ray and Joe stood in my backyard calling my name. When I walked out on the porch Ray mysteriously said, "C'mon. I wanna show you something."

We walked part way through the side alley running along Chandler schoolyard, turned into the alley between Belvidere and McClellan and stopped at a telephone pole.

"Take a look," Ray said, gazing down at the pole's base. There was a white, wrinkled, flattened-out, elastic tube lying there. I started to pick it up and Ray grabbed my arm. "Hey, don't touch it, you clown! It's a rubber! You don't know what a rubber is?!" The only rubber I ever heard of was on the end of a pencil.

They both laughed when I admitted my ignorance. Ray explained in detail their primary use and then pointed to the nearest house behind the telephone pole and asked, "You know who lives in that house, don't you?"

I knew. Old Laura. I was at once both disappointed and excited. I pictured Laura and Dick Tracy in an obscene embrace and flushed a little.

Ray chortled and said, "Hey, didn't I tell you?"

As we walked home Ray gave me more information about the white elastic tubes including their various names; how, just for fun, they could be blown up like balloons or filled with water, and where they could be purchased. I only half-listened. My mind kept returning to beautiful Laura. Though convinced Ray was right and Laura's standards weren't the highest, I didn't care. She was still the most gorgeous woman in the world.

* * *

Joe introduced us to a game called Step-ball. Three to ten kids played at a time, although we considered five or six ideal since that's the number we usually had available. Besides kids, the only necessities were porch steps and either a rubber or tennis ball.

I don't know why Joe always had tennis balls. He didn't play tennis nor did anyone else we knew. We classified tennis in the same category as croquet, badminton, hopscotch or jump rope; games suitable for girls, boys who wished they were girls, and rich people. Nevertheless, Joe always had the needed balls and we always used his front porch steps.

Step-ball resembled baseball in that each participant took turns trying to score runs before making three outs. The person "at bat" slammed the ball into the porch steps and it ricocheted back to the waiting fielders. If one of the other players caught it before it hit the ground or if it hit the ground and infielders fielded it cleanly, it was an out.

Infielders positioned themselves between the sidewalk and curb while outfielders covered the street and sidewalk across the street. If a batter bounced the ball through the infielders or lined it past the curb so it bounced between the curb and half-way across the street it was a single; the other half of the street, a double; between the opposite curb and far end of the sidewalk, a triple; past the opposite sidewalk, a home run.

The width of Butler's house determined the boundaries and if a ball rolled or soared outside these imaginary lines it counted as an out. The batter loudly kept track of the number of men on base and his score, and if he made a mistake other players loudly corrected him.

I couldn't decide which would be more thrilling — fielding a hot grounder or snagging a line drive as an infielder, running down a long fly as an outfielder, smashing a home run as a batter, or mongering Laura. A home run was only possible if you struck the sharp edge of a step with a ball at exactly the proper angle and with enough velocity. Joe accomplished this feat quite often, and some of his blasts sailed across the street and into the horse chestnut tree on my front lawn, well into home run territory. Joe was becoming very easy to resent.

Different factors determined the game's length. One was

Mrs. Butler's patience. The intermittent noise of the ball banging into wooden steps eventually frayed her nerves enough to bring her to the front door to suggest we discontinue our game. Another was an insensitive adult parking his car in single or double territory. And, finally, mothers were always calling sons home to eat or run errands, leaving us without the mandatory players. The one disadvantage of playing games around your house, instead of the playground, was your availability to mothers.

Something else began happening to break up our games. Joe would leave. In the middle of a game he'd suddenly announce, "Hey, I gotta go."

We'd ask, "Where ya going?"

He'd grin and vaguely answer, "To hell, if I don't pray," and pedal away on his bike.

Ray said he thought Joe had a girl friend, a believable theory. Joe had grown tall, and with his light brown hair, almost honey-blond, and his quiet demeanor he seemed to be attracting the gentler gender at our schoolyard baseball games. He was almost as good-looking as his twin sister Gladys, who developed in other, more provocative ways.

Joe's suspected involvement with girls gave me another reason to be envious of him. With varying degrees of failure, I already tried to emulate his athletic ability and common sense. Now I began to seriously consider how I'd fare with girls if I spent any amount of time with them. I had a particular girl in mind.

My sister Pat's best friend was a dark-haired girl named Jeanne Murphy. They sometimes roamed the neighborhood trying to appear sophisticated and grown-up while licking dribbling ice cream cones. When passing Chandler playground, they engaged boys their age or older in flirtatious, and frivolous conversations that sounded extremely dumb. They talked about school activities, school subjects, and their favorite recording artists, movie stars or songs. They smiled and giggled a lot. Not once did they mention batting averages or whom they considered the best pitcher in baseball — Bob Feller or Hal Newhouser — nor did they discuss the relative merits of Messerschmitts and Spitfires. But if that's what it took to talk to girls, I'd try to get interested in school, recording artists and songs. I already liked movie stars, especially Barbara Stanwyck.

Jeanne Murphy had a sister my age named Doris, a miniature movie star with long blond hair, a cute nose, dazzling smile and though not fully blossomed, she certainly was budding. Occasionally Jeanne and Pat took Doris along with them on their neighborhood walks. When they passed the playground, I tried to think of something witty or interesting to say to Pat that might impress Doris, but I never thought of anything. My mind blanked, throat constricted and face burned. If any words escaped they sounded croaky and silly.

Jeanne often visited Pat at our house, and once she brought Doris when I was there. I choked out a "Hi" and quickly fled the premises. I imagined derisive chuckling as the screen door closed behind me.

The Murphys lived on Belvidere not far from Cairney street, so when going to church, the Roosevelt theater, or anywhere else in the world, I started taking either the route that passed in front of the Murphy house or the alley that passed behind. Perhaps Doris would hail me from her front or back porch, we'd talk about Nativity or recording artists, I'd ask her to go to the Roosevelt with me (it wasn't necessary to talk a lot in a theater), and suddenly I'd be holding hands with the best looking 12-year-old girl in the neighborhood. The only hitch was I rarely saw Doris on my excursions past her house, and when I did, she failed to hail me.

Yet I still had hope and patience and began planning for the future. If you're going to have a girl friend you need money for movies, popcorn and sodas afterward and I doubted my mother would be eager to pay movie fare at the Roosevelt for any of my romantic entanglements. She wasn't too happy about giving me an extra nickel for Milk

Duds every week and strongly suggested I should wait for movies to appear at the Arcadia or Dawn where the admission was cheaper. Explaining that the Roosevelt showed better cartoons and "chapters" didn't faze her. She also didn't care that the Roosevelt treated us to an Our Gang, Charley Chase or Harold Lloyd comedy, and we could count on a Movietone news with a feature story hosted by Lew Leher, a comedian with a bad German dialect, who ended his segment by exclaiming, "Monkeys is da cwaziest people."

Joe told me the Morning Star Dairy was hiring jumpers — kids who helped the milkmen deliver milk — and he heard they paid two dollars a day. Joe already had a job delivering papers, but he said he'd walk over with me to apply. We knocked on the back door of the dairy owner's house, his wife answered, and, after I explained my strong desire for a money-making job, she told me, "Okay. It's six days a week. Report tomorrow at 5:30."

I thanked her, thanked Joe for this great job tip and ran home to tell Mom. She was very proud and mentioned it to the whole family at supper. She also cautioned, "You'll have to go to bed at nine tonight so you'll get enough sleep."

Hearing this, the job lost some aura. Who wants to go to bed at nine during summer vacation? But then Ed remarked, "When I worked for old man Ronkhol he used to buy me anything I wanted for lunch, mostly hamburgers and fried potatoes, and fish and chips on Friday," which was standard fare in many taverns.

Maybe I could do it for a month or so, I thought. Carrying heavy bottles of milk and eating anything I wanted for lunch, like hamburgers, would give me muscles. Large biceps would be very noticeable, and I'd start wearing short sleeve shirts when passing the Murphy house. I laid in bed that evening thinking pleasant thoughts while trying to ignore the happy shouts of other kids, including Chuck, having a good time outside. The sun hadn't fully set, and I was in bed trying to sleep. Yet the thought of money, muscles and Doris made me smile, and I knew it would be worth it.

My mother quietly shook me awake at 5:15. "You're going to be late," she whispered. She whispered to avoid arousing Chuck who slept peacefully beside me. I couldn't believe it. No kid with a brain gets up before the sun during summer vacation, but I concentrated on money, muscles and Doris and struggled out of bed. While dressing I thought of waking peaceful Chuck just to share my misery. Instead I pictured myself later in the day, flashing dollar bills and bragging about my purchasing power.

After washing my face and hands I hurried downstairs into the kitchen. Dad sat drinking coffee and Mom had a glass of milk and toast ready. I gulped the milk, grabbed a half slice of toast and headed out the front door with Mom following: "You have to eat! You can't work on an empty stomach!"

"I'll eat a lot at lunch," I promised.

I ran to the dairy where loaded milk trucks already were pulling away from the lighted bottling plant, turning onto Holcomb, fading into the darkness. I knocked on the dairy owner's back door and his wife again answered, complaining, "You're late. Some trucks already left. C'mon."

We walked swiftly to the plant, and she started asking each departing driver if he needed a kid. The first two drivers looked at me and shook their heads. Just when I began to feel unwanted, the third and last driver agreed to accept me. I stepped up into the truck's cab, and we started out on the driver's route.

It was noisy. The truck motor whined as gears shifted, and milk bottles rattled inside low, wooden, sectioned crates. I glanced behind me and saw crates stacked more than half-way to the top of the enclosed truck bed. A large block of ice crowned each stack.

The driver had dark hair and a pasty face. He loudly asked my name, told me his name was Christopher Cole, and I could call him Mister Cole. I thought of humorously calling him "Old King" but quickly changed my mind. He didn't look like a merry old anything. He explained my job duties and for the next five hours, well into daylight, we delivered quarts, pints and half-pints of white, chocolate and buttermilk to front porches and milk chutes. He covered the left side of streets, and I covered the right. At times we carried cases of milk into the front or rear of grocery stores, restaurants and sweetshops, returning with empties. I stacked the empty cases and soon saw progress as full cases depleted and empties grew.

I felt my stomach growling from hunger and wished the truck motor wasn't so loud. Then Mr. Cole could hear the growling and take the hint. I had a strong desire for a hamburger and fried potatoes, and we had delivered to, and passed, many inviting and not-so-inviting restaurants. Perhaps he has a favorite eating spot not yet reached, I contemplated. He finally pulled up in front of a grocery store and said the words I starved to hear: "Are you hungry?"

I nodded.

He said, "Okay. I'll be right back."

Leaving me slightly confused, since I never heard of grocers cooking up hamburgers and fried potatoes, he entered the store.

Returning shortly, he handed me a small, brown bag and said, "Here ya go. Ya can have a couple of those half-pint milks if ya want," gesturing to the remaining cases of milk behind us.

I opened the bag and pulled out a cellophane-wrapped package containing two snowball-shaped chocolate cakes with a gooey marshmallow covering, one white and the other pink. They were sprinkled with bits of coconut, and as I ravenously devoured them a pleasant thought flitted through my brain. Maybe Mr. Cole is a rare person, like me, who believes kids should eat desserts first. We'll drive to a restaurant later when he gets hungry. At that moment he pulled a large beef sandwich and a thermos from a lunch

216

bucket hidden behind a couple of milk cases, sat on the driver's stool and contentedly chomped while staring out the windshield. I silently said farewell to my hamburger dream and came to a conclusion: Mr. Cole isn't a very generous person.

We covered the remainder of his route the way we began, with a minimum of conversation. We returned to the dairy at 4:30 in the afternoon, and I helped Mr. Cole unload empty cases. When we finished he said, "Hey kid, ya did swell. Here. Hold out your hand."

I extended my hand, palm upward, he dropped a fifty cent coin into it and said, "I'll see ya tomorrow."

He turned, walked away and I came to a stronger conclusion: Mr. Cole is more than an ungenerous person. He's a penny-pinching prick — and I silently thanked Ray for teaching me this new, descriptive word.

Walking home my stomach still growled, my arms and legs ached, there was no noticeable change in my biceps, and I had just worked eleven hours for less than a nickel an hour. I could accumulate money faster and easier by bartering with junkmen, cashing in bottles and begging from my mother. I never saw Mr. Cole again.

Mom didn't seem too upset with my decision to forego the work-a-day world. She simply smiled and said I was too young to be working such long hours anyway. She didn't even ask for half of my day's pay. She only said, "Spend it wisely."

I found a way to spend it the next day. Red told me the Lutheran church on the corner was showing a movie in its basement. The movie was the *Last of the Mohicans* and the admission only three pennies. I asked Mom if I could go, fully expecting her to refuse. Impressionable Catholic children weren't allowed to go into Protestant churches lest they lose their faith to smooth-talking ministers.

Mom hesitated until I told her it would be in the church basement, and I'd avoid the main worship area and any clandestine religious instructions. Also I'd take Chuck along. This convinced her. The thought of both of us out of sight and sound, yet in a safe place, appealed to her.

This Lutheran church intrigued me. It was a square, white-painted, clapboard building extending from a small front yard all the way to the alley and, except for the front double doors, multiple side windows, and the plain wooden cross on the flat roof, it could easily be mistaken for a large, boxy house. I had difficulty accepting it as a church, having become accustomed to Nativity's huge size and splendor with its red-brick exterior, arched doors and windows, green-slated roof and lofty domed bell tower. Gentlemen tipped their hat when passing this edifice.

I had glimpsed inside the Lutheran church when its doors were flung open on Sunday to welcome parishioners and could see that Protestants believed pews, a pulpit and small altar were the only necessities to inspire reverence. With no majestic, variegated marble pillars holding up a gold-leafed ceiling, no tall candles and candelabra, no larger-than-life statues of holy people interspersed around the altar areas, no stained glass windows, no stations-of-the-cross along the walls, and no mysterious, guilt-freeing confessionals, I thought Protestants were being gypped. They didn't even have hard wooden kneelers to inflict kneecap pain, pain that could be offered up for poor souls in purgatory. I couldn't help thinking of what I had heard Dad say so many times about Protestant churches: "They're not churches. They're meeting houses."

The most surprising thing about this Lutheran church was that its exterior wasn't covered with the red or yellow artificial brick siding that graced half the frame houses on our street. Salesmen saturated every neighborhood in Detroit, talking thousands of people into cloaking their homes or places of business with this siding. The biggest selling points were increased insulation and never having to paint the outside again, but I suspect people bought this siding for a deeper reason — The Three Little Pigs syndrome. Most people were aware of what happened to the pig in the wooden house, so I figured many people unconsciously camouflaged their homes with this siding to keep the wolf from the door, although a wolf would have to possess extremely poor eyesight indeed to mistake that siding for real brick. I, personally, never believed that a wolf could level a wooden house with huffs and puffs. Straw maybe — not wood.

Red, Chuck and I walked over to the church when we saw about fifty boys and girls congregating in front. The minister, a middle-aged man in gray pants and white shirt, came out on the front steps and told us to go around to the rear entrance and line up.

He appeared again at the rear door and allowed us to enter and descend a short flight of stairs to the basement where his wife eagerly waited to collect our pennies. She was an angelic-looking woman with a sweet smile who, if put in a nun's garb, would be a candidate for canonization. She sat at a card table and collected our coins in an open cigar box. I paid admission for Chuck and myself, and she told us to choose any of the available folding chairs set up facing the movie screen, adding, "I hope you enjoy the movie."

As we sat down, I had some odd conflicting feelings. I felt brave for entering the church, even if just its basement, but also fearful, because my soul could be slowly turning black the longer I remained. I couldn't remember if nuns called it a major venial sin to enter a Protestant church or a full-fledged mortal one. This could be my first mortal sin, and I had always hoped it would have something to do with the sixth or ninth Commandant. I hated jeopardizing my soul for just watching an Indian movie.

While waiting for the movie to start, I planned my next confession. I'd try to avoid telling the priest what kind of Protestant church it was because this one, started by a wayward priest who turned church doors into bulletin boards for radical ideas, wasn't exactly a favorite of the Catholic hierarchy. I'd explain I only visited the church basement, it wasn't a religious movie, and there was no preaching.

I looked at Chuck talking with Red about Indians, and he didn't appear worried about the state of his soul, but then easy-going Chuck didn't seem to worry about anything. I scanned the room to see if I could spot any other worried-looking Catholic kids. If there were others present, they were all like Chuck. The minister's wife turned out the lights, and the movie began.

It was a thrilling, penetrating movie. People got penetrated by bullets, arrows, knives and tomahawks. Randolph Scott played the good scout "Hawkeye," and Bruce Cabot played a villainous Mohawk chieftain, with hairdo to match, whose motto seemed to be, "The only good Mohican is a dead Mohican." The movie taught us all an invaluable lesson — there are good Indians. Up until then movies taught us that all Indians, except Tonto, were murderous, wanton trash. Sadly, the two good Indians in this movie ended up deceased.

I was relieved the minister allowed us to depart without an invitation to pray with him. Feeling magnanimous I bought the three of us a bottle of pop at the corner store across from the church, which left me with twenty-nine cents, hardly enough for a Roosevelt movie date with Doris. My hoped-for romance would have to wait.

Two days later, on a Saturday, I started to church and confession. I walked to the dairy, ran through its parking lot to avoid the owner's wife, not caring to explain my absence from work, and trotted through a narrow passageway between a dairy building and garage, emerging into the alley.

The big black-on-brown setter in the yard across the alley saw my approach, rushed barking and growling and, as usual, slammed into the gate at a full gallop. Only this time the gate swung open. I froze, the dog froze and, as the gate slowly swung back, the dog stopped the gate with its body by stepping into the alley. It totally ignored me and trotted slowly down the alley toward Chapin street.

I waited until it was a hundred feet away before exhaling. After a few tentative steps to make sure my weak-kneed legs still moved, I continued my journey. Two backyards later the small white terrier barked and snarled. I looked at it with contempt, having just stared down a dog four times as large. The big setter must have feared me so why worry about a little mutt with yellow stuff flowing from bloodshot eyes.

I went to confession to Father Wolbur, a young, dark-haired priest. He gently told me going into a Protestant church wasn't a mortal sin, but it could weaken my faith and I shouldn't get into the habit, (the same advice he'd give a man who confessed to kissing a nun.) "I hope you enjoyed the movie," he added. Father Wolbur seemed like an okay guy!

I said my penance for all my swearing, lying and disobeying and started for home. Turning onto Belvidere I passed Doris' house, then crossed the street intending to shortcut through Blaso's yard, when I saw the white terrier. It sat on the lawn in front of its owner's house near the sidewalk. I considered recrossing the street to avoid it; then reconsidered since I'd learned barking dogs are more frightened of you than you are of them — with the exception of Mitzi. As I got closer the dog began a low, continuous growl. This worried me a little, but it remained sitting on its haunches, so I knew I had it petrified. Grinning, I stopped in front of it and said, "I ain't scared of you," and drew back my leg to give it a good-natured kick. Its teeth sank into my stationary leg just above the knee and I received a not-so-good-natured bite. I never thought an old muck-eyed dog could move that quickly. I let out a howl, shook the dog loose and didn't stop running until reaching home. Then I switched to a limp, hoping someone in my family might notice and ask what happened. Nobody noticed or asked, so I limped upstairs to my room and surveyed the damage.

My knickers and leg were both punctured in two places. I pressed my thumbs around the wounds making them bleed to remove any germs and to make the wounds look more serious, then called Mom. I needed sympathy. After four plaintive cries, she came upstairs and examined the bite as I explained what happened. "We have to get the iodine," she said.

I was sorry I called her. I needed sympathy, not more pain. Iodine hurt. After a few whines she relented and used Mercurochrome instead. It didn't sting like iodine, but was the same color. Friends were always horrified when shown a sore smeared with bloody-looking iodine or Mercurochrome and the first question they always asked was, "Did it hurt?" I'd answer, "Yeah, a little," as I smiled heroically and fought any urge to say, "Only when I laugh."

Mom seemed more upset about my torn corduroy knickers than my lacerations. "Why did you wear your good pants to confession?" she asked. "I don't know if I can sew those rips so they won't show. I wanted you to save those pants for school and Sunday Mass. Why didn't you wear your short pants or old knickers?"

"I thought ya meant I should wear 'em anytime I went to church," I said, not mentioning I had to look my best when passing the Murphy house.

She told me to change into an old pair and bring the knickers downstairs, and she'd try to repair the damage. This was a little more complicated than it might seem since Mother wasn't a Betsy Ross with a needle and thread. If the flag chore had been left to her, we'd still be saluting a Union Jack.

When Dad came home from work that afternoon, she mentioned my dog bite, and he called me into the living room to inspect my leg. "What did you put on it?" he asked.

As soon as I said "Mercurochrome," I knew I should have lied.

"Well, it looks bad. You have to be careful with dog bites. Go get the iodine."

After he finished smearing me with that searing, stinging, skull-and-crossbones labeled poison, my mother, who

222

had left the room, returned and showed him my torn knickers. "I don't know if I'll be able to fix these," she said. "Maybe we should buy him a new pair. You know, a Betsy Ross I'm not." She read my mind.

My dad then said words I'd been half-dreading for months. "Okay, but why don't you get him some long pants. He's certainly old enough."

I realized I'd eventually have to give up my beloved knickers, but wasn't in a hurry, because they were the closest thing to jodhpurs I'd ever wear. Jodhpurs, worn by many movie and comic strip heroes, were close-fitting from the knee to ankle and always covered with knee-high boots, so I easily imagined my knickers were jodhpurs and knee-high socks were boots. Long pants were necessary to join the adult world, but I worried that the pant bottoms would flap around my ankles when I ran, slowing me down. Baseball or football players never wore long pants. But the worst thing about wearing them was giving up any dream of ever owning a pair of high-top boots. No one wants to wear high-tops covered by long pants. I had mixed feelings about this rite of passage into the adult world, but maybe it was for the best. If I ever owned a pair of high-tops I'd probably end up begging Mom for a pith helmet.

XIX

Long pants flapping around my ankles made me feel mature. Joe, Red, Cliff and Ray already wore them most days so I wasn't conspicuous and eventually grew to like them enough to ask Mom to buy me another pair. Surely, now that I sometimes dressed as an adult, Doris would notice me as I passed her house, being careful to stay clear of the mangy white dog's house. I also dreamed of Laura beckoning me into her house as I passed but knew that dream bordered on lunacy. I didn't look that grown up. In the meantime I met Roosevelt Rosie.

At Roosevelt theater matinees children gave the screen full attention only during cartoons and serials, or during war, gangster, comedy or western movies. Otherwise we socialized, changed seats, and wandered. Consequently the theater management tried to schedule two action or comedy movies at matinees to keep us in our seats. Sometimes they slipped in a dull love story. The only applause during these movies came at their finish when lovers embraced and indulged in a long, drawn-out kiss. We lustily applauded the words "The End."

Rosie was one grade behind me at Nativity. I'd noticed her at morning Mass during school and now noticed her at the Roosevelt's Saturday matinee sitting five rows in front of Red, Chuck and me. Rosie was very noticeable because, unlike two girlfriends with her, she was maturing rapidly.

She had long wavy jet-black hair, full lipsticked lips and stood taller than her friends.

And Rosie had noticed me. One of her girlfriends giggled to Red at the candy counter that Rosie liked and wanted to talk to me. When Red returned to his seat and gave me the message, I couldn't believe my very own ears and thought he made it all up. Then Rosie's girlfriends began twisting around in their seats, smirking and gesturing in our direction, and I couldn't believe my very own eyes. Red didn't make it up. Rosie really wanted to talk.

It took a great deal of courage to rise and walk toward those young ladies. When they saw me coming, the grinning girlfriends left their seats and headed up the aisle leaving Rosie sitting alone. I sidled and lurched along the row of seats until I stood at a vacant seat next to her and began a never-before-recorded, less-than-intellectual conversation.

"Hi," I said nervously. (Now there was a real super, all-American, opening line. I'm sure I overpowered her with my erudition.)

"Hi," she said with a slight smile. (Well, at least she didn't top my line.)

"Can I siddown?" I asked.

"Sit down!" yelled a kid a couple rows behind us.

"Yeah! Siddown!" another kid agreed. (Damn! I thought. This dalliance is only one minute old and we've got half the theater involved.)

"Sure," she replied. I thanked her, and the two kids who yelled, and sat.

"What school do ya go to?" I asked. (I already knew but had to say something and nobody had yet thought of "What sign were you born under?" or "Do you come here often.")

"Nativity," she said.

"Yeah, I thought I saw ya in church." (I knew I saw her in church. I tried to remember if I saw her going to confession, and if she took a long time to say her penance. It could be a helpful clue.)

"Yes, I saw you too," she admitted.

"You going into seventh grade?" I asked.

"Yes," she answered.

"Just hope ya don't get Sister Rosella."

"Yes, I hear she's tough." (It was at this point that I said to myself, Robert, if you ever write a book, leave this conversation out.)

"How old are you?" was my next question because, though she wore a loose white short-sleeved blouse, she definitely was taking on a womanly shape.

"I turned twelve in February. How old are you?" she asked, while swiveling towards me for the first time. Our elbows on the seat arm lightly touched.

"I'll be thirteen in December," I replied and thought, geez, she's almost as old as I am.

This fascinating discussion continued with many uneasy gaps while I frantically thought of other questions. I learned she was Italian, she disliked school, she liked the Roosevelt, she lived on Cooper street, and she didn't want to be a nun. When I told her I'd like to be a priest, it seemed her elbow pressure increased.

There was activity behind us. Red and Chuck lobbed popcorn in our direction, and her two friends giggled and, I thought, hissed from three rows back. When the hissing got louder we found out it wasn't hissing. They were saying, "Kiss 'er, kiss 'er, kiss 'er."

Other kids in our vicinity joined in the "kiss" chorus and Rosie whispered, "Should we?" as she leaned closer.

I flushed, nodded, and before figuring out where or if my arms should go around her or where or if I could touch any part of her body when our lips connected, she grabbed my shoulder and pulled me halfway into her seat. My one arm automatically went around her neck and the other across her body, my hand grasping her waist.

The kiss was long — longer than any I'd ever seen adults do in real life or in a movie's reel life. My heart thumped and body trembled. She must have given her lips a quick lick

227

before we started for they were damp and soft, and I figured that this wasn't the first lip-lock she ever put on a boy. I lost all thoughts of germs, though I kept my lips loosely closed. The kids behind us made mocking remarks — "When they comin' up for air?" and "Your minute's up!" — but Rosie and I ignored them. I discovered I loved passionate kissing and didn't want to quit.

When we gently disentangled our upper torsos we leaned back, held hands, and I stared blankly at the screen. When I calmed down and reality returned, along with steady breathing, I whispered, "Let's do it again."

"No, the movie's almost over," she said. "I'll see you next week. You have to get back to your friends."

I really didn't have to return to my friends, but I got a distinct impression a dismissal bell rang. I unsteadily left her after she promised to return to the same seat the following Saturday.

Chuck and Red did their best to tell everyone about the "Rosie and me" incident, and for several days I suffered much ribbing from acquaintances and family, who thought it a real hoot that I had a girlfriend. Ray asked intimate questions about how Rosie felt and how it affected me. I didn't get too specific when answering.

The following Saturday, Red, Chuck and I were joined by Joe and Ray on our Roosevelt trip. Ray said he wanted to see a great lover in action. The theater's inside lights were still on when we started down the aisle, and I saw Rosie with her two friends, so I led the way into a row of seats ten rows behind her, out of popcorn range. I figured the empty seat next to Rosie was reserved for me.

Ray asked, "Where is she?"

I told him I didn't know, but Red pointed and said, "There she is. The one with the black hair!"

Ray started making uncouth commentary that I didn't want to hear so when the lights dimmed and screen lit up I arose and joined Rosie. I sat down next to her and said, "Hi." (My opening hadn't improved in a week.)

We held hands, and it seemed better than the week before, with one exception. Ray sauntered down the aisle all the way to the screen, then sauntered back while staring at us with a wide leer. After that bit of unpleasantness the time with Rosie was wonderful. The screen dimmed during a night scene and we united in a long drawn-out kiss. This happened three times before she said, "You should go back to your friends. I don't want them to think I'm easy." I didn't tell her Ray already thought she was easy. I did get her promise to meet me again the following Saturday.

Walking home Ray noted, "You really got it made. She pays her own way into the show and lets you maul her." Then he asked, "Did you get your hand up her dress?"

When I told him "No" he remarked, "She's probably rotten to the core. Good to the Army, but rotten to the Corps." Since this was an old wartime joke, we all ignored him.

I had big plans. I told everyone remotely interested that I'd most likely get at least five kisses the next time I saw Rosie. She seemed to really admire me. I even planned to buy her popcorn or a candy bar if I could talk my mother out of extra money.

Thankfully, Ray didn't accompany us on our next Roosevelt trip. He sometimes got on my nerves. I knew if he came anywhere near Rosie he'd say something to ruin our romantic relationship. My mother gave Chuck and me an extra dime without too much begging, so I knew some-how the day would be perfect — no Ray and an extra dime to spend on Rosie!

Joe, Red, Chuck and I got our usual seats near the middle of the theater, and I waited for Rosie's appearance. The lights darkened, and the movie began with no sign of her.

It was an Andy Hardy movie. Mickey Rooney, who played Andy, became enamored with a lovely, sophisti-cated female while neglecting his faithful girlfriend Polly Benedict, played by Ann Rutherford, but Andy and Polly got back together at the movie's end. Andy didn't seem overly bright. I'd never have left Polly in the first place. With her long black hair and savory lips she reminded me of Rosie.

Resenting Andy Hardy came easily. He not only had Polly and a bevy of other attractive girls, but also a 1931 Model A Ford convertible coupe with a rumble seat. I would have given my left anything to be old enough to own and drive that car.

After a newsreel, cartoon and serial chapter, the second movie started. It starred a paunchy Gene Autry in tight pants, flowery shirt and dazzling gun belt, yodeling, singing songs and playing guitar — not my idea of a real cowboy. I preferred realistically dressed cowboys like Ken Maynard and especially Tom Mix, the only good guy who wore a black hat. When Gene started singing his second song, Red went to the lobby candy counter and returned with some good and bad news. The good news — he had spotted Rosie in the back row. The bad news — she was kissing another boy.

A sense of loss and anguish prevented me from saying more than, "Well, I didn't like her anyway." No one believed me.

Joe and Chuck left their seats, returned with candy bars and verified Rosie's presence but I had to see for myself. When I passed them, Rosie and her new boyfriend were staring at the screen. He was as hefty as Ray so I estimated his age to be at least fourteen. Why was Rosie with a kid that old? I wondered. Maybe he kisses better, I answered.

Returning to my seat I tried to concentrate on the movie. Gene continued strumming, singing, riding and shooting. It was an especially long movie, and I wished to be elsewhere.

On the walk home from the theater we cut through the alley between McClellan and Belvidere, passed behind the Murphy residence, and saw Pat and Jeanne in the backyard. Pat hailed us by asking how we liked the movies. Standing near the alley fence we described the Andy Hardy movie as okay and the Gene Autry one as terrible, although Chuck liked it. My depression abruptly changed to joy as Doris came out on her back porch, noticed us, walked over to the fence with her gorgeous flaxen hair shining in the afternoon sun, and gave me a sweet "Hello." I instantly forgot Roosevelt Rosie and returned her greeting with my biggest smile and a suave, "Hi, there."

Sadly, that was the extent of our conversation. Doris spent two minutes talking to Joe, spurring another bout of jealousy and disappointment. Twelve-year-old girls must like older guys, I thought. Mercifully Joe didn't appear too interested in Doris and broke off their conversation by saying, "We gotta get home." As we slowly continued down the alley I thought: This day hasn't turned out quite as well as planned.

A backyard gate unexpectedly flew open twenty feet in front of us and Laura appeared in all her hair-dyed loveliness. She had cut through a backyard from McClellan, heading home. She gave us a disdainful look, shut the gate and started down the alley. We silently trailed behind, admiring the grace of her carriage and sway of her hips (which is really a lot like the grace of her carriage).

What happened next, I can't explain. Perhaps it could be blamed on the day's frustrations, disappointments and secret pain, or maybe I experienced an innate wish to publicly recite poetry. Whatever the reason, I suddenly shouted, "Laura, the whora!"

I immediately realized that the world, and especially Laura, wasn't ready for my first attempt at rhyme, publicly or otherwise. She spun around glaring and shrieked, "Who said that?!"

A reasonable question, I ruminated, while gazing skyward, trying to appear like I enjoyed studying cloud formations. No one answered her question. They didn't have to. Joe, Red and Chuck were all staring at me in amazement.

Laura growled, "Why you little bastard!" and rushed at me. I had to admit her adroit use of the vernacular was quite impressive but could see this was no time to compliment her on it. A survival instinct took over my body as, whirling, I headed in the opposite direction. Garages on both sides of the alley blurred as I sprinted past. Realizing she had sturdy legs, I imagined hearing footsteps gaining on me and borrowed a Stepin Fetchit line, "Sneakers, don't fail me now!"

Reaching the alley mouth I turned left onto Cairney street and risked a quick glance behind me. She stood fifty feet away in the middle of the alley, fists on hips, glaring. I kept running until I got to Holcomb, then trotted home.

Red, Joe and Chuck came through our backyard and saw me sitting despondently on our back porch. Joe said, "We have a message from Laura," and they all started laughing.

When Joe was partially laughed out he gave me her message. "She said you tell — ha, ha, ha, — that little bastard —ha, ha, ha, — I'm going to — ha, ha, ha, — kill him when I catch him — ha, ha, ha, ha." Obviously Laura had some misgivings about my ancestry.

I looked at my unsympathetic laughing friends and concluded that some unfeeling people are amused by others' misfortunes. With Laura and the white terrier wishing me harm, much of Belvidere became absolutely dangerous.

We stayed away from Chandler school for a few days to let Laura cool down and played baseball in the alley behind Butlers' house. The alley was so narrow we could hone our timing and skill at hitting directly to center field. There was another advantage. When our timing was off we often hit the ball into backyards lining the alley and when retrieving it had opportunities to notice which neighbors had ripening fruit trees. We relayed this information, along with the baseball, to other players. If the cherries, apples, pears or plums appeared ready for harvest, we planned our fruit raid for after dark that evening. If it appeared that no one was at home, some casual harvesting might even take place along with ball retrieval.

The most convenient trees were ones growing partially over a garage. Once we gained the garage roof, either by an adjacent telephone pole or standing on the alley fence and pulling ourselves up by our elbows, we leisurely hid in branches and filled our brown paper bags or knickers.

Knickers served a useful purpose not generally known to parents. When stealing apples, pears, plums or peaches the wily knickers wearer could loosen his belt one notch and drop fruit into his pants. Each pant leg carried about a dozen of the ill-gotten fruits without noticeably hampering running speed if running became necessary.

If the tree stood in the middle of a yard we quietly entered through or over the alley gate, climbed the tree and started picking. This was more perilous. If a tree owner heard us we easily could be trapped. Ray said it happened to a kid in another neighborhood. The tree owner waited at the trunk until the kid came down, confiscated a bag of plums, gave the kid a kick and sent him home.

We had certain rules. Never hit the same tree more than twice and don't take so much fruit that it would be noticeable. We broke the rules only once when we discovered a yard with large, black, plump cherries that were so delicious we raided the tree three nights in succession. Each night I brought an extra bag of cherries home to my mother. We sat on our darkened front porch steps eating them and every once in awhile she worriedly asked, "Robert, are you sure the man said he didn't mind you picking his cherries?"

"Yeah, Ma, he really did." Joe, Red, Ray and Chuck would nod in agreement. Just in case, Mom probably said a silent Act of Contrition and a couple extra prayers while biting into the tasty fruit.

On the fourth night we found the owner had sneakily and selfishly stripped his tree of all cherries. The following year he bought a watchdog.

* * *

A twelve year old, Jerry Wolschon, lived directly across the alley from Butlers. He participated at times in our alley baseball games and fruit tree raids and was my classmate at Nativity. Underweight and a slow runner, he nevertheless was a nervy little guy who learned to hit well, though his fielding left something to be desired. He received good grades in school and nuns and students liked him. It was rumored he talked through clenched teeth because he had contracted lockjaw a few years before — an ailment brought on, according to medical expert Ray, by getting your body punctured with a rusty nail — and it affected his weight and height. (Forty-five years later, Jerry arranged a Nativity class reunion celebration and presided as emcee and chief speaker. During a lengthy speech, I wondered if a tiny lockjaw relapse might not be in order.)

Jerry had one of the best comic book collections in the city. His massive accumulation lined one side of his enclosed back porch in three-foot high stacks. Along with the usual collection of super heroes — Batman, Superman, Captain Marvel, Plastic Man, The Green Lantern, Flash, Human Torch, Sub-Mariner, Hawkman, Captain America and Blackhawk — his collection included comical comics like Archie, the Disney characters, Powerhouse Pepper, Little Lulu, Henry and Scribbly. He also had every Wonder Woman comic book ever printed. Except for her black hair and costume, she looked like sweet, even-tempered Laura and could rescue me anytime.

Jerry rarely traded comic books but allowed friends to borrow them or read them on his back porch. The rest of us traded with each other so much that the books became worn and tattered. We never knew if publishers realized they lost money because of this trading, but I'm sure any losses sustained were more that made up by selling advertisements on the back covers, especially the Charles Atlas ads.

Charles Atlas billed himself as the world's most perfectly developed man. A small comic strip in the ad depicted an event early in Charles' life when, as a 97-pound weakling, he took a lovely female acquaintance to a beach to bask in the sun and, presumably, her charms. A hand-

234

some, aggressive bully deliberately kicked sand in Charlie's skinny face causing him embarrassment and loss of his girlfriend to this bully. Soon after, he invented dynamic tension, a form of exercise that miraculously turned him into a powerfully-built Adonis. He returned to the beach some months later, punched the bully's chin and won back the girl's heart.

To become muscular like Mr. Atlas I just had to fill in a coupon, mail it with a small stipend, and he'd reveal the secret of dynamic tension. An actual picture of Mr. Atlas dominated the ad, and I really didn't think he looked as muscular or perfectly built as the comic book Captain America or comic strip Tarzan, but I seriously considered answering the ad. Maybe his tension program could at least make me look as good as the bully who had a girlfriend while Mr. Atlas spent lonely hours at home building up muscles and weight.

I mentioned my intentions to Ray. He laughed and said, "Don't waste your mother's money. Dynamic tension is pushing one hand against the other, like this," and he demonstrated. "This is supposed to develop your biceps. Push-ups do a better job. It's also lying on the floor on your back and pressing your legs against the wall to develop leg muscles. Knee-bends work faster. Then Atlas says in between this dynamic tension you should lift weights and he'll be glad to sell you some. It's a come-on, for chrisakes. Like I said, don't waste your mother's money."

I appreciated Ray's well-versed advice, but I wished that he would be a little less cynical about my financial resources.

* * *

Once or twice a week, throughout the hot months of summer, fruit and vegetable trucks traveled slowly past our houses. These trucks were roofed, but completely open on their sides, and were operated mainly by Italian gentlemen

235

with loud, resonant voices announcing the day's bargains. My mother loved corn-on-the-cob, as did we all, so when she heard the truck driver proclaim, "Alabama sweet corn — ten cents a dozen," she'd send one of her kids out to hail the truck with a "Hey, Mr. Fruit Man!" while she searched for her change purse. The driver would stop his truck, my mother would come out of our house, pick out two dozen ears of corn and then haggle for other fruits and vegetables, but her primary purpose was buying corn.

The only drawback to eating corn-on-the-cob at the supper table was watching brothers and sisters eat it. Dolores and Ann were especially sloppy; many half-chewed kernels ending up sticking to their nose, chin and forehead. No one at our table appeared too concerned about it, but I was, and in order to avoid looking as repugnant, every ten seconds I furtively ran my hand lightly over my mouth area to dislodge loose kernels.

Ed had another type of corn eating problem. His upper two front teeth were much farther apart than nature's law allows, so with each gnaw around the ear he left a row of kernels. When he arrived at the cob's end he went back and forth like a typewriter until all kernels were accounted for. Ed also knew how to play the harmonica.

I concluded the only way to enjoy corn-on-the-cob was to eat it in private. This is what I was doing one afternoon, sitting alone on our back porch steps, when Ray came into the backyard.

"You had corn for supper?" he asked.

It was obvious, so I nodded and continued gnawing, chewing and, because he now stood in front of me, furtively wiping my mouth.

"What did your mother do with the corn leaves?" he asked, lowering his voice.

"You mean all that green stuff wrapped around the corn?"

"Yeah."

"It's in the garbage. I took it out before we ate."

"C'mon. Let's go get it."

He still whispered, which piqued my interest. Ray only whispered when something was dirty or illegal, so I quickly finished my corn while we walked to the alley garbage container. Lifting the top steel door, I threw in the cob and pulled out the bag of corn shucks. Ray rummaged around in the bag and withdrew handfuls of corn silk.

"What the hell ya gonna do with that stuff?" I asked.

"We're gonna smoke it," he answered, "like cigarettes."

We carried gobs of silk into our garage and piled it on the cement floor. From the kitchen, Chuck noticed our activity and came out to investigate. Ray explained what we intended to do, and Chuck pulled a kitchen match from his pocket, scraped the tip along the cement floor and shoved the burning end into our pile. "This stuff won't burn," he said triumphantly, like a teacher giving a science lesson.

"I know it, for chrisakes, Ray snapped. "We have to dry it out for a few days in the sun. We have to find a place where your folks won't notice it, or they'll throw it away."

After rejecting four or five locations, Chuck came up with a perfect drying spot. We'd lay it out on the back porch roof outside our bedroom window, the same roof where we lofted and scuttled our model airplanes before Mom shot us down. Chuck and I jammed all the silk we could into our pants pockets, sneaked upstairs and spread it thinly on the roof.

For four full days we patiently let it bake and brown in the sun. Once, when it started to rain, I ran home from Chandler schoolyard to temporarily pull the silk into the bedroom to protect it. On the fifth day we were ready for our smoke-out.

Chuck and I transferred the silk from the roof back to our garage and with Ray, Joe and Red, we began manufacturing cigarettes. After rolling portions of the silk tightly in small squares of newspaper, we each stuck one end in our mouth and lit the other with a kitchen match.

Boys always carried wooden kitchen matches to the

237

dismay of parents who were afraid their sons would inadvertently start a major fire. We didn't worry about that happening since we were so intelligent and responsible. We did worry about the possibility of matches accidently igniting in our pants pocket. We heard this once happened to a boy at Nativity. The matches were in his back pocket and when he sat down they rubbed together and blazed up. The nun slapped the fire out before his immolation but, to his chagrin, he still had to doff his knickers. After hearing that story we always carried matches in side pockets. When passing alone through the kitchen, we automatically grabbed a handful from the box sitting on the gas stove. They seemed to beckon to us and say, "Grab us. We're fun," and they were. You could build miniature houses with them that resembled log cabins, hold them loosely in your fingers and slam them hard onto the sidewalk to ignite them, and, of course, light the ends of corn silk cigarettes.

We sat around in a circle, like Indians at a war council, sucking in smoke, quickly blowing it out and lying to each other about how great it tasted. In reality it tasted and smelled like burning newspapers, newsprint and corn. With varying degrees of success and laughter, we all tried blowing smoke through our noses and blowing smoke rings. We all agreed to start saving silk anytime we had corn for dinner because smoking was daring and fun. No one tried to inhale.

Later that week Ray took me over to a small store named Momo's located on McClellan in the midst of residential dwellings near Chandler schoolyard. It was an oasis for tired and sweaty children who had played baseball or other schoolyard games and needed a cooling soft drink, Popsicle or ice cream cone. If kids needed to replenish energy the proprietor sold them potato chips, peanuts and candy bars. I'd been in the store many times, but with Ray it became a different experience. I discovered the owner sold a small pack of ten Sunshine cigarettes for ten cents. If you didn't have a dime he'd break open the pack and sell you one cigarette for two cents. Ray bought a couple, and we went home, hid out in our garage and experimented with real cigarettes. We even tried inhaling. It was lung searing, dizzying and breathtaking, but I knew I'd try them again. I especially liked the dizzy feeling.

Now that I occasionally wore long pants and smoked, I had no doubt I'd soon be an adult. Before long I'd be shaving and drinking coffee, maybe even drinking beer, which would make me happy and uninhibited enough to loudly sing "My Wild Irish Rose," much like my dad.

* * *

The Swartz family moved into a house four doors from us and they had two sons, Carl and Kenneth. Carl was fourteen years old, 5'5" tall and weighed 160 pounds. He had straight black hair, a ruddy complexion and, though overweight, had calves and thighs solid enough to carry excess poundage. In contrast, his brother Kenneth, though weighing the same, was four inches taller, two years older, had a pale complexion, wavy sandy-colored hair and wore horn-rimmed glasses, which instantly marked him as intellectual. He was smart, but what made him stand out was his woodworking ability; something his parents must have recognized since their basement work bench contained an array of tools.

Ken endeared himself to the neighborhood boys by building a homemade scooter for his brother. The scooter featured two lengths of 2-by-4 wood nailed together at a right angle forming an L-shaped vehicle not unlike a regular scooter. For strength he nailed two triangular-shaped brace boards on both sides where the wood intersected. He dismantled a steel roller skate by removing the shoe clamps, ankle strap and chunk of hard-rubber from between its front wheels, separated the back-wheel from the front-wheel section and nailed them near each end of the scooter's bottom. For handles, he nailed a sanded, wooden strip to the top of the vertical 2-by-4, and Carl had a handsome, homemade scooter.

It created a sensation. When we saw its simple construction the neighborhood resounded with pounding nails and hounding wails, the wails from sisters who wanted brothers severely punished for roller skate conversion. Many girls were reduced to angrily pushing themselves along the sidewalk on one skate while their brothers happily raced in the street on newly-made scooters. My sister Dolores lost both her skates when Chuck and I built our scooters.

To make scooters distinctive and colorful we nailed orange, red and green pop bottle caps to their front and sides. The corner store proprietor, who had a pop bottle- and ice-filled cooler with an opener on its side and a good-sized bottle cap catcher beneath, provided us with all caps needed. Ray and Joe replaced their vertical 2-by-4s with orange crates giving themselves a double shelf to carry things and more scooter to paint and decorate, but I personally didn't like the effect. Their crate scooters were cumbersome, bulky and aerodynamically inferior with more wind-resistance, a slow bomber compared to my speedy pursuit plane.

We found another decorative use for discarded bottle caps. Using our pocket knives, we carefully dug out the thin circle of cork inside the caps, placed the caps against our shirt fronts and, from inside our shirts, pressed the corks back into their caps. After we all roamed Holcomb for a few days looking absurd with orange, lime, cherry, Pepsi-Cola, Coca-Cola, root beer and ginger-ale pop bottle caps stuck to our shirts, Ray topped us all, so to speak. He stole one of his dad's old fedoras, cut off the brim, removed the hat band and lining, notched and folded up the edges, and attached dozens of caps. Triumphantly showing off his masterpiece, he called it his pop's pop bottle cap cap. His Pop would never have recognized it.

Ken Swartz turned us onto another homemade toy. After watching us play a game of "guns" with the resultant "You missed me, you only got me in the arm, heads don't count" arguments, he suggested using rubber guns. They would eliminate any questions concerning if, or where, we were shot. He took all players into his basement and with a scissors carefully cut an old bicycle innertube into half-inch wide bands. This was our ammunition, he explained, although they looked like oversized red rubber bands. He sawed a foot-long piece off an old broomstick to use as a gun barrel and cut two oblong shaped pieces of half-inch thick hardwood to a 2-by-5 inch size to use as a gun butt.

He carefully nailed the extreme top portion of an oblong piece to one end of the barrel. It now resembled a crude gun. He lined up the remaining oblong piece over the one nailed to the barrel, held them together by wrapping two innertube bands tightly around both pieces near the barrel and slipped a two-inch piece of wood the thickness of a pencil stub horizontally between them. The oblong pieces were now held tightly together at the top and, because of the pencil-thin wood in the middle, open at the bottom.

He loaded the gun by slipping an innertube band over the barrel end, stretched it until it reached the butt section, squeezed the butt bottom which, because of leverage, opened the top, and pushed about a half-inch of rubber into the gap. He relaxed his grip and the top clamped down on the half-inch of rubber. The gun was primed to fire.

He squeezed the lower butt section releasing the band and it sailed the basement length, smacking against the opposite wall. We were delighted. He made two more guns before we all went home to talk our mothers into buying new brooms. We didn't tell them why we wanted the old brooms, just that we wanted to make something, because mothers loved that we made stuff but weren't too fond of the word "gun." Every boy on the block built at least two rubber gun pistols.

Chuck and I didn't own bikes so we depended on others for an ammunition supply, but all bike owners had a few overpatched innertubes hanging from nails in their garages.

241

With the ongoing war, an innertube shortage developed, so old ones weren't readily discarded. Cliff mentioned that he had a couple old innertubes somewhere in his garage, but no one volunteered to search for them, figuring they were probably hidden under a mass of antiques or junk.

Joe and Red cut up a couple of their most patched ones and gave Chuck and me a dozen rubber bands each. I found a seldom-used belt in my Dad's closet and looped my extra ammunition onto it before tying it loosely around my waist and, with three loaded guns stuffed inside the belt, I knew I resembled a South American bandito.

We started gun games from our front porch, choosing up sides. One side disappeared, hiding somewhere on the block, while the other side counted to one-hundred, then searched for them, sort of a violent hide-and-go-seek. The boys who got shot had to return to our porch and await the next game. There were ambushes and shoot-outs and heads counted. We shot each other from garage roofs, trees, bushes and porches. Cliff once used a half-empty garbage container for concealment, thrilling Mrs. Combs when he walked into his house that evening for supper.

The clacking noise of homemade scooters, the muted splat of innertube rubber striking bodies, the shouts and glee of high-spirited boys filled these precious summer days. There was also an uneasy, almost foreboding, feeling among us that these enjoyable boyhood games were winding down, that possibly, in a year or two, our preoccupations would change and we'd consider these games "kid stuff." We'd soon be older guys, like Ken, who showed kids how to build toys, yet didn't play himself. I strongly suspected this feeling had something to do with girls.

XX

As I grew in weight and stature and neared teenage status my attitude toward girls changed. Earlier in life I became aware that females were smarter, in school and out, and their composure, appearance and self-confidence caused boys and men to act and talk differently. Not wanting to act and talk differently, I avoided them whenever possible. Now I made a conscious effort to be where they'd be, except in the case of Laura. I still loved looking at her, but far from mutilation range.

After the unrequited, passing passions for darling Doris and Roosevelt Rosie, other affections were developing, and age didn't matter as long as they were twelve years old or older. While sitting on Butler's front porch I'd hope no one suggested any games that would take us away from the vicinity because Red and Joe's sisters, Mary Jane or Gladys, might make brief appearances. On these occasions, they'd emerge from the front door, greet us, then walk briskly toward either Gratiot or Chapin, and I'd feel my day fulfilled. Mary Jane was sixteen, Gladys, thirteen, older than I; yet their presence roused warm, pleasant feelings.

Catherine Kaltz had the same effect on me. She lived across the alley, one yard over. We were the same age and in the same grade at Nativity. She was pretty, quiet, studious and saintly. During the school year, when attending morning Mass, she never missed receiving communion and even went to church and communion during vacation weekdays. She was one of very few students who deliberately sought out Father Geller's confessional, and she'd be in and out in a fast minute-and-a-half. She looked like the perfect-featured saints illustrated in religion books. She wore her straight, brown hair parted in the middle, sometimes in one or two braids but often hanging unencumbered straight down her back, well below her waist. This made her hair resemble a veil, and I readily imagined her developing a stigmata in a cloister or leading a French army against the English and, later, smiling at tormentors while being burned at the stake. She had a bedazzling smile, and on one occasion turned it on me. It happened in the alley as I passed her backyard. The smile, accompanied by a melodious "Hello" as she dumped a bag of garbage, caused my tongue to dry and swell, heart to accelerate and kneecaps turn to pulp. I returned her greeting with an involuntary, short, high-pitched noise. She smiled more broadly and turned back to her house.

I quietly muttered, "goddamnit," and concluded I needed more close association with a variety of girls to learn the technique of effective communication. I only had to finish one more year at Nativity, the ninth grade for boys had been discontinued two years previously, so after the eighth grade I'd have a choice, according to my mother, of two high schools, both requiring a daily Gratiot streetcar ride towards downtown. One was Saint Joseph's, an all-boy school taught by a religious order of Brothers. The other was Saint Anthony's, a co-ed school taught by nuns. Ed hadn't fared too well at Cass Tech so I didn't have a third, public school choice.

I chose Saint Anthony, not only because I yearned to be with girls, but also I didn't need any religious Brothers pounding on me. I had heard some were almost as intolerant as Father Geller. But first I had to get through Nativity.

Returning to Nativity's flats to start eighth grade depressed me. Our nun, Sister Mary Leocadia, a tall gaunt woman who wore a scowl and brooked no unauthorized student remarks or actions, portended another year with few joyful moments. For this last Nativity school year my mother had kept her promise and bought me another pair of long pants for school and also a too-large, double-breasted suit, "just in case you grow and graduate from the eight grade" she said humorously. She had more faith than I did.

Ed also got a new suit, and we finally got a service flag for our front window when he enlisted in the Navy. After going-away parties with going-away gifts, including a silver cameo ring and a shock-proof, water-proof military wristwatch (if you were blown-up or drowned your watch kept ticking), he left by train for Idaho's Farragut Naval Training Base on September 18th. I knew such a talented harmonica player would be successful and appreciated in the Navy because everyone who'd seen war movies knew the harmonica sound boosted the morale of lonely, home-sick servicemen.

Ed's Navy enlistment created lively discussions between Red and me concerning which service contributed most to the war effort. Red, with his older brother Frank in the Army, believed the Army did most of the fighting and winning. We both avidly scanned newspapers for details of Army and Navy victories to use in our ongoing "service superiority" arguments. Every time hundreds of Flying Fortresses bombed Germany or France, Red gloated that the Army Air Corps had struck again. He emphasized "Army." These air raids happened two or three times a week, and I imagined the Germans had lots of sand buckets in their attics. Red also cited the Army's land victories in Sicily. I, on the other hand, bragged about Japanese ships, planes and bases destroyed by our Naval forces, and Japanese islands invaded by Marines, a branch of the Navy. Whenever Red seemed to be besting me in our Army/Navy dispute I had a simple way to silence him. A popular song entitled *They're Either Too Young or Too Old* had one line:

"What's good is in the Army; the rest will never harm me," that I paraphrased to, "What's good is in the Navy; what's left is in the Army." It wasn't very inventive and didn't rhyme, but when I sang it it irritated old Red. He was aware much of the Army consisted of draftees while the Navy, made up of mostly volunteers, chose the best. Arguments aside, we were both very proud that each of our families had contributed a serviceman.

Meanwhile, on the home front, even the United States mint acquired patriotism. To save copper, it issued pennies made of steel with a zinc coating. These coins were a dull silver color and everyone in the country with larcenous hearts tried to figure out how to pass them off as dimes. Some succeeded.

Overseas, U.S. troops, after sweeping through Sicily, invaded Italy, and the German army was their sole resistance. The Italian soldiers tripped over themselves trying to surrender. The soldiering ability of the Italian army became the subject of jokes on radio and in print. One comic said, "I know where there are Italian rifles for sale...like new. Some have only been dropped in the mud once or twice." I couldn't understand this because it seemed that all Italian boys I met wanted to fight. Mussolini, the Italian dictator, should have recruited his soldiers from our neighborhood. You couldn't walk down the street alone without Italian kids challenging you with their favorite words, "Hey, ya wanna fight?" Three times I said "sure" and three times ended up with a bleeding nose and tear-filled eyes.

After that I'd say, "Why would I wanna fight? I don't know ya." I recoiled from any violence which could lead to the loss of my teeth, blood, equilibrium or consciousness.

They'd say, "'Cause we don't like your looks."

Luckily my looks included two fast legs, and I rarely met a kid my age who could outrun me.

* * *

246

As days got shorter, nights cooler and Halloween neared, we started planning prank strategy. Ringing doorbells was fun but we wanted something that created a little more adult aggravation; so Ken Swartz showed us how to make a ticktack, a device that, when used correctly, frightened or enraged the most even-tempered individuals. It was made using a wooden spool of thread (with thread removed), a long flat-headed nail and a length of cord. With a pocket-knife, we cut notches around both spool ends, wound the cord around the spool and inserted the nail all the way through the spool hole so a good portion extended out the other end.

Ticktacks were perfect for dark, chilly, peaceful evenings when people settled in warm, lighted living rooms for a pleasant relaxing time reading newspapers or listening to Fibber McGee and Molly, Bob Hope, Red Skelton or Henry Aldrich on the radio. We chose only lighted living rooms with shades partially raised for we had to see our victims' reactions to fully appreciate the ticktack attack. Living room windows were ideal, not only because that's where families gathered after supper, but also because the windows usually were adjacent to front porches we could stand on, enabling us to get as near as possible to the windows and survey the tranquil scene inside. It never occurred to us that we were guilty of Peeping Tomism until Ray mentioned it. He complained, "If we're going to get caught looking through windows, let's look through bedroom windows."

Once we silently gained the porch, gazed through the window and were satisfied no one inside was aware of our scrutiny, one of us placed the ticktack gently, but firmly, against the window pane, held onto the extended nail, grasped the cord end with his other hand and jerked it with all his strength. This caused the spool notches to spin and slam into the glass at terrific speed setting off an ear-piercing clatter.

People inside always reacted the same. Their heads swung toward the window, eyes wide, mouths agape. Our reactions also never varied. We leaped over porch railings or took steps two at a time, gathering at a predetermined, concealed spot to laughingly compare descriptions of what we'd just witnessed. After all the hilarity died down, we'd select our next victim. No one ever suggested his own house.

Another homemade scare device was fashioned from two empty tin cans and a length of string. The tin cans, retrieved from alley garbage containers, had to have their jagged open tops still attached. The string ends were tied to the can tops with enough string between to cover the width of a sidewalk. After dark the cans were placed upright just beyond each side of a selected section of walk with the string stretched taut between. We lightly covered the cans with fallen leaves and waited innocently on porch steps for pedestrians to trip the string resulting in cans rattling around their ankles. The unexpected noise usually elicited mild profanity. For a stronger response, we filled the cans with water.

* * *

In mid-November Ed arrived home on a fifteen-day leave. He had gained weight after eight weeks of boot camp and family and friends chided him about how well he filled out his uniform. Too soon he had to return to The War, and with aching smiles and tearful hugs we bid him farewell, knowing he'd be gone for a long time.

Ed was on the winning side according to newspapers and newsreels. German cities were bombed daily, sometime in thousand-plane formations; Marines invaded and occupied the Gilbert Islands with heavy casualties on both sides; Japanese ships and planes were destroyed in raids on other Japanese-held islands; the Russian army stopped the German advances; Allied armies were slowly breaking through the German defenses in Italy; and headlines blared a tongue-twister: Patton Slaps A Shell-shocked Soldier!

In keeping with the state of the world, rather than the spirit of the approaching season, Chuck and I both requested war toys for Christmas.

Chuck received a small, metal pursuit plane, a set of twenty plastic soldiers and a heavy cardboard fort with tabs and slots. When assembled the fort was a formidable, two-tiered structure with a stone block appearance, standing about a foot wide and ten-inches high. The plastic soldiers wore brown uniforms and black helmets, the sort worn by British and American World War One soldiers, and all aimed rifles from standing or kneeling positions on green bases.

I received a flat box containing thin cardboard sheets imprinted with left and right sides of thirty American soldiers. Each soldier had to be punched out, folded over and positioned in a slotted base. These were modern American soldiers with pot helmets, khaki uniforms, ammunition belts and canvas leggings. Some charged with fixed bayonets, but most fired rifles from standing, kneeling or prone positions. Included were two machine gunners and an officer pointing a .45 automatic. The standing soldiers stood three inches tall, a half-inch taller than Chuck's plastic soldiers.

I also received a box of thin cardboard cut-outs with tabs and slots that folded into a battleship, two cruisers and two destroyers. They had hulls, superstructures, gun mounts, masts and smoke stacks. When assembled they were flat-bottomed and resembled an armada in dry dock on top of my bedroom chifforobe.

I waited patiently, and when Chuck became tired of playing with his fort and soldiers, I quietly confiscated them, set up the fort in an uncluttered corner of our bedroom and filled it with the plastic soldiers, who now represented Germany. Their guns stuck out of every bulwark, rampart, tower and embrasure. I'd use my American cardboard soldiers to attack the German fortress.

I rounded up twenty-five rubber bands from different

drawers and doorknobs and positioned my men for a charge.

From behind the Americans I shot all my rubber bands at the fort and knocked down two Germans. I gathered the rubber bands and, from behind the fort, shot back at the charging Americans and hit four. I was getting to be a sharpshooter; not bad from a seven-foot distance.

Moving the Americans closer, I continued firing, this time picking off three more Germans. They spun around and fell to the fort floor. I felt like Gary Cooper in the Sergeant York movie. From a lofty post on the edge of my bed an American sniper did a lot of damage to the fort below, but the Germans regrouped and, after three unsuccessful shots, the sniper was hit. He dropped to the floor screaming, like a Japanese sniper in the movie Bataan.

As the battle raged, and my accuracy improved with each rifle exchange, I almost ran out of charging soldiers. So I changed the rules. If a soldier fell on his right side he was only wounded and could return to battle. Subconsciously, my aim suffered when shooting for the Germans, so there always were more American survivors at battle's end.

There were two dangers in this game. Shooting required that I loop one end of a rubber band around my left thumb tip, draw back the other end squeezed between my right thumb and forefinger, aim and release. At times my left thumb knuckle inadvertently interfered with a smooth, unencumbered rubber band flight and received a stinging blow from the band. At other times the band broke when sighting along its length resulting in a portion snapping back into my open eyeball causing excruciating pain, bright yellow and red flashing light behind my abruptly closed eyelid, and salty tears. But, however painful, I realized this is war and war is rough.

I played this game often, once talking Chuck into shooting for the German army, but, after a time, he said he preferred playing snow games outside. "A snowball smashing my mouth is better than a rubber band smashing my eye," he added.

The snow was deep that year providing opportunities for snowball fights, snow forts and snowmen. I created a five-foot tall snowman that actually resembled a man. He stood in our backyard like he waited to cross a street, wearing a topcoat and tie, with one hand in his pocket and the other holding a leash attached to a small snowdog sitting at his side. The only part of both figures not made of snow was the leash, fashioned from two thin belts commandeered from my sisters' bedroom.

Mom admired my creation and said, "Someday you'll be a sculptor," words that made me wonder anew what I'd be when I grew up. Most of my schoolmates and acquaintances didn't brood about it. They wanted to get well into high school before choosing their life's work.

Chuck, Red and I found a new, semi-exciting diversion to occupy us on a cold, snowy, late afternoon. Soon after celebrating New Year's people untrimmed Christmas trees and tossed them out in the alley where the trees patiently pined while awaiting the arrival of city dump trucks to cart them away. As we walked home through our alley, complaining about the cold, I suggested we warm up the vicinity by burning one of these dried-out trees. Chuck and Red thought it a sterling idea and we pulled a large spruce to the middle of the alley. I shoved a lighted kitchen match into its branches and an amazing blaze spread so rapidly and reached such heights we staggered backward to avoid a scorching. The heat felt wonderful as we removed our snow-soaked gloves, warming numbed fingers. This was the best idea I ever had.

In too short a time the fire died, and the sooty, charred remnants though still smoking emitted no warmth. The weather seemed colder than before the blaze, so we kicked the tree over to the alley's edge and looked around for another to burn as we walked toward home.

Some trees weren't dry enough and some were too small.

We burned a three-footer, and it blazed and died before we remembered to get our gloves off. As we neared home we noticed Combs' tree reclining against their garage. It was a perfect candidate — a dry, brittle scotch pine. We moved it to the alley's center and applied a match.

We watched silently, ecstatically. Flames roared and soared, flicked and licked, threatening to singe our clothes and eyebrows.

As the crackling fire diminished, Chuck and I heard Mom calling our names from the back porch. Chuck ran over to our gate and returned to say she wanted us for supper. Red said, "Yeah, I'm getting hungry too. I'll see you guys," and he took off running.

"Are you coming, Robbie?" Chuck asked.

"Sure, as soon as the fire's out," I told him. I was never in a hurry to eat, but when I did I liked to eat fast and get on with life.

Chuck departed and I stood in the alley alone as the flames burned down and snuffed themselves out. It was suddenly cold, gloomy, quiet.

After a time I grew impatient with drearily staring at the blackened skeleton of the smoldering tree and began throwing handfuls of loose snow on it. I booted it back toward the garage, tossed a few more handsful of snow on it to smother any wisps of escaping smoke, then ran for home. A half-hour later I heard the approaching fire sirens.

It was a glorious fire attracting a large segment of the neighborhood population. Flames shot from the Combs' garage roof and some items inside didn't burn cleanly for thick black smoke billowed and rolled skyward mingling with low, dark clouds. One fire truck sat in front of Combs' house, another in the alley, its headlights lighting the scene as deft firemen manipulated hose and axes. It only took fifteen minutes to control the fire, but by then the garage's roof and alley doors had collapsed. All non-metallic items inside were destroyed. I watched the firefighting activity from my backyard, shivering, not just from cold but also from dread. There was a distinct possibility some vigilant neighbor saw our earlier bonfire actions and might assume we were involved in this conflagration.

The next morning I stood with Cliff in the alley shaking my head as we looked at the shell of his family's garage. The three walls still standing were propped up with wooden beams. Furniture, appliances, toys, dishes and sundry other items stored within had taken on a decidedly blackened hue. "Have they figured out what started it?" I asked.

"Nah, but it coulda been anything. Someone in a car going through the alley coulda flipped a cig, or maybe a spark from someone's chimney. It coulda been anything."

"Yeah," I said. "It was probably a chimney spark."

Chuck and Red never made a connection between our tree burning and the garage fire, or at least we never discussed it. Three months later Mr. Combs had his garage razed and the whole charred mess hauled away. It didn't seem prudent to mention to Cliff or anyone else that I might have been responsible for the destruction of his garage and its contents. I didn't ask Cliff, but I sincerely hoped his family had a hefty insurance policy for they must have lost a thousand dollars worth of antiques and other valuables. Then again — maybe five dollars worth of junk.

XXI

Soon after Christmas vacation Sister Leocadia startled the class by announcing what many considered good news. Nativity High School would become co-educational. Any eighth-grade boy wishing to continue a Nativity education should discuss it with his parents and, if they approved, register for the September freshman class. We discussed it with our fellow students first.

Jerry Wygocki, a big, blond, good-looking boy, said his mind was made up. He intended to attend St. Joe's because of its traditionally good academics and football team. He was one of few. The majority of our class elected to remain at Nativity. When I told my mother the news she was overjoyed. She hadn't relished paying for my daily streetcar fare to St. Anthony's.

I noticed something. The subtle changes in my body and a drastic change in voice were accompanied by a change in personality and values. No longer did I strive for high report card marks — Bs and Cs were acceptable — and I was more outspoken in class, a typical rapscallion; although Sister Leocadia probably thought the words "incorrigible obnoxious nork" more appropriate. I was regularly detained after school to write 200 times "I will be quiet in class" or "I will not interrupt class."

After one such infraction a fed-up Sister Leocadia called me to the front of class and, after a warning to keep my arms at my sides, gave me a face slap that propelled me through the cloakroom doorway. It reminded me that Father Geller would soon be passing out report cards, and maybe my devilish ways should be toned down.

With much toning in the following weeks I managed a C-minus in Study and Courtesy. When Father Geller handed me my card I could see he was measuring me for one of his famous slapshots as he firmly suggested, "Get the Courtesy and Study marks up, Robert." That's when I made up my mind to be an altar boy.

I'd been thinking about it seriously for months. Pat, Mary and their girlfriends were uniform crazy, raving about servicemen on leave and even sacrilegiously raving about how cute Nativity's young priests looked in their cassocks. Maybe girls my age would be attracted to a young boy in a cassock. It was worth a try. With my huge pompadour — kept in place by using gobs of pure Vaseline that added an appealing luster —I already looked respectable. Memorize a few Latin prayers, and I'd have soon-to-be-freshman girls pursuing me. Furthermore, Father Geller rarely slapped saintly altar boys.

Father Wolbur was in charge of altar boy training. He made out the weekly serving schedule that religiously appeared every Sunday in the church paper, The Nativity News, and taught new altar boys the correct pronunciation of Latin prayers and their duties during high and low masses.

I had talked Stellon into joining with me and was surprised how quickly he learned these prayers. He explained that Latin was similar to the Italian language his parents spoke at home. We memorized the prayers together and soon felt confident enough to tell Father Wolber we were ready to serve our first Mass.

Father Wolber felt differently so he assigned us to serve with a couple veteran altar boys at three successive 6 a.m.

masses. Bill and I had little to do except stand, kneel, pray, watch and learn.

The next week we were on our own. The 6 a.m. Mass went by swiftly in a flurry of prayers, moving a large open book from one altar end to the other, pouring water and wine over the priest's fingers, lifting the priest's chasuble, genuflecting, ringing bells, holding patens under communicants' chins and trying to remember what to do next. My only major mistake was ringing the bell at the wrong time resulting in a glare from Father Burroughs, one of the young priests my sisters thought "cute," and a grin from Stellon. Fortunately the pews at this early mass weren't filled with young maidens witnessing my humiliation. Instead the sparse attendance consisted of black-shawled widows and a sprinkling of religious devotees going to Mass before work.

My mother, pleased that I became an altar boy, willingly purchased the required black sneakers. We wore them when serving Mass to muffle noise, but the chief reason was that other footwear left nasty black scrape marks on the sanctuary's marble steps and floor, enraging the nun assigned the daily task of keeping it dusted and mopped. In an alcove of the sacristy where we donned cassocks and albs stood a wooden, pigeonholed cabinet for sneaker storage, the logic being that each altar boy would have his sneakers available for mass at all times. The cabinet wasn't locked. Some altar boys, who failed to take seriously the "Thou shalt not steal" Commandment, wore worn-out sneakers to church and went home with new ones. I only used my new sneakers three times before they disappeared, or "took-a-hike" in my case. After that I grabbed any old pair that fit.

Mom sometimes accompanied me to church when I served these early morning Masses. She implied that the time I spent on the altar side of the communion rail enjoying the closeness to God might prod me to consider a priestly vocation. She watched me piously perform the altar boy duties and dreamed that someday, in answer to her prayers, she'd proudly watch me, dressed in clerical vestments, celebrate my first mass. It never happened. I felt the word "celebrate" sounded too much like "celibate."

* * *

Ed was stationed in San Diego, California, where he graduated as a Medical Corpsman. The Navy assigned him to a Marine battalion, putting him in a unique position of having a choice between wearing a Navy or Marine uniform. He sent Mom a tinted, glossy photograph of himself wearing the Marine dress uniform, and she placed it in our living room next to his Navy photograph. When I showed Red the new picture he said Ed looked like a bellhop — an envious reaction I ignored.

Ed hinted in a letter that he'd be going overseas, so I assumed he'd soon be fighting the "Nips," a kindly word used to describe our Japanese enemy. I read the letter over and over trying to figure out if he included a secret code to tell us his destination, for military mail was heavily censored. I tried using the first letter of each sentence but it came out IWITDBH. Even Japanese islands didn't have names that bizarre. I concluded Ed didn't know his destination either. It disappointed me because there were patriotic posters in most business places in town and one depicted a sinking, burning ship with the words, "Loose Lips Might Sink Ships." I longed to know the sailing schedule and destination of Ed's transport ship to give me a patriotic opportunity not to tell anyone.

A three-week period went by when Ed failed to write, which worried Mom. We finally received a letter in March. He was safely stationed in Hawaii enjoying sand, sun, surf, poi, hula dancing, grass skirts and leisurely leis. Old Ed was stuck on an island with thousands of beckoning, nubile maidens. Military life had redeeming features.

* * *

When eighth-grade graduation loomed, the classroom became more relaxed. Sister Leocadia even smiled at times although I believe it hurt parts of her face. I imagined her thinking, "Soon I'll be rid of these ruffians and hooligans for three glorious months. I hope my next class has more class." Now that our relationship would soon end I sympathized with her.

* * *

There was uplifting news from Europe. Allied armies captured Rome without blowing up the Vatican and other religious treasures. Four months before, following much soul searching and a long stalemate with the German army dug into the Alban Hills high ground, American generals decided to bomb the ancient Benedictine monastery of Monte Cassino, suspecting it harbored an artillery-directing observation post. After air strikes leveled the historic edifice, it was discovered that there weren't any German soldiers in or around the monastery, angering Italians and Catholics worldwide. But you can't argue with success. Our pilots received bombing practice, our army broke through at Cassino and now had captured the Holy City.

Two days later, D-day, United States, British and Canadian troops invaded Normandy and thousands of paratroopers landed behind German lines. Hitler's days were numbered.

* * *

Eighth-grade graduation ceremonies were held in the church after mass on the last day of school. All boys wore suits, some with ties, others with sport shirt collars open at the neck and neatly folded over suit coat collars. Girls wore their favorite Sunday dresses, mostly white, with ribbons and barrettes in their hair. Nobody wore lipstick.

259

Father Geller, standing at the communion rail, called our names and handed us diplomas. He then gave an eloquent speech directed at those who chose to attend other high schools, entreating them to: set a moral example for others, remember moral lessons learned at Nativity and be moral the rest of their lives or be damned and burn in hell forever through eternity. For the rest of us who would continue our education at Nativity, he offered congratulations for our wisdom and assured us he would always be there to discipline and guide us on the righteous path to our heavenly reward. I suddenly felt I should have enrolled at Saint Anthony's. On this cheerful note the ceremony ended.

We returned to our classrooms to pick up final report cards, graduation pictures and any personal items in our desks and gathered with parents in front of the main school building for picture posing and the I'll-see-you-next-year good-byes to our classmates who were returning to Nativity and "Good luck" and "You lucky guy" remarks for those who weren't. The school year was over, and we gradually drifted home.

Only one student in our eighth-grade graduating class ever gained anything close to local celebrity status. He was a light-haired, dimpled kid named Peter Waldmeir who voluntarily stayed after school a lot. When I involuntarily stayed, sentenced to write "I will not—" sentences, he cleaned erasers by clapping them together out on the flat's back porch or washed blackboards with wet rags. I thought it strange that he deliberately spent a second more than required in a schoolroom. At lunch hour, when warm spring days arrived, about twenty boys in our class often rushed to the empty field adjoining Nativity's recreation building for a quick game of slowpitch softball. One of the students who lived near the field, provided a softball and bat. We didn't use gloves. Pete sometimes joined us, and we quickly learned right field was commensurate with his ballplaying ability. Most batters were right-handed and usually hit the ball to left field so the worst fielders were assigned right field. It amused us to watch Pete try to cruise under a fly ball. He'd take a few steps out, then start running in toward the infield and the ball would fall ten feet behind him. He also misplayed ground balls. Left-handers had a distinct advantage when playing against Pete. Hitting the ball past infielders into right field assured a triple or home run.

Pete didn't continue at Nativity, instead choosing to attend Denby, a public high school on Detroit's northeast side. Three years later I heard Pete was writing a sports column for Denby's school paper. This information astonished me because, at the time, I assumed you had to be adept at sports before you could write authoritatively about them. I later learned that most writers, if they played ball at all, played right field.

A few more years passed, and I became more astonished when Pete got a job writing about college sports for a local newspaper. After a time this newspaper, The Detroit News, gave him his own by-lined sports column. He was mildly successful, but one day an observant person in Detroit News management determined that perhaps sports wasn't Pete's strong point, and they offered him an opportunity to write a general interest column instead. He wisely accepted.

As with most general interest columns, many of Pete's were thought-provoking and many weren't, but he did get a reputation as a hard-hitting, plain-spoken, opinionated pundit. He sometimes employed descriptive street language in his columns about city crime, words like "Jacktown" for the state prison in Jackson, Michigan; "slammer" for a prison cell; "copper" for policeman; "beef" for complaint; and "dude" for a street gentleman. He wrote columns about his family, friends, politics and city problems. Infrequently he even wrote derisive comments about his old grade school and Father Geller, possibly forgetting that Nativity was where he learned to spell, punctuate and diagram sentences.

Detroiters elected a new mayor in 1973 and the complex-

261

ion of city government changed. Pete Waldmeir was the first writer from either of Detroit's two major newspapers to mention in his column that all wasn't well in the new city government.

Through subsequent years, Pete's popularity increased as he continued to expose and publicize the follies and irregularities in Detroit's city administration as appropriation money disappeared, food rotted in warehouses, accountants stopped counting, police arrested police, and buses ran backwards.

Pete may have slowed the city's decline by forcing administrators to ask: "If I'm wrong, how will this decision appear written up in Waldmeir's column?" It's a theory which, if true, proves that you can have triumphs in life, even though, as a youngster, you aren't sure whether a baseball is blown up or stuffed.

XXII

A young couple moved in three doors from us. They both worked an afternoon shift, he as a policeman, she as a factory worker, and they kept to themselves, neither friendly nor unfriendly, according to Carl Swartz, their next door neighbor. I thought it nice to have a policeman, Mr. Combs, on one side of us two doors away and another on our other side, three doors away. It gave me a secure feeling to know that two of Detroit's finest, the keepers of peace, law and order and the scourge of criminals, were within a stone's throw of our house.

One week into summer vacation I sat alone on our back porch steps after playing baseball all morning. It was a sunny, early afternoon, and I lazily pondered how the rest of the day should be spent. A brilliant idea struck me. I'd sit on our garage roof and wave to Catherine if she happened to take out garbage. She'd probably be awed by my roof-sitting casualness. Or maybe she wouldn't — but then this really wasn't a brilliant idea as ideas go, since brilliance wasn't my strong suit.

I stood up and noticed a large, dark-gray rat meandering along the base of the garage two yards over. Grabbing the broom from our porch I headed toward the rat, knowing that when it saw me it would surely scamper for home. At least I hoped it would. Every kid had heard the story of the woman who hit a rat with her broom, it ran up the broom handle, bit her hand, and within three days she turned bulbous and died of black plague. I always thought myself faster than any rat, and by the time a rat scurried half-way up my broom I'd be a half-block away. As I climbed the first fence, and the distance diminished between me and the gray rat, I had nagging doubts about my speed. I scaled the second fence and dropped lightly to the ground and the rat saw me. It was the biggest, fattest rat in Detroit, a town that could win "rat size" contests. It gave me a defiant glare, reversed itself and slowly shuffled toward the young policeman's yard. It was five feet away from his fence when I hit it with the broom's twig section. Nothing happened except it walked a little faster. I hit it again and it slipped through the fence. Hastily climbing the fence I jumped into the yard and continued hitting the rat as it headed toward some long wooden boards stacked against the policeman's garage. It almost reached the boards and safety, but the broom beating must have addled its brain for it suddenly reversed direction. I stopped it by pressing the broom bristles into its body and it began an agonized squeaking.

I lifted the broom and started hitting it again. My heart pounded, the broom pounded and I thought, I ain't got nothing against this rat. Why am I doing this? Everyone always says, 'kill rats.' Why? It never did nothing to me. Hell, the damn thing's probably a grandfather.

I was ready to stop bashing it when the policeman came out his back door. He wore a white undershirt and dark blue uniform pants. He was tall, muscular, with black hair and moustache and grinned as he approached. "Nice going, kid," he said. "Kill the sonovabitch. Boy, you sure had a tough time with the bastard. I was watching you through the window. Keep hitting it."

I kept hitting it with his encouragement, and it finally stopped moving, squeaking, breathing. After rolling it over with his shoe, the policeman picked up the body with some newspaper and walked me to his back gate. He tossed the paper-wrapped rat into his garbage container, opened the gate and let me out into the alley. "You did a nice job, kid. I appreciate it. If you see any more rats in my yard you're welcome to kill 'em anytime. Nice going."

Walking home with my broom I felt happy because the policeman treated me like a hero, sad because I'd murdered a grandfather, and proud because the police department had commissioned me as our neighborhood's first "Rat Hit Man."

Soon after that episode I discovered Butler's dog Mitzi and I weren't the sole rat killers in the vicinity. During the previous winter Mr. Combs had rented the upper section of the house next door to a man named Dale Shulack. His living quarters consisted of a bedroom, bathroom and kitchen. Years before Mr. Combs had changed this single home into double occupancy by building an additional rear bedroom for his downstairs tenants and converting the upstairs into another rental unit. The lower bedroom addition had a gently slanted, almost flat roof that became a back porch for the upstairs tenant. The only upstairs entrance was accessible by climbing a long wooden flight of stairs from the backyard to this roof-porch.

Dale was thin, as was his premature gray hair, and he wore eyeglasses and a constant smile. When he came home from work in late afternoon, he always gave a friendly greeting to anyone he saw in Combs' yard or ours.

At twilight, a few days following my rat bashing, Dale sat on his porch in a kitchen chair holding an air rifle. I watched from my back steps as he leaned forward, carefully aimed at Cliff's chicken coop/garage, and pulled the trigger. He quickly shot twice more, and I knew he wasn't trying for a chicken dinner. No one killed their landlord's chickens, and besides, the chickens were already in their coop and settled down for the night. Walking over to the fence separating us, I looked up and asked, "What ya shooting at, mister?"

He smiled, pointed and answered, "I think I just shot a

rat. Why don't you walk over to that bush near your fence and see if I got 'im."

I jumped the fence and found the rat where he said it would be. It had tried to crawl to our yard before it died. One BB had penetrated its throat and another was imbedded in its side. I yelled up to him that it was dead, and he asked, "Do you want to take a shot at the next one?"

"Heck, yeah!" I shouted. It had to be easier than brooming them to death.

I ran up the stairs as he brought out another chair for me. He cocked the air rifle, showed me how to aim, and pointed to the rat hole at the coop's base. "There'll be another one coming out in a minute," he assured me. "Did you ever shoot a BB gun before?"

I told him about shooting Joe's Red Ryder model at a cardboard target in the Butler basement.

"Well, this'll be a little different," he explained. "Moving targets are harder to hit, and the distance is a lot farther than in your friend's basement."

We sat whispering and waiting, he patiently, me impatiently. It was getting dark. Suddenly his voice lowered still and he said, "Get ready. Here comes a rat."

A suspicious rodent poked its head half way out of the hole, turned its head left and right, sniffed the air, probably looking for its departed relative. I waited until its fat body cleared the hole before I hurriedly lined up the rifle and pulled the trigger. The BB smacked into wood above the rat's head and the noise sent it scurrying home.

"You need a little practice," Dale said. "Just a second."

He went into his house and a minute later returned with another air rifle. "Here. You can have this. It's old and hasn't much power but you can practice with it."

I couldn't believe it! Someone was giving me a BB gun! He also gave me a cardboard tube of BBs and showed me the loading hole in the rifle's top. "Be careful what you shoot at," he warned. "Don't shoot at people or birds."

Thanking him profusely, I left before he changed his

mind. As I headed down the stairs he called out, "Do me a favor tomorrow. Get rid of the dead rat in the bushes."

I promised, climbed the fence, ran to our darkened garage and safely stashed the rifle in the Model A's back seat. Tomorrow I'd start blazing away at anything that moved, but first I had to get permission to keep it.

In the kitchen the next morning my mother looked skeptical as I explained how I got the gun and how responsible I'd be when firing it. At first she said, "I don't think so," but after many "C'mon, Ma. Pleeease. I'll be careful" entreaties, she relented. "Well, if Mr. Shulack gave it to you…You are thirteen now. Just don't shoot at people."

I promised and ran out to the garage to get my rifle, thankful that she didn't mention not to shoot at birds. I always thought the world had too many English sparrows.

I drew a target on an empty cardboard box with crayon and placed it on the ground next to the garage wall with the target facing our house. BBs could be saved in this way for they'd smash through the target and rattle around inside the box.

Sitting on my back porch steps, I noticed how effortlessly the rifle cocked, not like Mr. Shulack's rat-killing one. The distance from back steps to target was about 30 feet. I lined up the sights on the bullseye, pulled the trigger and the BB hit six feet in front of the target, rolled up to the box and stopped. This definitely wasn't the most powerful BB gun in the universe. I actually saw the fired BB float through the air. After a few more shots with the same results I discovered aiming at a spot two feet above the box was the only way to hit my target. I had the only BB gun in Detroit that could do a lob shot.

Chuck and Red joined me and took a few shots but rapidly lost interest when they discovered what you aimed at wasn't what you hit. I started shooting at sparrows in our tree near the garage by aiming over their heads and occasionally hit one. I knew they were hit when they angrily flew away, cursing me in their cockney squawk. Or maybe it was cockney laughter because they seemed to also be slapping their knees.

After all birds left our tree and Red and Chuck left our yard, I walked down the alley shooting at birds in backyard trees and on telephone wires. It was a challenge to judge how far over a bird's head I had to aim in order to hit one.

I walked from one alley entrance to the other, shooting all the way. The gun got weaker so I shot at garage windows. Even from two feet away the BBs couldn't chip glass. I was almost home when a BB jammed the rifle. I'd cock it, pull the trigger and a poof of air escaped from the barrel, but no BB.

I was too busy banging the barrel on a cement garbage container to hear the car coasting toward me; a black car uniquely decorated with the word "police" spelled out in gold lettering. A uniformed officer braked, flung open the door and told me, "Don't move."

Another officer came through a yard at the same time, held out his hand and commanded, "Give me the gun." When I did, he said, "We hear you've been shooting at birds."

"It doesn't even work," I told him.

"Bullshit," he said. "Let's try it." He shook my rifle to make sure it had BBs, cocked it, aimed downward and pulled the trigger. Nothing came out but a weak puff sound. He tried it again with the same result.

"What's your name, kid?" he asked. I told him and he said, "Well, Robert, we're taking your gun. You don't know how to treat one. According to the neighbors you were shooting at birds. Let this be a lesson for you. Never shoot at your fine-feathered friends unless you intend to eat them."

He smiled, his partner chuckled, and they got in the patrol car and drove off with my first BB gun. I experienced a heavy feeling of loss walking into my backyard, then had a most satisfying thought. If one of those policemen took my gun to give to his son, that kid was going to be very annoyed at his hero-dad when he discovered it wouldn't shoot twenty feet, even if they managed to unjam it.

Four days later I built a fly zoo out of three wine bottle corks found in garbage containers and a supply of straight pins from my mother's sewing basket. With my pocket-knife I cut a quarter-inch slice from the top of each cork and pushed pins completely through the perimeters of the tops, spacing them at small intervals. I pushed the pin points into the cork bottoms, resulting in three round fly cages that needed flies; an insect our neighborhood had in abundance. It was simple to catch flies when they stopped flying. Get your cupped hand as close as possible to your prey and when it braced its little feet to take wing, swiftly sweep your hand over its resting place, simultaneously closing your fingers. Sometimes you'd miss them and sometimes you'd squish them, but eventually you'd catch one intact.

I took my cages out to our alley garbage container and quickly caught a large blue and a large green fly and incarcerated them. While patiently stalking a large, black and white striped one I heard footsteps. It was a fully uniformed policeman walking swiftly toward me. My heart started thumping and I wondered what did I do now? Is there a law against imprisoning insects? Is he going to confiscate my fly cages? And then I recognized him, my friend and neighbor who praised my rat-killing ability. "Hi," I said.

"Did you do this?" he asked furiously. He held up a dead robin by its tail feathers.

"No," I whispered, my heart speeding up again.

"The hell you didn't! Someone told me you were killing birds with a BB gun!"

"The police took that gun three or four days ago," I quavered.

"You're a liar! If I ever catch you shooting at birds again I'll kick your sorry ass!"

As he whirled and walked away carrying the dead robin, the realization dawned that if you kill a rat you're a hero...if you kill a bird you're a rat. I also realized I was developing a hardy dislike for cops.

269

XXIII

America had a new giant bomber, a B-29 Superfortress, half again as large as the B-17 with more armament and bomb capacity. Flying from a China base, a sizable force of these long-range planes, unescorted by fighter planes, bombed steel mills located in southern Japan, the first bombing of Japan since Doolittle's Tokyo raid. Four B-29s were shot down.

U.S. troops, mainly Marines, invaded two of the Mariana islands, Saipan and Guam, to secure the islands and build airfields. The islands were near enough to Japan so that short-range fighter planes could fly round-trips while escorting and protecting B-29s on future bombing raids. The Japanese fought savagely for these islands and suffered horrendous losses in troops, ships and planes. Newspapers reported the fierce battles and Ed stopped writing again, which worried most of our family.

I wasn't concerned. Ed probably didn't have anything interesting to write. He couldn't write about military matters — his V-mail was heavily censored by over-zealous officers —so all he could write about were sandy beaches and coconuts, not exactly fascinating subjects. I had my own war problems. My cardboard soldiers were handled and smacked with rubber bands so often they became worn, wrinkled and bent. I wanted to buy a new soldier set, but

271

invariably bought cheaper comic books instead. I mentioned this dilemma to Ray and he said, "Hey, save up for your soldiers. I'll get you free comic books. C'mon."

We walked toward Gratiot and I asked, "Ya know somebody giving away comic books?"

He said, "Don't worry about it."

Puzzled, I remained quiet until we turned onto Gratiot. "C'mon Ray, where we goin'?"

He answered, "To a dime store."

There were three dime stores lined up near the Roosevelt theater. Neisner's, the largest, stood in the middle with Kresge's and Woolworth's on either side. Originally they were called five-and-ten-cent stores, later five-and-dime, eventually "dime stores."

"Why're we goin' there? I only got a quarter. I told ya I have ta save my money," I protested.

He said, "Don't worry. You want comic books? You'll get them."

"How are we gonna get 'em with no money?"

"We're going to steal them," he calmly declared.

This remark was good for a heart rate acceleration. I mentally questioned Ray's sanity — and my own for getting mixed up in his schemes. "Geez, Ray, I don't know how ta steal."

He gave me a superior grin and said, "Well, watch an expert and learn."

We entered Neisner's, passed the soda fountain near the front door, and slowly worked our way to the toy and comic book section at the rear, examining uninteresting merchandise en route. When we reached the toys there was an open display case of hundreds of plastic soldiers, the kind Chuck had received for Christmas. An adjacent case held stacks of thin, flat boxes of cardboard soldiers, like I'd received, along with similar boxes containing cardboard tanks, half tracks, tents, Red Cross ambulances, nurses, howitzers, machine guns and gunners, all waiting to be punched out, folded, assembled and used with my soldiers at home. They were way out of my price range. Ray nudged me and whispered, "Let's get the comic books," which were further down the aisle. "We'll go out the back door," he added.

Facing the comic book racks, we casually made selections, thumbed through them and returned them to their rightful place, like two boys with limited funds searching for comicdom's holy grail. Nervously I watched Ray from the corner of my eye, waiting for him to suddenly walk out the back door with comic books in hand. No doubt he'd get caught and we'd both end up in the juvenile detention home. He squatted down, glanced through a few more on the bottom rack, replaced them, arose, came over to me, grabbed my arm and hissed, "Stick that book in your pants and let's go. Goddamnit, nobody's looking! Let's go!"

I jammed the book into my waistband and we both walked swiftly out the back door. I had an urge to sprint when we stepped into the alley, but Ray said, "Just keep walking. We're okay."

Resentment replaced fear. He said he'd show me how to steal, and I did all the stealing. This resentment was instantly replaced with admiration as he pulled comic books from his socks, sleeves and shirt front. "How'd ya do that, Ray? I was watching ya!"

"Simple," he replied. "Pick up two; put back one."

Ray was a shoplifting magician who relished sharing his tricks. For two weeks, moneyless shopping trips to dime stores became regular events. I became almost as adept at stealing as Ray, concentrating on comic books and plastic and cardboard soldiers. When Mom asked where all the extra soldiers came from I had a ready answer, suggested by Ray. "Ray loaned them to me." My thievery was called "being willingly led down the primrose path," a phrase later changed to "succumbing to peer pressure."

The excitement of stealing gradually wore off, replaced by conscience attacks and warnings from Joe, Red and Chuck about the eventual fate of thieves. Joe even hinted some parents might be told if Ray and I continued our wanton ways. Nevertheless, I decided on one last shoplifting trip.

I headed out alone. No one, including mentor Ray, wished to accompany me — a possible ominous omen. Crime always feels safer with accomplices. It was a typical summer day. Birds chirped, squirrels chattered, dogs yapped and mothers screeched at kids. I walked slowly, my enthusiasm waning. I considered turning around and regretted bragging to Ray, Red and Chuck that this would be my last trip. Now I felt I had to go through with it.

At Neisner's I went directly to the toy section and was relieved to see the usual cardboard army equipment, nothing new. I already had a box or two of everything displayed. The clerk asked if she could help and I mumbled "Just looking." I wandered around the counter intending to head home — until I passed a huge pile of penny balloons waiting to be grabbed and stuffed in pockets. The clerk had her back to me, so I looked left and right, grabbed a handful and started stuffing. A big hand gripped my right shoulder and an authoritative male voice said, "Put those back!"

I pulled the balloons, still clutched in my hand, out of my pocket, flung them back on top of the pile, jerked my shoulder loose and fled for the front door. The authoritative voice behind me hollered, "Stop that kid!"

Soda fountain customers spun around on their stools, jaws agape, as I sped past. None of them, nor the aisle customers, obeyed the authoritative voice. Someone had propped open the front door and I shot out onto the sidewalk and didn't stop running until half-a-block from home.

I found Ray, Joe, Red and Chuck in Butler's backyard and told them what happened. Ray laughed and asked, "Why would you try to steal cheap, penny balloons?"

Joe said, "See. I told you."

Red said, "You'd better cut it out."

Chuck said, "Yeah!"

I didn't need lectures. I was now sincerely convinced of the correctness of the "Thou Shalt Not Steal" Commandment. I had learned that stealers eventually got caught and I was very lucky not to be in custody. I wasn't as convinced about The Shadow's warning, "Crime does not pay." I was sorry I'd stolen, but pleased I'd accumulated all that merchandise before my short-lived criminal career ended.

* * *

On days leading up to Independence Day we spent every penny mustered on fireworks and tried to save some for the actual holiday. But usually, by the big day, our cache of firecrackers, pinwheels and sparklers was largely depleted. The farsighted among us always bought a few rolls of caps, though we didn't all own cap guns. They were a poor substitute for firecrackers, but if you folded a piece of the roll so a number of caps were directly on top of each other, placed them on concrete and slammed them with a hammer a satisfying explosion ensued.

Ken Swartz had a better way to make noise. He taught us how to make a bomb out of kitchen matches, a nut and two corresponding bolts. We screwed a bolt two turns into a nut hole, used a razor blade to cut off match tips, filled the remainder of the nut hole with these tips, and screwed another bolt into the other side of the hole, trapping the tips inside. Dropping this bolt bomb onto concrete resulted in a loud bang as the match tips ignited.

Joe, Red, Chuck and I made many of these bombs in our basement, using Dad's nuts and bolts, and we soon had a litany of explosions rocking the house, which resulted in Mom yelling down the basement stairs, "You boys take your firecrackers outside...right now!"

Joe, Red and Chuck obeyed her, but I wanted to make one more gigantic bomb since small ones wouldn't sound so loud outside. Searching through every drawer in the work bench I found what was needed — a huge nut and two bolts. I overpacked the nut with a slew of match tips, crushing them into the hole between the two bolts. Tighter packed meant louder noise. I pictured the astonished look on everyone's face when this device was dropped outside on the sidewalk and it exploded like a cherry bomb.

I was right. Giving the bolt one more twist it exploded like a cherry bomb. The noise deafened me as flames shot out of the nut and scorched my left hand. I dropped the bomb and rushed for the basement sink to soak my hand in cold water. Through the ringing in my ears I heard my mother's voice screaming, "I told you boys to take those things outside!"

After my teeth stopped gnashing and the pain diminished to a throb, I inspected my violated hand. The thumb, forefinger and area between were black and it didn't wash off. I was a little miffed that Ken didn't warn us about the dangers of bolt bomb manufacturing. He could have said, "Hey, guys, don't screw the bolts in too tight. They might go off a little early and burn hell out of your fingers."

But, in retrospect, maybe he did me a favor. I eliminated one more glamorous and exciting career possibility — Bomb Defuser.

* * *

Ed's long awaited letter arrived informing us that he was safely encamped on Saipan. The Marines had secured most of the island, mopping up scattered pockets of resisting Japanese who felt losing face by surrendering was more demeaning than losing extremities or life. This attitude made little sense to kids, yet we admired their fanaticism, and hoped if a foreign army invaded Detroit we'd be as courageous and fight to the last boy.

My parents were happy Ed was temporarily safe, but they knew Saipan wasn't far removed from Japan, and he'd be with the United States invasion forces, so they and my older sisters wrote cheery letters to keep up his morale, a practice all home front people were encouraged to do by our government.

276

Betty was writing servicemen all over the globe. She corresponded with a cousin, an uncle, Ed's friends from Detroit, two of Ed's buddies from his naval training company, and servicemen she'd met at United Service Organization's dances downtown and at Selfridge Field, a military air base outside Detroit. Ed graciously gave her address to a couple more buddies from his Marine battalion on Saipan and they were added to her list. She and her young female coworkers in Detroit's downtown Prudential Insurance office had weekly contests to see who could receive the most mail. "Anything for our boys in service," was their adopted media motto, a motto that competed with "Support our fighting men."

Mary had graduated in June and now worked at an insurance office in the Roosevelt theater building. Having slimmed down considerably she began to attract an occasional wolf whistle from crude idlers while walking to and from her job. These admiring whistles made her feel very mature for her seventeen years, and she began to believe herself ready for serious romance. Unhappily, the five servicemen she wrote to regularly were in Europe or on ships or Pacific islands and weren't expected home until war's end.

But Bill, a solidly-built 22-year-old, lived in the upper flat right next door. Mary liked him from the day he moved in. Bill had migrated from a southern state, and Mary was determined to help him adjust to city life. On summer nights they had long whispered conversations, she while leaning out her open bedroom window, he while sitting and leaning his elbow on his front porch railing. Because of the close proximity of the neighborhood houses — most were less than five feet apart —they easily whispered. Ray observed that all Bill needed was a six-foot plank and they could get a lot closer. Ray's one-track mind always wanted to turn "social" intercourse into another kind. I patiently explained that Betty, who bordered on sainthood, also slept in that bedroom and if Bill tried anything so rash he might find

277

himself doing a two-story free-fall.

Bill wasn't in service because, three years before, a truck had sideswiped his car while he was driving with his arm out the window, neatly severing his arm above the elbow. He braked, walked back to his arm, picked it up, threw it into his car's back seat, applied a tourniquet, then let the truck driver take him to a hospital. "I jest din't want ma arm layin' in the middle of the road," he explained modestly.

Mary also was having a budding correspondence romance with an Airborne soldier named Roy "Bud" Davis who had glider-landed in France during the Allied armies invasion. I thought Bud was serious about Mary when he mailed her his sergeant stripes. I knew he was serious when he sent her his screaming eagle pin and she proudly wore it attached to her sweater. I suggested she buy a jacket, sew on the stripes, along with additional emblems and patches wangled from the remainder of her and Betty's correspondents, and be in style. Many young ladies sported jackets covered with armored division, air force, infantry, airborne and cavalry patches. I thought it patriotic and neat, but Mary laughingly refused, saying, "I wouldn't know which end of the needle to thread."

* * *

In mid-July Pat got an office job at Buhl Sons Company, a wholesale hardware distributor located in a warehouse on the Detroit riverfront. She enjoyed working, and I hoped she'd continue to enjoy it because after three months she would be eligible to buy a refrigerator from Buhl's with an employee discount. It seemed everyone had a refrigerator except us. Ray's family not only owned a refrigerator but also a new floor model radio, and he allowed Red, Joe, Chuck and me into his living room to show us this electrical phenomenon and boast about its modern features. After showing us the large, round, green-lighted dial and pointing out tone adjustments, he laid the tour de force on us. "This is where you plug in television," he said, indicating two round metal holes in the rear, plainly marked "TV." He explained that television sets would be sold right after the war ended. They'd sit on, and be plugged into, these types of radios and everyone could watch their favorite radio shows. I wondered aloud how they'd get Silver, Scout and all those other horses galloping through a studio, but Ray assured me someone would figure it out.

* * *

The stifling July heat was dispiriting. Everyone went home after only two hours of playing ball at Chandler school. The Fire Department hadn't attached any spray nozzles to the fire plugs so we couldn't cool ourselves off. I decided to get my wooden flat boat with a rubber-band-powered paddle wheel that Ken showed me how to build and sail it in our bathtub. At least the water would be cool.

I filled the tub half full, wound my boat and watched it shoot across the water. Even this bored me. Then I remembered the five flat-bottomed cardboard warships gathering dust on my chifforobe. Maybe they'd float.

The battleship turned over on its side and started filling up with water as soon as I placed it in the tub. The ships obviously needed ballast and water-proofing to be seaworthy. Taking them to our basement workbench I filled all hull cracks with model airplane glue and then gathered handfuls of small pebbles from the backyard and dropped them down the ships' smoke stacks. The pebbles went all the way through to the flat bottoms and I had my ballast.

Returning to the bathroom, I found the ships floated nicely. I pushed them around the tub pretending a momentous sea battle was taking place, my mouth providing booming big-gun sounds. But more realism was needed.

I found Chuck's small metal pursuit plane under our bed and flew it slowly from our bedroom back to the bathroom. The lone American dive bomber would heroically attack the arrogant, unsuspecting Japanese fleet.

The Japanese were taken completely by surprise. Swooping out of the sun the dive bomber dropped incendiary bombs (lighted kitchen matches) onto ship decks and down smoke stacks. Billows of gray smoke poured from crippled ships as they vainly tried to fire back at the relentless, avenging plane that returned again and again raining fire and destruction. Confused Japanese captains sounded "abandon ship" alarms as crewmen leaped into shark-filled waters. The wooden paddle boat wouldn't burn but it too was the recipient of a couple bombs. It was a war scene right out of a Pathe newsreel.

I don't know whether it was sound effects or smoke that attracted my mother, but the battle abruptly ended when she flung open the bathroom door and hurled a staccato of questions at me: "Are you crazy? Are you trying to burn down the house? Have you lost your mind? Why do you do these things? Are you trying to kill yourself?" Followed by instructions: "Put out those fires! Clean up that tub! Don't ever light matches again!" Followed by resignation: "I don't know what I'm going to do with you. After you clean up this mess, go play outside!"

As she ranted I splashed water on the burning ships and sank them. After she left, shaking her head and coughing, I grabbed a towel and waved all the smoke out into the hallway since our bathroom lacked a window.

Dad wasn't due home from work for a couple hours so I worked hard scouring the tub's soot and scum rings. I even caught most pebbles and bits of ships before they escaped down the open drain. Eventually our tub sparkled and I carried pebbles and ship remnants in the towel and dumped them into our alley garbage receptacle. Mom accompanied me upstairs for an inspection and was pleased. "You did a nice clean-up job," she said. "I probably won't tell your dad about this unless he smells the smoke, but don't ever do it again."

I sincerely promised. How could I do it again? My entire

fleet was destroyed.

I found Red, Joe, Chuck, Ray and Cliff in Butlers' backyard, sitting under their only tree, shady and cool. Joe asked, "Where've you been?"

I told them about the bathtub battle and they all looked oddly at one another. Joe asked, sounding a lot like my mother, "Are you trying to burn down your house?"

Ray laughed and remarked, "I bet the ships ain't the only thing you were playing with in the bathroom." I didn't know what he meant, but then Ray always said dumb things.

We sat around for a couple hours talking about movies, war and baseball and seeing who could make the loudest noise by clamping a blade of grass between the thumbs and balls of our hands and blowing through the small, remaining crevice. Mrs. Butler opened the back door, let Mitzi out and asked if we wanted lemonade. There was a chorus of "Yes, Ma'ams" and "Heck yeahs," and Red went into the house and returned with tumblers and a full pitcher of lemonade with ice cubes floating on top. As we filled our tumblers I kept a wary eye on Mitzi, expecting her to join us. Instead she laid down on the porch's third step and began sunning herself for the last time while vigilantly guarding the back door against any intruding strangers.

The lemonade was sweet, cold, and delicious. Mrs. Butler sure can mix, I thought. What more could be asked on a hot day than grass, shade, a cold drink and baseball talk.

No one heard the car in the driveway except Mitzi. She barked, jumped off the steps and met Mr. Butler's green sedan just as it rolled into sight. The right front bumper knocked Mitzi down and the right front tire rolled over her head with a sickening bone-crunching sound.

Red and Joe leaped up screaming and waving their arms at their father who immediately braked. Red ran in front of the car, and Joe leaned into the garage wall, his face buried in his arms, sobbing. Mitzi lay on her back, four legs sticking straight up, one leg still trembling. I turned to Cliff and said, "Maybe she can be saved."

He muttered, "Nah, she's dead."

Mr. Butler, who wore a hearing aid, looked confused and thought Red's continued waving and wailing meant Mitzi was under his car in front of the wheels. He put the car in reverse and neatly ran over Mitzi's head again. The bone crunching repeated, and the moving leg was stilled. Red's waving and wailing became even more energetic and loud.

Mr. Butler got out of his car and held his weeping sons, with Mrs. Butler joining them. Ray, Cliff, Chuck and I left them to their grief, with Ray sincerely saying in passing, "I'm sorry" as he patted Red on the shoulder. When we got to the front sidewalk he said, "I always hated that fuckin' dog." We all nodded.

The following morning, a Saturday, Joe and Red solemnly invited their friends to Mitzi's funeral. She would be buried in a little clearing behind their garage at 11 a.m.

Ray couldn't attend, he had some errands to run for his mother, but Cliff, Chuck and I were there. Mr. Butler, Joe and Red had already dug the grave. We stood back from it, in deference to the family. The sealed wooden box containing Mitzi's remains sat next to the waiting hole. Red, Joe, Gladys, Mary Jane and Mr. Butler lowered their collective heads in prayer and said farewell to old Mitzi. If the Butlers were Catholic they would have covered all statues and crucifixes in their house with purple cloth and, if available, would have dug Mitzi's grave with a silver spade and lowered her down with a golden chain. Still, they had a nice ceremony.

After prayers the box was placed in the hole, spaded over with dirt, and we straggled off. Joe and Red remained indoors for the rest of the day, mourning their beloved pet.

There were other creatures who took notice of Mitzi's demise. That evening, squeaking sounds emanated from rat holes up and down the Butler alley as rats, in their unique fashion, lamented Mitzi's fate. There was also music and singing, and if you listened carefully you could make out the words: Ding, dong, the Mitz is dead! The wicked old bitch, the Mitz is dead.

XXIV

Sensitively, I allowed Red two days to recover from his despair over Mitzi's death and then recommended he accept, at no charge, one of two kittens I'd accumulated the previous week. The first, donated by a neighborhood woman aware of my love for cats, was completely white. The other, found skittering around the dairy, was pitch-black except for a small, white spot on its chest. They were both about six weeks old.

Red refused my offer, saying, "I don't need any of your lousy cats," but I didn't mind. I wanted to keep them both. Using all my imaginative power I called the white kitten "Snowball." The black kitten with the little white spot was easier to name. I called it "Spot." Watching Snowball and Spot chase each other, wrestle and frolic captivated me.

When I noticed Ray, his mother and their old tomcat sitting on their front lawn I carried my kittens across the street to show them off. Their tomcat, sleepily stretched out on the grass, did its best to ignore the kittens as they jumped on its back and chewed its tail and ears, but now and then it rose, swatted a kitten with its big paw sending it tumbling, and moved to a new grassy resting place. The kittens invariably followed and resumed their devilment. Ray's mother, a stout woman, enjoyed their antics, laughing and slapping her knees, which amused both Ray and me. Eventually she asked the kittens' names. I told her.

"I can see Snowball, but why did you call the black one Spot?"

I pointed out the small white chest spot and she looked dubiously at Ray, who shrugged. I explained I considered calling it Blackie but, because of an unpleasant experience with a dog so named, rejected the idea. After picking up and checking both kittens she laughingly told me I should have named them He and She — Spot was a male and Snowball a female — and I should get ready for future kittens. I told her this possibility was appealing, yet remote, because my cats always ran away before reaching kitten-bearing age.

Besides the cat play and hearing Mrs. Allis laugh I had another reason to go to Ray's. I hoped to get a close-up view of a new tenant in their building, a naturally redheaded woman in her early twenties. She had created a minor sensation by simply roller skating in the street. Once or twice a week during early evening hours she donned a purple skating outfit and practiced glides, pirouettes and jumps. She wore the first pair of roller skates I ever saw that weren't made of steel and didn't have to be belted and clamped to shoes. Her skates had wide, wooden wheels affixed to the bottom of white, laced-up-the-front, calf-high boots. It enchanted me to watch her gyrations as her short skirt surged outward. And I wasn't alone. Every pubescent boy on our street volunteered to go on errands for mothers if the errands entailed walking by this skating display, and many husbands in the vicinity chose to read evening newspapers on front porches, ostensibly because of pleasant weather. When my father took his first look at the skater he made an astute observation: "That girl isn't wearing enough to flag a handcar."

We boys concluded she was lovelier and a better skater than Sonja Henie and were sure she'd end up in movies since Sonja proved a knowledge of acting wasn't a prerequisite. We were wrong, of course, for she never appeared on the silver screen, but she certainly brightened Holcomb's scenery during that summer of '44.

* * *

Three families near our house didn't have a garage abutting the alley. One was the Combs family who lost their garage because of an ill-fated fire, probably started by chimney sparks. Another was the Kaltz family who never had a garage, making Mrs. Kaltz perfectly happy because it gave her ample room to grow Victory garden vegetables. She tilled half her yard and I cautioned everyone to refrain from raiding this garden because her daughter Catherine was in my grade at school. Mrs. Kaltz periodically interrupted our alley games by calling us over to her fence to share her tomato bounty and even said we could enter her yard anytime and harvest all the rhubarb we wanted. We didn't often take advantage of her offer because of rhubarb's acrid taste but appreciated her generosity. The third garageless house sat directly across the alley from my house and next to the Kaltz residence. People living there obviously valued privacy, for a six-foot, green, board fence loomed along the entire length of their alley line. Their fence gate, also made of six-foot boards, was always latched shut from the inside effectively barring us from using their backyard for easy passage to Chandler playground. A concrete garbage receptacle presented the sole break in the green board monotony. A small portion extended through the fence into the alley giving garbage men access to its front steel cover.

A twelve-year-old named Sammy lived there, a dark-haired, Italian boy who didn't go to Nativity school and I never saw him in church so I figured he wasn't Catholic. This was odd for an Italian, but odder still, he didn't try to participate in any of our games. The few times I passed him in the alley he avoided my eyes and turned his head. This failed to bother me since he didn't look too likeable anyway. He did discover a way to make his presence felt though. Once, in an alley duck-on-the-rock game behind the Combs' residence, stones began sailing into our group.

Sammy, crouched on his garbage receptacle behind the green fence, periodically popped up and pelted us, then ducked down and listened to us accuse each other of throwing stones. After it happened a couple times we spotted him, rushed the fence, pulled ourselves up to its top and, hanging by our elbows, watched him run for his back door as we rained colorful curses on his retreating shoulders. Afterwards, when discussing what mayhem we'd visit upon his person if we caught him, Red modestly told us he'd already punched him out two years before when both attended Chandler school. Sammy had an unsportsmanlike habit of starting fights with smaller boys during recess, Red explained, and made the mistake of picking on one of Red's friends. In Red's opinion Sammy had an IQ comparable to a winter centigrade reading. Red had good character judgment of bad characters.

When my kittens were nine-weeks old, I stood on our back porch and called them for their usual morning saucer of milk. Only Spot showed up.

"Where's your girlfriend Snowball?" I asked.

Spot ignored me and kept lapping so I began a fruitless search. Snowball had vanished.

Snowball stayed away the rest of the day and by nightfall I was certain she wouldn't return. Usually my cats deserted me when they were a little older, but maybe Snowball found people who allowed pets in their house. Sleeping in a garage or under a bush at night, even for a cat, wasn't exactly living luxuriously, so I sincerely wished Snowball happiness, wherever she was.

I called Spot the next morning, and he bounded out from under a thick bush next door and scampered onto our back porch. As I watched him drink from the saucer I heard a weak meow coming from the same bush. It had to be little Snowball. She no doubt felt guilty about staying away so long, so guilty she wouldn't even come near me. I scaled the neighbor's fence and, on my hands and knees, peeked under the bush.

Snowball crouched there, teeth exposed, hissing. I reached for her and she swiped at my hand with unsheathed claws. Lying on my stomach I stuck my head under the bush, murmuring, "Take it easy, 'Ball. I'm not mad at you. You can come out."

That's when I saw her problem — a large section of her beautiful white fur completely ripped from her back leaving nothing but pink, raw flesh. I recoiled in anguish — I mean, who wants to pet a bald cat? — and called my mother.

While I held up the bush's lower branches, Mom got down on her knees and examined Snowball. "There's nothing we can do for the poor thing," she said. "We'll have to call the Humane Society."

"Will she grow new fur?"

"I don't know. They'll know what's best for it."

Within an hour a Humane Society man arrived. I watched from our back porch as my mother showed him the harboring bush next door. He put on heavy gloves and gently captured Snowball and spoke quietly to Mom as they left the yard heading to his truck parked in front. I remained on the back porch, holding Spot, and heard the truck pull away, feeling an intense sadness. Mom returned and asked, "Are you okay?"

"Yeah, I guess so. Will they be able to fix her?"

"No. I'm sorry. The man said they'd have to put her away. She's in misery. He said the gas they use is quick and painless."

"How did it happen? Did he say?"

"He said someone cut part way through her tail, then pulled, ripping the skin off her back. Who would do something like that?"

I shook my head. No one I knew, not even Ray, was that rotten. She went into the house leaving me wondering what kind of person could cut off a kitten's tail; so when Red came into our yard, I told him what happened and asked, "What kind of bastard could cut off a kitten's tail?"

"Well," he said, "when I was over at the school yard

289

yesterday I saw Sammy playing with a small white cat on his front porch. He sure could do it."

Centigrade Sammy! Who else?! We ran to the alley and pounded on the green fence, calling, "Sam-eee-eee, Sam-eee-eee," with no results. From time to time, for the rest of the afternoon, we did the same. If Sammy heard our call he didn't heed it, and I went to bed that night thinking of violated Snowball and violating her violator.

The next afternoon Red, Chuck and I sat on our garage roof. From this lofty post we could see over the green fence into Sammy's backyard. The roofing was hot, the inactivity wearying, and we figured Sammy probably heard we wanted him and intended to spend the next fifty years inside his house. I had just started hoping Catherine would take out her garbage, to break the monotony, when Red nudged me. "There he is," he whispered.

Sammy stood on his back porch steps playing with a yo-yo. We vacated the roof, Red and Chuck by sensibly using the telephone pole, me by jumping Supermanlike into our yard, and met at Sammy's gate.

"Here's what we'll do," said Red. "I'll call him, and when he opens the gate I'll pull him out here, and you punch him."

This sounded like an excellent plan. Red sang out, "Sam-eee-eee. Sam-eee-eee" and my heart drummed in anticipation. I wasn't sure I could just punch someone, so I worked up some anger about poor Snowball, picturing her under that bush, hissing in agony. Mom had cautioned me often not to fight but even she would probably agree this was a unique case. We began to think Sammy wasn't going to appear when a voice above us asked, "Wha'cha want?"

Sammy stood on his garbage receptacle staring down at us from inside his fence, wearing his usual sneer. We stepped over to him, Red did all the talking, and got right to the point.

"This guy wants to fight you."

"What for?"

"'Cause you killed his cat."

"I can't fight him," Sammy said. Astonishingly, he didn't even deny it.

"Why not?"

"'Cause he's too big." This was the first and last time anyone ever referred to me, or any part of me, as too big.

"How about me," Red said. "I'm your size."

"You're too tough."

"Well then, how about Chuck here?" motioning to Chuck.

Sammy looked at Chuck's small, almost-twelve-year-old frame and said, "Okay, but you two sit over there." He indicated our garage.

Red said, "All right," and we walked to the garage.

Chuck seemed bewildered. He didn't even like cats. I told him, "Don't worry, Chuck. As soon as the fight starts I'll jump in and punch his face off."

Chuck looked dubious as Red and I sat down, leaning against the garage doors. Chuck stepped over to Sammy's fence and waited as I thought, Sammy will never fall for this. Then we heard the latch sound and the gate slowly opened. "Sammy's not only a bastard; he's a dumb bastard," I told Red.

Sammy glanced at Red and me, then walked up to Chuck, who hesitantly raised his fists. Sammy punched him in the forehead. Chuck was stunned for an instant and then started swinging wildly, landing a couple swings on Sammy's body with nice sounding thuds. Sammy, taller with a longer reach, backed up and tried to guard his face.

Red said, "Let's go."

"Wait a minute," I said. "Chuck's winning." It was one of the best fights I ever saw!

Chuck's fists moved like pistons, but he was tiring, red-faced and teary. Sammy got in a punch to Chuck's nose and blood started flowing.

I leaped up and at that moment my dad appeared at our open gate. "You!" he said, pointing at Sammy. "Get outta here!"

291

He walked swiftly over to me saying, "And you, c'mere!"

He grabbed my shoulder, pulled me into our backyard and jerked me silently, all the way to our back porch, interspersing jerks with an occasional kick to the slats with the side of his shoe. I didn't understand. I was getting picked on, and I hadn't even started fighting.

He ran me up the steps, through the kitchen and into the foyer with a few more kicks, then let go of my shoulder and slapped me on the head. I dropped to the hardwood floor, assumed the fetal position and started my usual wailing. He soccer-kicked me, and I slid part-way across the room. My mother stood in the doorway wiping her hands on her apron and quietly said, "Don't kick him, Sree."

"Kick him? I oughta kill him! He was standing out in the alley watching some imbecile beat hell out of his little brother!"

"I was gonna—," I tried to explain, but he cut me off.

"Shut up and get upstairs, goddamnit!"

I arose swiftly, ran to my bedroom, sat on the bed and muttered, "Damn! I shoulda nailed Sammy as soon as he walked out his gate."

Listening to the faint sounds of my mother tending to Chuck's wounds in the kitchen and my father still grumbling, I concluded I now owed Sammy for three things: skinning my cat, punching my brother and getting my ass kicked.

From that time on, when playing ball at Chandler, I watched for Sammy. I also started building myself up for our coming set-to. After ball games, along with Cliff, Ray and Joe, I headed for the chinning bars for a few chin-ups. As usual I frustratingly came in second to Joe. No matter how many I squeezed out he always did a couple more.

With the exception of two baseball backstops located in far corners, Chandler schoolyard had all its playground equipment concentrated in a section near the school's rear doors. There was a small slide, sand box, and four-seat swing set for the younger kids; two seesaws, large humped slide, six-seated swing set and chinning bars for us older types. The chin bars, made of galvanized metal, consisted of four vertical, three-inch-thick poles aligned at three-foot intervals and embedded in concrete. The poles were connected at the top by three thin horizontal bars set at four-, five- and six-feet heights. Outside of chin-ups, you couldn't do much on these bars other than a slow flip-over or hang upside down by your knees. Often boys warily tried walking on top of the horizontal bars in tight-rope fashion, but usually a wise person discouraged this practice by mentioning the substantial damage possible if boys slipped and straddled the bars. The subsequent plunge to the ground would be relatively painless.

We older boys thought seesaws monotonous and rarely used them except when a seesaw novice, usually a younger boy or girl, entered the playground. We lured them onto one end of the heavy wooden board, warned them to hold tight to its iron safety grip, gently raised and lowered them a few times, and when they were relaxed and at the apex, we slipped off the board. Their fast and unexpected drop to the ground rattled teeth and spine causing crying and cursing. We apologized insincerely, concealing our mirth, and justified this sadistic practice because someone had done it to us in our younger days. On a positive note, Ray once pulled this ruse on a girl and it inadvertently launched her entertainment career. Her name was Mitzi Gaynor and she attended Chandler school with her younger twin brothers, Phul and Haf. After thudding to the ground she avoided all playground equipment and concentrated her youthful energy on safer activities like singing and dancing. Eventually she gained fame in Hollywood musicals.

The six swings for older children hung from a long horizontal bar about twenty-feet high, braced by three converging poles on each end and two in the middle. Ray swore he saw a guy pump so hard that he swung all the way around the horizontal bar. I spent many hours surging to and fro, at times developing minor headaches, trying to duplicate this feat, until Joe told me it was humanly impossible. Listening to Ray not only got you in trouble at times, it also made you feel foolish. Oddly, Ray never taught me about the other use for this swing set. Cliff did, unintentionally.

After a ball game, Cliff was the only one to accompany me to the chinning bars and challenged me to a contest. With much effort he managed to chin himself eight times, a figure I easily topped by five. Being two years older and thirty pounds heavier, Cliff was not graceful in defeat. He said, "I know one thing you can't do! Climb up one swing pole and slide down another!"

"What's so tough about that?" I asked.

We walked to the swings and he explained the difficulty. The smooth and slippery poles prevented a tight grip and I'd have to climb one all the way to the top, then swing over to another for the downward slide. Ignoring the kids using the swings, he selected one of the end poles and demonstrated his technique by grasping it with both hands, wrapping his legs around it and pulling himself upward. He reached halfway to the top before he slid to the ground puffing.

"What's the matter?" I asked.

"You try it, damn it," he said testily.

Emulating his style, I started up the pole. For someone who'd spent considerable time shinnying up door jambs, tree trunks and telephone poles, this feat seemed relatively easy, and it was, except my hands began to perspire on the unpainted polished metal and I had to tighten my grip. Halfway up I stopped to rest, slid downward a little and experienced an unbelievably pleasurable warm sensation that permeated my groin, and I lost all interest in reaching the top. The feeling surged strongest when sliding downward, so every three feet up, I slid down two.

After a long while of shinnying and sliding, I bumped my head on a converging pole and realized I'd reached my forgotten goal. Forcing the glaze from my eyes, I looked quickly around the playground from my high vantage point, suddenly worried that someone might be observing my up-and-down romance with the pole. Though many children played below, none seemed interested in my antics, including Cliff who leaned against the chin bars watching a couple boys trying to launch a kite. I yelled to him to get his attention, then reluctantly swung over to the other pole and swiftly descended. When I hit the ground my knees felt weak and my arms ached. Walking slowly over to Cliff, shaking my head I wearily remarked, "God, it was hard." He thought I meant the pole climb.

For awhile I visited the pole every time I visited the playground and never told anyone the reason. I realized even worldly Ray would be hard-pressed to understand my love for this swing pole.

XXV

S pot was 11-weeks old when the accident happened. During cool morning hours, we used the Model-A in our garage as a combination meeting place, comic book library and driver training school. Sunlight streaming through rows of windows lining the top section of the alley entrance doors lighted both the garage and the car's interior. On the morning of the accident Red and I slumped in the back seat reading while Joe sat in the driver's seat making car noises. He was practicing clutching and shifting gears, even though it would be another year and a half before he'd be 16 and eligible for a driver's license.

Spot lay on the back seat between Red and me doing what bored cats do best — sleep. Spot wasn't the only one bored. Having read the same comic books six times, so was I. "I need new comic books," I said to Red. "I'm gonna ask my mother for a quarter."

I opened the car door, stepped off the running board, slammed the door behind me, and Red started yelling, "The cat! The cat!"

I turned as Red opened the car door from inside and Spot flopped onto the running board and then the floor, trembling and making low-throated choking sounds. Kneeling down I gathered Spot in my arms and asked, "What happened?"

"He tried to leave behind you and you slammed the door on his face," Red answered. "I didn't know what was going on for a second. He didn't make much noise."

How could he with his mouth clamped shut. I carried him outside in the sunlight, examined him, and saw the sole damage was concentrated between his jaws. They were partially open and connected with thick, yellow mucus. I sat him on the backyard grass and he didn't try to walk — just made quiet throw-up noises and motions.

"You'd better tell your mother," Joe advised.

"Nah, she'll just call the Humane Society and they'll give 'im the big whiff. Maybe if he drinks some milk and washes down that yellow stuff, he'll be okay." I knew I didn't know what I was talking about.

"Well, it's your cat," Joe said, "but he looks bad."

I went to our kitchen, returned with a fresh saucer of milk, and placed it in front of Spot's damaged face. He ignored it. We watched him retch for a few more minutes, then Joe said, "We gotta go. C'mon, Red. I still think you should tell your mother."

Once they left I picked up Spot, carried him into the garage, sat on the floor and petted him gently, telling him how sorry I was, how I should have known he'd follow me out of the car and how I should have looked before shutting the door. The Humane Society wouldn't get him, I promised, and held him for a long time.

I got up, wiped my eyes, grabbed a shovel hanging from the garage wall and carried it and Spot to the alley. Laying him tenderly near our garbage container I petted him, told him again how sorry I was and lifted the shovel above my head with both hands.

There was a loud clang as the shovel hit Spot and the concrete alley simultaneously. I brought it down twice more before he stopped quivering and I hoped Sammy would appear at his fence so I could throw the damned shovel at him. Tears blurred my vision as I realized I'd lost two cats in two weeks, and I silently vowed I'd never bring home another. Stuffing Spot's beautiful, desecrated body inside an empty Shredded Wheat box, I buried him at the foot of a backyard fence post, marking his grave with a small square piece of cardboard imprinted with the words: Spot. August 3, 1944. My friend.

I kept my vow. Except for a tin mechanical cat, the sole toy I received the following Christmas, I never again owned a cat. This mechanical one held a red, wooden ball between its front paws and when I pushed down on its tail it scooted across our kitchen floor. It was a fun toy. It broke within the hour.

* * *

Allied armies overran the German defenses in Belgium, France, Italy and Poland; B-29 Superfortresses bombed Manchuria and Japan; and Navy task forces sank Japanese shipping wherever it was sighted. It definitely appeared the war wouldn't last another four years, long enough for me to reach enlistment age. We were going to win without me.

Ed remained on Saipan preparing for the inevitable invasion of Japan by lifting weights, playing softball and cutting hair of fellow warriors, along with his regular medical duties of giving shots and passing out Aspirin.

As Ed gave his all for home and country, I had fun playing rain-on-the-roof, a new alley game Joe taught us. A tennis ball, three or more players and a reasonably steep, high garage roof were needed. Our garage was ideal. One player threw a ball onto the roof and called out another's name. The named player had to catch the ball after it rolled off the roof and before it hit the alley floor. If he didn't catch it, he received a point. He then threw the ball and called someone else's name. When a player accumulated three points he had to bend over facing our garage and the others each had an opportunity to throw the ball once at his vulnerable form before starting another game.

This is the game five of us were playing when we noticed

a neighbor had discarded a wooden crate. It was so large it must have contained a refrigerator and we walked over to inspect it. It consisted of thin plywood edged with heavy, hardwood. "Let's build a clubhouse," Joe suggested, and everyone else agreed.

Pulling, lifting and shoving, we got it into our backyard where a site was selected and building plans formulated. We all scattered to our homes and returned with the necessary tools for our project.

Ray brought a claw hammer and crowbar, Red and Joe brought saws, and Chuck and I supplied nails and another hammer. The site chosen was between our garage and backyard tree. The tree provided shade, and the garage provided one clubhouse wall. We worked for hours dismantling and erecting and when finished we had a seven-foot-long, four-foot-high enclosed structure with a hanging-burlap-sack entrance. A small window, cut from one wall and covered with cellophane, faced our house. A guard could be posted at the window to warn of approaching parents or sisters. Newspapers were spread thickly on the cold ground to ward off hemorrhoidal evils.

We crowded into our clubhouse, tired but proud of our labor. Red said he knew where we could get some paint and suggested we paint both the inside and outside. We talked of providing rugs but Ray said they'd only get soaked with the first rain. We then discussed slanting the roof using real roofing material and digging a moat around the outside to redirect rain. There was a proposal to add a No Trespassing sign over the door. Chuck wondered if we could find a lantern and use our clubhouse at night, maybe a couple of us even taking turns sleeping there. We debated if we could make it mosquito-proof for we hated mosquitoes, considering them miniature vampire bats. We thought of calling ourselves The Flub Club, the Alive Start Kids or The Clod Squad. We agreed our clubhouse was the next best thing to having a tree house.

It was a pleasant, relaxed, cheerful conversation until,

during a lull, Ray asked, "Do you guys know how to churn your chicken...you know...jack off?"

Did he really say what he said — JACK OFF?! We looked at Ray in astonishment and then at each other to see if anyone nodded. No one did. I'd heard about it. It was a mortal sin and if you did it hair grew on your palm.

Ray, who sat lounging against the garage wall, glanced at each of us awaiting an answer. "What's the matter? Don't you guys get hard-ons?"

I thought of the swing pole but didn't mention it, just nodded like everyone else.

"Well, I'll show you what to do with them. Someone keep watch at the window," Ray said, and placed a sheet of newspaper over his stretched-out legs.

Joe, who looked like he wanted to be elsewhere, reluctantly stationed himself at the small window as Ray unbuttoned the front of his trousers and pulled out a two-inch wide, nine-inch long truncheon that would have made Tess Trueheart faint. It was as if our club suddenly gained a new, unwanted member.

"Now say something to get me hot," Ray ordered.

Geez, I thought, you mean you ain't?

Joe, embarrassed, said, "I can't think of anything," and the rest of us remained silent. I doubted describing a swing pole's charms would have helped.

Impatiently, Ray growled, "Okay, I'll do it myself." With half-closed eyes he began describing out loud the beauty of a school friend's sister he once saw swimming at Belle Isle beach and, with some satisfaction, I noticed the truncheon only lengthened a couple more inches, but I'd still never stand next to him at a urinal.

When it was over we all sat transfixed until I asked, "What's it feel like?"

Ray goofily said, "If God made anything better He kept it for Himself."

At the mention of the Deity we all looked and felt guilty, with the exception of Ray who still grinned with half-mast

301

eyes and reached for a cigarette. Joe shook his head and said, with undisguised disgust, "Let's go play some more rain-on-the-roof."

As we crawled out of our clubhouse I thought, this explains why the church is against it. No wonder it's a mortal sin. It looked revolting. I couldn't wait to try it.

So once the rain-on-the-roof games were over, I ran into my house, up the stairs, into the bathroom, tried it and made a momentous discovery. I didn't want to be a Mountie, artist, inventor, sculptor, architect, cowboy, priest or milkman. I wanted to be a full-time chicken churner.

As I started down the stairs, realization of what I'd done struck heavily. I'd just committed my first, full-fledged mortal sin. My soul was completely black with not one dot of white remaining. Then I recalled the fifth-grade nun's words: "That's as black as it gets. It doesn't matter if you commit one or one-hundred mortal sins." I returned to the bathroom —and broke up with the swing pole.

In movies, Lon Chaney, the Wolf Man, on the eve of a full moon, would stare into a mirror hoping his face wouldn't get excessive hair growth. Somewhat like Lon, every morning upon awakening I checked my left palm for evidence of undesirable fuzz. After a few days I stopped checking and my belief in this tall tale went the way of the Bogeyman, Easter Bunny, Sandman, Jack Frost, Santa Claus and dragonflies sewing lips together.

Joining the sexually active world presented three worries — communion, confession and staying alive. I wasn't scheduled for a Saturday confession for ten days, plenty of time for layering my soul with blackness, but I did have to serve mass once before this confession, and altar boys were expected to receive communion. I shuddered at the consequences of receiving a sacred wafer in my sinful condition. If not struck dead at the holy altar, my tongue would no doubt turn black and fungusy when I extended it. The fifth-grade nun had told of nighttime thieves who'd robbed a church tabernacle and escaped with gold chalices. They didn't realize they were dropping communion hosts as they rushed to their lair. These hosts took on a ghostly glow in the darkness, leading policemen directly to the thieves before they could dispose of their loot. Misusing hosts led to dire punishment.

I considered going to the rectory prior to serving mass and asking a priest to hear my confession, but a face-to-face confession would be too embarrassing. Besides, mortal sins were fun, and I wanted to put off confessing as long as possible.

On the morning of serving mass I found a solution. I'd lie. One small lie, a venial sin, wouldn't even show up on my blackened soul. Before we entered the sanctuary to begin mass Father Gentner asked Stellon and me if we were going to receive communion. I told him I couldn't, that I had accidentally swallowed some water while brushing my teeth, thus breaking my midnight fast. I blushed reciting this story, because the priest stared at me as if he read my soul and didn't like what he read. I looked away and noticed Stellon smiling knowingly.

It was a long, guilt-filled mass — I felt unworthy to be on the altar — and I swore never again to commit a mortal sin. That afternoon I added two more to my growing total.

After a few days I stopped worrying about dying with a coal black soul and trusted to providence. If God didn't let Hitler and other bad people get killed, why would He let me? Nonetheless, I looked both ways twice when crossing streets.

Now my hardest-to-handle problem was my scheduled confession. Would the priest be shocked and start yelling at me through the screen for all to hear? Surely no other Catholic was as sinful. Would I have to say twenty-five rosaries for penance? Would he recognize my voice and expel me from the altar boys? And school? It was a horrible, dreadful scene to imagine.

By Saturday I had my strategy worked out. Though deceitful, I figured no one ever said you had to confess the big ones first. I'd bury them among a mass of venials.

When walking to church I thought many times of turning around but forced myself to continue onward. Once inside I sat apart from other students and concentrated completely on making a perfect confession. I especially avoided looking at female students. Sincerely sorry for all transgressions, I searched my conscience thoroughly for every sin committed in the prior two weeks. My memorized list was ready and I arose and stood in Father Wolbur's confessional line.

Entering and kneeling in the darkened cubicle, staring at the closed screen as perspiration poured from every pore, heart pounding, I prayed words would pass through my constricted vocal cords when my turn came. I heard the murmur of Father Wolbur's voice cease, the muffled sound of a sliding door, and the door in front of my face opened.

My words gushed out. "My last confession was two weeks ago and I have committed the following sins: I swore and cursed thirty-six times. I had impure thoughts thirty-three times. I disobeyed my parents twelve times. I did impure things twenty-four times. I lied six times. I cheated at games twice. For these and all the other sins of my past life I am heartily sorry."

Father Wolbur was paying attention and went right for the mortals. "These impure things you did...did you touch yourself?"

"Yes, Father," I whispered, wishing he'd lower his voice a tad.

"This is a very serious sin. Your body is the temple of the Holy Ghost and shouldn't be abused. You realize that, don't you?"

"Yes, Father."

"Do you recall the biblical story about dropping seed on a rock?"

"Yes, Father."

"Well, it's wrong and it has to stop. I want you to go to communion often and pray for strength to break this disgraceful habit. For your penance say a rosary. Now make a good Act of Contrition."

I smiled while reciting the Act of Contrition, for a great weight lifted from my body and I actually felt lighter. I left the confessional, knelt down in a pew, swiftly said the rosary using my fingers for beads, then ran home elated. My heart rejoiced for my soul was pure white, and if death came I'd go directly to heaven. I resolved to sin no more, avoiding even venials. It was the most magnificent feeling in the world to be in the state of grace!

The next morning, Sunday, I went to communion to strengthen my resolve and felt even more chaste and holy. Sainthood beckoned.

This rapturous emotion persisted until late afternoon when the red-haired skater appeared and started pirouetting in the middle of the street. Lusty feelings and thoughts flourished, battling pious righteousness. Sainthood still beckoned but, now, so did the bathroom. The bathroom won.

That afternoon was the first time I mastered the art of changing hands without missing a stroke.

In later years, when asked to describe my first sexual experience, I answered with a single word — "Lonely."

XXVI

As summer vacation waned we jammed in as much recreation time as possible with pom-pom-pullaway games played exclusively in front of Chandler school on a large grassy section edged by low hedges. This playing surface was ideal, and the games sometimes attracted 20 to 25 players ranging in age from 12 to 15. The person designated IT stood at mid-field facing the others lined up in an imaginary safety zone at one end of the playing area. IT sang out, "Pom-pom-pullaway, get your horse and runaway," and those lined up ran to a safety zone at the opposite end while trying to avoid ITs tag. Those tagged joined IT in the middle, helped sing out the pom-pom ditty and tag the remaining players as they repeated their charge across the field. After a few back-and-forth rushes there would be more taggers than taggees and the last tagged would be declared "winner," and the first tagged would be IT for a new game.

I loved pom-pom-pullaway. I relished slipping by taggers with quick fake-step maneuvers leaving them stymied. These moves, the same ones learned in alley touch-football games, worked even better on a wide grassy field.

The game's sole irritation was being IT. To stand alone in the middle of a field and sing out that moronic, mis-rhymed pom-pom chant, especially when girls played, completely flustered me. This chant was equalled in inanity only by "Run my sheepy, run" and "Red rover, red rover, let (some named person) come over" chanted in other games. When we changed the game to pom-pom tackle the embarrassment was somewhat alleviated because all the girls quit.

Tackling added an exciting dimension. No longer was it necessary to evade reaching hands. Staying on your feet became the challenge. And once tackled it became a challenge to tackle others, especially boys who outheighted and outweighed you. I learned head-on slamming into a large person caused shocking pain and extra pain if he used your suddenly prone form for turf, so I adjusted my technique by tackling big kids from the side or behind. Pom-pom-tackle became our favorite game — we played it three or four times a week — and summer vacation died.

* * *

I faced returning to Nativity with mixed emotions. High school was adulthood's training ground, a condition both dreaded and anticipated. Adults had more freedom to act, but also more responsibility for their actions. They had money, but parceled it out to threatening bill collectors, cajoling churches or begging children. In order to get this money they worked at uncaptivating jobs requiring long, humdrum hours, even longer than the humdrum hours we spent in school. Yet if they had cash remaining after doling out to collectors, churches and children, they freely spent it on pleasurable comforts like confections, cars, cigarettes, clothes and cabarets. I felt both envy and sorrow for adults. I wished to participate in driving, drinking, smoking and other grownup things, but hated the thought of abandoning childhood games and pleasures.

However, at thirteen years old, soon to be fourteen, I knew the inevitable was happening. I noticed changes in my attitude and taste and a subtle loosening of morals. I began to appreciate the big band sound in music. I closely listened to dialogue during movie love scenes. My all-consuming passion for candy, ice cream and pop diminished. I became more selective in buying comic books, only choosing those that featured female characters. I started listening to adult-themed programs on the radio, like Lux Radio Theatre, and often skipped the Lone Ranger and Green Hornet. And I stopped listening to The Shadow entirely. He was crazy. He had power to cloud peoples' minds so they couldn't see him, and he wasted it fighting crime. I would have clouded women's minds and spent all my time in bedrooms watching them disrobe. I even began reading my older sister's True Story, True Romance and True Confessions magazines. The stories were bland, but I found their feminine hygiene advertisements for Unitex sanitary shields and Fibs tampons intriguingly mysterious and their beautification advertisements fascinating, especially the kind that guaranteed three- to five-inch bust enlargement. I wondered if males could also use these enlargement methods. I asked Ray why a woman would even want to stick out three to five more inches in front and, after he explained the use of tape measures, he told me the ads were fraudulent. He said women who mailed money were sent a picture of a hand, meaning they should knead and manipulate their breasts. It didn't work and neither did secret formula bust enlargement lotions.

* * *

Stellon told me that Nativity's two freshman classrooms would have a mixture of boys and girls, but I believed we would be separated. How could a school that segregated boys and girls for three years, suddenly thrust us together again? But I hoped Stellon was right, and I was in for a wonderful, traumatic shock.

I arrived fifteen minutes early for the first day of school, and everyone else had the same idea. Masses of students stretched the school block's length, walking swiftly, slowly, bumping into each other, milling, jostling, looking for familiar faces. Knots of high school students stood in ragged circles in front of school and church, greeting, smiling, chattering. Mothers with reluctant first-graders in tow walked them into the main school building. The remaining grade school children reluctantly walked themselves in. Most nuns were already inside classrooms, but at times a straggler left the convent and swiftly walked toward school with students respectfully clearing a wide path, adding many "Good morning, sister" salutations. Some of these nuns actually smiled, as though they looked forward to fulfilling their religious vows. Dominican nuns belonged to the Order of Preachers and if they had to teach in order to preach they'd do so gladly.

I found Stellon standing with a small group of boys near the school's front entrance. I recognized Leroy Kolassa, Donald Fleming, Reynold Rimoldi and Frank Baccala, all returnees from the eighth grade. A round-jawed, sharp-nosed, hefty boy was with them who I'd never seen before. We all wore somber-colored shirts, ties, slacks and either oxford or loafer shoes. It seems strange now, but we had no advertising on our clothes, little alligators on our shirts, or Nike, Reebok or L.A. Gear emblazoned on footwear. The nearest thing to that present day practice was the picture of Buster Brown and his dog inside our shoes. Stellon even donned a plaid suit coat for the occasion, though it promised to be a warm day. We all held a loose-leaf folder or had one tucked under an armpit.

They gave me some loud "HIs" and "HOW-YA-DOIN's?" and I answered with an almost-whispered greeting learned from Ray over the summer — "How's it hangin'?" There were so many girls nearby I dared not shout it out. Frank Baccala was a tall well-built boy with black wavy hair, deep voice, and he already sported a hint of a moustache. (When I showed Dad my eighth-grade class graduation picture he pointed at Frank and asked, "How many children does he have in school?") Frank seriously

310

observed, "Do you guys realize we're the first class of high school boys in the history of Nativity?"

We'd previously thought of it but not in an historical perspective. We all nodded at the gravity of the pronouncement and noticeably stood a little taller, some even taking hands out of pockets, allowing feelings of importance to sink in. Then I silently decided that this fact would have little effect on the world as we knew it, and resumed my normal slouch.

We bantered with new arrivals and admired the high school female students. Many wore school uniforms, although uniforms weren't mandatory the first week. The rest, taking advantage of this opportunity, sported a multicolored hodgepodge of dresses, skirts and blouses. All modestly covered their legs with nylon or rayon stockings, some adding thick, white, folded-over bobby socks, and a small minority, perhaps not realizing or caring how unattractive, wore thin, pink or blue or anything-but-white anklets. I thought anklets made girls look like they'd just arrived at Ellis Island or stepped out of the Appalachian mountains. Most girls wore loafers, but a few opted for saddle shoes, the white parts of which had been thoroughly, deliberately dirtied.

The girl's uniform consisted of a navy blue skirt and bolero jacket with a white blouse open at the neck. The skirt was full and knee length, and the jacket sleeves reached almost to the wrist. There was one other small, but very important, uniform part. Each girl needed a navy blue beanie hairpinned to the top of her head when attending Mass for it was considered extremely disrespectful for a female's head to be completely uncovered in God's presence. If a student misplaced her beanie, she could wear a handkerchief pinned to her hair or wear a babushka, but it had better be an infrequent happening.

Stellon asked, "Hey, Bob, what homeroom did you get?"

I checked my registration slip and told him "Two-oh-one."

"You're lucky," he said. "You're with the rest of these guys. Me and Reno here (pointing to Rimoldi) got two-oh-two — Sister Richards. She's miserable."

Reno, tall and thin as a cue stick, another Italian with light-colored hair, laughed and said, "Aw, she couldn't be that bad. Besides, we'll be moving around to different classes."

I didn't know what he meant when he said we'd be moving around, but if they were in a different classroom then the two freshman classes would have both boys and girls, and I felt a surge of happiness. My eyes wandered to the inspirational words engraved over the school's entrance, THE TRUTH SHALL MAKE YOU FREE, words a confessed bank robber would dispute, and at that moment the first school bell clanged.

As we filed in, I nudged Stellon. "Who's the new hefty kid?"

"Oh, that's Jack Heffner. He's from Barbour. Seems like a nice guy."

Barbour Intermediate, a large school about a mile away, absorbed students from the area's public elementary schools. All public school kids on Holcomb went there after completing the sixth grade at Chandler and Joe and Ray told me it had a seventh, eighth and ninth grade. I vaguely wondered why Jack didn't finish the last year there. We crowded up the stairs to the second floor and I wished Stellon and Reno good luck with Sister Richards.

Room 201 was near to capacity when we entered. All good window seats overlooking McClellan were taken, but we spotted some empties at a rear corner and quickly grabbed them. With few exceptions, most boys sat bunched in islands among a sea of girls. The eight o'clock bell sounded as the nun closed the door and took attendance.

Nativity had 92 freshmen divided alphabetically into two classrooms. Nineteen boys and 27 girls named Alampi through Kraft were in room 201. Sixteen boys and 30 girls named LaDuke through Zotter were in 202. Each room had

312

six front-to-rear rows of seven or eight desks in close, claustrophobical proximity. This was advantageous for some mind-wandering, education-resistant students, such as I, lucky enough to have cooperative, scholarly seatmates who didn't begrudge moving an elbow allowing you to see a test answer or prompt you with whispered hints when called upon to define "isogony" or something equally as banal. However, on my first day of high school, I wasn't looking for educational advantages. I'd vowed to make serious attempts to assimilate a maximum of knowledge. The presence of female students would not deter me. I'd watch the blackboard, not girls. I was there to learn, not yearn. This noble attitude lasted for a minute and a half. Our first class was Religion, and as the nun expounded on this riveting subject, her voice droned, faded, and I began to surreptitiously examine the few girls I could see clearly. They were of different sizes and shapes with hair ranging from jet black to tawny. All were 13 or 14 years old and maturing nicely, except for one who could have put her brassiere on backwards and it would have fit. Gamic thoughts crept into my brain.

At 8:45 Religion class ended and we marched two by two to church for 9 o'clock Mass with girls leading the procession. Any activity outside classrooms still necessitated sex separation. As freshmen, we were required to fill up the front rows of pews, with sophomores, juniors and seniors seated progressively behind us. Being so close to the altar no longer constituted a major problem since Father Geller rarely officiated at 9 o'clock mass so we boys felt freer to make under-the-breath comments concerning nuns, fellow students and school life in general. Yet we remained wary because Father Geller, though a large man, walked silently and could materialize before we had time to stop grinning.

After mass we returned to our homeroom, and I learned why Jack, the hefty kid, came to Nativity. With the addition of boys the high school curriculum changed. No longer was it called Nativity of Our Lord Commercial High School.

The word "commercial" was dropped and college prep courses were added or planned. College didn't appeal to me but did to some far-sighted students like Jack. He explained this to me as we prepared to leave homeroom for our next class, an experience completely foreign to me. Every year through grade school we were taught all subjects in one room by one nun. Now we moved to other classrooms during the day to be taught specialized subjects by different nuns.

I saw her for the first time in the first class after lunch. We filed into the classroom, selected desks, and as the nun greeted us and made clear how much we'd appreciate her General Business course, I noticed a girl sitting in the row to my right, three seats forward. She had shifted in her seat so her calf was pulled back and partially in the aisle between us. Her uniform skirt, tight around her thigh and four-inches above her knee, caused me to temporarily lose interest in General Business. I had the distinct feeling I'd never laid eyes on this girl before, even though I couldn't see her face. After studying last year's eighth grade girls whenever possible and from every angle, I knew she was new to Nativity. Her hair — neck-length, dark-brown and ending in thick, ratless waves that circled her head — was a style I didn't recognize. Every time she moved I tried to see her face. No luck. In the meantime I studied the rest of her. Nature had compressed her waist making her hips flare, so, out of curiosity, I mentally removed her uniform, blouse, shoes and slip, but because of our religious surroundings, allowed her to retain her bra, panties, nylons and garter belt. She looked gorgeous! She had rounded arms and rounded thighs to go with her obviously rounded calves, and I fervently hoped, if we ever became acquainted, she'd have rounded heels.

When the school bell sounded ending class she squeezed out into the aisle, turning sideways. I was enthralled! Her lipstickless lips were full, her eyes deep brown. Her nose, holding clear plastic-rimmed glasses, tilted slightly up-

314

ward. I was pleased she wore glasses. Many boys weren't attracted to spectacle wearers so, hopefully, this would eliminate some future competition. She smiled at the girl on her left and I noticed her teeth protruded a little, but so did everything else in front that started with a "t." Although she measured only five-feet tall and I was a little under six-feet — a mere seven-inches under — I felt adjusting to this height difference could be easily accomplished. I was wholly smitten and all thoughts of Doris, Rosie, Catherine and even Laura vanished.

Returning to homeroom for my last class, I discovered her again. I'd missed her on my morning cursory classmate examination. After dismissal I waited outside the school doors and watched her meet another uniformed girl and walk toward Gratiot. I started home wondering if my feeling inside was a lovely lust or lusty love. Whichever, it felt good, and I knew the romance of the century had just begun.

Stellon, at my urging, talked to her whenever possible and for two weeks he garnered information. Her name was Kathleen Kelly. She and her sister Lois, a sophomore, took the Gratiot streetcar to and from school. She wore her uniform skirts short to save cloth, her small patriotic contribution to the war effort. She was quiet in class, seldom volunteering answers unless called upon, and when called upon, seldom giving correct answers. My admiration grew. Unscholastic girls were a rarity at Nativity.

Then Stellon discovered a discouraging fact. She lived way up Gratiot near Six Mile Road. I'd be wasting my time if ever I developed nerve enough to ask for a date. It was too far to walk, I couldn't afford the round trip streetcar fare, and I didn't own a bicycle. The romance of the century slowed before it flowed.

There were neighborhood activities to partially distract my thoughts. By early autumn, pom-pom-tackle at Chandler school gave way to tackle football. Football became an obsession. On Saturdays, if the Chandler field was occupied, Red, Joe, Carl, Ray and Cliff rode their bicycles, carrying Chuck and me on their crossbars, about 20 blocks up Gratiot to Detroit City Airport. There was spacious grass, just made for football, between an airport hangar and Gratiot Avenue. Boys our age from a nearby trailer court sometimes challenged us to a game. Joe called plays with handoffs, laterals and fakes, and we rarely lost.

One Saturday, when the others weren't available, Joe and I walked to Chandler school and found older boys, 16 to 18 years old, playing football, six to a side. Joe said we should ask if we could join them. I couldn't believe he'd say something so dumb. "Geez, Joe. Those guys are big. We'll get killed!" One even punted the football with a grass-stained bare foot and looked like he chewed railroad spikes.

Joe just said, "Don't worry about it. We'll do okay."

Joe jumped the two-foot high hedge surrounding the grass and talked to the barefoot punter who glanced at me and yelled out to the other team, "Okay if we take on a couple kids?"

A sophisticated speaker answered, "We don't give a goddamn."

Barefoot's team lined up on defense and he positioned Joe and me behind the right side of the scrimmage line, warning, "Stand over here and don't let 'em run over ya." He grinned, and I noticed two front teeth missing, probably from chewing those spikes. He wandered over to a safety position and Joe, who stood two yards behind me said, "If they come this way, you hit 'em low and I'll hit 'em high."

I thought he was nuts and asked myself, what am I doing here? A couple guys in the other team's backfield must have weighed a ton. We'd be trampled! After an incomplete pass the thing I dreaded occurred. They ran a play around our end. The ball carrier's blockers were knocked down at the scrimmage line, leaving him alone and bearing down heavily on me. As I ran forward, Joe, right behind me, yelled, "Get him! Get him!" I couldn't remember if I should tackle high or low and chose low.

The ball carrier veered outside a half-second before our collision, and Joe and I smacked him at the same time, driving him into the hedge. Barefoot stood over us chuckling and shaking his head. He helped Joe and me to our feet saying, "Nice going, guys," and to the ball carrier, who arose slowly while examining a bloody gash on his forearm, "My kids did okay, eh?"

Gash answered churlishly, "We'll be back."

They ran six more plays around our end and each time Joe and I stopped them with little gain. Joe timed his tackles so we hit the runner simultaneously, reducing the impact on our bodies. They specifically assigned a guy to block us, but then Barefoot joined in our tackles. Finally the other team's captain complained that it was eight against six and said, "Give us a young guy."

"You can't have my kids," Barefoot yelled back, "but I'll give you Ralph here," and motioned for a slow, overweight lineman to join the other team.

At game's end Barefoot discovered Joe could catch a pass thrown anywhere in his vicinity and run like a cheetah. Joe scored two touchdowns and we won the game handily.

As we limped home Joe enthusiastically blurted, "Let's go back next Saturday. Maybe they'll be there again. That sure was fun, wasn't it?"

"Yeah," I said aloud, while silently debating which of my bruises and lacerations throbbed the most.

Joe was serious. He rounded up Red, Cliff, Ray, Carl, Chuck and me, and the following Saturday morning we trooped over to Chandler looking for the older guys. Joe believed we all should have an opportunity to get maimed. Disappointed when they weren't there, he organized two teams, and we played an energetic game among ourselves. However, the day's highlight happened after the game as we sat on the grass exhausted. Ray asked, "Hey, do you guys wanna get high?"

We looked puzzled, so he added, "You know, like drunk."

A couple of us nodded. Ray explained that all a potential sot had to do is take three deep breaths, hold the last one, let Ray squeeze his chest from behind for 50 or 60 seconds, and when he let loose, the person squeezed would experience an intoxicated feeling. We all expressed disbelief because Ray lied a lot, but he swore it was true. "I saw it done at Eastern," he said. (Ray, Joe, Carl and Cliff attended Eastern High School.)

He called for volunteers to try it, tempting me, but I wasn't sure I wanted anyone embracing me from behind. The beastly episode with Blackie the dog was still fresh in my memory. Big Carl grudgingly agreed to participate. They both stood up and Ray encircled Carl's chest with his arms. Carl took three deep breaths and Ray clamped his hands together, squeezed and started counting out loud. By the time he counted to forty Carl's stoic face had turned crimson. At fifty Ray released his grip and Carl released his breath. He smiled, dropped to his knees and then flopped onto his face. Joe, looking worried, asked, "Are you okay, Carl?"

Ray grinned. "I told you it worked. He'll be all right. See! His eyes are still open!"

Ten seconds passed before Carl shakily regained his feet. "That sure was a funny feeling," he muttered.

We asked for more details, but all he could say was it made him weak and dizzy. I tried it next. When I exhaled after Ray's one minute squeeze, I didn't feel any different. I took two steps before hitting the grass.

Losing control of extremities, even for a short time, was an odd sensation. I didn't know the word "torpor" so I explained it felt freaky, and then, with the exception of Joe, the rest of us tried it on each other and all agreed it was an interesting, but not excessively pleasurable, experience.

Later Ray mentioned the squeeze slowed blood supply to heart and brain and, he heard in rare cases, could lead to dangerous consequences, including death. We told Ray he had a quaint, warped sense of humor and should have his dumb ass kicked.

XXVII

As promised, once Pat became a probation-passed employee of Buhl's, she purchased a Crosley Shelvador refrigerator. No longer would we empty a sloshing drip pan from under an icebox. No longer would we place an ice card in our front window. No longer would the iceman cometh.

I admired Pat's work ethic. She worked full-time at Buhl's during summer vacation and continued part-time when school started, including a half-day on Saturday. Monday through Friday she arrived home at 8:30 p.m., ate, and did her homework. To become as industrious when I reached her age became my long-range ambition.

* * *

At school we detected a subtle demeanor change in Nativity's younger priests, Fathers Wolbur, Burroughs and Gentner. Where once they exuded a serious, business-like, yet saintly air, now they were friendly toward, and active with, the nuns, parishioners and students — especially boy students. They laughed and bantered with us, and we expected them at any time to break into a catchy song, such as *Swinging on a Star*. We were sure they'd seen Bing Crosby in the movie *Going My Way* and realized they could be both priests and relaxed regular guys. They began participating with us in lunch hour and after-school football or handball games at the Recreation Center playing field, even allowing an agitated expletive, damn or hell, to escape from their priestly lips if someone dropped one of their football passes or slapped a handball out of their reach. We relished the priests' participation except for two minor annoyances. We had to be careful of our own, much stronger, language, and the priests always wanted to be quarterback. Father Wolbur and Father Gentner specialized in long spiral passes that passed ten-feet over the receiver's head, and Father Burroughs threw accurate, short wobblies, difficult to catch. Yet we appreciated the camaraderie with these clerics and were happy Bing had made the award-winning movie about a down-to-earth priest. We waited in vain for Father Geller to take on the crotchety, but loveable, ways of Bing's co-star, Barry Fitzgerald, who played the pastor. Father Geller apparently didn't see the movie.

Up until *Going My Way* Bing Crosby had starred in many lightweight movies including three comedies with Bob Hope entitled *Road to Singapore, Road to Zanzibar* and *Road to Morocco.* Now critics hailed his Going My Way performance, predicting he had a rosy future as a dramatic actor. It happened at an opportune time, for a new singer threatened to replace him as America's premier crooner. This singer, Frank Sinatra, entranced the teenaged female population. Many girls who attended Sinatra's concerts had emotion-control problems, most screaming, some crying, a few floor-flopping in ecstasy. Newspaper columnists who reported this swooning phenomenon questioned whether mass hysteria was a healthy outlet for young innocents.

Sinatra didn't have the same affect on adults and teenage boys. The adults agreed with the critical columnists and we boys couldn't grasp what attracted girls to a thin, sunken-faced, unhealthy-looking, 4-F military reject who in no way resembled our muscular comic book and movie heroes. We believed the Selective Service System should have classified him as 2-D for draft dodger (How could a singer have ear drum problems?) and we jealously assumed our sisters and female acquaintances would eventually come to their senses, and his career would be short-lived. But, just in case, some of us secretly considered a starvation diet and singing lessons.

* * *

The war news for the free world was generally good in November of 1944. German forces were driven from Greece, Russian troops advanced through Hungary, and Tokyo was bombed three times by B-29s based on Saipan. General Douglas MacArthur, referred to as "Dugout Doug" by resentful servicemen because he fled during the 1942 Japanese invasion of the Philippines while vowing "I shall return," returned with U.S. forces and crumbled Japanese resistance.

There was bad news. Germany had bombed England from June to September with inaccurate, pilotless V-1 robot bombs launched from France. Now they had long-range V-2 rocket bombs, accurate and aimed at London.

In politics, President Roosevelt was reelected to a fourth term.

There also was news at our house and several family members considered it bad. Mary's platonic friendship with Bill next door turned serious. The car accident that relieved Bill of his left arm hadn't relieved him of his love for driving cars, though conspicuous left turn signals were a problem. He and Mary started taking long leisurely drives to distant Detroit suburbs, two or three evenings a week. When Mary came home past curfew after one of these drives, Mom waited. "Where have you been, Mary?" she began.

"We just went to St. Clair Shores, Ma. We stopped at Tony's Popcorn Stand and talked.

321

"You talked for four hours? What could you talk about for four hours? You talked to him every night this summer from your bedroom window. He's too old for you. He knows too much. He must be flink or he wouldn't bother with a young girl."

"He's only twenty-two, Ma."

"Well, you're only seventeen. This is going to stop."

"We're not getting married, Ma. We're just friends. He's homesick."

"Let him be homesick with someone his age. Besides, he's not Catholic." Bill's lack of proper religious affiliation was Mother's second strongest argument against the relationship. She gave Mary the first. "I'll have to get your father involved if you don't come to your senses."

Mary fled to her bedroom, dampened her pillow with tears, cursed life's injustices and plotted how she could continue the warm, but still relatively innocent, affair.

The following afternoon Mary found Bill parked outside when she left work. They drove out Lake Shore Drive, a scenic winding road in the Grosse Pointe suburbs, and Mary tearfully recounted the previous night's conversation with Mother. He listened silently, parked on a side street, held her in his arm, kissed her and said, "Maybe it's fer the best. Ah'm going home soon fer Christmas anyway. We'll tawk about what to do when Ah get back."

They pledged undying admiration for each other and returned to Detroit where he dropped her off a half-block from home. Two weeks later, in mid-December, he headed south.

Mary felt forlorn. Bill hadn't given her an address so she could write to him. "It'll be less than a month," he'd said. She busied herself at home by writing long letters to Bud Davis and other servicemen. Unfortunately Bud couldn't respond. The German army launched a desperate but powerful surprise offensive against the western front, pushed the U.S. Army back sixty miles and effectively surrounded and trapped a garrison of Airborne troops at Bastogne in

Belgium. The troops refused to surrender. Bud was among them.

* * *

I submitted my usual bicycle request and Christmas morning received my usual two items of clothing along with a surprise gift, fitting for one who'd attained the lofty age of fourteen, a leather wallet containing a one-dollar bill. I felt very mature as I folded and thrust the wallet into my hip pocket while wondering what else would fit into its many slots and crevices.

Later in the day, Dad and Mom gave their children an extra Christmas present — news that we were moving to a larger house in three weeks. They were buying, not renting, a house near Gratiot and Six Mile road. Pat and I would continue at Nativity, but Chuck, Dolores and Ann would transfer to Assumption Grotto grade school in the new neighborhood. The house had four bedrooms, a sunroom, large kitchen, dining room with table and chairs, living room, driveway, two-car garage, large upstairs bathroom, and basement shower. The best news was the shower. I'd never experienced one that didn't originate from clouds.

I asked Mom to write down the new address on a piece of Christmas wrapping paper and stuck it in my wallet. The street name, Cedargrove, conjured up woodsy images and I knew I'd like it. I also knew it was in the Detroit section where Kathy Kelly lived, and pleasant fanciful thoughts of future befriending filled my brain.

Two days after Christmas the besieged Bastogne garrison was relieved by U.S. armored forces that cut a corridor through German lines. Bud Davis survived.

Mom insisted she'd not move into a dirty house so, prior to our moving date, she and Dad, accompanied by Betty, often drove to the new house after supper with a broom, mop, buckets and rags to scrub floors, ceilings and walls. Growing impatient to see the house, I begged to go along to

323

help them clean, but Mom insisted school homework was more important than any dubious assistance I might supply.

Ten days before we moved, Bill returned next door. It was a long, distressing ten days for Mary. Mom's character assessment wasn't quite as flawed as Mary previously believed. Bill returned accompanied by his new wife.

* * *

Sometimes an ordinary day can turn miraculous. After school, one week before we moved, as Chuck and I sat in the kitchen watching supper preparations and pumping Mom for new-house details, Dolores entered and said, "Robbie, there are two girls outside who want to see you."

"Don't kid me, Dolorie."

"Honest. One of them said, 'Tell your brother Robert that Kathy wants to see him.'"

I shot out to our front porch and gazed at the backs of two girls in matching dark brown coats with black velvet collars walking swiftly, already more than halfway to the Chapin corner store. One was Kathy Kelly. I'd stared at her hairdo so often at school I easily recognized it, even from a distance. Back in the house, I briefly contemplated what to do. Surprised at my nervy decision, I grabbed my gray plaid jacket and tore out the front door.

They weren't in sight. They had either rounded the corner or were in the corner store. I slowed my sprint to a lope, not only to better avoid sidewalk ice patches, but also to allow time to practice my opening gambit; except my impassioned brain wouldn't permit logical ideas. Anxiety settled in, and I told myself to turn around and go home. If she wanted to see me she would have stayed in front of my house. Go home. Yet my legs moved forward. I rounded the corner, and they had already crossed the alley apron. I stopped and heard myself yell out "Hey" and instantly regretted it. A "Hey" yell at girls sometimes earned an embarrassing retort of "Hay is for horses." Happily, they weren't familiar with this clever comeback for they stopped, turned, smiled and Kathy waved.

Rapidly covering the distance between us I asked, "Where ya going?"

"We're just walking around the neighborhood killing time 'til basketball practice," Kathy said. "It starts at 6:30. Lois knows one of the girls on Nativity's team. This is my sister Lois, by the way."

Lois smiled attractively and said, "I'm pleased to meetcha."

"Hi. What practice?"

Lois answered, "At the Recreation Hall. A lot of kids go there to watch."

"Can boys go?" I asked Lois. It was easier speaking to her. If I looked at Kathy she might notice the naked craving in my eyes.

"Sure. Everyone's welcome. Bring your friends."

"Okay, I'll call Stellon."

Lois turned to Kathy. "Stellon? He's the guy you—"

Kathy broke in. "Yeah. He's nice. Bill Stellon. I talk to him in school, and he jokes around a lot."

Lois smiled. "Great! Bring him. We'll see you later."

I forced a nervous grin, said "Okay, see ya" and turned, trying to walk away naturally on unsteady legs, realizing why people referred to those they love as "my heartthrob." My heart beat faster than a Gene Krupa solo. Although the weather was cold and overcast, I became aware of an exceptional amount of armpit perspiration. Perhaps a bath was needed. Six-thirty was a little more than an hour away, and I had much to do. I turned around at the corner, admired their retreating calves, and sprinted for home.

I phoned Stellon, and he said we'd meet in front of the Rec building. He also explained that Kathy had asked for my address just before he'd left school. I ate supper, told Mom about watching basketball practice, was told to be home at 8:30, bathed, donned clean clothes, greased down my cowlick, grabbed my coat and slipped outside.

It was dark and moonless as I quietly cut through our alley and Blaso's backyard. Running across Chandler school playground, I kept my eyes on the beckoning, lighted, Recreation Center building, then slowed to a walk while memorizing questions I planned to ask Kathy and subjects we could talk about. It was a short list, and I hoped Stellon would fill in any conversation gaps. Emerging from the playground I spotted Stellon standing on the Rec center's concrete steps leading to its front doors, his feet stomping, arms crossed and gloved hands slapping at his heavy, fur-trimmed coat. Bill always griped about cold weather and was one of few boys who still wore a hat during winter. His was brown leather, fur-lined with ear flaps. Most boys wore earmuffs and disdained hats, feeling it unmanly to yield to weather. Some bravely declared, "The only weather I worry about is whether she does or whether she doesn't," a witticism often spouted by we pseudo-sophisticated boys who had yet to date a girl. I actually didn't wear a hat because it collapsed my Vaseline-stiffened pompadour.

"Hurry up! I'm freezing!" Bill shouted when he saw me.

I ran across McClellan, up the stairs, pulled open one of the double doors, entered and stood in a dimly lit vestibule. Through closed doors leading to the gymnasium, we heard muffled sounds of high-pitched voices punctuated by a coach's whistle and basketball thumps on a hardwood floor. I whispered, "Are they here?"

"Yeah. They told me they'd meet us in the balcony."

The balcony was right above us. As we started up the stairs, my heart sped up, and I asked fearfully, "What'll I say?"

"Hey, you've wanted to talk to her for months. You'll think of something." Bill wrongly believed that the more you liked someone the easier it was to converse with them.

There were a dozen high school students, all girls, standing and elbow-leaning on the cement block barrier overlooking the basketball courts. The Kelly sisters were noticeable, solely because they still wore school uniforms.

They hadn't gone home to change. Bill and I walked up to them and voiced our mandatory greetings. Bill moved to Lois' side, I to Kathy's and we watched the girls below practice passing, blocking, shooting and dribbling. The players wore white, short-sleeved uniforms and I wondered why no one had ever told me of the attractions of basketball. Their hems were six to eight inches above their kneecaps.

Bill explained the game's rules, and I half-listened. It was getting warm. I asked Kathy what she and Lois did with their coats, and she turned and indicated a darkened corner behind us where many coats hung on three maneuverable spotlights used to illuminate school plays. Stellon and I hung our jackets with the rest, and I noticed he sported his beige sport coat with dark brown sleeves. He looked good, and so did I wearing my favorite black and white, houndstooth, long-sleeved shirt with zipper neck. I whispered, "I still don't know what to talk about."

"Why don't you take her down to the basement and show her the swimming pool?"

"I never heard of a pool down there."

"There isn't, but so what? She's never been in here before and you want to get her alone, don't you?"

"Good idea," I said. Sometimes Stellon was inspired.

Kathy agreed to accompany me when I quietly suggested checking out the basement pool. When told where we were going, Lois snickered and said, "Take your time and have a nice swim."

We descended to the vestibule, found the basement door and pushed it open. I struck a match and led Kathy down the darkened stairwell to the swinging doors at the bottom that opened effortlessly to a room as huge as the gym. It was noiseless and dark, the only illumination provided by rooftop floodlights that bathed the building's outside and dimly deflected through basement windows. Our eyes adjusted to the murkiness and we saw rows of long, wooden tables and folding chairs lined up for church dinners or bingo games. "Where's the pool?" Kathy murmured.

Christ! I thought. She actually believed me. "I was only kiddin'. I just wanted to talk to ya alone." I blushed, glad that she couldn't see me clearly.

She wasn't upset or disappointed. She even smiled and said, "I thought so. Let's look around."

We entered the kitchen area and, with lighted matches, admired the huge stove and stainless steel refrigeration units. We found a cold storage room stacked high with full cases of orange, cherry and root beer pop bottles. I asked if she wanted to drink one and appreciated her "No" answer, since I didn't have a bottle opener. We returned to the main basement area and she stopped, leaned back against a table and said nervously, "It's certainly quiet. Do you think we should be down here?"

I told her it was okay and began asking questions, not wanting to leave. I learned she was ten months older than I and had seven brothers and two sisters. Three brothers were in the army and her oldest sister was in the Woman's Army Corps. Kathy graduated from Assumption Grotto grade school and could have attended Dominican, an all-girls high school closer to home, but chose Nativity because Lois enjoyed it so much. I mentioned my younger brother and sisters were going to attend Grotto when we moved into her neighborhood, and she said they'd like the school. Then I asked what street she lived on.

"Cedargrove."

"Cedargrove?! That's the street I'm moving on," I said excitedly, reaching for my wallet. "What's your house number?"

"One-four-one-five-one."

Holding the small piece of paper with the new address up to the scant window light I read aloud the numbers. "One-four-one-six-one. God! I'm moving next door to ya!"

"I don't think so. I haven't heard about any next door neighbors moving out."

I didn't want to doubt her word. "Maybe I wrote the number wrong but I know the street's right. Anyway, maybe we'll be able to take the streetcar to school together."

"That would be nice," she said, smiling. She licked her lips, and I had a strong urge to kiss them before they dried. Reluctantly I put aside the urge. Girls in movies sometimes slapped boys attempting a first-date kiss, and this phony pool-viewing couldn't even be considered a date.

We talked for a couple more minutes and then, sighing softly, she said, "We'd better go."

Soft sighing was one of my favorite things, but not followed by "We'd better go." Little did I know how many times in future years I'd hear those words of finality: "We'd better go."

A crisp, crystal-like, snowy mantle covered the hushed outside world when the four of us emerged from the building. As we took the long walk to Gratiot's streetcar stop, closely following Lois and Bill, Kathy and I listened to their chuckling conversation and our crunching footsteps that sounded louder in the church-like silence surrounding us. Even the few slow-moving passing cars seemed muted. The purity of air and snow matched the emotions I was experiencing. A four-word refrain, "She really likes me," kept meandering through my mind. I knew I'd never again be happier or feel as blissful, and nothing could corrupt my love for this chaste girl at my side. The street lights, encircled by glistening halos, added to my spiritual feelings. I realized a heavenly-influenced miracle had occurred. Surely God had something to do with moving me to Cedargrove so close to my love. As we passed Nativity Church our gloved hands touched, and she caught my hand in hers. I looked at her, admired her virtuous, shadowed loveliness, squeezed her hand, and an odd, outrageous thing occurred. I got a hard-on.

I couldn't believe it! I'm not even thinking of anything like that, I told myself. Why is this happening? Thank God I wore my long jacket! Then I thought, maybe I'm involving God a little more than necessary in this. He probably had

329

much to do with moving me to Cedargrove, but I doubted if He was concerned with hiding my embarrassment with a long jacket.

I held Kathy's hand until the streetcar arrived, shouted to her and Lois as they boarded that we'd see them tomorrow, and the damn thing went down.

Bill and I started for home and he said Lois told him Kathy liked me, and he hoped I'd made the best of my opportunity in the Recreation basement. I explained about the moving-onto-her-street miracle, and he, too, was astonished. "I don't know if it's a miracle," he said," but it certainly is a heckuva coincidence."

We parted in front of Nativity church and I gleefully trotted home.

XXVIII

The moving van sat in front of our house, and I sat on Butlers' front porch silently watching furniture being loaded. Joe, Red, Cliff and Ray sat with me, our frigid, pink faces exhaling blue, steamlike clouds. The sole warmth I felt was my warm thoughts of Kathy. She and I now exchanged smiles and quiet greetings between classes, and during one lunch hour I briefly spoke with her at Taylor's Sweetshop on McClellan near Gratiot. She'd discovered our new house was two doors from hers. This somewhat disappointed me. Songs and stories were written about girl- and boy-next-door romances, not about girls and boys with a house in between.

Earlier, on this Saturday moving day, Chuck and I helped Dad load his car with small household items — dishes, silverware, pots, pans, clothes, ash trays — and Dad had driven off to our new house with Chuck, Dolores and Ann. Betty and Mary were already at the Cedargrove address, and Pat was at her part-time job. I waited for Dad's return. Chuck had said a quick good-bye to our Holcomb friends, and, with the exception of broken-hearted Mary, who couldn't get away fast enough from good-neighbor Bill, he seemed the most anxious to leave Holcomb street. I'd garnered this opinion from a conversation the night before. Chuck and I were in bed speculating about our new house when I mentioned, "I'm really gonna miss this neighborhood."

"I won't," he said.

"Why not?"

"I hate it. I can't wait ta leave."

"Why?"

"Why? 'Cause everybody here wants to beat my ass. I go to school and the nuns beat my ass. Father Geller beats my ass. Everybody in school beats my ass. Then I come home, and Pa beats my ass."

"I didn't know Geller hit ya."

"Yeah, he did. Last year. He didn't like my report card. It hurt me bad."

"Did ya tell Ma?"

"Nah. She'd tell Pa, and he'd beat my ass. I want out of this rotten neighborhood. Ya take a walk somewhere, see someone on the next block, and he beats your ass. They're always waiting for me. I try to go down different streets, and they catch me anyway. I walk down the street and here comes a whole gang of kids wanting to whale on my ass. I try to run...they catch me...get me down...beat my ass...hurt me. Christ! What a crock. No matter what I do here, somebody wants to beat my ass. We climb garages, someone gets pissed off and beats my ass. You know the wop cop down the street?"

"Yeah."

"The summer before last me and Red were stealing cherries off the tree next door to him. I was standing on his fence picking cherries, and that bastard came out and grabbed me. I jumped and he caught me in mid-air right by the ankle. That sonovabitch hung me over the fence for awhile, pulled me up, sat me on his porch and said, 'Sit there while I go call the cops,' and he was going to go call his buddies and take me to prison. I was so dumb I sat there."

"Why didn't ya just leave when he went in the house?"

"'Cause I didn't know any better. I was only ten. I musta sat there for an hour. You know that dago who used to own the store on the corner?"

"Yeah."

"He smacked me one day and knocked me silly. I don't know what I said to him, but geez! He rattled my teeth. I can't even go to the damn grocery store, ya know? One way or another I always say the wrong thing. One time I went with Red to see the old woman down the street…He said he liked to do things for her 'cause she was so nice…Gave him cookies and things. He said I'd like her. We weren't there five minutes before she started yelling at me, 'You get outta here! I don't like you! Get outta here!' I still don't know what I said, and neither does Red, but she wanted to beat my ass. This is a lousy neighborhood. If someone isn't beating your ass, some damn dog is biting your ass. I hate this place. I'll be glad to get outta here."

I never realized Chuck took life so seriously nor felt so strongly about the neighborhood but, after I stopped laughing, I gave him some brotherly advice: "Ya really should learn how to run faster and not talk so much."

Dad returned and parked behind the van. It was time to go. I stood and said, "I'll see you guys after school sometime."

"Not if we see you first," Ray said. He grinned, but I still detected sadness in his face, like a disappointed teacher watching a favorite student leave school. I was leaving before he'd completed my corruption.

Joe shook my hand and said, "Take it easy." Cliff echoed, "Yeah, take it easy," and Red joked, "I'd like to say I enjoyed knowing you, Bob. I'd like to, but…"

I nodded, forced a smile and repeated, "See ya," then turned and loped across the street.

Dad and I went through the garage and house, a final check, to ensure we weren't leaving anything, then helped Mom carry boxes of folded linen and curtains into the car as the van pulled away. Dad locked up the house, put the key in the mailbox, and the three of us got into his car. From the back seat I waved at the guys as we drove away.

With the exception of Red who visited me on Cedargrove

a year and a half later, I never again saw my Holcomb friends. Mary kept in touch with Mary Jane Butler for a few years so I learned Joe went to a small Michigan college and played wide end on its football team. I'm sure when he graduated he went on to better things. He was talented, confident, and a leader-type. I can only speculate as to the others. Cliff probably went into chicken farming; Red, a favorite of the ladies on the block, could have opened a home for aged widows; and probably Ray, with his flair for disseminating truths of life, ended up in an educational position. Sadly, I never had an opportunity to beat hell out of "Centigrade" Sammy, who, in later life, would have been perfect at wielding a slaughterhouse sledge hammer.

Dad was cheerful while driving up Gratiot to our new home, a perfect time to ask what prompted him to buy the house so close to Kathy, so I did. "Hey, Pa. Why'd ya buy the house on Cedargrove?"

I expected him to say, "I was mysteriously drawn to it." Instead he said, "The real estate agent recommended it. They had a study done and northeast Detroit will be the last section to turn black."

In retrospect his statement is amazing for this was January, 1945, long before the emergence in the '60s of the Stokley-Rap-Eldridge types who targeted ancestors of slaveholders and everyone remotely resembling those ancestors, declaring it permissible to rob and steal from them to atone for years of repression — slave reparations of a sort. In Detroit, many targets sought suburban safety. This was before Detroit's 1967 rebellion when many black leaders declared a need for more housing and jobs; then, during the rebellion, their followers burned down houses and businesses. More targets moved out. This was before representatives from newly-formed organizations visited small neighborhood stores and subtly suggested that regular contributions to their particular group would keep the stores flame-free. Many store owners closed and relocated outside Detroit's city limits rather than pay this additional fire insurance. This was before Detroit's mayor, in his 1974 inaugural address, loudly warned that his less law-abiding constituents should "hit Eight Mile," a thriving boundary between Detroit and some suburbs. Most people realized it was his quaint way of saying "Crooks, get out of town," but some constituents misinterpreted his words. With pointed weapons they hit Eight Mile liquor stores, gas stations, banks, motels, taverns, markets and restaurants. After most of those businesses closed or sported ghetto gates, bricked-up windows, buzzer doors, bullet-proof material and designer plywood, ladies of the evening hit Eight Mile and started plying their trade. More targets moved. This was before well-meaning judges, living in safe suburbs, decided Detroit's black and target children should learn to socialize and swap cultures while at school, and decreed an elaborate busing program. For Sale signs popped up on Detroit lawns faster than dandelion puff-balls. A few daring, less-scrupled, enterprising targets found a simpler, more-profitable and speedier way to move. Their heavily-insured homes and businesses mysteriously caught fire, and at times a faint gasoline aroma could be detected in the ashes. This was before 1989 when over thirty Catholic churches closed because their parishioners had deserted them in a "mass" exodus. Yet the 1945 real estate demographers, who couldn't have predicted these events, were correct. There remains a section of northeast Detroit, cuddled on two sides by suburbs and virtually all target. It's partly peopled by a contingent of current and retired city employees and is sometimes called "copper canyon" because many policemen reside there. Its undefined boundaries are steadily shrinking and eventually it will, as they say in the movie world, fade to black.

Despite my father's astonishing reason for buying the house I preferred to believe a more spiritual force influenced his decision, that a vaporous shining dove cooed into his ear as he slept, "Buy ye a house at 14161 Cedargrove. It will make thee and thy family happy and one son ecstatic."

335

Dad turned onto Cedargrove and slowly drove toward our new home. Tall leafless trees lined both sides of the street, meeting and meshing at their crests, forming a twiggy tunnel. I noticed most houses we passed had separating driveways and wide front porches and some were brick, a sign of wealth. As we crossed the first intersection at Grover street we saw the moving van parked at the curb three-quarters of the way down the street, and I began checking addresses watching for 14151. I hoped Kathy wouldn't be sitting on her porch while the van unloaded. I doubted she'd be awed with our home furnishings since we didn't own chaise lounges or Chippendale armoires. But then again, she might be impressed with our new refrigerator and electric wringer washing machine.

Kathy wasn't on her porch as we passed, but five boys near my age were. They sat on her steps clothed in Ace caps, parkas, windbreakers and lumberjack jackets and watched the activity at our house. As Dad pulled into our driveway I thought, this neighborhood's going to be fine — Kathy so near and guys to hang out with.

By February, Cedargrove living became routine. Pat and I walked to Gratiot every school day morning and caught the streetcar for the three-mile ride to Nativity. The Kelly girls sometimes left their house at the same time, and we walked and rode together. Kathy and I didn't talk much — she was naturally quiet, and I was afraid I'd say something dumb and she'd discover I was dumb — so our romance didn't progress. Perhaps when I became more accustomed to her presence I'd get up the nerve to ask for a date. But what if she refused? She was fifteen years old, almost a year older than I, and I'd noticed most girls wanted to go out with older boys. I wasn't aware that she had a boyfriend, in school or otherwise, but maybe she did. So I devised a clever plan. I asked Bill Stellon, who sometimes bantered with her between classes, to find out if she dated.

Bill waited for me outside school at lunchtime. "I did

336

what you told me," he laughed. "I asked if she'd go out with any guys from school. She said, 'Sure. Where are we going?' I told her I wasn't asking for me — that YOU wanted to know. She said, 'Tell him to talk for himself!' She was a little upset. Damn! You almost got me a date!"

Mortification and jealousy shot through me. I recalled a pilgrim story where Priscilla told some guy to speak for himself. "Ya shouldn't have mentioned me. Ya ain't taking her out, are ya?"

"No, but you'd better date her quick. She's ripe."

Now I was positive she'd turn me down. No one wants to go out with someone who sends emissaries. It also sounded like she liked Stellon. I was hurt and began to avoid her, hoping she'd be curious enough to ask why, so I could tell her I was sorry and embarrassed by the whole thing. Then she'd say, "It's okay, you're forgiven, but you should talk for yourself. Don't you realize that you're the only one I care about. I've had a crush on you since I first saw you, so I'd be more than happy to go out with you."

Unfortunately, this fantasy conversation never occurred. It seems she wasn't that interested in why I stopped talking to her and spitefully ignored me in return.

* * *

My mother developed an aching lower back that she believed was caused by the rash of cleaning she did in the new house. By late February when her pain continued, a friend suggested she see a chiropractor. It didn't help, and the pain worsened.

* * *

In March, Father Wolbur joined the Army and became a chaplain, an instant officer. When he returned to say farewell to Nativity's nuns and priests, the high school girls, who thought him handsome and adorable in priestly garb,

337

were rapturous when they saw him in uniform. At lunch-time, as he walked from rectory to school, he had to wade through an excited throng of infatuated female adolescents.

Father Wolbur chose an apt time to enlist. Our enemies weren't faring well. America was so confident of winning that two months previously the ban on Japanese-Americans living on the U.S. west coast was lifted. We'd soon be pulverizing Japanese cities as we were Germany's, and complete victory would be ours.

In April, President Roosevelt died of a brain hemor-rhage, and the country grieved. He'd led us for so long that no one visualized another person in the White House, though he was quickly replaced by someone named Harry S. Truman, a person only familiar to politicians and his immediate family. People worried that Roosevelt's death could affect the war effort. It didn't. Russian armies reached Berlin, and Russian and American soldiers met and em-braced at the Elbe river. Meanwhile, the U.S. Marines and Army steadily drove Japanese troops from Okinawa. Italy's dictator Benito Mussolini and his mistress Clara Petacci were executed by Italian partisans and strung up by their heels in Milan's public square. I stared at hazy pictures of this grisly scene published in Detroit's newspapers and disappointedly wondered what prevented Clara's skirt from immodestly flopping over her head.

On May 1st German radio declared Hitler had died in Berlin and the free world rejoiced; but the next day, with Berlin completely captured by Russian forces, Hitler's body couldn't be found.

Germany surrendered on May 7th, and an Associated Press correspondent, Ed Kennedy, announced it and was promptly suspended by Allied Supreme Headquarters. He'd broken a pledge not to release the story until authorized. The next day the unconditional surrender was formally ratified in Berlin and the European war ended. America now concentrated its full power on Japan.

Three of the five boys sitting on the Kelly front porch when we moved onto Cedargrove were Kathy's brothers: Jim, age 13; Jack, ll; and Tom, 9. The other two boys were Albert Przybylski, age l5, and his brother Alfred, two years younger. Since both Przybylski brothers had similar "Al" names, the younger, chunky one was nicknamed "Butch." Albert, who we called "Alby," attended Denby, a high school located a mile away on Kelly Road at Cedargrove. Butch went to Robinson, the neighborhood public grade school, and the Kelly boys went to Assumption Grotto.

Sunday Mass at Assumption Grotto church contrasted with Nativity's. The church exuded a quiet softness and warmth. The outside was gray, buttressed block and the inside cheery yellows and browns with white statues, marbled altars and colorful, reverence-raising stained glass. The church property included a grade school, rectory, convent, rear parking lot and a small cemetery where earlier church members lay buried under elegant tombstones. The cemetery reminded parishioners of their eventual fate, so they'd best heed the church's message. Near the cemetery's rear, among graves, elms and pines, loomed a large, stone, arched shrine containing an altar, small statues and vigil lights behind iron lattice gates. A Blessed Virgin Mary statue stood inside a cupola gracing its top. This shrine was referred to as "the grotto," and miraculous cures of ailing faithful were rumored, rumors supported by abandoned crutches at the site.

On Sundays, Assumption Grotto students were required to attend the 9 a.m. Mass, but all other parishioners could go to later Masses. My older sisters and I cheerfully chose these later Masses. To get to church we walked to Grover, turned right, crossed Troester, Seymour (Six Mile Road) and Spring Garden streets and entered an open gate in the cemetery fence. A short walk through parts of the cemetery and parking lot brought us to the church's rear doors.

Sometimes Grotto's pastor, Monsignor Marx, gave the sermon, another welcome change from Nativity, for his voice rarely rattled rafters with promises of nether world damnation for wrongdoing or for shorting the collection basket, and my mind and eyes often wandered seeking the Kelly girls or other similar congregation attractions.

Robinson school had a large, fenced, pebble-covered playground, not unlike Chandler, and as the Major League baseball season began so did ballgames at this playground. Neighborhood boys engaged in games from after-supper hours to nightfall and sometimes all day on weekends. Alby, soft-spoken with straight blond hair and a thin athletic build, was an excellent player. His dark-haired brother Butch was almost his equal in ability though shorter, huskier and vociferous. Alby, Butch, the Kelly boys, Chuck and I, would play against boys who lived across our alley on Troester street, and we spent hours at Robinson trying to smash baseballs over cyclone fences and sometimes succeeded.

When not playing ball on Saturday we went to the Ramona theater across Gratiot at Six Mile. The two-story theater building and parking lot covered a whole city block. Besides the theater, the building included a sweetshop, restaurant, dry cleaners, shoe shop, dress shop, barber and beauty shop and men's clothing store, all facing Gratiot. A dentist, chiropractor and optometrist, among others, had office space above these stores.

The theater ticket booth sat back from the corner. On one side a row of entrance doors faced Gratiot, on the other a row of exit doors faced Six Mile. Each row of doors ended with glass-encased coming-attraction posters. The ornate marquee projected well over the sidewalks and curved above and around the booth, doors and poster cases. The movie fare, spelled out with large black letters on both street sides of the lighted marquee, was framed by lines of orange flickering lights that continuously undulated in snakelike movements. A vertical, block-lettered sign, similarly lighted, soared higher than the building, spelling out the theater's name, "Ramona.". During hot-weather months, paper blue and white icicles hung from the marquee heralding air-conditioning, and at night hundreds of electric bulbs drilled into the marquee's underside illuminated the entire intersection. A large, tiled-floor lobby inside, its walls lined with more encased posters, led to red padded doors, all closed but one where an usher collected customer tickets. A well-stocked candy counter stood just inside these doors. The floor to the counter's left, covered wall-to-wall with deep-red carpeting, led to a balcony and the main viewing area. The movies were second- or third-run, the same as the Roosevelt, but the Ramona had a much more alluring attraction. Most employees were usherettes.

* * *

On warm spring days, I often delayed taking the streetcar home after school and instead Stellon, Heffner, Reno and I walked a few female classmates to their homes. If their parents were both working late we would be rewarded for carrying schoolbooks with quick, semi-passionate kisses on secluded back porches. In my case, these romantic flirtations rarely lasted more than a week before I noticed another lovely classmate needing a book carrier. Because of this lack of fidelity, I developed a reputation for being fickle and untrustworthy, putting a definite crimp in my underdeveloped love life.

As the final minutes of Nativity's last school day ticked away, smiling students cleaned out desks, discarding stacks of old test papers, pencil stubs and any other paraphernalia accumulated during the previous nine months of enlightenment and quickly judged worthless. As each classroom's trash containers were stuffed to overflowing, student volunteers dumped their contents into large drums at the rear of school. It was a time for relaxation and a throw-off-the-chains exuberance. The students weren't the only happy ones. The nuns lost some of their unapproachable aura and even joined in lighthearted merriment. Anyone standing in school halls could hear muffled bursts of laughter from several classrooms and the perfect weather, a warm, breezy, clear-blue-sky day, contributed to our mood.

The final bell sounded, and the high school emptied onto McClellan with many students reluctant to leave now that freedom was theirs. My sister Pat, who had the day off from her after-school job, had asked me to wait for her in front of school. I scanned the crowd for her but also, with the help of Stellon and Reno, tried to determine who was the prettiest girl in school. There were numerous sophomore and junior candidates. Pat abruptly appeared, ending our amateur beauty contest, and she and I headed towards Gratiot. Crossing Shoemaker street, a voice behind us said, "Hey, what's your hurry?"

It was the Kelly girls, both smiling, both lovely. Lois said they were going to walk home and asked if we wanted to walk with them. Pat said "Sure" and I flushed and nodded, not believing my luck. Three whole miles walking with Kathy! The sky became bluer, the breeze cooler and sunlight brighter, a tremendous way to start a summer vacation!

As we walked up Gratiot, Pat and Lois, the mature upper-classmen, fell in next to each other leaving Kathy and me walking behind, hesitatingly generalizing, then conversing as though we hadn't ignored each other for four full months. It was a thrilling trek I wished would never end. I didn't notice my feet ached until we arrived home.

XXIX

Ed participated in the assault on Okinawa. The 2nd Marine Division was assigned the task of faking an invasion of Okinawa's southern end to draw Japanese troops away from two actual invasion sites farther north. One of two troop ships transporting the division's personnel to the southern end was sunk by a kamikaze pilot. The remaining troop ship's personnel, including Ed, rescued the shipless marines and sailors and then completed their diversionary tactic mission. They feigned an invasion by launching fully-manned landing craft that sped towards the Okinawa shore and, at the last minute, U-turned back to the ship, hopefully deceiving the Japanese.

Ed and the rest of the 2nd Marine Division returned safely to Saipan, but Army personnel continued fighting on Okinawa, resulting in a surplus of wounded at Saipan's 148th Army Hospital Unit. The ever generous Marine commandants loaned the 148th half their Marine Medical Battalion personnel. Ed had been Company B barber in this battalion for over a year and had developed a reputation for giving the best haircut on Saipan. However, no one ever accused him of being diplomatic. When he insisted his company commander wait in line for a hair cut, his tonsorial days were numbered. One does not ask an officer to wait in line with enlisted men, especially when he is one's company commander. Ed was in the first group of medical corpsmen to be transferred to the 148th; his barber job turned over to a redheaded, freckle-faced, brown-nosed kid who couldn't carry Ed's razor strop.

But fate sometimes has a way of balancing events. When Ed reported for hospital duty at the 148th he found that the Company B warrant officer in charge was one of his steadiest hair cut customers. The officer asked, "What the hell are you doing here when they need barbers back at battalion?"

Ed explained the company commander problem, and the officer said, "I'm not surprised. He's an asshole. So screw 'im. You'll be our barber here because we have more men needing haircuts than the Army barbers can handle. There's an open chair available at the Army barber shop where the hours are eight to five, or I'll have a jeep bring your barber chair over here and set it up in the recreation hall."

Ed, though lacking diplomacy, wasn't stupid. He set up his chair in the Army recreation hall, established his own hours, and enjoyed life while working for the Army, Navy and Marines simultaneously.

Mom went to the hospital for an examination, and the doctors diagnosed her pain as cancer. Madame Curie, a French chemist, had discovered radium killed cancer cells so the doctors recommended a new treatment. A vial of radium was inserted in her uterus for a three-day period, and when her hospital stay ended she came home feeling fine and pain free. Dad had health insurance that didn't quite cover all hospital treatment but Ed's barber sideline was profitable, and the cost of living on Saipan wasn't exorbitant so he mailed home $200 a month from his service pay and barber fees, money that more than offset hospital expenses. Mom was smiling again.

Mary's broken heart also healed. Pat spent her work lunch-time at a snack bar on Kercheval avenue and met a gang of boys nicknamed Denny, Brownie, Jolly, Jerry, Jimmy and Louie. Denny, the nineteen-year-old leader of these youths, asked Pat to return to the snack bar some evening to continue their conversations. She did, taking Mary with her, and soon youths were spending evenings on our front porch flopped like rag dolls on our railings, steps and new glider swing. They all combed their long hair straight back at the sides and wore narrow-cuff trousers with an inch or two of material above the belt line, very similar to the sort worn by California "zoot suit" gangs.

Zoot suits consisted of knee-length, one-button, usually pin-striped, double-breasted coats with long lapels and wide, padded shoulders, and baggy pants that fit tightly around ankles. A thin chain, attached to a belt loop, hung down below the knee, ending up in a side pants pocket and on the chain's end was usually found a switch-blade knife; not used for mumblety-peg or whittling. Two years before, in 1943, unsavory California zoot-suiters discovered a way to supplement their income by rolling servicemen stationed in the Los Angeles area, and the servicemen eventually took offense and formed gangs of their own. Soldiers, marines and sailors roamed the city attacking anyone wearing a zoot suit and sometimes left them lying suitless on bloodstained sidewalks. To halt this bedlam, Army and Navy authorities declared Los Angeles temporarily out-of-bounds to servicemen.

Although Mary and Pat's new friends only wore peg pants, not the whole zoot outfit, I still admired the friends' pluck since, because of our victory in Europe, discharged servicemen were coming home, and some could still harbor resentment against those wearing this radical attire.

I also admired Denny because of the adventurous tales Mary and Pat related about him. He was tall, rangy, strong and enjoyed fighting. When problems with other gangs developed he hid his associates outside the other gang's hangout (usually a snack bar or sweetshop), boldly walked inside, started an argument, punched rival gang members and blindly trusted that friends would burst in and rescue him before he sustained excessive damage.

Some believed Denny wasn't always law-abiding. Mary told me whenever a neighborhood break-in occurred, the first person police questioned was Denny. The station detectives had a reputation for extracting detailed confessions from suspects who often tried to escape and injured themselves tripping over rubber hoses. To spend time at the McClellan police station, where this questioning took place, and not confess was admirable.

I believed Denny was too nice a guy to be involved in anything disreputable, that he and his friends were just high-spirited, genial, Dead End kids in peg pants. My dad believed they were hoodlums, and he mentioned it quite loudly and often. That Denny was of Irish extraction didn't influence Dad's opinion, so Mary and Pat, to avoid problems with Dad, began spending less time on our porch and more time in the Kercheval neighborhood, often staying out beyond curfew. This caused even more conflict because Dad thought teenage girls had no business out past 11 p.m. Some rancorous late night conversations between Mary, Pat and Dad ensued, with Mary and Pat contending they were responsible enough to set their own hours and Dad contending they lacked the mental wherewithal to "scratch a damned itch." The debates ended with two young ladies grudgingly coming home from limited weekday dating by 10 o'clock, 11 o'clock on Saturdays. Sunday outings were out. Peace again reigned on Cedargrove.

* * *

Alby, Butch, the Kelly boys, Chuck and I spent some of our lazing time on the Kelly front porch. Unfortunately when Kathy appeared my buddies didn't instantly disappear. Being a conniver I patiently bided my time waiting for an opportune moment to pose my request for a date, and Kathy provided the moment on a middle-of-July evening by asking if I'd walk with her to a Gratiot store to buy potato chips. Before we returned I'd elicited her promise to ac-

346

company me to a late afternoon movie at the Ramona the following Sunday.

Three days later I nervously stood ringing her doorbell while praying her father or brothers wouldn't answer the door. Praying worked, for she emerged smiling, called out, "I'm leaving, Ma!" and we walked down her front steps. She wore a white, short-sleeved blouse and black, short skirt, obviously still doing her patriotic best for the war effort by conserving skirt material.

Sometimes in life everything goes perfectly. I had worried that Mom couldn't afford to bankroll my first real date, and that if she did, Kathy and I wouldn't have anything to talk about. I worried needlessly. Mom cheerfully gave me a dollar and a half, and as Kathy and I walked to Gratiot, though our conversation didn't exactly flow like curbside storm water, we still managed a strained, self-conscious exchange.

We sat before the silver screen watching a Dennis O'Keefe romantic comedy, and I had trouble concentrating. When the movie crowd laughed she'd smile, look at me, and I'd choke out a chuckle. My mind was focused on something else, namely, how to casually take her hand in mine. Instead I got up and returned with a box of buttered popcorn.

By the start of the second movie I'd progressed to resting my right elbow on the back of her seat. From that position it was easy to feign a stretch and stretch out my arm so it laid completely across the back of her seat where it remained like a useless slab of liver. Mentally, I asked this liver if it intended to stay motionless forever. No reply. Later Kathy shifted towards me, and the liver automatically came alive encircling her shoulders. My left hand, moving independently of any brain commands, crossed over and clutched her left hand as her head came to rest on my shoulder. Afraid to break the spell, I stayed frozen in this heart-pounding, hand-sweating, arm-aching position until the movie's end.

347

The marquee lights were blazing as we exited the theater. The setting sun, reflecting off strings of purple-orange clouds, promised another ten minutes of light, a disappointment. I hoped we could walk home in darkness. "Wanna go next door for a soda?" I suggested.

"No, I ate too much popcorn. Let's go to Grotto cemetery and I'll show you where my grandfather's buried."

It didn't seem like the most pleasant or romantic place to end a date, but I sure didn't want to walk her home so soon. We crossed Gratiot at the traffic light and headed towards the church. "How'd you like the movies?" she asked.

"They were great!" Both movies blurred in my mind. I couldn't even remember the plot of the *Tom and Jerry* cartoon.

"The Ramona's where I learned to tap dance. Lois and I used to take lessons there. They also taught acrobatics."

That's how her legs got so solid and shapely. "Ya learned right on stage?"

"Yes. It was fun. We can go in here."

We turned into the driveway between church and school. When we reached the rear parking lot, twilight shadows deepened, and Gratiot street noises muted. We entered the cemetery, and the night became deathly quiet, except for cricket love songs and mosquito whines. We took a path leading to the shrine and stood admiring its hallowed beauty, adorned with fresh flowers, vigil lights flickering. I fought a strong desire to genuflect. "C'mon," Kathy whispered, taking my hand. "It's getting dark."

We circled the shrine, walked a short distance and stopped in front of a large monument. Through the dim light I read the chiseled name *John A. Kelley.*

"They misspelled his name, but it's nice, isn't it?" she said.

"It's beautiful," I answered, looking at her.

"Did my brothers tell you Kelly Road is named after him?"

"No," I murmured, while wondering if another of her attributes was a lively imagination.

348

"It's true. He bought a farm on a dirt road called Pumpkin Hook—"

"Pumpkin Hook?"

"Yes. His friends had a hard time finding him so he nailed a sign to a tree near the road that said 'Kelly' with an arrow pointing to his farm. For years people called it 'Kelly's Road' instead of Pumpkin Hook. When the city bought his farm and paved the road they named it Kelly."

It was a logical story. I was holding hands with a girl whose family had a major thoroughfare named after them. Detroit had other major streets named after dead people: Washington, Jefferson, Madison. Although not standing with the granddaughter of a president, I was deeply moved for it still had aspects of immortality.

"Did he come from Ireland?" I asked.

"No, he was born here, but his wife did. She came from County Down. Actually he was mostly German, with an Irish name."

She changed the subject. "Have you ever seen the Saint Joseph shrine here?"

"Nah, I usually try to avoid graveyards, even in daylight."

She laughed politely, and I silently wished for a more ready wit. "C'mon, I'll show it to you." She turned and led me past shadowed tombstones, our feet crunching on pebbled paths. A full moon, filtered through rolling clouds and leaf-swollen trees, struggled to light our way.

The small, simple shrine stood a short distance from the Spring Garden street entrance. I'd noticed it when going to Sunday mass. Now up close in the murky light it resembled a giant holy card.

"It's pretty," I whispered and turned towards her. As Saint Joseph's blank eyes looked on, we reached for each other and everything fused — lips, chests, thighs, knees. Pure rapture triumphed as every conscious and unconscious dream I had since first seeing her came true and more! Her lips were softer and the smell of her hair sweeter than I imagined. Her arms around my neck and mine around her waist clutched and tightened. My lips must have been slightly ajar for suddenly her tongue darted into my mouth sending me into wide-eyed, momentary shock. I'd never had a tongue in my mouth, except for my own, and I wondered where a German-Irish girl learned Gaulish affection techniques? After that short, shocking moment, it became the most natural thing in creation, two active tongues, and I savored every drop of alien saliva.

A long time passed before her arms loosened and gently separated us. I stood staring into her eyes, gasping like I'd just won a 300-yard dash against Jesse Owens. She smiled and whispered, "It's getting late."

All I could think to reply was, "No, it ain't."

She kissed me lightly, said, "C'mon, we have to go," grabbed my hand and pulled me toward the Spring Garden gate. I obediently followed. I would have followed her to the North Pole at that moment and melted ice floes in my condition.

We did little talking while slowly walking home. I think we both knew something perfect and mystical was transpiring and neither of us wanted it to end. A heavy rain began, but even this failed to quicken our steps. I considered it a godsend because it cleared neighbors and friends from front porches and steps; so there were no hoots or snide remarks as we neared her house.

At her side door we said goodnight with a gentle, rain-soaked kiss before she smiled and slipped inside. Buoyantly, I walked the short, splashy, distance home.

* * *

Somewhat humanely, the U.S. Air Force began notifying Japanese people in advance of B-29 bombardments. In early August when a lonely B-29 flew over the city of Hiroshima the bomber probably appeared relatively harmless to townspeople and soldiers below. Maybe they expected a rain of leaflets warning that the city be evacuated. It dropped an atomic bomb.

The explosion killed, maimed and vaporized tens of thousands of people and demolished miles of the city. The world waited for Japanese leaders to strike their "setting sun" flag and capitulate. They didn't, so three days later a B-29, christened *Great Artiste,* dropped another atomic bomb on Nagasaki. This explosion got the Japanese government's attention. They asked for and received surrender terms. While they pondered the terms, U.S. carrier planes pulverized sections of Tokyo. The following day Japan surrendered unconditionally.

The war was over, and America celebrated. In Detroit, factory whistles blasted, car horns blared, and little children, banging pots and pans, cheered. On Gratiot, streams of cars packed with young men and women, many perched on fenders, roofs and trunks, slowly moved toward downtown. They joyously whooped, shouted, laughed, some waving American flags, others beer bottles. Among them were uniformed servicemen home on leave or from Selfridge field or recently discharged veterans. It was an opportune time to be in uniform.

While standing on the curb with crowds of other happy spectators watching this boisterous display of patriotism, I yearned to be old enough to join in. A good portion of the excited maidens hanging out of car windows looked primed for debauchery or better. Many other Americans of a more spiritual bent overflowed churches to thank God for our victory and for sparing their sons. By the time President Truman proclaimed the 2nd of September as official "Victory in Japan" day, it was anticlimactic.

When the Japanese war officially ended, Ed was already in Japan. He'd enlisted in the Naval Reserve for the duration plus six months, and the Navy was determined to get full use of him. They sent him to Nagasaki to help establish a naval hospital to treat our Marine occupying forces. This duty gave him and fellow marines and sailors opportunities to gather Japanese artifacts and to ingest good doses of any remaining radioactive particles. American authorities weren't fully aware of radiation dangers. Luckily, after only a week in Nagasaki he, with a contingent of others, were transferred to Miyakonojo to set up another hospital in an abandoned Japanese army barracks, using local tradesmen for labor.

Other American servicemen, not in the occupation forces, came home. Joyful reunions took place at train stations, airports, harbors and front porches. Tears, kisses and embraces welcomed brothers, fathers, sons and daughters. The five Przybylski and three Kelly brothers, wearing rows of battle ribbons, returned safely to Cedargrove.

Some ex-servicemen were impatient to get jobs, marry or go to college under the G.I. bill of rights. Others opted to join the "fifty-two twenty club," a government program allotting $20 per week for 52 weeks to those in no rush to join a labor pool.

Hank Greenberg was a returning serviceman I especially admired. He'd been a sergeant in the Army Air Force and rejoined the Tigers in the middle of baseball season. With his help the Tigers engaged in a pennant race with the Washington Senators. In the ninth inning of the season's last game against the St. Louis Browns, trailing 3 to 2, he hit a bases-loaded home run to clinch the pennant. He also contributed immensely as Detroit beat the Chicago Cubs to win the World Series. The city had another reason to celebrate, and happiness flourished.

I was even happy returning to school. Because of lack of money, nerve and opportunity I hadn't dated Kathy since July, but we both tacitly knew we were going steadily. Nearly every school day morning she and I traveled to Nativity together and spent lunch times with groups of other students squeezed into booths at Taylor's sweetshop. She even looked beautiful with a cannoli crumb stuck to her lip.

A new kid named Marty often joined us. He was tall,

slim, dark-haired, of Italian descent, with a flat nose, ear-to-ear toothy grin, wide shoulders, a cool demeanor and a slightly anti-academic attitude. He felt, as I, that school learning was tolerable but shouldn't become obsessive or interfere with more portentous matters. I noticed he wasn't intimidated by nuns or priests, a trait I was trying to cultivate, so I liked him instantly. He also had an industrious quality I admired in others but lacked myself because he worked part-time at a Harper street market. My sister Pat probably described him best when she said, "He's so ugly, he's cute." Most of Nativity's high school girls felt the same.

Marty suggested he and I buy some pegged pants. My mother agreed new pants were needed and willingly gave me the money, although I neglected to mention the type I intended to buy. There were two Detroit clothiers who sold these pants, Todd's and Sam's, both located downtown near the foot of Gratiot, so after school Marty and I took a streetcar downtown, bought black pegs at Todd's and returned home. I worried that Mom might think fourteen-inch cuffs were too extreme, but worried needlessly. She simply sighed, "Well, if that's what they're wearing in school now—"

Marty and I were the first to wear pegs at Nativity, and not many other boys rushed to follow our noble example. I personally enjoyed the feeling of dressing differently. What could be sharper than black pegs, white bobby socks, black penny loafers, a shirt with upturned collar and a burning cigarette dangling from one's lips, smoke drifting into squinting eyeballs? I knew I looked mature, exciting, and I imagined every perceptive female wanted to know me intimately.

Besides dress-style changes, our speaking style began to change. For years adults used odd expressions we understood, even if the words made little sense: No skin off my nose. That's the ticket. You've got another think coming. Wet behind the ears. Bury the hatchet. Young whippersnapper. That's using the old noggin. Stuff that in your pipe and smoke it. Go sit on the floor and let your legs hang over. He knows what side of the bread his butter's on. I gave her a piece of my mind. Pleased as punch. If you don't like it you can lump it. Mind your own beeswax. Crazy as a bedbug. Cute as a bug's ear. Cat got your tongue? Raining cats and dogs. They also used contradictory expressions: Ain't it a small world? It's a big world out there.

However, there were some remarks from much older adults I didn't understand at all: He's getting long in the tooth. Your legs are the second thing to go. Going to bed with my wife is like shooting pool with a rope. If you can't cut the mustard you can always lick the jar. The thicker the cushion the better the pushin'.

Now, as worldly high schoolers, we began working our own semi-humorous, slangy or profane phrases into conversations: Made in the shade. Know what I mean, jellybean? She'd break your back...your front too. He's a wolf. That's as funny as a crutch. I'm warm for her form. Up your gump stump. I'm in the nude for love. Pitch a maul. She's square. Screw that noise. On the prowl.

And snappy, clever comebacks: (You going to the game tonight?) What do you care...you writing a book? (Are you serious?) No, I'm Roebuck. (Where are you going?) That's for me to know and you to find out. Or, Crazy! Wanna come along?

Although many Nativity students used profanity and/or slang, few dared to carve or write graffiti on school lavatory walls, at least not anything like the poem beginning, "Here I sit all broken-hearted..." We feared nuns might recognize our script. One brave scamp did pencil over the urinals *For a good time call Mary Magdalen, TU. VI IX VI IX,* but it was erased the following day.

We didn't know where we first heard it, but Marty and I increased our monosyllabic vocabulary for a time by calling each other "pimp," a word that had a nice, derisive, slangy tone to it — much better than "simp," short for

354

simpleton. One day, while walking to school after lunch, I called out to Marty, "Hey, pimp! Slow down!"

A female classmate walking between us turned and said, "You two use that word a lot. Do you know what it means?" Confused, I took a stab at, "Yeah. It means dumbhead." With a superior smile she said, "No it doesn't. You'd better look it up."

I told Marty about this weird conversation, and after last class we consulted a school dictionary. Pimp meant "procurer." Procurer meant "pander." Pander meant "a go-between in love intrigues." Our interest piqued as the definitions spiced. Our knowledge search was suspended by a curious nun who magically appeared, hovered behind us and asked, "What words are you boys interested in?"

Marty calmly replied, "Panda, Sister. Someone told us it wasn't a bear."

After a quick animal-life discussion Marty and I left school still puzzled. "It's gotta be a dirty word," I told him. "Hey, don't jump to concussions. I'll ask George."

The next day Marty said his army veteran brother had explained that a pimp was a guy who fixed up other guys with women for immoral purposes. We hastily dropped this word from our everyday vocabulary, but for a short time we half-wittedly called each other "procurer."

* * *

With the exception of traveling to and from school and lunch hours, always with others present, I rarely socialized with Kathy. During cool autumn evenings after touch football games, when we lolled and slumped on the Kelly front porch, Kathy, Lois and Mrs. Kelly sometimes sat on their glider listening and adding to our cleaned-up conversations. Neither Mr. Kelly nor the older Kelly brothers ever joined us, for which I was grateful. I wasn't in a hurry to meet them. These "sits" lasted well past "sundown, moon up, streetlights on" hour, our voices automatically lowering as working neighbors and other sensible people doused lamps, yawned and went to bed. Eventually the other boys departed; Mrs. Kelly and Lois herded Jim and Jack Kelly inside, and Kathy and I were left alone. We then had about 15 minutes of glider time to hold hands and whisper before Mrs. Kelly came to the screen door to remind us of the late hour. Our heads, silhouetted between the street-light across the street and front room windows, were visible to all inside the Kelly house so kissing wasn't attempted until we parted at the door. There would be an innocent brushing of lips and whispered Good nights, and I'd go home happy, though dissatisfied. These frustrating, but appreciated, times ended with the onset of winter.

I did manage another excuse to see her outside of school. Her mother owned a sewing machine and agreed to peg all my regular-cuffed trousers, so I took one pair at a time to her house. Sadly, I only had three pairs needing alterations and Chuck crankily declared, "Keep your hands off my pants. I don't wanna wear no stupid pegs!"

A week before Christmas I spent two of the three dollars my mother gave me for presents purchasing a thin, flexible, gold-colored, metal bracelet at Woolworth's. Holding the bracelet together was a small heart-shaped padlock with a tiny flat key and engraved on the lock were the words: Key to My Heart.

We stood at her side door after dark on Christmas Eve, she in a hastily donned sweater, me in an Eisenhower jacket. We were both shivering, either from cold and falling snow or trepidation and desire.

I'd arrived at her house earlier, ostensibly to admire the Kelly's Christmas tree — always immense and elaborately trimmed. Bountiful, beribboned gifts around the tree and the blazing fireplace added to the festive setting. Kathy introduced me to her dad and home-from-the-war brothers. I mumbled "How do ya do," added a "Hey, it's pretty!" about the tree, wished everyone a merry Christmas, and then she mercifully led me through their dining room into

356

the kitchen saying, "C'mon. I'll get you a cookie."

I was glad to escape the older brothers' presence. They seemed to study me, wondering about my intentions with their little sister, trying to read my less-than-honorable mind.

I nervously ate a Christmas cookie and asked if she'd come outside with me for a minute. She nodded, grabbed a sweater hanging near their side door, and we stepped out onto their snow-covered, shadowy driveway.

"I got ya a present," I muttered, reaching into my jacket's breast pocket, pulling out the carefully wrapped bracelet.

She crumbled the wrapping paper, opened the box, and the bracelet glittered in the soft glow shining through the side door window. Raising her eyes, smiling, she said, "It's beautiful...but I didn't get you anything."

I'd already noticed, but didn't consider it an over-slight of the highest magnitude. "That's okay," I said, adding, "There's words on the lock."

She held it up to the faint light, read the inscription, whispered "I love it," and suddenly we were embracing, kissing, increasing body temperatures. Our lips would part, we'd stare gasping at each other, she'd say "We have to stop" or "It's getting late," and we'd start again. She never said "It's getting cold." It was a long time before we separated completely.

Reluctantly crunching home through five inches of sparkling heavy snow I clearly realized two things: People can't freeze to death while kissing, and being in love is the greatest Christmas present of all.

The army Eisenhower jacket I wore that Christmas Eve I'd received from Roy "Bud" Davis, with whom Mary had exchanged letters throughout his army service. After his discharge he'd returned to his home on Detroit's west side, and they began to date. I liked him, not only because of the jacket gift (it went well with my black pegs), but because he was a cheerful outgoing type. This surprised me. He'd survived the German assault on Bastogne (Chuck and I called him "Battle of the Bulge" Bud) and didn't act overly serious or shell-shocked, although he avoided talk about military skirmishes, preferring to dwell on less dangerous experiences like thrilling glider landings or happy times in London pubs.

After Mary and Pat's Kercheval gang relationship faded, my parents regarded Bud as a godsend. He was employed, respectful, mature, and wore ties, argyle socks, oxfords, regular pants, sweaters and, when appropriate, a Glen plaid suit jacket. He also introduced Betty to his best friend, an ex-Marine named Joe Dolan, whom my parents also liked.

Bud and Joe were a "Mutt and Jeff" combination, Bud five and a half feet tall, dark hair, 140 pounds; Joe over six feet, light hair, rangy and 40 pounds heavier. They both had one common failing — a willingness to ride buses all the way from the west side once or twice a week just to take out my sisters.

My love life ended in mid-January. I saw Kathy talking and laughing with a boy in school — an action I interpreted as flirtatious — which produced a snit fit on my part. I again began avoiding her and, after a week of silence between us, she stopped wearing her heart bracelet, either because our twosome was now two onesomes, the bracelet broke, or because it discolored her wrist. Maybe all three.

* * *

World War Two finally ended for our family. Ed came home in March bearing souvenirs. After emotional greetings he unpacked his sea bag and, besides uniforms, it contained a slew of Japanese coins, three silk pillow cases embroidered with dragons, a bolt action Japanese rifle and two swords in scabbards. The longest, a Samurai sword, had rust colored stains on its blade. Disappointingly the sword hadn't been pried out of a dead enemy's hand. The stains were rust. A Marine had given it to Ed for a good haircut. The other sword, a shorter and thinner ceremonial type with a fancy hilt, Ed had liberated from a Japanese policeman.

The most fascinating item he brought home was an English translation of a final message from Lt. General Saito to his troops defending Saipan. It was delivered at 8 a.m. on June 6, 1944, two hours prior to his death. It read:

"I am addressing the officers and men of the Imperial Army on Saipan:

"For more than twenty days since the American devils attacked, the officers, men and civilian employees of the Imperial Army and Navy on this island have fought well and bravely. Everywhere they have demonstrated the honor and glory of the Imperial Forces. I expected that every man would do his part.

"Heaven has not given us an opportunity. We have not been able to use fully the terrain. We have fought in unison up to the present time, but now we have no materials with which to fight, and our artillery for attack has been completely destroyed. Our comrades have fallen one after another. Despite the bitterness of defeat, we pledge seven lives to repay our country.

"The barbarous attack of the enemy is being continued. Even though the enemy has occupied only a corner of Saipan, we are dying without avail under the violent shelling and bombing. Whether we attack or whether we stay where we are, there is only death. However, in death there is life. We must utilize this opportunity to exalt true Japanese manhood. I will advance with those who remain to deliver still another blow to the American devils and leave my bones on Saipan as a bulwark of the Pacific.

"As it says in the Senjinkun (battle ethics), 'I will never suffer the disgrace of being taken alive' and 'I will offer up the courage of my soul and calmly rejoice in living by the eternal principle.'

"Here I pray with you for the eternal life of the Emperor and the welfare of the country, and I advance to seek out the enemy. Follow me."

The Japanese opinion of our troops' humanity wasn't much higher than ours of theirs. A postscript, added to the message by the translator, stated: "After U.S. troops secured the island of Saipan they gave General Siato a full military funeral."

When the excitement of his homecoming abated, Ed explained that metal against his skin caused a rash and gave me his waterproof, shockproof wristwatch and cameo ring. The watch now sported an elaborately engraved sterling silver band made by a Japanese silversmith. The accoutrements added a certain worldly flare to my attire and I thanked him profusely.

XXX

Marty got a driver's license in March on his 16th birthday and bought a black Model A Ford. I suggested girls would pay more attention to us if we painted clever comments on it like *Hubba, Hubba!* or *Oh, you kid!* He declined, pointing out, "Cops also notice 'Hubba!' cars."

He frequently parked the car on McClellan not far from the school's entrance and at lunch hour he'd drive a group of us to a nearby YMCA building that contained two pool tables. Reno, who'd discovered these tables and whom we secretly believed invented the game, gave us lessons on bank, carom and masse shots. Eventually, after many of these misspent lunch hours trying to master 8-ball and rotation, we all improved our cue stick ability. We thought it deviously daring and rebellious to spend a Catholic school lunch hour shooting pool in a Protestant building.

On one of our lunch hour sojourns the smiling YMCA caretaker invited us to use the building's swimming pool. His eyes held a zealous missionary gleam as he shuffled religious tracts making me wary of future Protestant sales pitches, but nonchalant Marty thanked him and said, "Okay, we'll be back Saturday."

Saturday afternoon, Marty and I paid a small fee for towels and a locker, donned swimming trunks and joined about thirty other males at the pool. It was my first swimming pool venture. I had cautiously left my waterproof watch and cameo ring on the top shelf of my rented locker since, with that many boys, the pool might contain a high degree of metal-corrosive liquid.

Two hours later we showered, dressed, turned in wet towels, left the building and entered Marty's car. En route home I noted the absence of my watch and ring. Marty did a quick U-turn, returned to the "Y," and the smiling caretaker accompanied us to the locker I'd used. Some young Christian had swung with my jewelry.

The caretaker took my phone number and confidently said he'd call me when the repentant Christian returned the loot. Faith in the human conscience seemed to belong exclusively to zealots. I felt differently, knowing "finders, keepers" was a stronger article of faith among my peers.

Marty tried to console me with, "All you have to do when your brother's around is wear long sleeves, keep your hand in your pocket, and hope he doesn't ask the time. He'll never notice."

"Thanks, Mart," I said, bitterly. "That's great advice. But I know one thing. Ed'll never give me anything else, except a hard time. I only had them for two damn months."

"Hey, don't cry about it. I'll tell ya what. My brother George is having a party tonight at our house. He won't mind if ya come. It'll cheer ya up. How about if I pick ya up around seven."

"What kind of party?"

"Just a party party. C'mon, you'll have a good time."

Marty was right. It cheered me. His basement and garage were packed with reveling older people, mostly in their 20s, laughing, smoking, singing, dancing, eating, drinking. He introduced me to parents, brothers, sisters, brother's friends and cold beer. Having tasted the warm remnants of bottled beer left uncapped overnight by my dad, I was always confident it could never become a favorite beverage, but at Marty's urging I had a couple "slugs" of a cold, full bottle, and a lifelong lager love was born. We drank this beer in the dark alley behind Marty's garage, away from any disapproving adults, then took turns smuggling more bottles from the ice-cube-covered cache in the basement sink. After each of us downed three bottles of Stroh's we rejoined the party and my psyche gradually changed and I became certain my words engrossed others. Two more beers made me realize I was uncommonly funny, especially when walking into basement posts. My humor grew and balance dwindled.

On one of my grinning bathroom trips I stopped in the kitchen to amuse Marty's mother. "You look like you could use something to eat," she said, unamused. "Do you want to try a pizza pie?"

Visualizing apple or cherry pastry, I answered, "Sure, I'll 'ave a piece. I love pie!"

She handed me a red and yellow topped slab and said, "You'll like this. It's Italian."

The pie had a strange spicy taste. She smiled at my facial expressions as I chewed and swallowed a mouthful. "If you don't like the sauce and cheese...here. Try plain pizza bread. It's good for you."

I exchanged slabs and bit into the sauceless, garlicky bread. It was much more palatable. She contended that people eventually developed a taste for pizza pie, that a lot of George's non-Italian friends liked it, and someday I would too. I tried not to look doubtful. I finished the bread, thanked her and reeled to the bathroom.

After two more beers, Marty stood over me in the alley as I shuddered and retched. "That pizza sure messed up my stomach," I groaned.

Marty's brother George drove me home, gently preached moderation, let me out of his car, and watched until I safely negotiated the steps and entered my front door. No family members sat in the living room so no one saw my cautious entrance or slow, deliberate walk upstairs to bed. I slept the sleep of the embalmed.

To pass time at Mass the following day I composed a verse: My head…it aches, my hand…it shakes, my stomach knows no peace. My knees…they quiver, my arms…they shiver, I doubt it'll ever cease. Hangovers are bad, I tell ya, Dad. With luck I'll be dead by noon. (But you can bet, that I'll forget, and be snozzled again — and soon). It wasn't very scintillating so I never wrote it down.

As the school year drew to a close, Sister Richard who taught science, mentioned my favorite beverage while discussing food. She said beer consumption in moderation was healthy, its ingredients had food value, and two beers a day benefitted your body. Recalling my hardy feelings at Marty's house, before eating pizza, I silently vowed to pour this beneficial elixir into my body whenever possible to ward off infirmity.

On the last day of school, a relaxed Sister Richard volunteered to answer any questions on nature or science. Marty asked an innocent, but somewhat embarrassing question: "Do trees, flowers and grass hurt when you cut them? Do they have feelings? After all, they're living orgasms."

Some astute students gasped, then broke into inane laughter. Even Sister Richard smiled. When the laughter diminished she replied, "The word is organisms, Marty…and no, I don't think so. They lack nerves."

On that cheerful note the school year ended.

My sister Pat was even more cheerful. She graduated and entered the work-a-day world, fulltime.

* * *

Two weeks into summer vacation my conscience pulsed with guilt. Depending on Mom and others for fun money humiliated me. My older brother and sisters worked. Why couldn't I? Getting a job seemed prudent. Alby told me the market at Gratiot and Troester was hiring, so I rushed over to see its manager. His office stood in the store's rear corner and at my knock he invited me in. I instantly disliked him. He was in his 40s, bulky, receding black hair, and spoke in short, staccato sentences. After writing my name and address on a card he said, "All right. You're hired. Stockboy. Start tomorrow. Eighteen dollars a week. Monday through Thursday, 9 to 6. Friday, 7 to 7. Saturday, 9 to 9. Half hour lunch. Be here tomorrow. Seven o'clock."

I thanked him, he grunted, and I departed feeling buoyant. Eighteen dollars a week! Wow! And Sunday off!

The next morning at 6:45 I stood with the manager in a rear storage area as he explained my job. "Mop. Dust. Unload trucks. Stack shelves. Dump garbage. Follow orders."

He handed me a white butcher's apron, introduced me to two other teenage boys, told them to put me to work, and returned to his office. A horn blared, we pushed open large wooden doors leading to a side alley where a truck waited stacked high with boxes of canned vegetables to be unloaded, and my work day began.

By noon my arches felt like they'd fallen and couldn't get up. Every step on the cement floor was agony, and I silently vowed to exchange my sneakers for arch-supporting loafers the next day. Deliveries tapered off later, and we had time to sit, but whenever we became comfortable the manager appeared with more jobs. By closing time every muscle throbbed, and $18 a week seemed to be an impossible goal. I'd never last a week. We finished mopping the floor at 7:30. I went home, ate and went to bed.

The following morning my smiling mother handed me a lunch bag with encouraging words, "Work hard! Get ahead!" Walking into the market at two minutes to nine appeared to rankle the manager.

Because it was Saturday there were more shoppers, and we were busier than the previous day, but the work became routine. Between jobs I sat down, relaxed and had a cigarette. The second time the manager caught me sitting and smoking he angrily told another stockboy to show me how

365

to stock shelves and price cans. While stamping prices on can tops I asked my companion, "Doesn't that guy ever smile?"

He answered. "Nah. I think someone pees in his Rice Krispies every morning."

My loud chortle brought an admonition from the manager, "Quiet! Get to work!" The guy was everywhere.

It became a challenge to last through the day. Even with loafers my feet hurt, but if I endured until 9 p.m., Monday's 9 to 6 would be relatively easy. I imagined how pleased Kathy would be if she walked in to buy a loaf of bread and saw me earning a living. She was my inspiration.

Between chores, when the other stockboys sat down on crates in the storage room, I leaned against a wall, since the manager apparently had an aversion to sitting employees. It was a long, arduous day and while mopping up at closing time I congratulated myself for persevering. The manager allowed us to leave at 9:15.

Monday morning was cool and refreshing, not exactly a day to be inside. I reluctantly pushed open the market's front door and headed for the rear storage area, my loafer's cleated heels loudly dragging. The manager stood in front of his closed office door watching my less-than-enthusiastic approach, then opened the door and waved me inside. Lifting the lid of a steel box on his desk, he reached inside, removed a five-dollar bill and said, "You ain't needed. Here." My hand automatically took the money as he added, "Someday get a government job. They sit more than work."

Bewildered, I stuffed the money in my pocket, turned and walked out. The weather, still bright and lovely, didn't help my confused, ravaged feelings. Half way home a thought struck me. Six days into $18 equaled three dollars a day. I'd worked the two longest days and only received five dollars. He should have paid me six dollars at least. I debated whether to return to the store and argue but decided it would lead to added mortification. It was too nice a day to be working anyway.

(For many months, when passing the market late at night, I resisted a tremendous urge to lob a brick through its plate glass window, figuring the first person they'd suspect would be a disgraced, disgruntled former employee who'd been boinked by an obnoxious manager.)

My mother wasn't happy with my job loss. She'd have to continue paying for all my tuition, carfare, church collection, clothes and recreation, but I assured her my search for steady work wasn't over. In the meantime there were good times to be had with five dollars, and I happily phoned Marty.

He picked me up that evening and many future summer evenings, and we drove to Eastwood Park, an entertainment center that covered a massive piece of land across Eight Mile Road at Gratiot avenue. It included a roller skating rink, outdoor swimming pool and elaborate Eastwood Gardens, a dance pavilion where, at times, nationally known big bands played.

The main attraction for Marty and me was the vast amusement park that attracted a vast number of girls. There was a carousel, whip, ferris wheel, dodge 'em and other body-jerking rides dominated by a life-threatening roller coaster. The coaster's cars reached awesome heights and speeds, soaring and plunging, rising and diving, on tracks supported by thousands of dried-out, crisscrossed slats of unpainted wood that visibly shuddered and wavered as cars hurtled above. Rumors abounded of tragic hushed-up derailments adding an element of danger for those daring to ride.

When we met unescorted young ladies we plied them with cotton candy, popcorn balls, candied apples, ice cream bars or hot dogs, then tested their morals by steering them to the Tunnel of Love. We were usually rewarded with two or three innocent, damp kisses and warnings to "Watch your hands."

We learned to avoid colorfully striped, open-faced tents that offered prizes for tossing rings at stakes, baseballs at lead bottles, and smooth-pointed darts at half-filled balloons. We noticed major prizes at these tents, frequently small radios and giant stuffed pandas, were covered with years of dust. We also avoided the "Test your strength— Ring the bell—Win a prize" game, having heard that the lead donger could be manipulated.

The only time we tried the Fun House we discovered it required groping through a pitch dark passageway to a door that opened onto a brightly lighted stage. An audience of grinning expectant spectators sat on rows of long benches watching each new bewildered arrival who, blinking from the sudden light, followed directional arrows painted across the stage floor. A gravel-voiced Fun House employee urged them to hurry. Women and girls wearing slacks had no problem reaching the opposite end of the stage and descending steps leading into the main fun area. Those wearing skirts or dresses, however, had them blown over their heads by hidden air blasters operated by the same mouthy employee. Leering onlookers thought this hilarious; the brunts of the jokes didn't as they valiantly tried to restore their dignity.

Marty and I quickly found an empty section of bench in the audience and settled down to watch this provocative display, hoping a Betty Grable look-alike would innocently cross the stage. Many of the prettiest women were seasoned Fun House patrons and held tightly to their skirt hems, disappointing observers, but when a novice appeared, it was time for cheers, whistles and applause.

Although welcoming this unexpected opportunity to study anatomy, I began feeling sorry for some of the more chagrined young women. They probably didn't appreciate becoming part of Fun House entertainment. At that pang-of-conscience moment Marty and I also became part of the entertainment as electricity surged through our buttocks and we leaped to our feet blurting out the name of God's Son. Faces in front of us turned, staring or smiling, and people behind guffawed. The Fun House operators had rigged our bench with a device capable of a high voltage charge. We sheepishly left to check out the other Fun House enticements that included two try-to-keep-your-balance devices: a large, slow-turning cylinder to walk through and flat, level-with-the-floor, spinning wheels to walk on.

We returned to the stage viewing area just as an overweight, frowning blonde woman in a thin blue silk dress stepped into the light. Clutching her purse in both hands she haughtily strode across the stage as the air gusts raised her billowing dress waist high. Gasps were heard, then stunned viewers reacted. Shrieks exploded, friends pounded each other's backs and three teenage girls sitting in front of me doubled over clutching their stomachs in convulsions of laughter. The blonde woman, in high-heeled shoes, was completely nude under her dress. It was the high (or low) note of our Fun House stay.

Another of Eastwood Park's several allurements was a Freak Show, housed in an immense tent. Huge placards illustrated its oddities — a sword swallower, a midget, a fat man and woman, the tallest man in the world at 8-feet 4-inches, an alligator-skinned woman, a tattooed man, a woman with a headless baby growing from her stomach, and Popeye, a man who popped his eyeballs outside his eyelids. At the Freak Show entrance, a flashily dressed barker loudly regaled potential customers with descriptions of the wonders inside. A bored, veiled dancer shared the barker's platform, sinuously rolling her hips, guaranteeing numerous male listeners. I'd received warnings from Marty and others that the alluring alligator woman probably wasn't as alluring in person as the artist depicted her on the placard — young, shapely and buxom, her green scaly body clad in a scanty bathing suit. I argued that in school we learned that misrepresenting a product was false advertising, a crime. Besides, even if the alligator woman wasn't a beauty, the barker had assured us the belly dancer removed much of her costume inside, and he'd refund our money if we weren't completely satisfied. I paid my quarter.

A small crowd inside moved from stage to stage. The sword swallower swallowed, Popeye popped eyes, the midget and tall man joked about their size, and the fat man and woman bragged about their blubberous weight. A phonograph record of Arabic music began, and we all moved to another stage to watch the belly dancer. She undulated vigorously for two minutes, but only removed her face veil. I began to feel screwed.

The barker's partner inside announced it would cost everyone an extra twenty-five cents to see the alligator and headless-baby women. I reluctantly gave him a quarter, was directed alone into a separate canvassed room and gazed at the alligator woman lying in a booth behind a pane of dirty glass. She was an overweight, dumpy matron in a modest two-piece black bathing suit with grotesque reddish-purple skin covering most of her visible body. She appeared to be dozing. The screw tightened.

In the next booth the woman with a headless baby protruding from her stomach was equally unattractive and also wore a modest bathing suit. She stared defiantly, daring me to doubt the headless rubber doll glued neck-first to her navel wasn't real and alive.

Swiftly exiting the tent, I decided to get the screw removed by standing at the platform's side and waiting for a gap in the barker's spiel. When it came, I yelled, "Hey, Mister! I want my money back!"

He ignored me. My second "Hey, Mister! I want my money back!" was louder and got his attention.

"Whadda ya want, kid?"

"I want my money. I wasn't satisfied," I said.

"Are you crazy? Beat it, troublemaker!" His eyes narrowed.

"But you said I could ask for—"

"Get outta here before ya get hurt!" This through gritted teeth.

He was getting churlish. Although I bemoaned the loss of 50 cents spent for six minutes of dubious entertainment,

I pictured this ape yelling "Hey, Rube" and a dozen carnies and grifters escorting me bodily to the park's entrance and giving me a vigorous toss. It wasn't a pretty picture.

The screw remained tightly embedded, and I discreetly slunk away.

The park's Penny Arcade, filled with delightful games, was where young boys usually received their money's worth. There were rows of pinball machines, a boxing ring machine that allowed a player to manipulate one boxer against another, a "Test your grip" machine, and an enclosed thick-glassed case with a fragile toy crane inside. Piled at the case's bottom were cheap plastic prizes and one expensive looking wrist-watch. Object: maneuver the crane using outside handles to pick up a prize, then drop it through an escape chute. There was just one chance to close the crane's teeth, and most players eventually realized the watch was too heavy to be lifted.

I wasted most of my coins and happy hours at the row of peep show machines, learning dance appreciation by viewing energetic, skimpily-clad, serpentine maidens. The "Dance of the Seven Veils" and "Bubble Dance" were favorites.

Marty's car allowed us to range farther from home for other pleasurable activities. In a rented canoe at Belle Isle we explored shaded, tree-lined lagoons and floated under vine-covered bridges while playing "dodge 'em" with other canoeing nature lovers. If another canoe held young ladies, we strove for "collide 'ems."

Lured by provocative newspaper advertisements, we drove downtown to burlesque shows. Box office attendants at the first two theaters we visited, the National and Gayety, declined our proffered money, citing an "18-years-old or older" admission law. The Avenue theater attendant wasn't so finicky. The show consisted of a scruffy clown named Scurvy Miller slapsticking through blue comedy routines. One memorable line had Scurvy facing a beautiful woman who wore western garb that included boots, short fringed

371

skirt, 10-gallon hat and a tin star pinned to her vest. "If you're the sheriff let me see your posse," Scurvy demanded.

These routines were intersticed by lovely and semilovely spotlighted women dancing to slow, jerky, band music while stripping down to pasties and G-strings; an eye-opening, heart-fluttering experience. Between shows the emcee strolled aisles selling overpriced boxes of popcorn, promising that a few boxes contained Bulova wristwatches. By coincidence, the second box sold held a watch, and his business immediately increased.

* * *

Marvelous technological strides took place and new phrases entered the country's language: rocket propulsion, two-way radio, jet engine, guided missile, robotic electronic computer. A unique Air Force bomber was built, shaped like a fifty-foot wing. Radio signals bounced off the moon and new aircraft speed records were set. Pride in America's scientific breakthroughs was rampant.

Gelatin Products, where Dad was now a superintendent, had its own modest project that, if perfected, would revolutionize medicine and dentistry — a needleless injection needle. Dad brought a prototype home to impress his children. Made of stainless steel, seven-inches long, it resembled a small grease gun. On the firing end was a tiny showerhead with barely visible holes. Underneath, at the opposite end, was a handle and trigger. He loaded it with water and fired it at our recreation room window from two inches away and water sprayed against the pane; a bead slowly rolling downward. He reloaded and demonstrated the injector's use by placing its head against Chuck's bare arm and pulled the trigger. Chuck flinched but didn't feel a thing. The water propelled through his pores into his system, a unique way to absorb liquid. He gave us all a drink in this manner and we confidently assured ourselves we were on the cutting edge of medical history. No longer would patients fear injections nor medical personnel fear accidental pricks from infected needles.

Meanwhile, America's composers wrote pleasant, relaxing music, a welcome change from wartime songs exhorting enemy obliteration. *The Old Lamplighter,* and *I Can't Begin to Tell You* received big plays on the nation's jukeboxes. *The Gypsy* stayed on radio's Hit Parade for a record twenty weeks. Listening to my favorite, *Full Moon and Empty Arms,* conjured up vivid memories of Kathy and Grotto cemetery.

Kathy and I waved and helloed the rare times we saw each other. Most summer evenings she babysat so she spent little time on her front porch. I was reluctant to approach her anyway. She earned money, and I didn't. She probably heard from her younger brothers about my abbreviated market job and noticed I didn't rush to seek other employment, so I was sure her opinion of me could be stated in one word: sluggard. It amazed me, therefore, when I came home from Robinson schoolyard one late afternoon and my mother said, "You just missed Kathy Kelly. She stood at our front porch steps a little while ago and called, 'Robbie-ee,' like you kids used to call each other. It was darling."

"What did she want?"

"She just said she wants to see you."

I dashed to her house, rang the doorbell, and she appeared in all her loveliness. Cheerfully, she stepped out onto the porch and invited me to sit with her on the steps. "Could you walk me to my babysitting job tonight?" she asked. "There are some boys on the street saying things to me every time I go there."

"What are they saying?"

"You know...things!"

I didn't know, but nodded. "Where's the house?"

"It's six blocks down Grover. I don't hav'ta be there 'til eight o'clock so you can go home and eat if you want.

Maybe they won't be hanging out there again, but I'd feel better having someone with me. Okay?"

"Sure," I answered. "I'll see ya at a quarter to eight."

Walking home, I imagined myself fighting four thugs while heroically screaming, "Run Kathy! I'll hold them off!" Another, less pleasing, vision intruded — being punched into a bloody pulp. Nah, it'll never happen, I assured myself.

While escorting Kathy, we talked so much of the coming school year that I almost forgot my bodyguarding duty required alertness. We wondered if our future homeroom nun, Sister Mary Jarlath, could be as pleasant as claimed by our older sisters, Pat and Lois. Neither of us recalled laying eyes on the nun since underclassmen rarely ventured to Nativity's top floor where Juniors and Seniors were taught. Now, in a week's time, we'd be Juniors, third-floor uppercrust upperclassmen, closing in on graduation.

I learned she'd be in my typing class. Using the argument that the schoolroom would be full of girls, and it was an easy course, I'd talked Marty into taking Typing I with me. Kathy and I also discovered we'd both be taking the dreaded Algebra class and expressed misgivings since we barely slipped through Geometry II the year before. Religion was the only other class we'd share.

Caught up in school talk, I was startled when she turned a corner and said, "There's the house," pointing to a flat, three houses ahead. Time had passed so swiftly that I wasn't fully aware how chilly, dark and foreboding it had become, the only illumination from house windows, lampposts and a clouded-over half moon. Reaching the flat's porch steps, she hesitated, turned and whispered sweetly, "Thanks for walking me."

As I gazed at her face, the clouds fully released the moonlight and it reflected off her glasses. She looked captivating, tempting me to croon, "Half Moon and Empty Arms," hoping she'd take the hint. Instead I said, "That's all right. It's probably too cold for those four boys to be out tonight, eh?"

"There were only two," she said, smiling.

"Well, I'll be glad to walk ya home. Give me a call when you're done. Do ya have my phone number?"

"I'd like that, but my dad already said he'd pick me up in his car. It'd be too late anyway. These people sometimes don't get home 'til midnight." She softly touched my arm. "I'd better get in there before they call another sitter. Thanks again."

She turned, ascended the steps, pressed the doorbell, and the door opened immediately. She waved and disappeared inside, leaving me kissless, alone and standing on a dark, unfamiliar street. Our time together was so short I'd forgotten to ask why she didn't get an older brother to walk her. Then jubilation reigned as the answer dawned. She really liked me! A lot!

Exulting, I turned onto Grover and felt a joyful leap and heel click were in order, like happy people did in movies. I succeeded in joyfully leaping, but clicked a heel into an ankle causing intense pain. Yet nothing, not even a shattered ankle, could dim my contentment.

As I limped past the first alley a hostile voice asked, "Hey, ya want a kick in the ass?"

Stopping, I peered into the dark abyss and saw two obscure figures leaning against a backyard gate. Stupidly I entered the alley, swiftly covering the sixty feet between us, while wondering why my legs kept moving forward and what I'd say when I got there. Stopping in front of them I saw one was my size; the other, standing behind him, four inches taller. They were glowering so I squinted and frowned, hoping my expression passed for a return glower. Using a Humphrey Bogart imitation I growled, "Did ya say somethin' ta me?"

"I didn't say nuttin," the one in front muttered.

I looked at the taller one. "How about you?"

He shook his head once, continuing to glower.

"Okay."

I turned away, trying to swagger naturally from the alley,

resisting the temptation to sprint, hoping not to hear charging footsteps behind. Back on Glover street I broke into a fast lope for two blocks, noting a miraculous absence of ankle pain. Nonetheless I passed up another leap-and-click try. This evening was almost perfect, I thought. Although no physical contact occurred between Kathy and me, at least I was in her good graces, and when she heard of the alley episode I knew she'd be impressed with my derring-do. Maybe I'd expand on it, perhaps adding, "And then I said, 'And stay away from my friend Kathy or you'll get what's coming to ya.'" Abruptly another scenario crossed my mind. What if, in answer to my "Did you say something?" question, the kid would have said, "Yeah. I asked if you wanted a kick in the ass, asshole." I had no idea what I, or old Humphrey, would have replied but surely unwanted physical hurt could have resulted. It was sobering.

I didn't see Kathy again until the following Sunday. She, Lois and their mother were at Grotto's eleven-thirty Mass sitting in a front pew. Hustling through the crowd after Mass I caught up to them, said "Hello" and Kathy dropped back to walk with me. "Did ya ever babysit at that house again — the one I walked ya to?"

"Yes. A couple nights ago."

"Did ya have any trouble with those guys?"

"No."

I described what happened after I'd escorted her, and she stared at me with an unfathomable look. After a pause she said, "Are you telling me you walked into a dark alley where two guys wanted to beat on you?"

I modestly smiled and said, "Yeah."

"You'd have to be crazy to do that!"

"Yeah, but I did."

"You expect me to believe you?"

This conversation wasn't turning out as expected. "Honest. It happened."

"Sure it did." She smiled and shook her head. "Are you ready for school tomorrow?"

My face burned as I said, "Yeah, I'm ready." She definitely didn't think me heroic. Judging from her reaction she thought me loony or a prevaricator. I think she settled on the latter. I felt grieved, but at least I was back in her good graces.

* * *

Of all the members of the Zewecki family who moved in down the street, Geri was the most conspicuous. She stood tall and slim with alluring blue eyes, pouty lips, throaty voice and long rippling red hair. Kathy introduced her as we walked to the Gratiot streetcar on the first day of school. Geri was enrolled at Nativity, a new Junior classmate.

XXXI

S ister Jarlath, gorgeous and perky, stood behind her desk and melodiously intoned, "All right, students. Take your seats. We have to get started. Sit down, please! Quiet!"

I already sat, staring at her face. I guessed her age as thirty. Her nose was perfectly shaped, not too long, short, spread, tapered, pugged or flat. Her lips were also perfect, not too thin, fat, pursed or wide. When she smiled her pure white teeth, a dentist's paradigm, seemed even whiter because of her naturally tanned skin. Her upper cheeks curved into enchanting half-circles. She had a trace of dimples, and her deep-brown eyes, framed by long black lashes, narrowed and turned upward at the corners, some-what like adding two more smiles. After she took atten-dance and began a discourse on American History, I glanced across the room at Marty to see if he too was enraptured by this stunning teacher creature, intending to shake my hand loosely and silently mouth "Wow!" I didn't get a chance. Sister Jarlath, her melodious voice unexpectedly changed, said, "Turn around and pay attention, Robert!" She glared.

"Yes, Sister," I murmured. She continued talking history while I pondered: What did I do? Just turning a head shouldn't rate a chew-out. Maybe she doesn't like my looks. I sure like hers. At least she knows my name. If it'll keep her smiling I'll never glance around the room again. Besides, sometimes history is engaging. I'll do anything to make her happy, even study. I'll start by listening right now.

Attentive for the remainder of class, I absorbed her every word, countenance and movement. Just before class ended she snapped at Marty for a minor infraction relieving my anxiety. I wasn't the only one she disliked.

Every day Sister Jarlath singled Marty and me out for criticism and disciplinary attention, and by week's end our classmates were commenting, "What did you two do to her? Why is she on you guys?"

We didn't know. It was peculiar because she was exceptionally pleasant to others, and I envied them. How could a person with a smile capable of brightening the Black Hole of Calcutta be unfair? It mystified me. Her selective discipline included demerit slips.

Nativity High School had a demerit system that affected a student's Courtesy mark on quarterly report cards. All nuns carried a small printed pad headed with spaces for a date, a recalcitrant student's name and homeroom. Beneath was listed every transgression conceivable by nuns and the amount of demerits for each. Two demerits were given for chewing gum, wrong stairs, excessive make-up, disorderly conduct, loitering, unexcused tardiness, running in building, misconduct in assembly, banging desks or books, and incomplete uniform. Opening others' desks and unexcused absence were rated five-demerit offenses. At the bottom of the list was a space for a nun's signature. Every student started each quarter with 100 merits — a potential A in Courtesy. This number diminished as demerits accumulated. If you fell below 93 you received a B, below 86 a C, below 75 a D and below 70 the horrid F.

The second week of school, following Thursday's morning mass, Sister Jarlath with relish and flourish, wrote out and presented "Misconduct During Assembly" demerit slips to Marty and me as we sat in her room with fellow students awaiting the ten o'clock bell. She returned to her desk and I politely asked, "What's this for, Sister?"

With a withering look, she said, "You and Martin were talking during Mass. Perhaps you'd like to let the class know what you were talking about. I'm sure it would be enlightening."

"Well, Sister," Marty lied, "All I said was 'Bob, I think Sister Jarlath is the best looking teacher in school,' and he agreed."

A flustered Sister Jarlath let our classmates' laughter die, then said, "Thank you, Martin, but you still deserve the demerits." From that moment she became our friend.

Geri Zewecki, my neighbor and the new girl in class, became an instant smash with us Junior boys, and she was congenial enough in return, but few of our boyish charms charmed her. She had a mature and sensible persona, and I gathered from our conversations that she sought males with these same attributes, which eliminated most Nativity boys. The only boy she occasionally dated was Bill Stellon. I didn't even consider an other-than-friendly relationship with her, having learned that most tall females harbored a bias called "sizism," a hesitancy to associate seriously with diminutive males.

* * *

"Here's money to buy a suit and shoes so you'll look nice for Mary's wedding," my mother said. Mary was getting married to Bud Davis in October, one month away. At Sam's Clothiers downtown, known to sophisticated adolescents as "Hot Sam's," I bought a navy blue, double-breasted, pinstriped "lounge" suit with long, wide, pointed lapels that buttoned once at the right front hip. The trouser cuffs narrowed to fourteen inches. At a nearby Flagg Bros. store I bought a pair of thick soled, square toed, oxblood-colored shoes, tastefully decorated with brass grommets. A cream-colored sports shirt completed my costume. No tie was necessary. With my long hair combed back and cut straight across at the nape, the only word to describe me was "sharp." So when Joyce, a classmate, invited members of our Junior class to a Saturday evening house party, I was ready. I did add a blue, Windsor-knotted, knit tie in case her parents were into formality.

The party was personally disappointing and embarrassing. A major disappointment was that Kathy didn't attend. Another was the case of beer. After nightfall someone brought a case from home and stored it in the back seat of Marty's car. It was warm and foamy so I only drank two bottles.

Most party goers congregated in the basement where a phonograph played soft dance music, and the sole light was a 40-watt bulb hanging over a sink full of ice-covered pop bottles. It may have been the beer, or the new thick-soled shoes, that made me feel so tall and confident, but I asked Audrey, a statuesque girl, to dance, and she accepted. We staked out a dark corner near the furnace, and I started in with the box step my older sisters had taught me. After I stepped on her instep for the second time, Audrey stopped. "Do you know how to dance slow...I mean really slow? Look, just hold me and don't move your feet too much. Simply sway. It's great for crowded dance floors."

It sounded like a fantastic idea. We swayed to the music, holding each other firmly, my forehead against her chin. I revelled in the slimness of her waist under my right hand and how her hip curved outward. The tune we danced to, *You Keep Coming Back Like a Song,* was prophetic, because Audrey whispered in my right ear, "Something's bumping my leg."

I pulled away, flustered. "What?"

"I felt something bumping my leg," she repeated. "What is it?"

Thinking swiftly I said, "Oh, that's my pocketknife."

"Small knife," she said, smiling sweetly.

Following that disconcerting exchange I allowed more space between our bodies.

382

The second embarrassing incident occurred near midnight as the party broke up. People crammed into the front living room and rear dining room to sit on sofas, chairs, end tables or lean against walls and door jambs, or simply stand while saying thank you, saying how much fun they had, saying we should have more parties, laughing, reluctant to say good-bye. Some had phoned parents and waited to be picked up. Others, like me, waited for friends with cars, like Marty, to stop blabbing and drive them home. Marty wasn't winding down, so I searched for a place to sit and relieve the blister pain caused by my new shoes. An elaborately-carved, glass-topped coffee table beckoned.

The loud laughter and conversation of slowly departing guests drowned out the cracking sound as the glass-top gave under my weight. Quietly rising, I wended my way through the crowd to a spot near the front door, as far away from the fissured coffee table as possible without leaving the house completely. Finally I caught Marty's eye, gave him a "c'mon" wave, and he drove me home, raving about his good time.

At school on Monday morning everyone who attended the party commented on what fun we had and how it was too bad we'd never again have a party at Joyce's house. Her parents were enraged because someone broke a coffee table, and they wanted the breaker to step forward, confess and pay for repairs. Joyce and her close friends questioned every party-attender in vain. The vandal, who'd been told many times that he talked too much, realized that no one had witnessed his misdeed and stayed uncharacteristically silent. His identity forever remained a mystery.

* * *

The Detroit Tigers with Hal Newhouser, Hank Greenberg and George Kell, won 92 games that year, 1946. They came in second. The Boston Red Sox, with almost an All-Star lineup including Ted Williams, Bobby Doerr, Rudy York,

Pinky Higgins, Johnny Pesky and Dom Dimaggio, won 104 games and the pennant. The World Series began and every American League fan was confident of a Red Sox victory. Granted their opponent, the Saint Louis Cardinals, had Stan Musial, Enos Slaughter, Red Schoendienst and Del Rice, but they also had unknown players like Martin Marion, Whitey Kurowski and Joe Garagiola. The Red Sox were a sure bet. Then something odd happened. Williams stopped hitting, his teammates stopped fielding, fly balls disappeared in the sun, and the Red Sox lost in seven games. I felt bad for the American League, and Boston in particular, but knew that someday the Red Sox, given another World Series opportunity, would surely win.

Chuck also played organized ball, although some parishioners used the more descriptive word "disorganized." He played halfback on Assumption Grotto's grade school football team. The team started out expertly coached by one of Grotto's youthful priests, who was also closely affiliated with the church's Young Ladies Sodality. The priest became extraordinarily close with a Sodality officer and they were last seen together traveling in the direction of Chicago. The football team was coachless before playing their first game. Grotto's pastor quickly recruited a substitute coach, an ex-Grotto player not much older than team members. A Knute Rockne he wasn't and, although Chuck starred (he finally learned to run), the team lost every game.

* * *

In late October, Mary married Bud Davis at Grotto church followed by a restaurant breakfast, followed by a celebration with friends and relatives at our house. My parents hadn't lost a daughter, though. Betty moved out of the bedroom she shared with Mary, and Bud moved in.

* * *

The rumor swept through school: Nativity was going to field a football team. Students questioned, "How can we have a team? The season's almost over." Two days later it was proclaimed that any boy wanting to play football should report after school to the Recreation Hall field.

Twenty-four boys from Junior, Sophomore and Freshman classes showed up. We milled around, inspecting the rocky field, glass shards glistening, and asked, "Are we supposed to play tackle on THIS?"

Jack McEvoy, a fullback on the Jerry Lynch All-Stars in a semi-professional football league, was hired to coach us and stood near the Hall's rear door talking to Father Geller and Bill Stellon. He was heavy and powerful. Stellon walked over to us, tossed Marty a football and said, "Play a little touch 'til the coach gets through with Barney."

We chose up sides and played for a half-hour trying to awe Mr. McEvoy with our prowess. Father Geller left and the coach approached, introduced himself and explained: "We'll be out here every day after school, getting in shape, running plays. We'll be in the Catholic League third division next year and anything we learn now will help us get ready. Maybe I can schedule a few scrimmage games this year if I think you're up to it. Okay, I want you to line up in three rows for calisthenics."

For an hour we did situps, kneebends, pushups, duck walks, stomach karate chops, running in place, body twists and other exercises making us all sorry we hadn't worn older clothes to school. Then Mr. McEvoy gathered us around him and declared that Father Geller would supply uniforms, but we had to furnish our own football shoes, socks and jockstraps. He said it was a good first workout, praised our enthusiasm, said we had the makings for a good team and dismissed us with, "Go on home now and I'll see you tomorrow at three o'clock."

As we left the field I asked Marty, "What's a jockstrap?"

One of Alby's older brothers gave me a well-used pair of football shoes with screw-on cleats and Ed, who worked as a salesman at Montgomery Ward, bought me a jockstrap from the sports department. While adjusting this strap I recognized it could have a dual purpose: protection from excruciating pain during athletic contests and from excruciating humiliation during social events, especially dances.

Besides hip and shoulder pads our uniforms consisted of black jerseys with gold numbers (our school colors), beige padded kneepants and khaki-colored plastic helmets with two holes in the inside padding that fit snugly over our ears. With all this protective clothing we actually looked forward to our first contest.

Following a strenuous practice session, Marty suggested we get the feel of high school football by attending a night game at Keyworth stadium in Hamtramck, a mostly Polish city located inside Detroit. His real reason was to meet big, blonde, friendly, Polish girls. So Jack, Marty and I expectantly went to a game and did see many big, blonde, Polish girls sitting in the stands. They were surrounded by big, blonde, Polish boys who could kick your ass from Caniff Avenue to Dodge Main. We concentrated on football.

(Tom Tyler, who played the mummy in the movie *The Mummy's Hand,* was raised in Hamtramck and often returned to his hometown. One of his ex-girlfriends complained he was too wrapped up in himself.)

Two more weeks of after-school hours were spent tackling, blocking, passing and practicing defensive formations and offensive plays before the coach told us he'd scheduled a game with a third division team from St. Clement High School.

Our starting team consisted of nine Juniors and two freshmen, Sammy Vacari and Tony Arcesi, both fifteen. Sammy, the left halfback, was a solid, 5'6", 150 pounder, built like a small viaduct, with black curly hair, a square jaw and a neck that melded into shoulders. His muscles had muscles, developed from working on a relative's beer truck. He was a trained boxer, having reached the Golden Glove amateur boxing finals the previous year. He rarely evaded tacklers, preferring to smash over them. The rest of our backfield was composed of Marty, 150 pounds, at quarterback; Bob Tersch, 155 pounds, at fullback with spin-out-of-a-tackler's-grasp ability; and me, 130 pounds, at right halfback, who wanted nothing to do with grasping tacklers.

The other freshman, "Tall" Tony, was a good natured, 6'3", 190-pounder. He slammed blockers down to get at a ball carrier, then helped everyone to their feet after his tackle. He became a pass-catching right end on offense because of his height and large hands. With Jim Manley, 6'4", 210 pounds, at the other end position, and the rest of the linemen under 5'10", our two ends stood out like book ends.

Don Jacobs, the center, was 5'6" and 230 pounds of solid suet. He was the only team member who took a block from Sammy without wavering or falling back. Our two tackles, Frank Baccala and Bill Kraft, each weighed 170 and our two guards, Bernie Harrington and Jack Whelan, weighed 160. Jack Heffner, our only platooner, weighed l65 and played first-string linebacker on defense and second-string fullback. We weren't going to terrorize any teams with our mammoth proportions.

We played our first game on a cold Sunday evening at a lighted stadium in suburban Mount Clemens. Following a short, locker room pep talk from our coach we ran onto the field to spectator roars from what looked like all of Nativity's parish. Floodlights, clustered high on poles surrounding the stands, turned everything a shade brighter than twilight. It had rained regularly for three days and the field was a morass of mud and flood. While watching Saint Clement's kicker prepare the ball for kickoff, I silently prayed he didn't boot it my way. In my nervous condition, I wasn't ready to fumble in front of all those people and could picture the headline in the Nativity News: "Kickoff Flubbed By...."

The referee blew his whistle, the kicker kicked, the ball

spun end-over-end in my direction and I, in a stationary stupor, watched its flight. It hit the ground five feet to my right, splashed up and rolled by. I turned around and yelled, "Get it, Marty!" Marty picked it up and sloshed forward nine yards before a half-ton of bodies squashed him.

In the huddle a muddy Marty asked, "Hey, Bob, how come you didn't grab that ball? You stood like a lump on the road."

"I was shaky," I said lamely but truthfully.

For spite he called a right halfback end run play. Our backfield shifted left into single-wing formation, I caught the snapped ball, faked an off-tackle run, slipped by the defensive end, a linebacker slammed into me, we both slid in muck, and I lost all nervousness.

After ten minutes spectators couldn't distinguish one team from the other. My parents were in the stands and every time an injured, mud-caked player was carried from the field my worried mother sent Dad down to the sidelines to see if he was me. Most of the game was played in slow motion for solid footing, except for small areas near goal lines, was impossible. St. Clement players got nearer goal lines more than we and beat us 26 to 6. Sammy scored our lone touchdown.

In the locker room Mr. McEvoy said we played well and mentioned that the St. Clement coach told him we were a good team and dreaded playing us next year. I was exhausted and only hoped there was enough hot water for showering when we returned to the Recreation Hall.

We had two days off from practice while our uniforms were cleaned. At Wednesday's practice, Mr. McEvoy told us he'd scheduled a scrimmage game with St. Rose of Lima the next day at 3:30. St. Rose school, in a nearby neighborhood, was a second division team. I silently questioned Mr. McEvoy's wisdom. We couldn't beat a third division team and now he wanted us to play one in a tougher division.

The next afternoon we dressed at the Recreation Hall, crammed into cars owned by Mr. McEvoy, Father Gentner,

Marty, Bill Kraft and Don Jacobs and drove to a school yard featuring a long, wide swath of sward running alongside a cyclone fence where the St. Rose players waited. The two coaches explained that each team would take turns running a series of plays and we lined up facing each other. St. Rose had the ball, and I eyed our opponents. They were big! Their linemen all looked heavy, six feet tall or taller and their backfield looked formidable. We're going to get killed I told myself.

Surprisingly, some St. Rose players were less than fast and agile. They ran ten plays and didn't gain twenty yards. Our line often overwhelmed their blockers and ball carriers. When their ball carriers broke through, the rest of us splattered them. When we went on offense our line opened gaping holes and I figured in a real game on a real football field we'd have scored a few touchdowns. I credited Viaduct Sammy for much of our success. He was all over the field, blocking, tackling, and when carrying the ball, if a hole wasn't open, he made one. We exchanged the ball many times.

Back at the Recreation Hall, Mr. McEvoy said we probably could beat St. Rose in a regular game. He'd try to get us one more practice game and sent us home.

A Detroit Free Press columnist, Neal Shine, later to become the newspaper's publisher, played football at St. Rose that year. In columns recalling his youth, he often gently mentions how his St. Rose Golden Warriors weren't Detroit's most proficient team. He exaggerates, of course, for some excelled, but on the afternoon we played St. Rose they boosted our morale so high we actually looked forward to our last game.

We played our final scrimmage in Saginaw County on a remote field surrounded on three sides by rows of harvested corn stalks. There were few Nativity spectators, either because of the threatening, late-autumn weather or the four-hour round trip from Detroit. We played without goal posts so extra points were eliminated. Father Geller, who liked Sammy's rough style, had promised him fifty cents for every touchdown he scored. Marty gave Sammy the ball on most plays and Sammy scored six times. But those farm boys were strong, could hit, we lost 48 to 42, and our abbreviated football season ended.

* * *

My parents began to socialize more frequently. Now that their children were growing up that had more time to spend together. They went to dances or movies on weekends and occasionally to a neighborhood tavern for a chicken-in-the-basket dinner on weeknights. Mom's stomach and back pain recurred but she loved these dates. Two movies she especially raved about were *The Jolson Story* and *It's a Wonderful Life.* My parents were two of the few people nationwide who actually saw the latter when it first hit America's theaters.

On Christmas Day Mom received a full length fur coat, a present from Dad and her working children. She tried it on and looked radiant.

* * *

President Truman proclaimed that World War Two hostilities were officially over as of December 31, 1946. The war had been over for so long, no one noticed.

* * *

On a cold January morning, Betty married Joe Dolan in a quiet ceremony at his west side parish, St. Vincent's, and immediately moved to a rented house in a west side neighborhood. Soon after this wedding Ed handed me his Navy peacoat. "I think this'll fit you now. Try not to lose it." The sarcasm was obvious, but I still appreciated the gift. It looked good on me, but more important, it was warm and

I was beginning to value winter outdoor activities.

One winter activity I enjoyed was hockey. A neighbor on Cedargrove flooded the empty lot next to his house so his daughter could ice skate, and when she temporarily relinquished it we boys changed it into a hockey rink. Alby and Butch provided a puck and, except for Chuck and me, the others owned skates, and we all had worn-out brooms. An open cardboard box at one end of our rink served as a goalie's net. With no referees to penalize us, tripping and high-brooming were common, mayhem and arguments proliferated, and Canada had few reasons to fear we'd usurp their national sport.

I next tried ice skating. A group of Nativity students planned a Friday evening ice skating party at Belle Isle, a perfect place to take a girl on a date since the costs were minimal. I borrowed Butch's ice skates, Kathy agreed to accompany me, she brought her sister Lois, and Marty drove us to the party meeting place, the Belle Isle casino. A couple hundred bundled up skaters haphazardly whisked around a floodlighted, frozen canal fronting the casino while others inside its lobby drank hot chocolate and coffee. Lois and Marty left to look for other Nativity students, and I talked Kathy into testing the ice before donning skates.

We cautiously followed an embankment until we reached a secluded channel far from skaters and casino lights and, sitting on a snow-covered fallen log, I put on my borrowed skates and knelt down to help Kathy lace up hers. It was a slow process. "Why are your hands trembling?" she asked.

Because your shapely, nylon-encased kneecaps and calves are mesmerizing, I should have boldly said. "'Cause I'm cold," I meekly said.

After her skates were laced, we put our shoes in the grocery bag she provided, and skated back to the casino area. Kathy skated well; I didn't. This was my first ice skating venture. My ankles turned inward, falling was easy, speeding was dangerous, and braking was impossible.

Reno skated up to us, braked, sprayed ice, spun, said hello, demonstrated his backward gliding technique, returned, asked Kathy to skate with him and they swept away. Shooting pool wasn't his only talent.

Marty, also an experienced skater, spotted Mary Jane, the blonde, lovely, leading scorer on Nativity's basketball team, and left me standing unsteadily wondering where they all learned to skate so well. An hour of floundering and falling, bumping and apologizing, along with aching ankles and frosted ears, convinced me of skating's folly and I retreated to the warmth of the casino and stayed there.

Kathy wasn't elated at my disappearing act, and, as we rode home in the back seat of Marty's car, she allowed space and silence to build between us. Our on-again off-again romance was off-again.

This personal ice skating misfortune didn't deter me from other winter games. When the same school group suggested a day of tobogganing I was ready. Sitting on a toboggan had to be a lot easier than standing on skates, with the added alluring possibility of squeezing between two females. The toboggan party was scheduled for noon on Saturday, five days hence, at River Rouge Park on Detroit's far west side, the sole hilly place in the city.

A major problem arose as Saturday approached. Skies cleared and much of the ground snow melted. "Don't worry," Jack Heffner said. "It always snows more on the west side."

On toboggan day, low gray clouds threatened to dump more snow on the city. "It'll probably snow four or five inches before we get to the park," Marty said confidently. We were in Marty's Model A on the way to pick up our school buddies. Streets and sidewalks were clear and front lawns had dead, brownish-green patches peeking through grimy, crusted snow.

We picked up Jack, Stellon, Frank, Leroy and Reno and headed west. It was an uncomfortable ride sitting in the front seat crowded between Marty and Reno because I had to be alert to shift my legs to avoid getting a crushed kneecap as Marty slammed the floor shift into first or third.

"Who's bringin' the toboggan?" I asked Jack who had helped organize the outing.

"Bill Kraft. He borrowed one from a neighbor." Bill Kraft, a sandy-haired scholar, played right tackle on our football team.

"How many are coming today?"

"I figure about twenty."

"How many girls?"

"About eight or nine. Kraft's going to have a car full and Don Jacob's picking up the rest. Why do you care? I thought you were going with Kelly again."

"Nah. I screwed up with her at the skating party."

"You could screw up a damp dream. Why do you bother with her? She's always cutting you off at the knees."

"As long as she doesn't cut me off higher."

"I hate to excite you," Jack smiled, changing the subject, "but I asked Veronica and she said she'd be there."

Veronica was a freshman, a slim girl of 14 who looked exactly like Veronica Lake, the movie star. Her long blonde hair partially covered one eye as it cascaded down in soft waves, spreading over her shoulders. Her name wasn't Veronica, but that was the only name we used when lauding her beauty. She sat in the front pews at morning mass and our admiring eyes followed her every move, including her walk to the communion rail.

"So where is she?" I asked.

"She didn't wanna be the only girl in a car full of guys so Don's picking her up. But she'll be there."

"You gotta lotta guts, Jack," I told him.

"It's not like I asked her out," he said modestly. "She was standing with Pat Mox and I couldn't just ask Pat and not her."

"She's too young for us," Marty said. Marty's seventeenth birthday was coming up, and he was feeling old since he started shaving once a week.

"If she's big enough, she's old enough," Reno philosophized.

As they debated merits and liabilities of dating much younger girls, I considered what a handsome couple Veronica and I would make. She was the right height, three inches shorter than I, and I pictured us attending the prom together, swaying to Dorsey music, her blonde hair nestled against my cheek, the envy of peers. I'd rather take Kathy, I thought, but with the prom three months away in May, I couldn't predict how our relationship would be faring. Jack didn't say he was interested in Veronica; so, maybe, if given the chance, I could charm her with my golden-tongued, glib dialogue.

At Rouge Park, Marty pulled alongside a row of parked cars. Bill Kraft's moss green 1936 Hudson Terraplane was already there, empty and with a toboggan still lashed to the roof. We headed for the tobogganing area, acutely aware that we weren't trudging through a foot of fresh snow; instead we walked gingerly over well-trodden mush mixed with flattened blades of grass. A crowd of about 70 adults, teenagers and children was spread out in small bunches overlooking the slopes. Nativity students waved at us, but no one seemed too happy. "Take a look," Kraft said.

We warily stepped to the drop-off edge and stared downward. It was almost as steep as a roller coaster dive and much farther to travel before leveling off. Kraft pointed out swatches of brown dirt showing through the thin covering of ice and said, "I'm not taking the toboggan down that mess. My neighbor just waxed it. There might be rocks in that dirt." Everyone who heard this grousing instinctively glanced skyward hoping six inches of new snow would suddenly plop down.

Disappointed, we watched fearless, giggling youngsters take turns plunging down the slope on sleds and inverted garbage can lids. Further to the right, serious adults on skis pushed off and schussed downward, miraculously staying erect.

"Why don't we borrow one of those kids' lids?" I said to Marty, hoping he'd say no. My peacoat would really get soiled on that dirty ice.

"Nah, let's go see what everyone else wants to do." The others had gathered back from the slopes, standing in loosely connected circles, trying to think of a substitute venture. Veronica was there in gay apparel like the other girls, who wore ski pants or slacks tucked into fur-lined boots and brightly colored fur-trimmed jackets, mittens, scarves, and tasseled knit caps. Veronica's flowing blonde hair set her apart.

Marty carefully scraped together some loose snow, crunched it into a compact ball, stood and flung it in Reno's direction. It splattered on Jack's shoulder, routing those around him. Jack ran to a relatively untrampled field of snow, made a snowball and sailed it past Marty's nose. Snowballs flew as other laughing, screaming Nativity students joined the good-natured fray. Boys chased boys chasing girls chasing boys, flinging snowballs or stuffing loose snow inside jacket collars. One shrieking girl grabbed Stellon's leather cap and hurled it skyward. It landed next to Reno who picked it up and tossed it to Marty who winged it to Leroy who lobbed it to me, while Stellon stomped around pleading, "C'mon guys, gimme my hat. You're messing it up. C'mon." Grabbing and throwing headgear became the new game until Jack shouted, "Let's play football!"

We chose two teams, five boys and three girls on each, and measured off goal lines and boundaries. Kraft, dressed as a hunter with a red plaid jacket and matching earflapped cap, volunteered his cap for a ball. I was disheartened when Veronica was chosen for the opposing team, but heartened when I saw its advantages. Carrying Kraft's hat she tried an end run, and Marty gently tackled her. He arose and grinned, knowing I envied him. I whispered to quarterback Jack, "How about sending her my way, hey?" He just laughed.

Two plays later she ran right at me, holding Kraft's hat like a 105-pound fullback. I upended her and laid her flat on her back in the snow before noticing my left hand buried between her upper thighs, and I quickly removed the brashly misplaced appendage. She smiled, and spoke her first and last words to me, "Nice tackle."

The game continued, a light, sleety snow started falling and all girls gradually quit. Consequently we lost interest and ended our outing.

We slowly wandered toward the parked cars, still gabbling, laughing, exuberant. I walked with Kraft to his car, ostensibly for a closer look at the toboggan, but actually to be the last one into Marty's car, not wanting to be dodging his gear shift on the way home.

Marty began revving his Model A's motor while Reno hung out the front passenger side window, exhorting me to "C'mon, let's go."

I opened the door, and Reno moved over to let me in. As I rolled up the side window, happy words burst forth: "When I tackled Veronica, did you guys see where I grabbed her?!"

My excited proclamation was greeted with complete silence. Marty concentrated on backing up his car, and Reno made odd, thumbing, chest gestures. "Whatsa' matter?" I asked, before realizing that his motions meant "Look behind you."

I turned and in back, seated tightly between Frank and Jack, sat Veronica staring straight ahead. Stellon, in one corner, shook his head, bit his lip and made coughing noises.

It was a quiet, disquieting return to the east side with the only conversation centering on weather and traffic. Any attempt to include Veronica received short, ambiguous remarks from her. The car's chill got chillier. We dropped Frank off at his house, and Veronica directed Marty to her house. Getting out of the car she said good-bye like she meant it to last eternally.

"Do ya think she heard me?" I asked as we pulled away from the curb.

This question started them laughing, except for Jack who said, "Yeah, she heard you, you dolt."

"How did she know I meant her? Her name ain't Veronica."

"'Cause I told her that's what we call her. You sure can mess things up. I was thinking of asking her to the prom."

"Yeah, me too," I said seriously, which brought more laughter.

Marty advised, "You gotta learn that quiet is golden."

"How was I to know she was there?" I protested. "The damn snow was sticking to the back windows. I couldn't see her. What happened to Leroy?"

"He wanted to ride with Audrey, so he and Veronica switched cars," Marty explained.

I never apologized to Veronica, though I tried. I passed her in a school hallway, said, "Hello," and she ignored me. I saw her standing in front of church at lunchtime, walked up and said, "How ya doing?" and she gazed through me, then walked away. I remorsefully accepted her subtle hints and never went near her again. It was frustrating. She wasn't like her namesake at all. The real Veronica Lake, who always wore a sly, amused smile, would have surely forgiven my minor indiscretion.

XXXII

With Spring's advent came cleansing rain, new creation, climbing temperatures and anticipation, but I developed feelings of trepidation. Junior year with Sister Jarlath would end within three months. It was an ongoing pleasure to enter her classroom, enjoy her plucky countenance, absorb her teachings. Often, at schooldays's end, Marty and I tarried awhile just to bask in her company. She was more worldly than other nuns, saw humor in school rules and delighted in counseling us in our mundane, idiotic, teenage problems. During one of these afterschool sessions, I asked why she was so harsh with us at the school year's beginning. She replied, "A couple of your tenth grade teachers warned me you two annoyed them the most. I don't know why they felt that way."

"Well, we did mature over last summer," I exaggerated. Actually she was too lovely to irritate.

Marty and I profited from our closeness with Sister Jarlath. Nativity's principal started an anti-smoking campaign when a pair of nuns (nuns always traveled in pairs) entered Taylor's sweetshop and found half the students puffing on the devilish weed. The shop was a couple blocks from the nearest school property, a distance that students considered outside the school's perimeter and jurisdiction. The principal believed differently. She officially extended the perimeter to Gratiot and threatened expulsion for any student caught smoking. Suspension wasn't an option. Marty and I complained to Sister Jarlath who sympathized, but suggested we either quit smoking or find another lunch hour hangout. She added, "There's another shop a block past the Recreation Hall."

"That's too far, Sister," I told her. "We'd spend half our lunchtime getting there and back!"

"Try running," she compassionately advised. "It's good exercise."

We compromised by walking fast or using Marty's car for the trip. Eventually other smoking students, both male and female, joined us.

The sweetshop was grubby, the wooden booths unpadded, and its former white walls had turned beige from age and tobacco fumes; yet there was a good selection of pop, sandwiches, potato chips, candy and ice cream. Anne, the middle-aged owner, was extremely congenial and appreciated this sudden customer influx.

Sister Jarlath defended students if she believed they were treated unfairly. When a grade school nun passed the rear of school and saw clouds of blue cigarette smoke wafting from an open second floor window she investigated by bursting into the boy's lavatory and took names of everyone standing near the window, including Marty and me, ignoring flustered boys occupied in other legitimate restroom pursuits.

Later Marty and I were questioned by Sister Jarlath privately in the school hall, and we assured her we never smoked inside the school building. She looked relieved as she said, "I told the principal you two wouldn't do such a thing, and she removed your names from the list. But please don't let it happen again. I may not be able to protect you next time." She truly was a cooperative, understanding person.

* * *

The handball court across the field from Nativity's Recreation Hall was a neighborhood attraction. Cool April weather was perfectly suited for strenuous handball games. Students gathered at the court after school to participate in games or observe, cheer or just jeer participants. The court consisted of a cement floor and three gray-painted, 8-inch thick wooden walls. A high, square main wall was enclosed between two triangular-shaped ones. Two games with either two or four players were played concurrently on each side of the main wall. Regulation handballs were in short supply; so tennis balls were usually substituted.

Nativity students weren't the sole people congregating at these games. Public school teenagers also appeared, and one of them, a 5-foot tall, 16-year-old beauty named Marie let it be known among other spectators that she thought me cute. I thought she was ravishing. Her ebony hair, full lips, thin waist, perfect teeth, dark eyes, shapely legs and boticeful bosom, assets capable of captivating any male, made me doubtful that she'd actually have a "wide on" for me, but Marty sagely advised, "Never pass up a gift horse."

Encouraged, I lost a handball contest, then edged close to where she stood in a small crowd of onlookers and voiced a question, "Do you like these games?"

She said, "No. I'm standing here waiting for a bus," but smilingly added, "Only kidding. I do like them. Actually I'd like to learn how to play...or at least how to score."

I explained scoring, we exchanged first names, she introduced me to her girlfriend at her side, I introduced them both to Marty, and soon we chatted like we'd known each other for hours instead of minutes. Later, when the sun set and the street lights lit, everyone else wandered off. She had to go home and I gallantly offered to escort her.

Marie lived four blocks away, and we walked slowly. She mentioned her Italian parents were strict. She was late for supper and would probably get yelled at. I told her I didn't have that worry. My mother was sick and rarely cooked supper. That chore was handled by my older sisters who didn't care whether I was late or even ate.

We parted in front of her house, promising to meet again at the handball court. I jogged to Gratiot, caught a streetcar and arrived home at 7:30. While warming up leftover food, a happy thought dawned. I might have a date for Nativity's prom.

When I went upstairs for my daily chat with Mom, she was fingering her rosary. "Did you have a nice time tonight?" she asked.

"Yeah, Ma, I met a girl and might ask her to the prom."

"I thought you were going to ask Kathy."

"I wish I could, but I can't. We ain't even talking. Are ya feeling okay?"

"Yes. It hurts, but not so bad. I even helped Mary with the supper. The doctor came today and checked me over."

"When did he say you'd get well?"

"Oh, he just said it was a good sign that the pain is less and that I looked better."

I didn't think she looked better.

* * *

Detroit's east side harbored many gangs, some with membership numbering over one hundred. These gangs proliferated during the '30s and early '40s and were made up of males in their teens or early twenties who banded together for fun and mischief. The fun consisted of beer parties, dances and shooting pool. The mischief, which they also classified as fun, consisted of loitering in front of business establishments creating a nuisance, and fisticuffs among themselves or with other gangs. Some members, who believed there is strength and safety in numbers, participated in high jinks they never dreamed of doing alone, like blatant pilferage and property damage, which added to their "undesirable low-life" reputation. A small minority of these ruffians eventually graduated to more serious crimes of breaking and entering, mugging, running numbers and operating illegal drinking emporiums called blind pigs, but seldom were guns involved. Their loss of respect for another's property didn't extend to another's life.

Most gangs, who's members weren't known for their inventiveness, named themselves after neighborhood streets or intersections and were seldom ethnically diverse. The ones with the least savory reputations were the Harper/Van Dyke and the Chene/Trombly gangs whose members were almost exclusively Polish, the hillbilly Conner/Jefferson and Mack/Fairview gangs, the integrated Field/Jefferson gang with Italian, Polish and German members, and the Italian Cagalupo boys. The Cagalupo's inhabited the Gratiot/Harper area, and their name, loosely translated, meant wolf defecation.

Generally gang members continued attending high school, and others had legitimate jobs. A leader of the Frontenac street gang who ushered at the Eastown movie theater in the Harper/Van Dyke area brought his own brand of gang expertise to his job. He volunteered to exclusively patrol the balcony, usually a boisterous problem arena in theaters, because he enjoyed throwing boisterous problems down balcony stairs.

World War II and the draft dissipated the gangs' ranks. Many members volunteered or reluctantly reported to the induction (they called it the "abduction") center for a more lethal type of fighting. Others, who appeared in court for minor offenses against society were sometimes given a choice by judges to "serve country or time." They all chose military enlistment.

At war's end gang life had lost it's appeal for these patriots. Returning veterans wished to settle down and become productive citizens. But for boys too young for the sobering military experience, gang life still had an exciting aura. I was one of these boys, which explains the following.

It was midmorning, Friday. Marty and I stood in Nativity's lavatory furtively waving our hands to break up smoke we

403

expelled as it drifted toward the partially open window. Across the room Reno held the door open a crack and peered down the hall, alert for wrathful black-and-white clad apparitions. "Whadaya wanna do tonight, Marty?" I asked.

"I don't know. What do you wanna do?"

"I don't know. I asked first. Whada you wanna do?"

"How about joining a gang. They're always doing things."

"What gang?"

"You know Johnny Maiuri?"

"Yeah, the zoot suit guy." Johnny was a sophomore. Early in the school year he created a minor stir by wearing a zoot suit to school including the knee length chain. The nuns, who considered minor stirs kindred to class disruptions, proposed he dress more conservatively in the future. He returned to wearing his usual black peg pants and hip-length sweaters.

"He says they're looking for guys for his gang," Marty explained. "I'm supposed to meet him at Anne's at lunch to let him know if we're interested. Whadayasay?"

"Do ya wanna?"

"It's imvenereal to me. What do you think?"

"Sure. Why not?" The word "sure" I used often and after using it, noticed that sometimes problems developed.

In a booth, at lunchtime, Johnny sat across from Marty and me extolling the benefits of gang membership. Johnny was medium tall, very thin with sunken cheeks and chest. Some joked that he had to move around in the shower to get wet. He had wavy black hair combed straight back and a whispery voice. To strengthen his case he pointed out that the two freshmen on our football team, Tall Tony and Viaduct Sammy, had already joined his gang. He also mentioned the fellowship among gang members and protection from other neighborhood gangs. Marty explained we already had enough fellowship with school buddies and gangs never bothered us. We weren't convinced until he mentioned his gang had parties attended by public school

404

girls. Catholic school boys dreamed of partying with public school girls and then marrying Catholic school girls. "Where do we sign and does it have to be in blood?" Marty asked. Johnny snickered and said, "I'll just introduce you to the guys tonight, and you'll be in. Anymore questions?"

"Yeah," Marty said. "Where do ya hang out?"

"You mean 'Where's our headquarters?' Right here. Anne's. We call ourselves the McClellan gang."

"Why'd ya ask us to join," I wondered.

"'Cause you wear black pegs. All our guys wear them."

I had hoped it was because we looked tough. I had another question. "How many in this gang?" Anne's was a small shop.

"Counting you two, there's 26."

At 7:30 that evening Marty and I were back in Anne's, sitting in the same booth, the jukebox blasting *Open the Door, Richard.* Johnny grinned at us across the table. There were a dozen males occupying or standing over the other booths with four more slumped on soda fountain stools. Anne stood behind the counter wearing a weary expression. All her customers were in their late teens or early twenties. Most had dark, slicked-back hair. A few wore mustaches. Some wore black leather jackets. They all wore black pegs. They looked like guys I'd crossed streets to avoid in the past.

Marty was still wary about gang membership. "So where's all the girls?" he asked Johnny.

"Don't worry...they'll be here. The whole gang's supposed to be here."

We waited, sipping Cokes. Every few minutes Johnny called out to two or three of those present, "Hey, c'mon over and meet our new members!"

The old members had names like Vinny, Dom, Dino, Paulie, Carmine, Guedo and Augie. When introduced some smiled and said "Hi," some grunted, others nodded. Most said a few friendly words to Johnny before returning to their seats. None seemed excessively impressed with their new members.

"Are all these guys Italian?" I whispered.

"Yeah. We have 25 Italians and you. You'll have to dye your hair black." He grinned to assure me he joshed.

"Even if Tony and Sammy show up I don't count no 26 guys here," I noted.

"They said they'd make it. The only one who won't be here is Vito. He had a little accident three weeks ago."

He waited for someone to ask about the accident so I did. "What kind of accident?"

Johnny smiled and said, "Old Vito found a way to make a little spare change. He was stealing a couple cases of empty beer bottles from a grocery over on Cooper street and selling them at another store. The grocer kept them stacked on his back porch, and Vito stole two or three a week before the grocer noticed. The next time Vito showed up late at night to relieve him of a couple cases the grocer was waiting and came busting out his back door with a rifle. Vito jumped off the porch carrying a case and the grocer, an old guy, chased him to the alley. Vito could really run and was half-way down the alley when the old guy yelled "Stop!" and fired a warning shot in the air. It hit Vito in the leg."

"You're kidding, right?" Marty asked.

"No, that's what the grocer told the cops. He fired in the air."

"I believe him," I said. "I useta have a BB gun like that." No one asked me to explain.

"Vito won't be around for awhile," Johnny continued. "From the hospital he's going to jail."

Sammy and Tall Tony strode in, greeted by, "Hey Tony! Hey, Sammy! How ya doin'? Whatsa good word?" Sammy came to our booth while Tony went to the counter to get a couple more cokes. "Well, whadaya think? Ya gonna join?" Sammy asked.

I said "Sure" and Marty nodded.

"Where's all the girls?" Marty asked.

In answer, two young ladies walked in the front door. With few exceptions they looked like other teenage girls with pleated skirts, baggy sweaters, bobbysocks and scuffed saddle shoes. The exceptions were that one had long hair the color of tar, the other the color of brass, and both wore black leather jackets, two layers of pancake makeup and a thick layer of mascara and ultra-red lipstick. They proudly exhibited their skill at simultaneously greeting friends while vigorously chewing gum.

"Those are a couple of our girls," Johnny said smugly as we watched them push into a booth near the front door. "They'll be at the party I'm throwing next week Saturday."

Whenever possible on the days leading up to his party, Johnny readied me. "You'll be the only one not Italian so you have to learn a few Italian words."

"What for?"

"So you'll fit in. Some guys wanted to keep our gang 'Italian only.' I'll just teach you a few easy ones."

He taught me relatively, friendly words, "Goombah, compadre, paisan," an understanding word, "Capieche," a gentle, derisive word "Chooch," and words and phrases not to be used in mixed company, "Scotta, bah fungoo, fungoola buetana."

"You don't look Italian," Johnny said, "so if anyone asks, tell 'em your mother's Italian and her father came from Milan. There's a lot of light-haired people in northern Italy." I began to suspect the sole reason Johnny invited me into the gang was at Marty's insistence.

There were six girls at the party, each surrounded by a gaggle of swarthies, so I stayed close to Marty and avoided use of my newly-acquired Italian vocabulary. The beer ran out at eleven p.m. eliminating the last vestige of enjoyment and Marty drove me home. Our first gang-life social event, devoid of expected bacchanalian pleasure, ended with a dull thud. I crawled into bed next to Chuck, mumbling, "Don't wake me tomorrow unless I'm dead."

To be a gang member and continue altar-boying seemed

407

ludicrous. I'd thought of quitting often since, having moved out of the parish, my serving was limited to school days, usually at nine o'clock mass. My sole altar boy pleasures were tapping attractive girl's under the chin with a cold paten so I could watch their closed eyelids snap open at the communion rail, and drinking wine dregs left in cruets after mass. Father Gentner, a premature balding young man, seemed visibly upset at my decision to quit, mainly because I couldn't give him a definitive reason for it other than, "It's too much trouble, Father." I couldn't tell him my "gang" reason or that I was rarely in the state of sanctifying grace when serving.

* * *

I walked Marie home from the handball court three times and received two chaste kisses before inviting her to be my prom date. She said she'd be happy to accompany me, and that she'd wear a white, strapless gown for the occasion. I cherished my good fortune. A night of up-close dancing, gazing at heaving cleavage. My older sisters said I was also fortunate in Marie's choice of a gown color because, since a corsage should always contrast with a gown, I could buy red carnations instead of expensive white gardenias. Everything was falling in place. Jack had permission to borrow his father's car on prom night, and he and his date would pick up Marie and me at our homes. After the dance we'd go to Lelli's, a restaurant Jack classified as classy, with Marty, Reno and their dates. The prom would be a night to remember.

It happens too often that the best laid plans get waylaid. Ten days before the prom Marie had second thoughts about her gown. "I have a pink one I'm going to wear," she told me over the phone. "The white one is too low cut."

"So what?" I said, thinking: How can a dress be too low cut?

"My mother said the nuns won't like it and won't let us

in. The pink one has wide shoulder straps and is a lot more modest."

This unnerved me. I certainly didn't want her striving for modesty. "Our nuns ain't like that. Honest, they don't care. Jack's girlfriend is wearing a strapless," I lied.

"No, I'd rather not. You'll like the pink one."

"No I won't. C'mon, Marie, I love white. I've always wanted to go to a prom with a girl in white. Please?" I tried to keep the wheedle from my voice as my close-up cleavage dream wilted.

"I just don't want to be embarrassed."

"You won't be embarrassed." Panicky, in desperation, inspiration struck. "I'll tell ya what. Wear the white dress and if the nuns say anything I'll have Jack drive ya home to change. Ya live close by so it won't be much trouble. Whadda-yasay?"

"I don't know. Why can't I just wear the pink? It's a pretty gown too."

"Cause I love white. Give me a break, Marie. You'd look great in white."

There was a short silence and then, "You're right. I do look good in it. Okay, but I'm going to have to wear a bolero jacket."

"That's okay," I said. Bolero jackets open in front. It still irritated me. Shoulders and arms are also attractive.

A slight complication arose when Bill Stellon told me between classes that Kathy wondered why I hadn't asked her to the prom. This depressed me. Just because we weren't speaking to each other was no reason for her not to write a note asking me to take her. It explained why she'd been giving me meaningful glances lately.

At lunch I sat next to her at Anne's and broke our long silence by saying, "Hi, Kath. Ya going to the prom?"

She answered, "No, it's too late to get a prom dress. Why didn't you ask me sooner?"

"I just figured you were mad at me."

She shook her head in exasperation. "Are you going?"

I confessed that I was, but said I'd take her the following year. She promised to go with me.

The night to remember began as Jack and his date, Joann, picked me up at home. I sat in the car's back seat wearing my blue, pinstriped suit, starched white shirt, blue knit tie, square-toed shoes, white socks, undershirt, boxer shorts and jock strap; holding a see-through plastic rectangular box on my knees containing a red carnation corsage, still cool from the refrigerator. Jack, chattering as he drove, wore a conservative navy blue suit and Joann an ankle-length, light blue gown with capped sleeves and high cut square neckline. Marie in her strapless is going to create a furor, I happily mused, and pictured every guy at the prom envying me. I silently wished Jack would stop gassing and step on the gas as I grew impatient for my eye banquet.

Marie's beaming porch light cutting through dusk welcomed me. Jack parked in front, I left the car and tried to walk casually, like an adult, in case anyone inside watched my approach. I rang the bell, Marie's mother, a smiling, short, plump, black-haired woman, opened the door, invited me in and suggested I sit on their living room couch. "Marie'll be down in a minute," she said.

While replying to her questions about what time I expected to have Marie home, if Jack was a good driver and what restaurant we were going to, I warily eyed the large, undershirted, overweight, Tony Galento look-alike sitting at a table in the connecting dining room reading a newspaper. I figured it was Marie's dad. He was probably listening to the conversation and I wondered what he thought of Marie's white gown. The sound of high heels descending focused all my expectant attention on the staircase to my left. A radiant Marie appeared in all her loveliness and in all her modest, pink apparel. Three weeks worth of fantasies crashed in a split second, replaced by disappointment, wrath and embarrassment. Not only was my cleavage dream canceled, but the red carnations didn't go with pink. With a forced smile I reluctantly handed Marie the corsage.

She had a lot of dress material to choose from so she pinned it to her left shoulder area.

In the car, Jack introduced Joann and himself to Marie while I brooded.

"What's the problem?" she whispered.

"Where's the white dress?" I whispered back.

"I told you I didn't want to wear it."

"Ya coulda called me."

"I just didn't think it necessary."

I thought, yeah, great! My first formal dance and everyone is going to say, "Look at the dummy who bought red flowers for a pink dress." Silence grew between us.

The prom theme, "Apple Blossom Time," was evident. Strings of fake apple blossoms hung from basketball backboards, ceiling beams and window drapes. An eight piece band, its members garbed in white jacketed tuxedos, played slow, romantic music from the stage. Behind them were white latticed frames trimmed with more apple blossoms. The band's vocalist put down his saxophone at times, grasped a microphone and, doing a passable imitation of Art Lund, sang tender ballads. The lights were romantically dimmed.

I didn't feel romantic. I felt remorse. Although Marie and I stood near the wall a foot apart, all conversation between us had ceased and our silence was getting on my nerves. When Reno asked her to dance it was a relief. Marty, with his date, Mary Jane, walked up and said satirically, "Ya look like you're having a blast. How come ya ain't dancing with Marie?"

"We ain't talking," I said.

"Why?"

"'Cause she said she was gonna wear white and she wore pink, and the red flowers I bought ain't right with pink."

"That's silly," Mary Jane said. "Pink and red go well together."

"Yeah?"

"Yes. She's very pretty, by the way."

411

Marty added, "What's with you anyway, Bob? Sometimes you really act dumb."

"I ain't dumb. Sister Richard said I have a high IQ."

"In your case it stands for intellect questionable. Stop fooling around and ask her to dance. You two have to go to Lelli's with us tonight. We got reservations."

"Okay," I said, relieved that everyone didn't think red with pink was a fatal fax pas. "As soon as she gets back."

The music stopped, Reno returned Marie to the empty space beside me, thanked her for the dance and took off. The band was well into their next number before I got up nerve to say, "Do ya wanna dance?"

She said "No," rather emphatically.

Marie and I spent the shank of the evening proving to each other that we could have a good time alone. She danced with Reno, Marty, Jack and Stellon, and I danced with their dates. I noticed none of my dancing partners wore strapless gowns. When the vocalist sang *Goodnight Sweetheart* (every band's "send them packing" melody) I wanted to continue merrymaking. Maybe some of the evening could be salvaged if Marie felt the same. I sidled up to her and said, "We're going to Lelli's restaurant."

"Maybe you are, but I'm not," she said tersely. "I'm going home."

Marty agreed to drive Marie and me home since Jack had made the restaurant reservations and had to be there early. When we parked in front of Marie's house, I jumped out of the back seat to hold the car door open for her, but as she exited she failed to thank me for this courtesy, instead saying, "Don't bother walking me to the door."

"Good night," I said formally.

"Buzz off," she said informally.

Marty tried to talk me into going partnerless to the restaurant, but I declined. "You have a knack for fouling things up before they get started," he lectured. "Worrying about the color of flowers! Geez!"

Mary Jane added, "I've noticed you have trouble devel-

412

oping, opposite-sex, long-term relationships."

I couldn't discreetly mention my main irritation, the cleavage disappointment, to Mary Jane so I just said, "Yeah, it was a dumb reason to get mad, over flowers, but at least her parents are happy. I got her home at a decent hour. How long should I wait before I call her to apologize."

"You're joshing, right? Let sleeping lionesses lie," Marty cautioned.

It sounded like good advice. Damn! I mused. Leave it to cleavage. It turned my big prom night into a night to forget.

But I began silently planning for next year's prom, weighing the odds of hoodwinking Kathy into wearing a white, strapless, low-cut gown.

XXXIII

Gang life, as exciting as watching dust settle, started to happily perk up. Late nights we surreptitiously entered wedding halls two or three at a time and indulged in free beer and food, leaving peacefully if discovered by hosts or invited guests. Gang life began to turn menacing when ten of us went to a well-attended dance at a Gratiot hall. I remarked in an aside to Marty that one of the jitterbuggers looked like he was suffering with D.T.'s. Soon after, "zoot suit" Johnny told me he overheard a restroom conversation between Sherwood street gang members about what they intended to do to some smartmouth in a blue pinstriped suit who disparaged a member's dancing skill. I swiftly persuaded Marty we should inconspicuously vacate the dance through a side door, which we did, with my smartmouth and teeth still intact. This incident convinced me hanging out with a large group wasn't always safe. Two nights later at Anne's another ominous element was added.

"We're going to have a gang fight," Johnny told Marty and me.

"With who?" Marty asked.

"The Dukes."

"Who the hell are the Dukes?"

"They hang out at a Gratiot store four or five blocks past Harper."

415

"Hey, I know those guys," I interrupted. "They wear blue jackets with 'Dukes' on the back."

"Yeah, that's them. Sal's arranging the fight right now."

"Whadda we wanna fight them for?" I asked. "They look like nice guys." I often saw Dukes walking on Gratiot when I stared out streetcar windows while traveling home in the evenings. Most had light-colored brushcut hair, and few wore gang-type peg pants. "I thought they belonged to a club; not a gang."

"Hey, don't pick a nit. Gang...club...what's the difference. We're still gonna fight 'em."

"What for," Marty wanted to know.

"'Cause a couple Dukes gave a hard time to some younger brothers of our members in front of the Arcadia. Knocked down their bikes and pushed them around."

"How old were these brothers?" I asked.

"About twelve or thirteen. We can't let them pick on our kid brothers."

If they were like most Italians I had met at that age they probably provoked and deserved it, I speculated. "How many guys in the Dukes' club, Johnny?" I asked aloud.

"They've got about thirty-five, so we're getting a little help from the Mack boys. That'll give us around 60."

"At least the odds are right," Marty said. "When's this big battle taking place?"

"Probably in three weeks, when we're out of school."

* * *

Near school year's end many children who desired a class memento bought thin, hard-cover, autograph books and had friends and classmates fill it with hokey sentimentality and good wishes. My sister Ann brought home such a book and requested I write something in it that she could replicate in her classmates' books at Assumption Grotto. Searching through the shallow pool of banal, off-colorful material stored in my memory bank, I extracted a simple

416

gem: Roses are red. Violets are blue. Mary's are pink, 'cause I saw them on the line. Ann thought this amusing and the next school day she wrote this gem in every autograph book offered to her. Later she started hearing cloakroom whispers about a "dirty poem." Her shocked little girl friends started to shun her and little boys flashed friendlier smiles. With one fractured verse I managed to transform my little sister into the fifth-grade strumpet.

Meanwhile, at Nativity, Kathy and Lois Kelly, who usually passed school lunch hour at either Taylor's or Anne's, found another place to spend this relaxing time — at the Dukes' hangout. They had company. Dolores DeWalls and June Narkus, attractive students from our Junior class, had formed a Dukes club auxiliary called Derbys and were recruiting new members. I learned this from Geri Zewecki who I talked to frequently, who knew my feelings for Kathy, thought Kathy and I made a cute couple and wondered why I continually said or did things to repel Kathy. I wondered the same thing. I also wondered why the Derbys named themselves after a horse race or hat instead of the more logical "Duchesses." I'd ask Kathy while persuading her not to join.

I caught up with Kathy after school as she walked toward Gratiot with Jackie, another bright-eyed lovely from our class. "Hey, Kath! I heard you might join the Dukes' club." I flashed her my most unbelieving smile, like it was such a stupid idea that I knew she wouldn't even consider it.

"I've been considering it," she said.

"You know that gang I'm in?" I asked.

"Yes."

"We're supposed to have a gang fight with the Dukes in a couple weeks."

In unison, Kathy and Jackie gasped, "What for?!"

"'Cause they beat up the little brothers of our members," I said triumphantly.

"They wouldn't do something like that. They're nice guys," Kathy said, miffed.

"Yeah, they're nice guys," echoed Jackie, also miffed.

"Well, that's what I heard they did," I said lamely, knowing I had elaborated the Dukes' sins.

"Tell your scuzzy friends to leave the Dukes alone," Kathy said as we reached the corner of McClellan and Gratiot. She shook her head. "You really irritate me, Robert. I'll see you tomorrow."

They turned up Gratiot, walking away from me, and I asked, "Ain't you taking the streetcar?"

Kathy turned around, backpeddling, and said, "Not now." She smiled. "We're going to see the Dukes."

Jealously, despairingly, staring at their receding forms, I realized I not only hadn't persuaded Kathy against joining the Dukes, but now she thought me part of the bad guys. I painfully knew I would lose her to one of those nice guys, and the thought of someone else kissing her almost gagged me. And I hadn't even settled the mysterious Derby/Duchess question. And suddenly I didn't care about the answer.

The school year ended; Lois graduated; our whole Junior class was promoted, and Marty and I sadly said farewell to Sister Jarlath.

* * *

Gang fight preparation is easy. No one did roadwork, jumped rope or sparred, at least in public. Our negotiators discussed rules and battleground site with theirs while the rest of us sat around Anne's exaggerating the justification of our cause. How could the Dukes be nice guys, we reasoned, if they'd punch out ten-year-old boys, demolish the boys' bicycles, steal their candy bars?

Tall Tony, Viaduct Sammy, Marty and I, having played football together, usually remained relatively apart from other members at Anne's. As new untried members, the four of us were insiders/outsiders, expected to gradually ingratiate ourselves. As a non-Italian, I found ingratiating especially difficult. At least Marty, Tony and Sammy had their heritage going for them. I suspected the coming Dukes set-to was a perverse, contrived initiation to test our membership mettle before we were completely accepted and I didn't relish the test. I tried to forget, but vividly recalled, participating in three, youthful, fist fights resulting in two losses and a draw, an ignominious record. I fretted to Marty, Tony and Sammy about personally flunking a fight test. They confidently told me to just stick close to them, keep swinging and I'd be okay. Or, if we got separated, I should try to find a little Duke my size.

I noticed other members weren't worried either. Some loudly bragged of their fighting prowess, of participating in previous gang fights. One smiled and said the Dukes probably wouldn't show up anyway. "The Dukes don't look tough," he declared. "They look like nice guys." I hoped he was right.

Fight conversation at Anne's slowed until after Independence Day, then flared anew. "Zoot suit" Johnny told us the fight was scheduled for the following Tuesday, at sundown, five days away. We'd all gather at Chandler schoolyard, march to the Dukes' hangout and have at them for maiming those seven-year-old boys and stealing their milk money. When Marty dropped me off at home after dark he asked, "Do you have a feeling this whole thing is rather stupid?" A half-hour later I received a stupid phone call.

"Is this Bob Beckwell?"

"Yeah."

"You in the McClellan gang?"

"Yeah."

"You gonna be at the fight next Tuesday?"

"Yeah."

"Good. I'll see you there. This is a Duke."

The phone clicked as I said, "Who?"

Irritated, I ran to Kelly's house, told Kathy about the phone conversation and wondered who had bandied my name about the Dukes' hangout. She assured me neither she nor Jackie mentioned me to the Dukes, she didn't know anyone who would, and it was probably one of my crummy acquaintances joking around. She finished with, "No Duke would make a call like that. They're too nice."

At Anne's on Saturday, three evenings before fight night, as I repeated the words of my strange phone call to Marty, Johnny rushed in and emotionally told us, "C'mon! Our guys got some Dukes surrounded in front of the 'Y.' Get your car!"

On the short ride to the Harper avenue YMCA, I pictured two or three Dukes, after a peaceful pool game, stepping outside to face a mob of bent-on-mayhem cretins. I was close. Marty parked on Cadillac street near Harper and he, Johnny and I stood behind five other members of the McClellan gang as they animatedly talked to two strangers whom I assumed were Dukes, though they weren't wearing Dukes jackets. The two leaned against the YMCA's brick wall, close to its corner entrance, looking crestfallen, shaking their heads, as accusations of child abuse bombarded them, coupled with threats to their flesh and life, either then or when we all met on Tuesday evening. After a short time the entrance doors opened and three more young men, two wearing Dukes jackets, left the "Y" and merged with their tormented friends. As the three newcomers loudly denied all charges, five more Dukes quietly vacated the "Y" and swelled their ranks. Our rabble rousers, realizing we were suddenly outnumbered, toned down their acerbic denunciations and warnings as a pre-fight fight became less desirable. Slowly the confrontation softened into a more conversational style and we began backing up. One Duke standing ten feet away, studying me, said, "Hey! Are you Beckwell?"

I nodded.

"I'll personally be looking for you Tuesday," he said with a touch of vehemence.

On the ride back to Anne's, Marty asked, "How come those Dukes want to kick your ass? What did ya do to 'em?"

"I dunno...it's making me paranoid. They not only have my name...they also must have my picture."

Marty laughed. "Well, I take back what I said. If they're all going to pile on you Tuesday night, don't be standing by me." He added, "You know I'm kidding."

"Yeah, you're as funny as a crotch, Marty!" A profound funk settled in, and I nervously lit a Chesterfield.

On Monday, Marty, Sammy, Tony and I stood outside, in the late afternoon sun, leaning against Anne's pane glass window facing McClellan, enjoying warm breezes, talking about everything but the next night's fight, expecting, as in the past, that ultimately a patrol car would stop at the curb and a cop would forcibly suggest we get out of sight — either go home or inside Anne's. Idle, slouching loafers upset a neighborhood's aesthetic autonomy. Before that happened we hoped young ladies would pass, trade friendly greetings with us, maybe even stop and talk. It never happened, but we hoped. We tried not to be obvious, but our eyes constantly swept the McClellan sidewalks, wanting to be the first humorist to spot a female and shout, "What's that coming up the road...a piece?" Unexpectedly a black Pontiac sedan pulled up and six young men piled out. Two wore Dukes jackets. "You boys in the McClellan gang?" their spokesperson, a tall, gangling specimen, asked.

We all nodded. I couldn't voice "Yes" aloud. A fear lump was blocking my vocal cords.

"Well, look," Spokesperson said in a friendly tone, "we got a deal for you. We don't want this fight tomorrow...it's been blown way out of proportion. You guys say two of our guys pushed some kids around...our guys say the kids bad-mouthed them, and all they did was accidently knock over one of their bikes, and the kids ran. Why don't we settle this right now. One of you guys fight one of ours."

We continued to stare, saying nothing. A quick glance told me I wasn't going to volunteer. Every one of them outweighed and outaged me by at least 20 pounds and 2 years.

"How about you, big fellow," Spokesperson said to Tony. "You want to settle this? Just fight this guy here and it'll be over, win or lose." His thumb indicated a solid, overweight, 5'9" gentleman with short dark curly hair who looked like a strong candidate for a college fullback position. I didn't know some Dukes had dark hair, I thought.

"We can't speak for our gang," Tony said softly.

"You look big enough to talk for them. How about it." Tony slowly shook his head.

"Anybody else?" Spokesperson's eyes swept over Sammy, Marty and me, and a thick, uncomfortable silence hovered.

"I'll fight 'im," Sammy said, pushing himself away from the pane glass, stepping forward.

"Okay. Good," said Spokesperson and, except for the full-back-type, he and the other Dukes stepped back.

"How do ya wanna do this," Fullback asked.

"Just fight," said Sammy and smacked a fist hard into Fullback's chest.

Sammy intended to box, but Fullback didn't. Using his 30 pound weight advantage he rushed Sammy, enveloped him and they both slammed heavily to the sidewalk, Sammy punching, Fullback grappling. Fullback managed to get a headlock on Sammy as they struggled to their knees and with Sammy's neck in a tenacious grip under Fullback's armpit, right hand squeezing left wrist, Sammy's punching became ineffective. Using both hands in a useless effort, Sammy tore at the choking arm around his throat and at the pressuring right hand. He bucked and twisted. Both battlers' faces turned crimson and they gasped audibly. Sammy relaxed all resistance, and Fullback hissed through gritted teeth, "Do ya give?"

We heard a muffled, "No, goddamnit," and Sammy resumed struggling.

Sammy eventually relaxed again, and we all knew the fight was over. Sammy couldn't break Fullback's hold. "C'mon, kid. Give up, and he'll let you go," said Spokesperson, bending over them.

Sammy, resorting to forceful profanity, choked out an, "Up your ass."

"C'mon, you can't win. You gotta give up."

Tony intervened. "Let him go, and I'll hold him," he said.

Spokesperson nodded. Tony got a strong grip around Sammy's waist, and Fullback let loose, scrambling upright. Sammy stood up slowly, unsteadily, face flushed, eyes teary, fists clenching and unclenching.

"Are you okay, kid?" asked Spokesperson.

Again using earthly language, Sammy said, "Fuck you."

"This should settle it, anyway," said Spokesperson as he and his entourage headed to their car.

"This don't settle nothin'," Sammy said hoarsely, rubbing his crushed larynx.

Spokesperson was the last one into the Pontiac. He looked at Sammy sorrowfully, shook his head, and they drove off.

The next evening, at seven p.m., Marty and I stood inside Chandler schoolyard's cyclone fence near the baby swing set speculating where all the humanity came from. Males stretched from the school's rear to its baseball backstop at the schoolyard's opposite corner, bunched up mostly at the backstop, but spilling onto the diamond. Children, ignoring this influx of older people, tried to make good use of the swings and seesaws before nightfall. "I gotta count these guys," I told Marty.

We walked along the masses' fringe all the way to the backstop, me counting, Marty looking for Tony and Sammy. I missed an accurate count when some guys shuffled around, but estimated the crowd at 110. We were supposed to have 60. Where did the extra 50 come from?

We found Tony and Sammy, part of a large group, and Marty asked, "Do you guys know what's going on?"

"Yeah," Tony said. "We're gonna start marching about seven-thirty. It'll start getting dark about then."

"Where's the fight supposed to take place?"

"In front of the church across from the Dukes' hang-out."

"Who are all these guys?" I asked.

"The Mack boys brought them in. They picked up some extras from other gangs."

Scanning the gathering I noted a prevalence of peg pants, while others, worried about trouser damage, wore denims. It was coolish, long-sleeve-shirt weather, but some added black leather jackets, probably more for body armor than warmth. The majority looked of Italian origin with slicked-back dark hair that older adults would say needed trimming, but there were some whose hair was as light-brown as mine. Brush cuts and flattops weren't prevalent. If the Dukes don't wear their jackets, how are we going to tell each other apart, I worried. I don't know 90 percent of these people, and they don't know me. In the heat of battle one of these goons might mistake me for a Duke and punch out my eyeballs.

I noticed a familiar, slow-moving Pontiac with two figures inside cruise into sight on McClellan and swiftly cut down a sidestreet. Some of the assemblage grew impatient. Cries of "Let's get going!" and "What are we waiting for?!" erupted. I looked through the cyclone fence, across McClellan, at Nativity's recreation building, its windows suffused in the sinking sun's orange radiance, and silently wished I was there watching a girl's basketball game, uninvolved with this whole hideous horror. It occurred to me that this was the first time I'd been in Chandler school playground since I'd moved from Holcomb street over two years before. My attention swung to the swing pole and I pondered if any other young boys had discovered its sensuality. As I considered testing my old pole love, the group nearest the corner fence opening began smoothly emptying out onto the McClellan sidewalk, like syrup pouring from a can, and headed in the direction of Gratiot. I caught up to Marty, and we walked along in the murmuring, serious crowd that reminded me of the group I joined during the '43 riot — quiet, law-abiding, everyone staying off the grass. I was lost in thought; my main thought — whether I'd lost my mind. I haven't anything against them Dukes, I told myself, outside of the fact that some desired to personally pummel me. Johnny, our designated messenger, scurried from the line's front to its rear repeating over and over the words, with minor variations, "We're gonna cross Gratiot with the green light, but don't stop marching when it turns red. Don't worry. The cars'll wait for us. Stay close together." His mission accomplished, Johnny ran to join the leaders.

We passed Momo's store and neared Cairney street across from Nativity's rectory, and I thought if Father Geller looks out his front window and sees this motley mass there could be early trouble. Then someone yelled, "Hold it up!," the long line stopped, and instantly grumbling started among our ranks. "What the hell's the matter?" "What's going on?" "What's coming off?"

The question should have been, "What's not coming off?" A black Pontiac had parked on McClellan and the driver conferred with our pack leaders. The word-of-mouth message travelled from the line's front to the last straggler. "The Dukes ain't ready. The fight's canceled 'til tomorrow." The Dukes had sent an emissary. If we showed up, they wouldn't be there.

While driving me home that night Marty questioned whether we should stay in the gang. "Gangs are trouble," he said. "If you hang with thieves, you wake up with fleas."

I told him we hadn't done much thieving yet, unless free beer at crashed weddings counted.

"How about the time 20 of us ate at that restaurant and walked out without paying?" he argued.

"That was only one time," I said. "Besides, Sammy, Tony and Johnny are gonna think we're scared if we quit before the fight."

"Okay," he said, "but I can think of better ways to waste time."

Wednesday evening at Chandler school started out as a duplicate of the evening before, except the sky was cloudier, temperature warmer and I counted 125 people standing around. After the count Marty and I leaned forward against the schoolyard's fencing, our fingers curled in its steel, zigzagged cables, staring across McClellan at Nativity's recreation hall, thinking. I hope I don't meet up with the fullback-type Duke tonight, I thought. I don't need that big clown neck-gripping me. I didn't know Marty's thoughts.

An automobile coasted into our vision and braked at the curb directly in front of us. "Damn! Look at that!" Marty said. "C'mon."

I followed as he rushed out of the schoolyard's confines to get to the car just as the driver and passenger stepped out. "That's one beautiful car!" Marty exclaimed.

The driver and passenger smiled at this accolade and the driver said, "Thanks."

"What year is it?"

"'31," the driver said.

"I own that '30 over there, but it's nothing like this," Marty said modestly, pointing to his standard Model A parked 50 feet away.

The car was impressive, a Ford Model A convertible, top down, dark blue with yellow wire wheels, rumble seat, almost a duplicate of the one Andy Hardy tooled around in. Marty peered inside, checked the dashboard, rubbed the seat covers.

"You two wanna take a ride?" the driver asked. "I can open the rumble seat."

"What about the fight?" I asked.

"Are you guys in the McClellan gang?"

"Yeah," Marty said.

"Look," the driver said, "there ain't gonna be no fight. This is gonna end up just like last night...nothing. These people don't know what they're doing. If dimwits made honey this playground would be a beehive."

He certainly convinced me. He pulled open the rumble

seat, I stepped on the fender step and piled in with Marty right behind. The driver and friend got in, and we roared off. Marty introduced us to Dave, the driver, and Phil, his friend who were in their early twenties, short dull-brown hair, unpegged blue pants, all-American Van Johnson types.

"You guys here last night?" Marty wondered.

"Yeah," Phil said, smiling. "Dave knows a couple Mack guys who invited us to watch the action. They're all nuts and no one knows what they're doing, especially the McClellan guys. You're leaders run a slipshod ship...and try to say that three times, real fast."

"Thatthatthat," I said comically, but nobody laughed.

While Marty talked about the car's V8 engine and riding smoothness, I enjoyed the wind blowing my hair awry. I swiveled around hoping to catch sight of potential Polly Benedicks to hail and wave at, knowing all girls are captivated by boys riding in an open air car. As if reading my thoughts Dave casually said, "Do you guys want to go visit a couple girls?"

"We sure would!" Marty said.

"They're not bad looking and sometimes have girlfriends over. They live off Kercheval in an upper flat."

"That reminds me of a hillbilly song," Marty said. "She Criticized My Apartment So I Knocked Her Flat."

Phil laughed and said, "How about, I Gave My Girl a Ring and She Gave Me the Finger. Or, The Shades of Night Were Falling Fast, But I got a Good Look Anyway."

Dave contributed, "Do you know whadda Hungarian is? It's a guy from Gary, Indiana, with one this big."

As they joked and snickered I thought, they're forgetting about the fight. I hope they're right, and there won't be one, but if there is and we miss it, how will we explain to Sammy, Tony and the rest? Then again, meeting girls beats getting beat on any day.

Dave and Phil regaled us with wild tales of the two ladies we'd soon see, and five minutes later we parked in front of a string of flats. "It's that gray one over there," Dave said.

"I'll be right back." At last my dreams were coming true and I'd finally meet girls intent on loosening my morals.

When an unsmiling Dave returned my dreams were again placed in lay away. "They ain't home," he said, sliding behind the steering wheel. "What do you guys want to do now?" he asked, starting up his car and turning on its headlights.

"Let's go back to Chandler," Marty said. "Maybe something's happening."

Only three boys about twelve years old remained just inside the fence of a darkened Chandler schoolyard. Dave parked, cut off the motor and called out, "Where did everybody go?"

"They left about a half hour ago heading that way," one boy yelled pointing towards Gratiot.

"I know a short cut to the Dukes' place," Dave said. "Maybe we can catch them." He keyed his ignition, shifted gears, turned off McClellan onto a sidestreet, made a series of left and right turns, and within minutes we ended up on a dark residential street that outletted onto Gratiot. He parked a hundred feet from the avenue and said quietly, "Let's walk the rest of the way."

We climbed out of the car and walked. The Dukes' dimly-lit hangout and a red-brick Protestant church were visible on the other side of Gratiot, the two separated by a side street. The church had a small lawn in front and two floodlights illuminated the front and side doors. That's where the fight's supposed to be, on the lawn, I recalled. There sure ain't nothing going on now. Maybe we're the first ones here, and no Dukes showed up.

The only discernable movement in front of us was Gratiot's moderate automobile traffic zipping by. We were forty feet from Gratiot when a black Chrysler came into view but didn't zip by. It pulled to the curb, a back door flew open and a man large enough to fill the opening yelled, "Come over here, boys!"

"Christ! It's the Big Four!" Dave whispered.

428

The Big Four! A phrase that convoked abject terror in the hearts of Detroit's wrongdoers and even rightdoers. This unique four policeman crew roamed the city in a large black unmarked car. Three of these veteran cops dressed in suits, ties, fedoras, the other in uniform. They shunned normal criminal justice and paperwork, preferring instead to mete out instant street punishment for sins against society. They considered disrespectful mouthing-off near the top of their major crime list. Rumors and arguments abounded among my acquaintances. Some said there was a Big Four in every precinct; others said the same four patrolled the whole city. Some said they only carried sidearms and shotguns; others said they included Thompson submachine guns in their arsenal. Some believed to become a Big Four member a cop had to weigh a minimum of 240 pounds; others said the minimum was 260. All agreed they didn't wish to meet them socially or unsocially.

Dave's whispered words "Big Four" caused me to have an adverse reaction, and I instantly turned and started walking in the opposite direction. If they don't notice me, and I can get close to that side alley, I thought, there's a chance my fast little legs can get a good headstart on any submachine gun bullets coming my way.

"Hey, you! Walking punk! Get back here!" a voice boomed. I ignored the voice and kept walking. Three more steps, and I'll start running.

"You take another step and you're in big trouble, punk!" He could have been politer by saying, "C'mon back here kid and join our discussion group," but nonetheless I consented to find out what he wanted.

The booming voice sat on the edge of the car's backseat, his body partially thrust out the open back door, one foot in the car, the other on the ground. He questioned our presence in the neighborhood because, he told us, a brawl had erupted recently across Gratiot in front of the church. Maybe we were in on it. Dave explained that we had heard of a pending fight and wanted to be spectators.

"Well, it's all over," the cop said, "so why don't you get the hell outta here. If I see you around here again I'll be all over your ass like a hip pocket."

We gave him some "Yessirs" and turned to leave.

"Wait a minute!" he said. "Walking boy! C'mere!"

I assumed he meant me and reluctantly returned. He picked up an altered baseball bat lying on the car floor, a foot of its handle sawed off, causing me great apprehension. He gripped it at its electrical-tape-covered, thinnest end. "Do you know what this is?" he asked.

It looked like a lethal homemade nightstick. "Yessir," I said.

"I'm gonna remember you. You ever keep walking again when I call you, I'll wrap this around your fuckin' neck! Understand?"

"Yessir," I said.

"Get going."

"Yessir."

Dave and Phil dropped Marty and me off in front of Anne's, and we stood outside watching limping, bedraggled battlers and stragglers return from the Duke wars. Most, including Johnny, were quiet, sheepish, others loud, angry. "Where the hell was the McClellan gang?" one Mack guy complained. "I looked around and mosta ya took off 'cross Gratiot."

"I stayed, goddamnit," said Sal. "Lookit here. A damned Duke cut it with a bottle when I was fightin' another one." He twisted and pulled on his shoulder to proudly flash the gash in his leather jacket.

"What happened?" Marty asked.

"Where the hell were you guys?" Sal asked.

"We took a ride, came back, and everyone was gone."

"You're lucky ya missed it. The Dukes kicked our ass."

"Where's Tony and Sammy?" I asked Johnny.

"The last I seen, Tony went down with three Dukes on 'im, and Sammy was fighting two more. Most of us ran."

"How many Dukes were there?"

"It looked like hundreds. They were spread out and came at us with baseball bats, pipes, chains, broken bottles; screaming like maniacs. It was bad."

"Did you stay?"

"Yeah. I got a Duke without a weapon, and we sparred around awhile, but I sure was glad to see the cops. It gave me an excuse to take off."

As the gloomy, wound-licking, ego-maimed warriors filed into Anne's, Marty said, "Let's go home. I don't want to listen to these guys whining because we weren't there. I've had enough excitement tonight."

He drove me home, dropped me off in my driveway and said, "At last the fight garbage is over."

Except it wasn't. Open Duke season was declared. A blue panel truck with the least wholesome-looking Mack gang members began stopping at Anne's at regular intervals to pick up anyone who wanted to go on Duke hunting trips. The truck full of revenge-seekers drove around looking for small groups of unwary individuals wearing distinctive blue nylon jackets with white lettering and, after roughing-up wearers, they collected these jackets like trophy pelts. The Dukes stopped wearing their jackets except in large crowds, and fight fever died.

Later, word filtered back to us why the Dukes called off the originally scheduled Tuesday fight. Their scouts informed them that they'd have to face over a hundred opponents. They enlisted help from the Harper/Van Dyke gang who added 30 more fighters to the Duke ranks and who suggested equalizing odds by arming themselves. One Duke armed himself with a sawed-off baseball bat. Wednesday evening the Duke contingent spread out and waited behind the church, parked cars and in a side alley running behind their hangout. When their Harper/Van Dyke allies saw about 120 stretched-out Mack and McClellan people resolutely approaching up Gratiot they opted to leave their posts and seek sanctuary elsewhere leaving only Dukes defending turf and honor. When the Dukes dauntlessly

431

attacked like an enraged ocean, waving chains, bats, bottles and screaming "Kill," at least 100 of their enemies decided inclusion of weapons canceled out the saying "There's safety in numbers" and chose fleedom. Police cars arrived soon after, scattered the remaining battlers, and the police confiscated all dropped weapons.

For a few weeks I felt guilt for missing this encounter, like a draft dodger probably feels when an army friend gets a Purple Heart. I often wondered if I would have stayed to take some lumps, but I suspect, being a follower-type, I'd have followed the majority, fleeing group. Those Dukes may have been nice guys, but they were also rough.

Marty and I never did feel like McClellan gang insiders and except for Johnny, Tony and Sammy, there weren't too many members we greatly admired, so we gradually stopped attending gang activities and considered ourselves officially ex-members by August.

XXXIV

A heat wave baked Detroit in late August of 1947. As the sun sank and sky blackened, temperatures slowly dipped ten degrees. People opened screened doors and windows either to allow scorching, shimmering heat out or cooler heat in. At these times Chuck and I, after a hard day of hard play, sat on our front porch glider, feet on railing, with minimum movement, and had quiet discussions about subjects ranging from the reason firs remained green year-round to the validity of Ripley's "Believe It or Not" claim that if all Chinese lined up four abreast and marched into the ocean, we'd still never run out of them. On this night of August 28th our discussions were occasionally interrupted by eruptions of feminine laughter, drifting through the open front windows of the Kelly house. Maybe Kathy's having a Derby party, I thought, as jealousy flickered. Maybe Dukes are there, too. There's certainly a few unfamiliar cars on the street. "What's going on at Kelly's?" I asked Chuck nonchalantly.

"Tom told me they're having a shower for the woman Don's marrying. Tom, Jack and Jim have to stay down the basement, and Don and Ken took Mr. Kelly to the Ramona bowling alley." Don and Ken were Kathy's older brothers.

A woman's party, no Dukes. Great! This information started us on a marriage dialogue. I lied to Chuck by saying

I never wanted to marry, knowing that I someday wanted to wed Kathy. He predicted that he'd marry and have eight kids before he died. I asked him how he wanted to die, and he said he didn't, but if it was necessary he hoped it was in his sleep after a party honoring him for being the world's oldest living human. I said I wanted to die in the army fighting whoever the United States picked on next, although I sure didn't want to be burned to a crisp with a flame thrower. It would be like an early preview of my eternal reward. We weren't sure we wanted our bodies laid out for viewing. We had both been to classmate's funerals and recalled the weeping, which would be nice, but there were always people who made dumb remarks like, "Except for not breathing or snoring he looks like he's asleep," or "She's prettier than she ever was." Our Dad once said that when a relative died, someone commented, "It's the first time I ever saw her sober." We both agreed we weren't in any hurry to be the main attraction at a funeral.

We fell silent and watched the activity across the street. Two dark forms, Waylon, a ten-year-old boy and Johnny, his eight-year-old brother, were quietly dislodging a porch slat by hand. They could have accomplished the job faster with a claw hammer but the two adults who raised them, their harried, middle-aged mother and 70-year-old grandfather, had locked up all tools capable of destruction.

We watched as Waylon and Johnny scampered from the porch and hid in the small, dark empty lot next to their house just before their mother's silhouette appeared at the screen door calling them for bed. The two boys were rowdy, uncooperative and outspoken, with Waylon always the instigator. Chuck and I, in our front porch sits, often watched them demolish structures, slingshot birds, punch each other bloody and tell their grandfather, "Go screw yourself." It was like watching a live Katzenjammer Kids comic strip.

On this night, Chuck made a dire prediction concerning Waylon. "He'll probably die in the electric chair in a few years," he whispered.

This was another of Chuck's predictions which, as usual, was a little off. Waylon grew up, chose the less-than-honorable pimp profession and, at 19 years of age, was knifed to death in a Philadelphia cathouse.

A car pulled into the Kelly driveway, and a figure jumped out and ran into the house. The laughing voices muted, then turned shrill, eerie. The Kelly's screen door burst open and screaming females rushed onto the front porch, holding each other, weeping.

"Go see what's happening," I told Chuck.

He walked over and stood near the Kelly's front steps. Two minutes later he returned with an explanation. "Mr. Kelly had a heart attack at the bowling alley. He's dead."

I stayed away from the Kelly family, dreading facing their sorrow. I wished I could hold Kathy and say something profound to ease her misery and I thought of words I'd heard others say about sudden death, "At least it was quick" or "He didn't suffer," but knew such statements would sound trivial after the loss of a 50-year old father. I couldn't imagine the pain of a parent dying. My mother was sick, but I knew she'd heal eventually.

But after two days I could no longer put off a funeral home visit. I put on my pinstriped suit and a black tie.

Mr. Kelly was laid out at the Weitenberner funeral home that sat across Gratiot from Assumption Grotto church. I paid my respects, consisting of many "I'm sorry" remarks to kin and a short silent prayer on a kneeler placed in front of the casket, which was as close as I ever got to Mr. Kelly. He looked asleep.

I deliberately searched for Kathy in the crowd of mourners, found her, and explained that I understood her grief, and she wistfully smiled and thanked me for coming, our first conversation since school let out. I left the funeral home feeling sad for the Kelly family's loss of their father, but selfishly pleased that Kathy and I were friends again.

* * *

435

Dad intended to become a thousandaire. He assembled a crude contraption at work that consisted of a tin cigarette case, with a thin wavy leather band fastened to one side and two clamps welded to the other. On one end was welded a metal tube the size of a toilet-tissue tube. He explained his invention could be clamped onto a golf pullcart handle, extra tees could be inserted into the leather band, extra balls could be stored in the tube and, with a pack of cigarettes in the case, it would be a great convenience for smoking golfers. The device would be easy and cheap to manufacture, could be painted colorfully and he was sure we'd soon be rolling in colorful greenbacks. Sadly the device didn't include a pair of wings and it never got off the ground.

Other creative Americans competed with the automobile industry. A man named Tucker manufactured a safety-conscious, sleek, low-slung affordable car with padded dashboard and three headlights. The middle headlight turned with the steering wheel when a driver turned a corner, greatly improving night visibility. This modern concept in automobiles was even advertised in the Sunday newspaper's comic section and excited Americans anxiously awaited an opportunity to buy one.

Two men named Kaiser and Fraser also manufactured cars named after themselves, and the birth of these cars led to this quip: Three swains discussed gifts for girlfriends. One bragged, "I'm buying my girl a Kaiser and surprise her." Another said, "I'm buying my girl a Fraser and amaze her." The third said, "I'm buying my girl a Tucker."

The hapless Kaiser, Fraser and Tucker cars, like my dad's golf gadget, also lacked wings.

Other creations were more successful. Expensive, seven- and ten-inch screen television sets filled electronic shops and started to sell. Shop owners always placed one or two operating sets in their front windows, drawing large, marveling assemblages. I only had one question about television sets. What happened to the wire to plug into the radio?

* * *

Disappointments prevailed upon my return to Nativity. Marty was assigned to the other Senior class homeroom, hurting our combo; Sister Mary Remegia, my homeroom nun, wasn't a jolly Jarlath-type, hurting my heart; and Viaduct Sammy and Tall Tony transferred to a public school, hurting our football team. But on the bright side, Kathy was in three of my classes and Jerry Wygocki, my grade school classmate who went to Saint Joseph's and became their fullback, returned to Nativity for his Senior year and brought along a teammate named Angelo Dicicco.

My biggest worry was Sister Remegia who wanted to die with chalk-stained, knarled fingers and felt grateful her Dominican order lacked a mandatory, retirement age. She was short, slightly overweight, with the disposition of a freshly-harpooned sperm whale. Since I only had her for first classes in the morning and afternoon I figured, with luck, I could endure my final year.

Two or three mornings a week my departure time from home coincided with Kathy's and Geri's, and we rode the streetcar together to school. At these times Kathy didn't say much, as befitting someone who had just lost a father, so Geri and I did most of the talking. I did get Kathy to agree to accompany me to a Ramona theater late show.

After the double feature she didn't suggest a Grotto cemetery stroll, so we headed home slowly, holding hands, saying little, the steamy, windless, late-summer weather causing our hands to blissfully mingle perspiration as we basked in the quiet, perfect, surreal aura that cloaked us. I resented every streetlamp we walked under that expelled darkness. At times we heard low conversations effusing from indistinct adult porchsitters, their cigarette tips and mosquito chasers flashing firefly-like, and I wondered if they too could have ever experienced the complete adoration for another similar to my simmering feelings for Kathy, feelings that produced such rapturous euphoria.

437

As we neared her house I asked Kathy if she still associated with the Dukes, and she said "sometimes." I asked her reasons, and she said because they're "nice" and "mature," two words I hated since neither described me. Before we parted at her side door she promised to attend some Nativity football games, quick-kissed my cheek and disappeared inside. Still feeling the sweet brush of her lips I regretted not suggesting a cemetery side trip.

* * *

Marty had trouble starting his Model A after school and noticed sugar crystals sprinkled around its gas tank. He paranoidly declared, "The damn Derbys or Dukes did it. We ain't even in the gang anymore, and they're still screwing with us."

I told him no Derby would do such a thing, and maybe the Model A just wore out. He traded it for a black 1936 Ford sedan, which delighted me. The younger Ford looked sleek compared to the boxy Model A, and it was a pleasure to ride in a car without a front that resembled a large pig snout.

* * *

For three weeks we spent afterschool hours writing X's and O's in notebooks, exercising, blocking, tackling and running through football plays. Marty replaced Tall Tony at left end; Bob Tirsch moved from fullback to left half making way for our team captain, Jerry Wygocki; and Hank Wouters, a Junior, replaced Marty at quarterback. Hank couldn't run too well. He believed in stationary jockeying and feinting to get by a tackler, a practice that allowed other tacklers to catch up and make jockeying players part of the landscape. But he could throw an accurate pass so coach McEvoy added more passing plays to our agenda. Our new guard from Saint Joe's, Angelo Dicicco, built like Viaduct Sammy and ten pounds heavier, was also an asset.

We played our first home game a mile and a half from Nativity at Chandler Park, named after the same gentleman whose name graced Chandler grade school. Father Geller had rented an old blue bus to transport our team, giving us a team feeling, but we were still nervous. The field had no stands so spectators thronged at the sidelines. As our opponents from All Saints high school lined up for the kickoff shouting encouragement to each other, I wished our team felt as confident. Jerry Wygocki kicked off, and the game started.

Jerry was a paradox. In school he was quiet, gentle and smiled easily. He not only took typing, but was the first male to take shorthand, two courses not considered overtly masculine. But as fullback he loved smashing through tacklers, and when he linebacked he aggressively made half the tackles himself, a hundred seventy-five pound dynamo who slapped down blockers and ball carriers. If Viaduct Sammy hadn't quit school I'd never have had to make a tackle.

The game seesawed until the third quarter when, on All Saints' 20-yard line, I rounded left end, got by two opponents and scored. In the fourth quarter Hank Wouters quarterback-sneaked into the end zone, and we won 14 to 0. Nativity fans, including Kathy and Lois, cheered, and I even saw Father Geller, standing next to coach McEvoy, grin.

Mr. McEvoy warned us during the next week's practice that Saint Patrick, a high school in Wyandotte, a downriver suburb, would be the toughest team we'd play all season. When we ran out on their field the following Sunday I commented to Marty, "They don't look so tough," a remark they must have overheard and resented. Their offense was on our 40 yard line two minutes into the game. They had two hard-to-stop halfbacks who ran all over us. Once one came through our line and I confidently said, "Where ya think you're going" and slammed my shoulder into his thighs. He showed me where he was going, ten more yards over my supine form. I caught the other halfback in an open field, grabbed him by the neck of his shoulder pads and flung him five yards behind me. He stayed on his feet, gained another 15 yards, and they scored two plays later.

On our first offensive play I lost three yards, and our team lost Marty who sustained a broken collar bone, sending him to the hospital. Bill Kraft replaced him, and by half-time we trailed 35 to 0.

We scored early in the second half on a 40-yard pass from Wouters to Wygocki, but it didn't seem to dismay Saint Patrick. They quickly scored again, kicked off, and the ball came to me. I ran to the left; their whole team converged, and I cut to the right. At the 50 yard line I saw an abundance of green grass and chalklines. I was almost in the clear with only two St. Patrick players to fake out, when Angelo Dicicco cut over to block for me and knocked me off my feet at the 25 yard line, where we stayed for four plays. St. Patrick took over the ball, and as their halfback ran for a long gain someone blasted me from behind at my knees, unnecessarily since I wasn't in the vicinity of the ball carrier. As I sat up to regain my feet someone kicked me at the base of my spine, a spot unprotected by hiked-up hip pads, causing a temporary, enfeebling nerve shock.

The game ended on a positive note. I intercepted a pass in our end zone, ran to theirs and, dazed and confused, lined up with the St. Patrick team for our extra point try. This evoked mirth among St. Patrick players and caused a referee to question my mental fitness by asking, "What day is it, son?" I couldn't remember so he banished me to the sidelines. A nice St. Patrick gentleman yelled at me, "You played a good game, kid!" I cherished these words after two ghastly hours of pain, mortification and a 49 to 12 rout.

Marty, his arm in a sling, received a lot of sympathy from female students causing me to wonder if a buttocks sling could be rigged for my spinal injury. At after-school practice Mr. McEvoy encouragingly told us not to worry; we still had a good team; every team has bad days and put it behind us. I didn't believe him, but the following Sunday at Chandler park we played Saint Hedwig and won 36 to 6.

Now we had to play a night game against Saint Clement in Mt. Clemens, the team that badly ripped us the year before. It could have been our cheerleaders' inspiring chant: "Fight, fight, black and khaki! Crack 'em, sack 'em, knock 'em wacky!" Or the scornful rejoinder from the St. Clement crowd: "Well, well! Do tell! Holy hell! What a yell!" Or maybe, unlike the previous year's game, the dry field and our more experienced team made a difference. We prevailed, I scored three times, and we won 32 to 6. Dad told me I played well, and Ed said if I blocked better maybe someone else could score once in awhile.

Sacred Heart. Two words that conjure an image of a gentle, lamblike, turn-the-other-cheek Jesus radiating goodness, wisdom and purity. Surely Sacred Heart's football players would fit this model. My assessment changed while we stood around with hands on hips (a football player's favorite pose) as the Sacred Heart team charged grunting out on the field and warmed up by banging their helmeted heads together. They were all huge, but one stood head and chest above the others. He's probably a guard or tackle and won't carry the ball, I hoped.

We kicked off, and a Sacred Heart receiver caught the ball and handed it to this behemoth. Mr. McEvoy had instructed me to hang back on kickoffs in case a ball carrier broke through; so I jogged towards the big guy happy to know someone on our team would surely tackle him. My mood changed to terror as teammates got blocked out or bounced off this giant who became more enormous the nearer I got to him, and suddenly he was in the clear at the sidelines, and I thought, where's Joe Butler when I need him? The collision with his midsection slammed me backwards, and he landed on top of me like a wounded redwood tree, effectively smothering my suggestion for him to "Get the hell off!" He took his time arising. Sacred Heart spectators smiled and applauded when they saw me still breathing. "Nice tackle, number eleven! That guy's two hundred forty-five pounds," one yelled. It was my last good tackle all day.

Sacred Heart rambled up and down the field using the T-formation with quick opening plays and even scored a safety. Their big guy played guard. Frank Baccala and Angelo Dicicco had the displeasure of trying to keep him out of our backfield and rarely succeeded. I learned shoulder pads don't always protect against injury when their fullback shot through a hole in the scrimmage line that I tried to plug, and he slammed so hard into my left shoulder, gaining five flying yards, that I lost complete use of it for a time. It had to be similar to being jarred by a charging Clydesdale. I kept telling myself not to worry; the throbbing shoulder will eventually line up again with the other, but in the meantime, I missed an open field tackle, and the ball carrier scored. It was a frustrating, fruitless game as we lost 43 to 6.

All week Coach McEvoy preached confidence to our physically-hurting, demoralized team, and by Saturday night we were ready. Saint Florian had lost to teams we'd slaughtered so how could we lose. The game was scheduled under the lights at an enclosed stadium, Mack Park, where a small attendance fee was collected. A crowd actually paying to see us play! Astonishing! It would be a consummate evening because Kathy would be at the game and attend a victory party at my house afterwards.

By game time, ominous signs arose to sap our confidence. The temperature plunged, gray clouds threatened atonement for Detroit's dearth of snow, and parts of the field resembled plowed farm acreage. The game began, and Saint Florian played like they too had scheduled a victory party. Both teams scored in the first quarter, we progressed nicely in the second, and I suddenly broke free and ran for 45 yards. Unfortunately, I was tackled five yards from the goal line. Four plays later we had only gained two more yards and gave up the ball. They scored again in the third quarter, but so did we on a long drive in which I contributed a 30-yard pass to our right end Bill Manley. Later I also contributed a thrill to the crowd by leaping over a prone St. Florian player who reached up and tapped my toe and I landed heavily on my head. The crowd groaned in frustration when I jumped to my feet uninjured.

In the last quarter, while on our 25-yard line, St. Florian's backfield started an end run. A lone player, their tall left end, broke from the pack in the opposite direction, and I suspiciously followed him. The ball spiraled lazily from behind the scrimmage line heading straight for the left end, giving me two choices: either bat down the pass or intercept it and run for a touchdown. Thinking slowly, I reasoned trying to intercept might lead to the end shoving me, catching the ball and scoring. I batted it down. They scored three minutes later anyway, and the game ended with a 20 to 14 St. Florian triumph.

Thirty people showed up at my house, a third of them girls, for our victory-turned-to-defeat party. Two cases of beer were smuggled through the basement window by an ex-Nativity student named Tim Reegin and stored safely out of sight in our coal cellar in case my dad visited our festivities. The beer would help us get over our game loss depression. Kathy attentively consoled me for losing the game and was so loving and considerate I wondered how much attention I'd get by throwing our last two games.

Following a close dance I suggested we sit on our porch glider that we stored in our basement and, to conserve space for other guests, suggested she sit on my lap. She graciously agreed causing my confidence and libido to soar. She really likes me, I reasoned, and it's time to take command of our relationship so, testing my new feeling of control, I whimsically whispered in her ear, "Ya look exceptionally fetching tonight. How about fetching me a beer."

She hissed, "Get your own beer and get bent," while rising from my lap. My depression returned as she spent the next half-hour talking to Stellon before quietly slipping out the side door to walk home. Romance's rocky road tripped me anew. You can't stand prosperity, I sorrowfully reflected, as I fetched my own beer.

Monday, during morning school hours, individual students were summoned from class and told to report to the principal's office. Rumors abounded that Marty and I had hosted a drunken soiree after the St. Florian game, and an investigation, including taking attendees' statements, was in progress. Having been forewarned, Marty and I had a chance to discuss the accusations and discovered we both believed honesty, with variations, to be the best policy. When called to the principal's office together we made the same statement: We did have a party; a former uninvited classmate who'd dropped out of school the year before, Tim Reegin, and a couple of his friends had brought the beer; current students weren't involved in drinking it, and we were offended that anyone thought otherwise. The principal, Sister Mary Verena, said no students had confessed to drinking; she didn't believe us, and she'd keep her eye on us from that moment on. Marty and I returned to our classrooms, congratulating ourselves for averting another crisis on our relentless march towards graduation.

Our second to last football game was played on Detroit's west side against a winless, non-league foe that shall remain nameless. I knew it would be an uncommon game when I charged through a hole in the line, and an enemy player, who could have tackled me, punched me instead, neatly splitting my upper lip. As the game progressed I noticed my body absorbing other unnecessary violence, especially when under a pile of tacklers, that included elbow thrusts to my neck, knee jolts to my ribs and particularly painful pulls on my helmet that ripped both earlobes. When I complained loudly to my tormentors a referee threatened to penalize us yardage for my unsportsman-like profanity. Our first time-out I told Mr. McEvoy what was happening and asked what to do since the referees seemed indifferent and I was weakening from loss of blood. He laughed and said, "Learn to play dirty." When I relayed this message to our team most linemen said they already had personal battles going on with individual opponents.

My only revenge opportunity came in the third quarter when, while stiff-arming a tackler, I managed to thumb-gouge his eyeball sending him to the sidelines. A few minutes later someone managed to wrench my ankle in a pile-up sending me to the hospital. We lost most of the fights and also the game, 20 to 13.

I still limped the following Sunday when we played Mount Carmel, but managed to get into the game for one play, throwing an incomplete pass. Our dismal season ended, to some degree, on a high note. Mount Carmel was the second best team in the league and we only lost 12 to 0. Miraculously my ankle healed the next day.

Mom only felt well enough to watch me play in two games, but my sisters, brothers and Dad were there every week so I had my own cheering section. Dad always knew more about football than any coach that ever lived, so when he told me "you did all right," I cherished the moment.

There were some Cedargrove success stories in football that year. Jack Kelly, Kathy's younger brother, quarterbacked Grotto's grade school team to a Catholic Youth Organization championship, and Alby Przybylski played second-string quarterback on Denby's team that won the city championship.

After the football season officially ended, Stellon was given the honor of presenting to each Nativity football player a large, gold-colored "N" to be sewed to a school sweater I couldn't afford. Failing to find my name listed among the Catholic league third division all-city selections published in the newspapers, I abandoned all thought of pursuing a football career. Perhaps a career of pool hustling would be more my style, I told myself. Delicately propelling numbered balls into table pockets with a lightweight cue stick had to be safer than banging helmets with I'll-make-you-regret-taking-up-this-sport Neanderthals.

XXXV

An announcement on November 29, 1947, intrigued me. The United Nations had approved a Jewish state in Palestine. My fifth grade nun had preached that Jews, instrumental in Christ's crucifixion, were cursed, so their ancestors were destined to roam the world forevermore; devoid of a homeland. Oddly, she never explained why the Romans, who did the actual crucifying, had a homeland that included the Vatican. I wondered how she reacted to this historic development and decided she probably snapped, "Yeah, but it's still being contested!"

* * *

Jack, Reno, Marty and I found a more preferable habitat to play pool, Schofield's Recreation on Harper off Gratiot. This hall was a stone's throw from the YMCA if you had a weak arm, but unlike the YMCA it offered multiple billiards and snooker tables and no religious tracts tempting repentance. From the sidewalk above we descended steep concrete steps to access this grand, underground sanctum. Mr. Schofield, a tall gray-haired gentleman with baggy pants who usually sat just inside the front door on a stool behind a counter, would lead us to a table, rack the pool balls, collect a fee for the game and return to his stool, all with a minimum of conversation. Marty said he was as quiet as a dog's hair. We not only spent a few school lunch hours in this place but also some evening and weekend hours. Marty and I had read and admired Willard Motley's book, *Knock on Any Door,* about a young man in Chicago who died in the electric chair and we had adopted the young man's motto, "Live fast, die young and have a good looking corpse." We considered shooting pool a "living fast" activity since pool halls had a reputation for harboring riffraff plotting or engaged in criminality and vice, although we didn't observe anything of that nature in Schofield's. His customers were cigarette-puffing teenage boys striving for sophistication and cigarette-puffing sophisticated men striving to win small wagers. All enjoyed pool competition and banter.

The Monday after Christmas, the four of us encircled a pool table, leaned on cue sticks, and waited for Mr. Schofield to re-rack our balls. "Old Schof" always delayed this chore. At least two shouts of "Rack!" were needed to rouse him from his front door perch, and when roused he never dashed to a table carrying his triangular wood rack frame. He ambled.

We watched him quietly welcome a new arrival whom we recognized as Tim Reegin, and they both started towards us.

Tim had quit Nativity the previous year with strong encouragement from principal and nuns. We still saw him at parties and Nativity sporting events but avoided getting too friendly since he had an undercurrent of violence about him, kindled by his fondness for displaying made-of-iron "brass" knuckles he carried in his front pants pocket. Tim's eyes weren't always happy, and some said he had a squid's personality and a numbie's brain. I personally liked him, especially after he supplied the beer at my victory-defeat party.

"Hey, what's the tune, goon?" Reno greeted him.

"How you guys makin' it?" Tim asked, smiling.

We mumbled "Okay" and watched as Mr. Schofield slowly slammed pool balls into the rack frame on the table's green felt. He centered the eight ball, mixed the stripes and solids, rolled all the balls inside the frame twice, positioned them, carefully lifted the frame, and we were ready for another game. Tim waited until Mr. Schofield headed back to his perch before asking, "Hey, Marty. You still working?"

"Nah, I quit about a month ago."

"Yeah, I quit my job too," Tim said. "I'm going in the Navy in a couple weeks."

After we congratulated him and wished him luck he continued, "Look, you guys know I've been going with Eunace. We're gonna get married after I'm settled in the Navy…they got a dependent allowance for married guys. We're getting engaged before I leave, and I need money for a ring. Her parents have a few bucks, and she has some rich relatives I ain't met so I sure as hell don't wanna give her some cheap diamond. So what I'm gonna do is pull a hold-up and I need a couple more guys. How about you, Bob?"

His words didn't register before a "Sure" escaped my mouth.

"What about you, Marty?"

"No way," Marty said.

"Why not," Tim asked.

"I'm not interested," Marty said, looking cool and disinterested.

"How about you two?" Tim asked Jack and Reno.

They both refused.

"What's the matter with you guys? I'm talking a thousand dollars each. Nobody wants a thousand dollars?"

Marty, Jack and Reno shook their heads.

"Okay, forget it...maybe I can do it with just Bob here. I'm telling you it'll be easy."

"Who ya gonna rob?" Marty asked.

"Can you guys keep your mouth shut?"

We all nodded.

449

"The place where I used ta work...this coming Friday. It's their payday."

"You gotta have a car," Marty said.

"I got one. Don Jacobs said he'd drive. C'mon, Marty. Whadaya say?"

Marty again refused, and I wondered how to gracefully say I had a change-of-mind without sounding like a complete, craven coward.

"Well, at least Bob here isn't chicken," Tim said, effectively crashing shut any change-of-mind. "Maybe we can do it with just three. I'll pick you up at your house at nine Friday morning," he told me. "I'll see you guys. Let me know if you change your mind, Marty."

After Tim left Jack shook his head and said, "You know you're crazy, don't you, Bob?"

"Yeah," I said glumly.

For three days I wished Christmas vacation was over and I was back in school where all I had to face was Sister Remegia. Even school had to be better than jail. I doubted amateurs could pull off a daytime, big money robbery, especially one conceived by Tim, and if successful, I doubted whether I could keep people from getting suspicious when I suddenly bought a school sweater and starting flashing ten dollar bills after a life of flashing dimes. Mostly I doubted my sanity. Why did I automatically say "Sure" when asked to participate? It couldn't be genetic. The only relative I had who engaged in outlaw activity was my uncle Hunsey who, at seventeen years of age, was arrested delivering bags of counterfeit silver dollars. He wouldn't tell the T-men where the coins were manufactured or who distributed them and, consequently, spent five years in a federal penitentiary. After gaining his freedom Uncle Hunsey was so law abiding he wouldn't spit on sidewalks.

So if it wasn't genetic it had to be purely moronic.

Prior to hold-up day I spent some time with Mom. Bedridden, she sat propped up by pillows, reading, listening to the radio, praying, sometimes weeping. When her stomach pain intensified she swallowed handsful of aspirin tablets from a brown-glass 1000-tablet-capacity bottle at her bedside. She appreciated my reading magazine stories to her because, she said, it helped her fall asleep. After her eyes closed I'd quietly kiss her warm, worn forehead and tiptoe from the room.

I also spent time at Schofield's waiting for Marty, Jack or Reno to give me a reason not to go through with the hold-up. They didn't suggest any, other than, "You could end up dead or in jail." I noticed it's difficult to concentrate on pool shots while anticipating pistol shots.

New Year's night I received a "We'll be there tomorrow at nine" phone call from Tim and he hung up before I could ask for robbery particulars. It dawned on me that I was caught up in something I couldn't get out of unless I just refused to go through with it. This wasn't acceptable. I knew I was a coward but didn't want anyone else to know it. I quietly planned my costume and disguise for the big heist.

The next morning Mary, Chuck, Dolores and Ann were in the kitchen. Mom was in bed and every other resident of our house had left for work by 8:30. I secretly transferred Dad's old tan trenchcoat and brown fedora from the basement to the closet next to our front door, donned my Eisenhower jacket and went upstairs to tell Mom I was going in search of a parttime job. I slipped into the bathroom and used mascara to paint an Errol Flynn moustache under my nose, quietly walked downstairs to the closet to retrieve the trenchcoat and hat and left the house just as Don's dark blue '35 Dodge pulled into our driveway. Icy winds and gray-purple clouds made it a perfect day for a funeral, possibly mine, and I climbed into the back seat.

After perfunctory greetings nothing was said until we turned onto Gratiot. Tim, sitting in the front passenger seat, turned around and watched silently as I flattened the brown fedora's crown and turned down its brim. "I like your moustache," he said, half smiling.

451

"Does it look real?" I asked.

"No," he said. "Are you ready?"

"Sure. Where is this place?"

"It's in the St. Jean-Vernor area. "You ever been around there?"

"Yeah, I think so. It's all factories and stuff."

"That's it. Look, I drew a picture what it looks like. It's a trucking outfit."

He showed me an overhead sketch of a street with a fence running along it and a box splitting the fence. Tim would never win a blueprint art contest. "This box is where the money is. It's a hut with windows on both sides and doors in the front and back. Trucks go in and out through gates on each side. Drivers stop at the hut's windows so the guy inside can record their going and coming time and check route sheets. You see this line through the hut?" He pointed at a line dissecting the box.

"Yeah."

"That's a wall like in a bank with a teller window and the guy inside has a little office behind that wall. Later today he's supposed to pass out pay envelopes to drivers through the side windows...except we'll have the envelopes."

He's serious, I thought. He really means it! "What do I do?"

"Okay, here's the plan. You're going in the front door and point the gun at the guy to keep 'im busy and I'm going through the back door and hit 'im over the head."

"What gun?!"

A small, black, 22-caliber automatic suddenly appeared in his hand and he removed its clip. "It only has this one bullet but be careful after you cock it," he explained, showing me the clip. "It has a hair-trigger."

"It sure does," said Don, chuckling.

Tim snapped the clip back into the gun's handle and passed me the weapon over the front seat. He's definitely serious! I thought, as I pocketed the gun.

More silence. Finally, "Show him what you're gonna hit

him with," Don said as he turned onto Conner street.

"It's a homemade blackjack," Tim said, handing me a thick, weighty, tubular, ten-inch long, stiffly-flexible cudgel completely covered with layers of white adhesive tape. Tim proudly explained that under the tape was a tightly coiled spring packed with bolts, nuts and gravel.

"What are you gonna be doing, Don?" I asked.

"I'm gonna be waiting for you guys with the motor runnin'," he said, chuckling.

I returned the white blackjack, and we fell still as Don maneuvered down sidestreets. I tried not to think, but a thought intruded. "Hey, Tim! Don't hit that guy too hard."

"Hard, hell. I'm going to kill 'im," Tim said quietly.

"What the hell are ya talking about? Are ya crazy?!" My voice matched my rising panic. "Ya never said anything about killing!"

"I have to…he's gonna recognize me."

"Then, goddamnit, I don't want nothin' to do with this!"

"Okay, okay, take it easy. I'll try to cover my face, but you keep 'im concentrating on you. Don't let 'im turn around."

I said "Okay" unenthusiastically.

We turned down a one-way sidestreet. "There's Vernor highway," Don announced, slowing his car, pulling to the left and parking 25 feet from Vernor. I wondered why they called it a highway since it looked like any other busy street in Detroit but didn't ask considering the circumstances.

Tim turned to me and smiled reassuringly. "You can cock the gun now."

"I don't know how to cock no goddamn gun," I said, still angry about his "killing" remark.

"Let me see it." I handed the gun to him, he snapped its top back, then forward, and returned it to me. "The bullet's in the chamber. Don't forget to keep light on the trigger."

"Where's the place we're robbing?" I asked.

"This is part of it here," Tim said, motioning to the dingy, windowless, two-story, gray-brick building immediately to our left. "You'll see the hut when you get around the corner up there. It's in the middle of the block. This is what we're gonna do. After I get out of the car you start counting to thirty, then follow me. When you get to the front door make sure you have on a glove...we don't want fingerprints. Relax, will ya? Are you ready?"

I nodded, not feeling ready.

Tim grinned. "Hey, just keep thinking of the fifteen hundred dollars you're getting. You can buy a lot with fifteen hundred. Don't worry. It'll be easy. Here we go."

He left the car and Don and I watched him walk to the corner and turn left. "Are you countin'?" Don asked.

"Yeah," I said. I wasn't; so I started my count at fifteen. I reached thirty and said, "Hope I see ya again," put on my hat and pushed open the door. I didn't hear Don wish me good luck.

The sidestreet we were on ended at Vernor because across Vernor was a four-story, red-brick factory stretching for two blocks with all its upper windows painted green. I put a glove on my right hand, grasped the automatic resting in my trench coat pocket with my left hand and turned the corner.

The first floor of the factory across the street included clear picture windows next to its entrance doors and behind the windows approximately ten men in police uniforms sat at desks or stood talking to each other. Except one. He stood inside close to the window staring at me. I faced forward quickly, turned up my collar and hoped he didn't notice my moustache wasn't hairy. I imagined him telling his fellow cops, "Hey, some kid just went by with a hairless moustache." Tim didn't mention a police station across the street, and I realized this added a strong danger element. I saw the gray, wooden hut up ahead, larger than visualized, with two steps leading to its front door. I reached cyclone fencing and saw a long dock area sixty feet behind the hut, with no trucks and little activity. The large gates on both sides of the hut were wide open, pulled inward. I hoped when I pointed the gun that the hut man became as frightened as me and wouldn't laugh, and I hoped Tim didn't lie about not hitting him too hard, and I was glad Michigan didn't have the electric chair, just in case. I thought of my mother's pain if she heard of my arrest, and I pictured a losing shoot-out with the cops across Vernor, using my gun with one bullet. I stopped at the hut, hesitated for two seconds, took a deep breath and placed my foot on its bottom step.

"Wait a minute...wait a minute," someone whispered. I froze as Tim came rushing from around the hut's rear. "Don't go in...wait a minute," he said in a low voice. "C'mon."

"Whatsa matter?" I asked as he led me across Vernor.

"There's someone in there with 'im. I heard 'em talking. It's probably a truck driver or dock man. Jesus, that was close! I was in back watching for you. We'll just stand here and wait 'til the guy leaves. They're probably drinking coffee."

We stood near the factory wall staring across at the hut and I silently prayed the hut man and visitor were long-winded, had lots of coffee and enjoyed screwing off. "I'm getting a bad feeling about this," I told Tim. "There's a police station in this building here, and one cop was looking at me when I went by."

"They ain't cops...they're factory guards."

"I don't care. They still have guns. C'mon, Tim. Let's call this off."

"Nah, we'll give it a few more minutes. That guy can't stay in there forever."

We waited, gazing at the hut's rear area, Tim wishing the visitor would leave, me wishing the opposite. "This ain't workin' the way ya said, Tim. Let's get the hell outta here," I whimpered.

"Take it easy, dammit. Give it a couple more minutes."

A minute passed. "Alright, the hell with it," Tim said, disgusted. "Let's go."

455

On the way to Don's car I glanced at the plant guard haven. The same guard peered out the window, watching, puzzled.

Inside the car, Tim explained to Don what happened; we pulled from the curb, and Tim voiced a lamentful complaint, "What am I going to do for ring money?" Neither Don nor I advised him. I didn't care if he ever got engaged, just so we were driving away from that hut.

"How about stopping at Schofield's," I suggested, changing the subject. "Marty's waiting for us."

"Gimme back the gun," said Tim.

Marty and Jack were shooting pool at a back table when we entered Schofield's. They seemed genuinely disappointed when we told them what happened (and didn't happen). I think they wanted our pockets to be stuffed with cash bundles. They laughed at my factory police station fears and at my moustache; so I went to the restroom and washed it off. When I returned Marty was telling Tim if he wanted money he knew of a Harper street market that was robbery ripe. "The owner takes his cash receipts home with him every Friday night so all you have ta do is follow him home and stick the gun in his face."

"What time does he close the store?" Tim asked.

"About nine o'clock. I'll go with you and show you where it is, but I don't want nothing to do with the robbing. He knows me."

Marty filled in more details, the owner's description and weight, the store's exact location, estimate of the take (500 to 1,000 dollars), the possibility of the owner objecting strenuously to giving up his money. "If the gun don't scare him, I've got something that'll tone him down," said Tim, smiling again. "And if my blackjack don't work, Don here can always sit on him. Anyway...thanks, Marty. It sounds like a good deal. We'll pick you guys up here tonight around eight-thirty."

After Tim and Don left, Jack gave his assessment of our plans: "I think all you people are demented."

I didn't care. It had to be a lot safer than heisting a place with a police station across the street.

At 9:15 I told Don for the third time, "Turn on the damn heater…it's freezing back here!" Winds lashed the car, whistling and slipping through minute cracks encircling windows and doors.

Don keyed the ignition and switched on the heater. "It's just gonna steam up the windows again," he complained.

Tim, sitting in the front passenger seat, also complained. "When's he gonna close that damn store, Marty? He just let two more customers in."

"The more customers he gets the more money he'll have when he comes out. Besides, the day after New Year's is always busy," Marty explained, then added, "We oughta be wondering what we'll say if cops stop and wanna know why we're parked here and why Bob has a mascara moustache." He laughed. "You almost look like Groucho Marx."

"I got some more mascara in my pocket if you guys want to use it. It's my sister's," I told them. They all refused.

"Hey, lookit over there," Don said. Across Harper on the sidewalk an overweight man shakily manipulated his legs as he clutched his coat collar securely against the frosty wind.

"He's staggerin' drunk," Tim said. "Drunks always got a lotta money. Whadayasay we roll 'im."

"Wait a minute…he's pretty big," I said.

"You guys still know how to tackle, don't you. You knock 'im down; I'll crack him a couple times and get his wallet. C'mon, Don! Get moving! He's turning down that street."

Don made a quick U-turn across Harper and slowed as we entered the dark sidestreet lined on both sides with packed together housing and parked together cars. We passed our prey while searching for a parking space. Don spotted an open space, guided his car into it, switched off the headlights, and we watched the vague shape of the oblivious reveler weave towards us.

"Hope he didn't spend all his money. Get ready," Tim said.

"He might start yelling," I cautioned.

"If he makes any noise I'll put the hurt on 'im quick," Tom said, holding up his blackjack.

Our hands clutched door handles as we waited for our fellow man to walk by the car so we could bound out and do him harm. And we waited.

"Where the hell is he?" Don asked.

A porch light snapped on two houses behind us, answering his question. We gazed through the rear window as an angry wife welcomed her lucky, wayward binger into their warm abode.

"Christ! This ain't my day," Tim muttered. "Let's get back to the market."

We returned to Harper and again parked half a block from the store's entrance. Ten minutes later the stake out ended when the store's lights doused, the owner locked the front door, entered his black panel truck and pulled away from the curb. "Stay close," Tim cautioned as Don turned on headlights and followed.

"Hey, Marty. Is the money in that paper bag he was carrying?" Tim asked.

"Yeah."

"Then this is gonna be easy," Tim said.

We stayed six car lengths behind until the market owner suddenly sped up to make the changing traffic light at Gratiot. "Damn! Step on it, Don!" Tim yelled.

Don floored the gas pedal and we shot through the intersection. "God, that light was orange!" Marty exclaimed. "I hope no cops saw us."

"It's too damn cold for cops to be out. They're all drinking coffee somewhere," Tim assured him.

Don yelled, "Open the windows...I can't see through this damn steam."

We rolled down all the windows and freezing air blasted our faces, but we hardly noticed. Don shortened the space between vehicles and we drove at a safe legal speed until the truck abruptly accelerated. "What the hell's going on?" Tim asked no one in particular. Don kept pace as we weaved around and flashed by slower moving cars. "He's either in a hurry to get home or knows we're after him," Marty observed. Don's speedometer passed fifty-five and inched towards sixty, and the truck still increased the space between us. "Floor the sonovabitch!" Tim yelled. The market owner was four car lengths ahead when he reached the traffic lights at Outer Drive, an island-divided, two-way street. He hit the brake, snapped the steering wheel to the left, swerved sideways and drove onto Outer Drive. We did the same, following closely, as he quickly left-turned at the first cross street, sped through the island median, slid to a sudden stop under a corner streetlamp, jumped out with paper bag in hand, and ran for the nearest brick house. Don slammed on the brakes, and we slid into the market owner's car with a gentle bump. I was halfway out the rear door when Tim shouted, "Forget it...it's too late...back up...get the hell outta here!"

Don was already spinning the wheels in reverse as I slammed the door shut. He swiftly backed onto Outer Drive, shifted gears and headed for Harper.

As we drove to Marty's car Tim said morosely, "I guess I'll buy a cheap ring and tell Eunace it's temporary until I can afford a good one. This sure has been a lousy day."

"Yeah," I agreed. "Now I can't buy a school sweater." In actuality I was happy, happy that my lucky golden horse-shoe stayed securely wedged up my goofka as our spate of attempted crime ended.

A week later, at school, Don told Marty and me that Tim had indeed become engaged to Eunace and left for the Navy. Don also said that two days before Tim departed to serve his country they were handling the automatic in Don's upstairs bedroom. It accidently fired and drilled a neat hole in the bedroom wall, just below the ceiling.

Except for a couple cursory conversations at social gatherings, I wasn't too familiar with Eunace, but I did happen to meet her soon after at a Gratiot store. I gave her my best wishes on her recent engagement to Tim, and I couldn't help mentioning the diamond ring on her finger. It was not only beautiful, but the largest diamond I had ever seen. She extended her hand so I could admire it more closely and I said, "Eunace, I don't wanna be nosey, but I happen to know that Tim was having great lack-of-money difficulties just before he departed this area to take up the maritime life." I also opined that I was quite surprised that he could afford anything more extravagant than a ring from a Cracker Jack box.

She gave me one of those smiles usually directed by wives to husbands who can't remember what time they got home last night. "Well, Bob," she said, "there's an engrossing story behind the ring."

"So, lay it on me," I said, trying not to sound too interested.

"Well, my uncle Charlie who is my mother's brother, and more importantly my godfather, has told me for years that when I found the man with whom I wanted to spend the rest of my life he would deem it an honor and pleasure to give that young man the price of a very large engagement ring, his wedding present to us.

"But this is not what makes this story so interesting," she continued. "What makes it interesting is that it almost didn't happen."

"Why was that?" I asked.

"Well, on the way home in his truck on a Friday night, with the ring money in his pocket, he was beset by a very inept group of robbers who he easily managed to elude…and that's why this beautiful, expensive ring is on my finger."

I felt beads of perspiration on my forehead.

"You see, Bob," she added, "my uncle makes good money. He owns a market on Harper avenue."

I stood quietly stunned. After a short silence she said,

"Would you believe that one of those assholes had painted on a mascara moustache?"

XXXVI

The first semester would end in a week, and I figured I'd have a straight "C" report card. What more could be asked of a student? Except for grouchy Sister Remegia the nuns were all tolerable, so with nineteen more weeks of me relentlessly slipping by, a diploma would be mine.

Even the weather cooperated to add to my contented mood. The temperature rose to 34 degrees, ashen clouds loosed four inches of new snow before clearing, and the sun transformed McClellan into a sparkling spectacle.

The school swiftly emptied at lunch time with most students wanting to bask in the elements. Marty, Jack, Reno, Stellon and I walked slowly to Anne's, breathing crisp air, enjoying damp snow invading our shoes, the sun reminding us of Spring, two short months away.

As we grudgingly joined a string of plodding schoolmates returning from lunch, girls' backs offered tempting targets for the good-packing snow. Snowballs sailed and girls shrieked, running. By the time we passed the church all female students were already in school, but a group of eighth grade boys challenged us to a snowball fight by throwing one that struck Marty solidly in his ear.

We peppered them. They ran for the flats; the bell sounded and everyone ran for school. Except Marty and me.

Marty was determined to give a snowy face wash to the boy who snow-stuffed his ear. I caught the kid; Marty washed his face, and we merrily returned to school.

Sister Remegia stood unmerrily at the top of the stairs blocking access to classrooms. "You're two minutes late! Turn around, go see the principal and get demerit slips!" she sputtered.

"We just passed her office, Sister. She's not there," Marty said.

"Then wait in her office 'til she returns," she commanded, and watched as we retreated down the stairs and entered the principal's office.

Twenty minutes later we were still there. "All this for a lousy two minutes," Marty complained.

"It beats sitting in Remegia's class," I rationalized.

We heard footsteps, and Sister Verena swept into her office and didn't seem surprised to see us. "What did you boys do now?" she asked.

We explained our two-minute transgression, and she said, "I'll have to talk to Sister about this. Stay here." It was plain she didn't trust our version.

Six more minutes passed before she returned, sat at her desk, brought out a demerit pad and started writing. When finished, she stood and handed a slip to both of us. "You're getting two demerits for being late and five for missing class."

Marty looked stunned. "Wait a minute, Sister. Seven demerits? That's not fair. We didn't ask to miss class."

"That's what Sister Remegia and I determined you should get. Go back to class and be happy I didn't decide to send you to see Father Geller." She looked down and picked up some loose papers. Apparently we were excused.

Marty was silent until we arrived at our classroom doors that stood across the hall from one another. When he spoke his persecuted words came through angry teeth. "Look, this is garbage. We didn't miss the class on purpose. These seven demerits are gonna give me a "D" in courtesy. I've had enough of this. Let's get the hell outta here."

"Whadaya mean?"

"I mean let's quit this damn school, okay?"

"Sure," I said.

"Then get your stuff outta your desk and I'll meet you right here. Let's go." I figured he'd change his mind once he was back in his classroom.

Sister Remegia ignored me as I entered, hung up my jacket and sat at my desk. Jack was beaming, and I hoped Kathy also thought it amusing. I was settling down to await the "change class" bell when the door opened, and an agitated Marty stepped inside with his looseleaf folder in hand. "Are you ready, Bob?"

I nodded, jerked open the drawer under my desk, pulled out everything I thought belonged to me, arose and grabbed my jacket. "Where do you boys think you're going?" Sister Remegia asked.

We ignored the question.

"If you two walk out of this room, don't come back!"

"Bunt off, Sister," Marty said.

We stood in wet snow in front of school and discussed the unfairness of our situation while having second thoughts about quitting. "Let's go tell Father Gentner. Maybe he can do something," Marty suggested, and we walked to the rectory.

Father Gentner invited us into his office and listened closely to our woeful tale. "I'm sure something can be done," he said sympathetically. "Let me talk to the nuns. Don't worry...we'll work it out. By the way, why aren't you in school?"

"We walked out," Marty said.

His kindly expression changed. "In that case I can't do a thing for you...nothing. What's the matter with you? You both have bad attitudes...especially you, Robert."

"Whadaya mean, Father?" I asked.

"What do I mean? That's easy. You lack judgment. You quit the altar boys for no reason...you didn't feel like serving. And the time right after a football game when you lit up a cigarette. Do you know how dreadful that looked?"

"No, Father...I mean yes, Father."

"Well, I can't do anything for you. I'm sorry, but you made your bed." He didn't sound that sorry. He escorted us to the front door.

Marty drove me home, and we told each other how great it was that we were out of that rotten school, away from nuns and priests, on our own, how we could get full time jobs, have money, have fun. And I silently wondered if he felt as bad as I did.

Our parents decried our quitting school so Marty enrolled at Eastern High School and I enrolled at Denby, a 4,500-student, public high school with a reputation for providing everything students desired, including excellent teachers and counselors, a solid academic curriculum and a strong sports program. Denby's spacious grounds included two baseball diamonds and a track that encircled a gridiron. The school produced many students who went on to become college and professional sports stars.

I didn't realize it at the time but I attended Denby with a student destined to become the hardest-hitting fighter in Michigan boxing history, with the possible exception of Joe Louis. His name was "Ducky" Dietz and I don't know why he was called "Ducky." He never ducked a fight or punch in his life.

Because Marty and I hadn't fully completed Nativity's first semester we had to start our senior year over and wouldn't graduate until the following January. This discouraged me, and so did transferring to an impersonal high school with ten times as many students. With plenty of non-uniformed girls, no crosses on walls, no daily mass, no robed nuns and no Father Geller, I should have been happy. I wasn't. I missed regimentation, familiarity and friends.

My assigned school hours were terrific, nine a.m. to one p.m., and I figured they could be terrificker. After my first week I pointed out to my counselor that if I dropped my last

466

class in chemistry I'd still have enough credits to graduate and I could leave at noon and get an afternoon job. He said that if he approved my dropping chemistry, and I failed one of my other three classes then I wouldn't qualify for a cap and gown. I told him I wouldn't fail my other three classes. He said that his decision requiring my attendance in chemistry class was binding and pointed me out his office door. I honestly tried for a couple days, but failed, to work up enthusiasm for chemicals, microscopes and Bunsen burners. I dropped chemistry from my school day routine, and Denby terminated my enrollment.

Marty had more perseverance than I. He lasted a month at Eastern before quitting. He quickly found work as a stock man at a candy machine company, while I searched for a soda jerk job. Wearing a white jacket and cap and being called "jerk" didn't thrill me, but it had to be a marvelous way to meet females, plus satisfy my secondary craving for sodas, banana splits and sundaes. I applied at every Gratiot establishment that had a soda fountain within walking distance of home. By mid-February, sad, discouraged, and just so I could tell Mom I was still looking, I asked the Ramona manager for an usher job. He hired me part-time for Friday, Saturday and Sunday evenings.

My usher duties included collecting and tearing tickets, standing outside at the ticket booth proclaiming "Standing Room Only" to lined-up movie buffs, filling the popcorn machine with pre-popped popcorn, mopping restroom floors, using a strainer to remove cigarette butts and phlegm from sandfilled ash trays, and any other chore the manager thought up. But I knew my uniform, consisting of a white shirt, black bow tie, rust-colored suit coat with gold buttons and gray pants with a rust-colored stripe down both sides, was attractive to all maidens. Another perquisite was free movies and a possibility of passing by the usherette's dressing room when its door was ajar. My neighborhood acquaintances shared in the free-movie bounty anytime I collected tickets and it really amused Butch to hand me grimy, trod-on stubs.

Two-and-a-half weeks after I landed this usher job, Marty phoned and said he'd pick me up for an evening at Schofield's. When he drove into our driveway an hour later I didn't recognize his car. His '36 black Ford was painted sky blue with cream-colored fenders. From a distance it looked fine. Up close it didn't. "Who whiskbroom-painted your car," I asked.

"I did. It ain't that bad," he said irritably.

"Yeah, you're right," I lied. "Why'd ya paint it?"

"It's a long story, and I'll explain it some other time. How'd you like a full time job? I'm trying to get a service route where I work, and they said they might have an opening next month."

"What's a service route?"

"That's when you drive around filling candy machines and collecting coins. I told my boss if he gave me a route I knew someone who might want my stockroom job. Whadayasay?"

What could I say? It was full-time. I said yes.

Jack and Reno awaited us when we entered Schofield's and gave us some unexpected, though non-startling news: Tim Reegin had been home for awhile. He had endured three weeks of Navy life and wouldn't divulge the reason for his discharge. After his marriage he was moving to California. We all felt he'd fit in well with the West Coast's wholesome normalcy.

I hadn't seen Jack or Reno since quitting Nativity and noticed our conversation was slightly strained. They were insiders; Marty and I were outsiders. We worked; they schooled. They anticipated and planned graduation; we anticipated and planned nothing. Worst of all, they saw Kathy more than I did. I envied them and missed Nativity. Marty and I went home early that night, never to enter Schofield's again.

Jack and Reno continued honing their pool shooting skill at Schofield's until the evening they witnessed an incident.

468

A rookie policeman had verbally annoyed a young, regular customer for a few weeks, and the customer stoically accepted this torment, saying little in return. But he took considerable offense when the policeman deliberately bumped his cue stick when he lined up a shot. He went berserk, plunged the tapered cue through the policeman's chest, dragged the body across the floor, up the back stairs and through an alley, and dumped his burden in front of a shoe store before fleeing. The remaining customers remained standing at pool tables, not wanting to leave through the front door where the policeman's partner waited, or the back door where they might trip over a body. They and Mr. Schofield were taken into custody by angry policemen and grilled incessantly at the nearest police station, but no one admitted seeing the assault. After a few hours, Jack and Reno's fathers were notified by phone to pick up their sons. The police initiated a sustained badgering campaign against Mr. Schofield, and he quietly turned over management of his establishment to his son.

* * *

The newspapers reported that America's national deficit, which had grown to $269 million by the end of 1946 because of war commitments, had shrunk to $258 million and the shrinkage was expected to continue. We'd soon be in the black; capable of lavishing total happiness on all citizens.

Driven by money madness and an unnatural ambition I kept my part-time usher job and accepted the candy machine company stockroom job. The company was housed in an aged, shaled, red-brick, two-story building and sat in a mid-Detroit industrial area. Its main floor contained an office and long shelves stacked with unopened cardboard boxes filled with a variety of candy bars and Chicklet gum. Marty and other route men carried boxes of candy and gum to their car's backseats and trunks during early morning

469

hours and vanished until late afternoon.

I enjoyed my job. Except for helping unload boxes of candy from delivery trucks and stacking them in the building's first floor storage area, most hours were spent in the basement with the other stock man sandpapering and re-painting heavy-metal, black-enameled, gum-machine stands. Each stand included a two-inch-in-diameter pole protruding from a flat round base. A gum machine could be bolted to the pole's small, hole-drilled plate on top. Trusting store owners often stood these company-provided penny gum machines outside their front doors hoping to attract pedestrian traffic. Exposure to the elements tended to rust the stands so every work day route men exchanged a few rusty stands for newly enameled ones. Since our boss seldom visited the basement, preferring to call down the stairs when needing unloaders, repainting gum-machine stands progressed at a leisurely pace. The only employee who came down to the basement on a regular basis was the janitor, push broom and dust pan in hand, to sweep up dust, burnt matches, sandpaper grit, cigarette ashes and butts scattered on the cement floor. He usually stopped for an extended social chat each morning and afternoon.

My fellow stock man and the janitor had much in common. Both were in their late thirties, weighed about 160 pounds, had familiar surnames, had similar southern accents, pronouncing "eye" as "ah," and both loved to talk. Yet they were as different as night and day. Climax Williams, the janitor, was Negro. Gillian Jones wasn't.

The main basement area had dusty, broken-down candy machines lining its walls waiting patiently, futilely, for repair. Gillian and I did our enameling in a smaller side room, half of which was stacked almost to the ceiling with flattened out cardboard boxes. Route men tossed empty boxes down the basement stairs daily, and we flattened and added them to our growing inventory. We also stacked a few to sit on while doing our painting chore and always slid one under the stand we painted to keep dripping enamel off the cement floor. The enamel we used was fast-drying and had to be thinned often so we kept turpentine nearby. Exposure to fumes sometimes bothered us, but we reasoned it had to be better than working upstairs exposed to our employer's baleful eye.

Another advantage was that rats rarely ventured down the basement, preferring to spend their time on the main floor gnawing through cardboard boxes to sample candy wares. Marty told me he discarded two or three pre-nibbled candy bars a day and that Clark bars were rodents' favorite.

Climax was the first Negro with whom I ever had extended conversations. He seemed to take a shine to me and told me his life's ambition. He and his wife were saving money so they could open up a combination barber/beauty shop and call it 'DOs and 'FROs. Climax thought it amusing that I was 17-years-old and still virginal and once gave me detailed romantic advice on how to approach women. Gillian advised me to ignore the advice, it was bull manure, and that it could lead to getting either physically slapped or slapped with an obscenity charge. I acquired a vague impression that Gillian's heart wasn't flowing with brotherly love for Climax. The impression grew the following week when I asked Climax and Gillian what they did during the '43 race riot, expecting some adventurous first person accounts. They both disappointed me by claiming they saw National Guard patrols but stayed safely indoors. Climax and I discussed how terrible it was that humans of different hues couldn't be more tolerant of one another. As he picked up his broom and full dust pan preparing to leave I asked, "Ya don't dislike white people do ya, Climax?"

"Nah, Ah loves white folk," he said, smiling. "If ya'll dint bring us over heah Ah'd be sittin' in front of a grass hut wit' a bone through ma nose."

When I heard Climax close the upstairs basement door I said to Gillian, "Do ya think Climax told the truth about likin' us?"

Gillian replied, "Everyone thinks them people are only good at barbecuein', dancin' and holdin' fashin shews.

471

What they do best is lah."

Being a tolerant person I gently took Gillian to task. "Geez, Gil...ya sound like a racist."

"No Ah'm a facist. Ah can't stan' their faces. Ya ever really look at Climax? He looks lak the rest of 'em—twelve miles of bad road. They're walkin' ahsores. You'll see iffin one ever moves on your block. The first nigra poisons a block lak a broke appendix poisons a body. Weeds grow fasta, paint peels and streetlahts lose wattage."

I told him about the nice Negro couple who lived on Holcomb, and I was sure that weeds grew, paint peeled and streetlights didn't shine brightly before they arrived.

"All Ah know is they homely up places," Gillian said, slightly exasperated.

"Climax ain't a bad-looking guy except for his nose that looks like a two-car garage...and he seems smart some-times," I said, not unreasonably. I had mulled and mused over racial matters and felt now was an opportune time to voice these thoughts. "I think we're all kin under the skin, and if we get together with Negroes, live with 'em, marry 'em, have lots of children, we'll be better off. After a hundred years or so women wouldn't haveta wave their hair, get permanents or sleep on hard metal curlers (think-ing of my sisters) because everbody'd have dark, curly hair...and they could dye their hair if they wanted a differ-ent color...and we'd all have natural suntans and wouldn't haveta lie around on beaches anymore...and we'd all have kissable lips...not fat like theirs or thin like ours...and we'd all have brown eyes...I like brown eyes (thinking of Kathy)...and we'd all know how to jitterbug...and besides, they're gonna have equality anyway 'cause my brother Chuck, who predicts things, said that although Malcolms One through Eight didn't do much, someday a savior named Malcolm Nine would inspire and unite Negroes and lead 'em outta want and oppression."

I waited for his reaction to my breathless, rational discourse. He stared, shook his head, half-smiled and said,

472

"Beckwail...all yer brain seeds ain't sprouted yet."

Gillian had a lower tolerance for Negroes than my dad did for the English. Gillian obviously needed to attend a block party with Climax, but I knew he never would.

* * *

My holding two jobs elated Mom, as much as a pain-wracked person can be elated. I gave her my first pay envelope from the candy machine company, and she said, "See, you can do it. You're just as hard-working as my other children. I'll save this money, and when I get well I'll buy you something nice."

In early May Mom complained there was something inside her that had to come out. She started hemorrhaging, Dad rushed her to the hospital, the doctors operated and a week later she returned home to recuperate. Though still eating more aspirins than food, she seemed in better spirits. She even smiled when I told her I had quit the usher job. "Working everyday is too much for anyone. Young men need weekends for fun," she said.

"Yeah, it was a lotta work, Ma," I agreed. My other reason: The usherettes weren't tripping over themselves encouraging me to ask for a date.

* * *

Marty acted restless and unhappy. I guessed he had spring fever. Spending an evening at Eastwood Park unsuccessfully searching for beautiful, unescorted girls didn't help his mood. When we parked in my driveway he asked, "Do you get the feeling we ain't going anywhere?" He didn't wait for my answer. "I'm sick of this life, my job, everything. All we do is go to work, look for girls, sleep, go to work, look for girls, sleep. I'm making two or three extra dollars a day collecting coins jammed in candy machines, but money ain't everything. There's no future in our jobs.

We need some excitement, but if we hang around here we're gonna get in trouble. Did I ever tell you why I painted this car?"

"No."

"I told a guy I met at Eastern about us trying to rob people that time, and he said he knew a store that'd be easy, and he had a gun. So we robbed it...I mean I did. That jerkoff stood inside the front door with his hand on the knob."

"How'd ya do it?"

"I walked up to the owner at the counter, asked for potato chips, and when he turned around I had the gun pointed at him. My damn hand wouldn't stop shakin'. He reached in the cash register, gave me a ten dollar bill and said, 'You'll be sorry for this.' When I ran to the car my buddy was already in the front seat. That's why I painted it."

"What about your license plate?"

"I had a wet rag covering it and took it off when I got a few blocks away."

"Damn, Marty, you're neat!" I said admiringly.

"No I'm not. It's just a matter of time until we do something stupider. Sometimes you haveta step back and scan the action. Whadaya say we get outta this city. Let's jump start our lives...join the Navy...you wanna? We're gonna get drafted anyway."

"Sure," I said.

Three days later we visited the recruiting station downtown. My parents seemed almost relieved that I was taking control of my life and gladly signed my permission papers.

After we took a written test and physical consisting of checking to see if our hearts beat steadily, if our blood pressured normally, if we had enough teeth, if we had flat feet, if we could spread wide our cheeks and could cough while a doctor finger-probed sensitive body crevices, the recruiter said we qualified to serve our country. He suggested we keep our jobs because we might not get called for a month or two.

Gillian always kept the paint room door open to disperse

enamel and turpentine fumes. He claimed fumes gave him a headache. He transferred turpentine from its original large container to two small empty soup cans that he placed near our feet, and he never filled the cans completely. "The less turps around the better," he said. The problem with his theory was that we had to get up and fill the soup cans three or four times a day, which wasted energy. I would have filled up a large empty paint can with turpentine and used it for a week. Also the cans were easily, accidently kicked over, soaking the surrounding area and causing more fumes. This vexed Gillian, but he still insisted on using the soup cans and I deferred to his age, seniority and experience.

The last time I carelessly knocked over a soup can happened on a Wednesday morning when I had other things on my mind. Nativity's senior graduation would occur over the coming weekend and I felt bad because I wasn't invited to any graduation parties. The spilled turpentine splashed on flattened cardboard boxes next to me. I got up, refilled the can, returned to sit on the boxes, struck a match to light a cigarette and orange flames whooshed up immediately to my left.

Gillian and I lunged to our feet, with him screaming, "Smother it! Smother it!" as he tossed unburned boxes onto the fire. This caused smoke and spread the fire. We can't stop this, I told myself.

The flames were reaching for the ceiling when Climax suddenly appeared, fire extinguisher under his arm, and foamed the whole conflagration. The fire was over almost as fast as it started. "Ya'll gotta watch dem matches," Climax warned, grinning.

Gillian said he thought about getting the extinguisher that hung on the wall outside the paint room just before Climax rushed in, and I thanked Climax profusely for rushing in, and the boss opened the basement door and yelled down, "You got a fire down there?!" and Climax yelled back, "It be okay, Boss. Ah took care of it!"

Climax waited around to assure all smoke wisps disappeared, broomed up our ashes, butts and used matches and returned upstairs. As Gillian and I separated burnt and foam-soaked cardboard from the rest I said, "It's a good thing Climax was around. This proves you're wrong, Gil. He really does like white guys. He sure saved our jobs."

Climax's heroic action didn't change Gillian's subtle animosity. "That's crap! Iffin this place burned down he'd be outta a job too," he replied cynically. "He's still slum scum."

Gillian and I had no problem understanding each other's words, only understanding and agreeing with each other's thoughts, opinions and ideology. I determined that Gillian was a poor receptacle for my enlightened wisdom.

* * *

I watched from my front porch as a glowing Kathy, clad in white cap and gown, climbed into her older brother's car with her brother, mother and sister Lois. She'll never go out with me again, I told myself. She's a graduate; I'm a drop-out. She'll get a prestigious job; I'll still be a stock flunky. Painful feelings of loss and frustration overwhelmed me as the car accelerated towards Gratiot, destination: Nativity's graduation ceremony.

* * *

Russia's Premier, Joseph Stalin, had communists infiltrating our government and Russian soldiers cutting off western allies' ground access to Berlin. A Berlin airlift began on June 28th. Marty and I quit our jobs at the candy machine company. With the tense world situation developing we knew the Navy would soon call us to defend our country against the bastardly Russian enemy, and we wanted to fully relax and enjoy ourselves before plunging into battle preparation. We mentioned to every patriotic-looking girl we met that soon we'd be off to war protecting our American way of life. Most were duly unimpressed. Hearts filled with anticipation, Marty and I awaited our call to the colors.

* * *

At 11 p.m., July 29th, I came home after an ineffective search for patriotic girls, climbed the stairs and saw Dad, Ed, Betty, Mary and Mom's doctor crowded in my parent's bedroom. I heard the doctor explain to Ed how much morphine to administer for Mom's pain. When I reached my bedroom I asked Chuck, who laid awake, "What's going on in there?"

"Ma's pretty sick," he said.

At two a.m. Dad came to our bedroom and loudly said, "Robert! Charles! Get up and say good-bye to your mother."

Chuck and I put on our pants and went to Mom. A blanket covered the bottom half of her frail body clothed in nightgown and quilted bed jacket. Her eyes were closed, and she didn't move, except for heaving chest and gasping mouth. I leaned over, kissed her forehead, Chuck did the same, and we returned to bed. We stared at the dark ceiling a long time before Chuck spoke. "She's dying, Robbie." he whispered.

"Nah," I said.

When we awakened, her long battle for life was over.

She was laid out at the Weitenberner Funeral Home in a bronze casket adorned with carved angel heads. She wore her favorite turquoise dress with sequins down the front, and she clutched her blue rosary. I should be crying, I told myself, but tears didn't come. I knew it was my mother lying in the casket, the body certainly resembled her; yet I also knew it wasn't her so I didn't dwell on it, just spent my time reading sympathy cards on flower arrangements placed near the casket and around the room and, in between, chatted with friends and relatives whose most common phrase was, "It's for the best...she suffered so."

On the second day at the funeral home, Marty, Jack and Reno were among the crowd who paid their respects, and after they left, Bill Stellon, Geri Zewecki and Kathy arrived. After they expressed their sorrow and went through the ritual of kneeling to pray at the casket, I managed to steer Kathy away from the others for a private chat in the funeral home hallway. I admired her navy blue dress with its short hem line and told her she looked pretty, and she said I looked nice in my pin-striped suit. She said, "I hear you and Marty are going in the Navy," and I said, "Yeah, any day now...Do ya wanna check out the bodies in the other rooms?" and she said, "No" and I said, "I wonder where these steps lead to...Let's find out, okay?" and she said, "Okay."

We walked up the carpeted stairs to the second floor and discovered a large room full of caskets, some with lids open to display their plush insides. "This must be the 'pick-out' room," I whispered. "They bring people up here to pick out a casket for dead relatives." We paused at a white casket with a split lid. "This one is called a half-couch," I said authoritatively, "and that one over there is a full-couch."

"Where did you learn that 'couch' stuff?" she asked, with what I hoped was admiration for my knowledge.

"I was talkin' to the funeral director. Let's go look at the full-couch."

We stopped at a black casket with its top fully open exposing satiny innards. "It feels soft and comfortable," I whispered, touching the satin, as sexual images of us accidently tumbling inside the casket flashed through my brain.

Funeral home or graveyard atmosphere must attune certain people to each other, or maybe Kathy wanted to relieve my sorrow, for a touch of our hands led to passionate moments of clutching, clasping, grasping, writhing. While people quietly mourned downstairs, we quietly moaned above them. We knew we had to cease, and we did, but it was difficult.

Funeral day, August 2nd, was bright and sunny. Grievers filled the funeral room, sitting on folding chairs, for a short

478

prayerful ceremony. The prayers ended, and friends and relatives lined up to touch Mom's hand or say a silent farewell. Dad, standing near the head of the casket, watched as his children slowly filed past. I stopped and stared at the lifeless figure, thinking that it can't be my mother. She's at home waiting for me to read her a story, get her some fresh water and aspirins, or hit her up for a couple bucks ("All right. Bring me my pocketbook on the dresser.") It was simply unreal.

"Kiss your mother, Robert," Dad said. I leaned into the casket and kissed her lips and it was like kissing cold marble. See! You're right! It isn't her! I told myself and walked across Gratiot to Assumption Grotto church for the funeral Mass.

Following the Mass, a blur of prayers, quiet weeping and blessing of the sealed casket, a long solemn procession of cars trailed a hearse to Mount Olivet cemetery. More prayers, tears, and it ended.

At home, relatives from Pennsylvania and Ohio assembled in our dining room. Whisky bottles slapped the table, and a boisterous reunion ensued, filled with banter and stories that began, "Remember when..." Their conversation eventually got around to Mom. They talked about how she had talents besides raising children. She played the piano by ear. If the Olympic Games included the game of jacks she would have won at least a silver medal. How she never lost her colloquial expressions: Turn off the spicket; I have to red up the house; Don't be nebby (curious).

Pat recalled how Mom loved to correct Dad's speech. He'd start a sentence with, "Irregardless and not withstanding and by the same token..." and she'd calmly interrupt with "Isn't regardless enough? Why irregardless? You're simple." He'd laugh and start over, "Regardless and not withstanding..."

Ed joked that Mom took particular pleasure in small smelly things, especially flowers and children, and batted .875 by raising seven fine children and me. (But no matter

479

what I did she always believed my redeeming features would someday come to the fore.)

Betty said that it was a shame Mom died at so young an age, 44, but at least Mom had the pleasure of seeing her first grandchild, Patricia Dolan, born to Betty eight months earlier.

Mary remarked that a doctor had told her perhaps Mom's having eight children in eleven years contributed to her illness. An aunt disagreed, saying that God ofttimes culled the most gorgeous blossoms before withering, and that measured in goodness Mom had achieved life's success.

Once during this reminiscing another aunt burst out sobbing and wailed, "Oh, Claire, why'd you die?" but others, comforting, returned her to a more jocund mood.

Someone remembered it was Chuck's 16th birthday, and an uncle took up a cash collection and presented it to Chuck with a terse, "For your birthday." No one sang the happy birthday song.

The party broke up by late afternoon. I never cried.

XXXVII

M arty was angry at the Navy's continued delay in
calling us to serve America. He wasn't used to
joblessness. I didn't mind a bit. Joblessness
seemed to be my natural state, and I stayed busy by playing
baseball and seeing movies. Ed told me the Navy required
personnel to shave daily so to get in practice I shaved every
other day.

Kathy didn't get a regular job, but babysat often, chiefly
on weekends. One afternoon in late August I saw her and
Lois from my bedroom window on a blanket in their
backyard, sunning themselves. Kathy, clad in a white one-
piece swimsuit, stood up, ala Betty Grable's pinup picture,
and the sight inspired me to ask Dad for a couple dollars
date money.

It was easy getting money from Dad. Every evening
since Mom died, he came home from work, ate supper, and
sat in the living room holding up the newspaper like he was
reading. Only he didn't read; just stared at the paper or over
the top of the paper. When I requested money, I'd have to
ask twice because he never understood me the first time.

Kathy remained the sole female capable of tying my
tongue so badly that I dreaded approaching her. I had a
certain amount of confidence with other girls but around
her I was still Bashful to her Snow White. So when I nerved

myself to ask her for a Saturday night movie date and she said she had to babysit, I felt downfallen. But she was quick to add that she'd be available the following Saturday.

It was another perfect date. We held hands walking home and kissed many times at her side door. The kissing loosened my tongue and I blurted out a whispered "I love you," and felt instant embarrassment, but she also whispered "I love you" and my chagrin changed to ecstacy. That she loved me too was much more than I expected. Between kisses we discussed marriage, either during my Navy time or when I finished my three-year enlistment.

Official letters arrived directing Marty and me to report to the recruiting station downtown on the morning of September 30th for eventual transportation to the Great Lakes Naval Training Center in Illinois. Ed told me to travel light; so the night before I packed a small satchel with toiletries, shaving gear and cigarettes. After laying out the clothes I'd wear, there remained one more thing to do, ostensibly say adieu to the Kelly household, actually see Kathy one more time.

Her older brothers filled me with the usual information of how to survive the military (never volunteer and never drop the shower soap), how tough basic training is, how every serviceman hated the rigid discipline but wouldn't trade the experience. Kathy got out the family album and gave me one of her photographs. Eventually, mercifully, everyone except Kathy talked themselves out, said goodnight and headed for bed. As Mrs. Kelly walked upstairs she warned us not to stay up too late, that I had to "get up" early.

And then it started. Alone at last, we turned off lamps, returned to the sofa and for two hours our bodies heaved, teeth clashed, tongues searched, hands rummaged, all this with our clothes disheveled, unfastened, but still on, sort of a dry run. We pledged love eternal, to write everyday, and she vowed to keep her knees crossed, and I vowed to keep my bellbottoms buttoned. My heart filled with wholesome desires to protect her, comfort her, hold her, shield her, marry her.

482

After her mother called down the stairs for the third time suggesting I go home and Kathy come to bed, Kathy and I parted at her front door with virginity intact. "I'll be seeing you," I murmured, adding, "Hey, that'd make a great song title!"

"Good night, darling," she said smiling, and closed the door. Darling! She called me darling! I felt like I was in a romantic movie.

I laid awake in bed thinking life can be kind. I was deeply in love, my love loved me, I'm heading for exciting naval exploits, and all is right with the world.

Ed drove me downtown and dropped me off in front of the recruiting building. Fourteen others besides Marty and me were sworn into the Navy's clutches and a Chief Petty officer led us to a waiting bus for the ride to the Michigan Central train depot. It was the first time since 1935 that I had entered its grandiose interior, and it was the same — busy, thronged.

The Chief, trying to mold us into some sort of military conformity, ordered us to can the boisterous chatter, stay together and follow him. He led us onto the train.

Marty sat across from me and wouldn't stop smirking. "We're going to finally get excitement in our life...see the world...meet women!" he gushed. "And you're finally getting a steady job. You quit this one; they'll shoot you. It's called desertion."

I nodded while silently contemplating my future. Maybe I'd found my niche in life at last as a mariner. Maybe I'd meet a trollop and get my ashes hauled. Maybe I'd become a petty officer. Maybe we'd go to war. Maybe I'd win a medal. Maybe I'd get killed.

Ash hauling seemed a more pleasant subject so I gave Marty some details about my last hours with Kathy, how we'd done everything but the thing, how close I'd come with her.

"Close only counts in horseshoes and hand grenades," he counseled.

I questioned if I'd ever again be capable of arousing her to such lofty passion. "Don't worry," he reassured. "A woman's like a batch of leftover spaghetti…always tastier when re-heated."

The train jerked, moved forward, slowly picked up speed. I stared out the window at the passing landscape, and with every cla-clunk, cla-clunk of the train's wheels, two words repeated over and over in my mind…words that promised to alter my dull life to one of action and adventure…words that could turn my life towards the maturity I craved…words that would also make a great song title, maybe sung by a skinny singer-dancer with a glass eye…words hundreds of thousands of others would gladly/sadly say in the future…words that sadden me still: Good-bye, Detroit.

THE END

Epilogue

One of Midland, Pennsylvania's few claims to fame is that it's close to Beaver Falls, the home town of Joe Namath. Midland is also close to the town of Beaver where the Beckwell family elders are buried, a fact that somehow escaped its city fathers. On my last trip there I didn't see any bronze plaque at the town limits to alert tourists.

As of 1993, many buildings mentioned in this book are still standing. Our houses on Belvidere and Holcomb look better than when we lived in them. The wooden Lutheran church on Holcomb was replaced by a larger, red-brick Baptist church. Nativity school was replaced by a new high school that is now used by the Wayne County Community College. Nativity Recreation Hall has been converted to a 4-H club. The Roosevelt theater and dime stores were torn down to make way for a freeway.

My sisters and brothers all married and all moved to Detroit's suburbs, save one.

Betty and Joe Dolan raised nine children.

Ed entered the trucking business and dabbled with singing, song writing and comedy. He retired and is currently the morning bartender at Tudge's Pub in St. Clair Shores where "songs and witty stories come through the open door."

Mary and Bud Davis had six children before Bud died of cancer. Mary met another man who died of a heart attack a few months after their engagement. She married another gentleman who was murdered in a suburban motel. For the last few years she has been keeping company with yet another gentleman who is starting to look a little peaked.

Pat is still living in a relatively safe section of Detroit. She's only had her purse snatched once and only witnessed one daytime shooting.

Chuck's prediction that he'd have eight children was wrong. He only had seven and is looking forward to his retirement so he can join Ed and me occasionally at Tudge's.

Dolores raised seven children and never owned a biting dog.

Ann, a glutton for punishment, had three children with her first husband, divorced and married a man with six.

Bob Durant and his band are still entertaining in the Detroit area.

Mrs. Hill was never pilloried.

One-armed, good-neighbor Bill had three children before his wife left him. He raised the children single-handedly.

Five months after I joined the Navy, Walter Stein, the class artiste, was killed when he accidently smashed his car into a northern Michigan bridge abutment.

A short time after Walter's death, William Stellon's rheumatic heart stopped.

Donald Blaso transferred to a public school following completion of Nativity's 11th grade. He later worked the nightclub circuit in Chicago and Miami playing piano in a Liberace mode. He intended to attend our 40th year (I didn't graduate but they invited me anyway) class reunion. He had a heart attack and died one week before the scheduled reunion, which dejected me. I wanted to apologize for not stemming some of the abuse he suffered at Nativity from some male students.

Catherine Kaltz married one of the Barshaw boys.

Leroy Kolassa and Audrey Hoch married three years after high school graduation.

486

Jerry Wolshon's mother threw out his comic book collection. He now has a beer can collection that covers every inch of his basement walls.

Jack Heffner graduated from the University of Detroit with a law degree, played a season as a Toronto Argonauts linebacker, then practiced law.

Reynold "Reno" Rimoldi, to this day, will not speak of the "Schoefield" incident. He resides in California.

Jerry Wygocki was the first Nativity male to qualify for a Gregg shorthand award. He suffered a fatal heart attack at an early age.

Bill Kraft retired after 40 years at the Michigan Consolidated Gas Company.

Frank Baccala owns and operates a FTD florist shop.

Bob Yahner retired from the Lake Orion Cadillac Plant.

Sam Vacari owns Vacari's Fireplace Sales in Utica, Michigan.

Tony Arcesi went into paving and construction.

Dolores DeWalls, a Derby, married a Duke.

Geri Zewecki married a man two years her senior who lived across the street from Nativity school.

Marty served four years in the Navy (they extended our enlistment because of the Korean war), became a meat cutter, owned a butcher shop, and retired to Naples, Florida.

Don Jacobs went into construction and, as foreman, helped build the Fermi nuclear plant near Monroe, Michigan. He now owns two laundromats in Erie, Michigan.

Sister Jarlath "leaped over the wall," so to speak. She quit the Dominican sisterhood.

Following 28 years as Nativity's pastor, Father Geller shocked and angered the 1963 senior class by retiring two months before graduation. After weathering his tutelage for years, not having Father Geller's signature on their diplomas infuriated them. He died 10 years after retirement.

Alby Przybylski became a carpenter.

Butch Przybylski went into the automotive repair business.

487

Eight months after I joined the Navy I altered a shipmate's leave record for a small stipend, it was discovered, I panicked and wrote a letter to Kathy advising her to forget me; that I was heading for a term in the Naval Portsmouth prison. The next day, when our division officer decided he couldn't pin the crime on anyone, I wrote an air mail letter suggesting she forget the previous letter urging her to forget me. It was too late. She had already taken my advice. Soon after she met a man with a yellow convertible. She married him and had five children. Twenty years later, on a steamy, summer afternoon, I was caught in a freeway traffic jam. In front of me was an open, yellow convertible driven by a young man. As the convertible inched under a pedestrian bridge I watched as two teenagers standing on the bridge dumped the contents of their pop bottles onto the driver's head. The language the young man used was horrid to hear and I giggled all the way home. I just figured out why it amused me so.

After completing four raucous years in the Navy, I worked for Chrysler, was laid off, went one year to college, then took the obnoxious market manager's counsel and got a desk job with Detroit's city government. At age 35 I married, begot a beautiful daughter, divorced, remarried, and lived happily ever after.